GENERAL EQUILIBRIUM GLOBAL TRADE MODELS

THE TRICONTINENTAL SERIES ON GLOBAL ECONOMIC ISSUES

(ISSN: 2251-2845)

Series Editor: John Whalley *(University of Western Ontario, Canada)*

Published:

Vol. 1 General Equilibrium Global Trade Models
edited by John Whalley

Forthcoming:

Vol. 2 International Trade Agreements and Political Economy
edited by Raymond Riezman

The Tricontinental Series on Global Economic Issues

Vol. 1

GENERAL EQUILIBRIUM GLOBAL TRADE MODELS

Editor

John Whalley

University of Western Ontario, Canada

World Scientific

NEW JERSEY • LONDON • SINGAPORE • BEIJING • SHANGHAI • HONG KONG • TAIPEI • CHENNAI

Published by

World Scientific Publishing Co. Pte. Ltd.

5 Toh Tuck Link, Singapore 596224

USA office: 27 Warren Street, Suite 401-402, Hackensack, NJ 07601

UK office: 57 Shelton Street, Covent Garden, London WC2H 9HE

British Library Cataloguing-in-Publication Data
A catalogue record for this book is available from the British Library.

The Tricontinental Series on Global Economic Issues — Vol. 1
GENERAL EQUILIBRIUM GLOBAL TRADE MODELS

ISBN-13 978-981-4383-67-7
ISBN-10 981-4383-67-8

In-house Editors: Mohammed Ashique/Sandhya Venkatesh

Typeset by Stallion Press
Email: enquiries@stallionpress.com

Printed in Singapore by World Scientific Printers.

Contents

Acknowledgments

I wish to thank the publishers of the following journals for giving copyright permission to reproduce previously published articles as individual chapters in this book:

Canadian Journal of Economics: Chapters: 5, 12 and 19.

Economic Journal: Chapters: 4 and 9.

Economic Theory: Chapter: 18.

Journal of Development Economics: Chapter: 10.

Journal of International Economics: Chapters: 1–3, 6, 13 and 17.

Journal of Political Economy: Chapter: 16.

Review of Development Economics: Chapter: 15.

Review of International Economics: Chapters: 8, 14 and 20.

The Review of Economics and Statistics: Chapters: 7 and 11.

I also thank my students, colleagues and coworkers in the Centre for the Study of International Economic Relations at the University of Western Ontario and elsewhere for their support and collaboration. Dana Medianu and Kun Peng have provided outstanding support.

I thank Sandhya Venkatesh and Mohammed Ashique and others of the World Scientific Publishing Company for enthusiastically producing the book.

Lastly, I thank my wife, YiHua, for her support and encouragement.

John Whalley

Introduction

1. Background

This volume contains 20 papers which are connected by the broader theme of application of general equilibrium computational methods to a range of policy and other issues involving the global economy and international trade. They reflect a long evolution in method and application from the early 1970's till today.

These all stem in one way or another from my experiences in graduate school in the early 1970's at Yale, where I took courses in linear models with Tjalling Koopmans and in general equilibrium with Herbert Scarf and wrote a thesis on general equilibrium computation applied to U.K. tax changes made in 1973 to accompany entry to Europe. Even though these two teachers of mine were among the leading economic theorists of their day, they both impressed on their students that the ultimate worth of even the most esoteric theory lay in its ultimate application. This emphasis was to remain as a central tenet with me in my academic and research career that followed.

In those days, general equilibrium theory had been raised to its high point of modern formalization by Kenneth Arrow and Gerhard Debreu who in 1954 had provided a proof of the existence of equilibrium, appealing to the Brouwer and Kakutani fixed point theorems, and constructing mappings of the unit simplex into itself whose structure ensured that at a fixed point the conditions required for a competitive equilibrium would hold. Herbert Scarf had taken this work a critical stage further by showing how constructive proofs of existence could be provided in which the argument for existence lay in the guarantee that a computational method devised by Scarf could be assured to find a close approximation to equilibrium. The challenge posed by Scarf to his students was to apply these computational methods to real world situations to aid in policy formation. This was the intellectual environment which provided the genesis for my thesis work, a portion of which was undertaken jointly with a fellow graduate student at the time, John Shoven.

The initial area of application I worked on (and emphasized in early years) was public finance, and more narrowly taxation. This direction had been suggested by another Yale faculty member, Peter Mieszkowski, who had pointed John Shoven and myself to the work of Arnold Harberger on the incidence and efficiency effects of the corporate tax for a term paper in his course. Harberger had formulated simple two-sector general equilibrium tax models which he had parametrized to reflect the US economy of the late 1950's, and then solved them for price and quantity changes induced by tax changes using local linearization approximations. Mieszkowski had suggested we improve on Harberger's work by applying Scarf's methods to his earlier analysis. Out of this, a career of numerical simulation activity in economics was to emerge, in which work on international trade and global issues progressively displaced taxation issues as the major focus.

What transpired in those early days of numerical simulation was that applying general equilibrium computational methods to policy issues of the day implied taking many steps outside the confines of then (and still) prevalent notions of what constitutes empirical analysis in economics. For a generation raised on Popperian–Friedmanian positivism in which econometric testing of model generated testable hypotheses played the central role in empiricism in the discipline, this was a major challenge. Prior econometric models used in empirical work had involved combining simple linear economic models with ever more complex statistical structures, but were nonetheless simple linear economic models lacking the nonlinearities and interdependencies stressed in economic theory. Perhaps the central theoretical construct in the discipline, the two person pure exchange economy, had never been either estimated or, to my knowledge, used directly in empirical work. The challenge of applying Scarf's computational methods was thus one of using far more complex structural models in which little or no room existed for statistical structure. And so evolved the use of deterministic empirical models based on integrated demand and production structures, with parametric specification using calibration methods that was to grow in the 1980's in the subfield of macroeconomics with dynamic stochastic general equilibrium models.

At the same time, there were important developments both in international trade theory and policy analysis which were also to lead to further evolution of global computational equilibrium models. In the 1950's, with the proposed and then actual creation of the European Common Market, major attention had been focused on the merits or otherwise of geographically discriminatory trade policy arrangements, and more specifically customs unions. In 1949, Jacob Viner had presented his famous analysis of the dual trade creating and trade diverting effects of customs unions in which the welfare effects of participation in regionally discriminatory trade pacts could be either good or bad. This was because the effect of a union in stimulating trade (trade creation) helped participating countries, while trade diversion (importing from within union countries at higher social cost due to the preferential tariff elimination within the union) hurt countries. In confronting issues such as whether the European Union was in the European interest, the conclusion of leading trade economists of the day was that this was an issue which could only be further analyzed using numerical methods involving simulation analysis. This was to lead to initial numerical analysis of the potential impacts of regional trade agreements.

In the years that followed, numerical international trade analysis was to flourish with analysis of GATT (and subsequently WTO) negotiating rounds and impacts of unilateral liberalization in a wide range of countries. These were supplemented with numerical analyses of developmental strategies and policies in a range of countries, and further global issues including climate change mitigation policies. Many other authors too numerous to mention here contributed in major ways to this emerging subfield, but it was from this background that the chapters presented in this volume evolved.

2. Content of the Volume

In organizing the volume, I have collected together 20 papers spanning a range of topics in global equilibrium analysis. Many are joint papers with valued colleagues and close friends whose contribution I simply acknowledge and greatly appreciate. I briefly present a summary of each.

In an early and critical piece for later work titled "On the Computation of Competitive Equilibrium on International Markets with Tariffs", a procedure is presented that allows a competitive equilibrium in international trade with tariffs to be calculated. The modeling structure incorporates the later central so-called Armington structure of country heterogeneity across goods. The procedure set out also serves to demonstrate the existence of an equilibrium.

The chapter "Optimal Tariff Calculations in Alternative Trade Models and Some Possible Implications for Current World Trading Arrangements" reports results of calculations of optimal tariffs with and without retaliation in a sequence of simplified two-good, two-country trade models. In the process, Nash equilibrium are iteratively computed, and the chapter considers these in both pure exchange models and models with production. It uses conventional functional forms for preferences and production sets and crudely calibrates parameter values to mimic current "empirical" knowledge.

"Interactions Between Trade Policies and Domestic Distortions in a Small Open Developing Country" reports results from a price-taking open economy numerical general equilibrium model of the Philippines. The purpose is to explore ways in which trade policies and other domestic distortions interact in a small open developing economy. The trade policies featured in the model include tariffs, export taxes, and import quotas, while the domestic distortions considered are rent seeking, and Harris–Todaro labor market dualism. Results reported indicate that interactions between trade policies and other domestic distortions are significant, and suggest they need to be more fully considered in numerical economic policy analyses for developing countries.

In "General Equilibrium Evaluations of Tariff-Cutting Proposals in the Tokyo Round and Comparisons with More Extensive Liberalization of World Trade" a numerical general equilibrium model of international trade involving major world trading blocs (the U.S., Japan, the EEC and the Rest of the World) is used to analyze the effects of alternative tariff-cutting formulae proposed by the major participants in the Tokyo Round negotiations under the GATT.

"How Reasonable are Assumptions Used in Theoretical Models? Computational Evidence on the Likelihood of Trade Pattern Changes" assesses the reasonableness of the commonly used assumption that in a multi-country, multi-good world, the direction of trade (import and export by commodity) is predetermined and fixed for each good for each country. It considers a simple three-country, three-good, pure-exchange model with CES preferences. Free trade competitive equilibria, three-country noncooperative Nash equilibria, and customs union equilibria for randomized parametrizations are computed and trade pattern changes between free trade and customs union equilibria in around 35% of cases.

In "External Sector 'Closing' Rules in Applied General Equilibrium Models" formulations of external sector behavior adopted in applied general equilibrium literature in the 1980s are examined. In many cases these models are constructed for single economies and the model-builder attempts to use a convenient external sector specification to close the model. Issues and difficulties with export demand and import supply functions for foreigners which satisfy trade balance and the modeling of small economy price taking behavior are explored.

"The North–South Debate and the Terms of Trade: An Applied General Equilibrium Approach" employs a price endogenous numerical general equilibrium model of world trade is to analyze terms of trade issues in the North–South debate. Seven regions are identified, the U.S., EEC, Japan, Other Developed, OPEC, New Industrialized, and Less Developed Countries. The model is benchmarked to a global 1977 micro-consistent data set. In the central case analysis, protectionist trade policies in the North inflict an annual welfare loss on the South of around 30 billion dollars per year with an associated terms of trade deterioration of around 9%. The annual welfare cost to the South from northern trade restrictions is somewhat larger than annual North–South aid flows. Protection in the South, and the potential terms of trade impacts of differential growth, are also analyzed.

"Trade and Environment: Bargaining Outcomes from Linked Negotiations" explores physical and policy linkages between trade and the environment. The chapter explores linkage through leverage in bargaining, whereby developed countries can use trade threats to achieve improved developing-country environmental management, while developing countries can use environmental concessions to achieve trade discipline in developed countries. A global numerical simulation model is used to compute bargaining outcomes from linked trade and environment negotiations. Results indicate joint gains from expanding the trade bargaining set to include the environment. Compared with bargaining with cash side-payments, linked negotiations on policy instruments provide significantly inferior outcomes for developing countries.

"Global Effects of Developed Country Trade Restrictions on Textiles and Apparel" reports general equilibrium estimates of national and global welfare costs of both developed country tariffs and bilateral quotas on textiles and apparel using an applied general equilibrium model. It covers quotas negotiated between three major developed importing countries (the U.S., Canada, and the EC) and 34 supplying developing countries under the provisions of the Multi-Fiber Arrangement applying in mid-1980's (MFA III). These results suggest that, despite foregone rent transfers, the vast majority of developing countries would gain from removal of restrictions on trade on their textiles and apparel exports, with some gaining proportionately more than others.

"Immiserizing Growth and Endogenous Protection" focuses on immiserizing growth; both the likelihood that it may occur and how its extent can be affected by the presence of endogenous protection; i.e., quota and other forms of protection for which the *ad valorem* equivalent level of protection is endogenously determined. It uses a general equilibrium model of the Philippines to compute counterfactual equilibria involving changes in domestic policies, terms of trade, and resource endowments.

In "Geographically Discriminatory Trade Arrangements" an eight-region numerical general equilibrium model of global trade is used to investigate the impacts of various geographically discriminatory trade policy arrangements (GDAs) on regional trade and welfare. Results suggest that the important factors determining gains and losses in any GDA are such issues as whether initial levels of protection are asymmetric, the relative sizes of participating regions, and the pattern of trade between participating and nonparticipating countries.

"The New Regionalism: Trade Liberalization or Insurance?" builds on the observation that several of the recently negotiated regional trade agreements contain significantly fewer concessions by the large countries to smaller countries than vice versa. Post-retaliation Nash tariffs by region under various regional trade arrangements are computed using a calibrated numerical general equilibrium model of world trade. Regional agreements constrain strategic behavior within each trading area, and (in the Customs Union case) enhance it outside the bloc. Results confirm the intuition that without side-payments large-small country regional agreements (such as the Canada–U.S. agreement) would not have occurred.

"How Often are Propositions on the Effects of Regional Trade Agreements Theoretical Curiosa?" uses computational techniques to assess whether or not various propositions that have been advanced as plausible in the literature on regional trade agreements may actually hold. The idea is to make probabilistic statements as to whether propositions of interest might hold, rather than to restrict assumptions so they unambiguously hold. The aim is to blend theory and numerical simulation and go beyond the ambiguous analytically derived propositions that dominate the theoretical literature so as to assess the likelihood of propositions holding for particular model specifications.

"Developing Country Benefits from MFN Relative to Regional/Bilateral Trade Arrangements" evaluates the benefits of most-favored-nation (MFN) treatment to developing countries in multilateral relative to bilateral or regional trade agreements. Using a general-equilibrium model of world trade, three sources of benefit are stressed. First, developing countries may be able to free-ride on bilateral tariff concessions exchanged between larger countries in MFN-based GATT/WTO rounds. Second, MFN benefits developing countries by restricting discriminatory retaliatory actions by other countries, evaluated here by a noncooperative Nash tariff game. Finally, MFN changes threat points in bargaining and hence affects the bargaining solution of multilateral MFN-based trade negotiation compared to a bilateral/regional arrangement. The benefits to developing countries are small in the first case as the tariff rates are already low, and the benefits are small in the second case as the optimal tariffs under unconstrained retaliation are asymmetric. Benefits from the third case are large as large countries can extract large side-payments if they bargain bilaterally.

"Tax Structure and Revenue Instability under External Shocks: Some General Equilibrium Calculations for Côte d'Ivoire" presents general equilibrium calculations for Côte d'Ivoire which explore the significance of tax structure for the relationship between external shocks and revenue instability, an issue little explored in the literature. Results suggest that a low-rate broadly based value-added tax, as advocated in World Bank structural adjustment lending, may be a poor revenue stabilizer compared with existing trade-based tax regimes in many lower-income commodity exporting countries. With high trade taxes, the external sector is smaller, and external sector shocks generate less revenue instability under existing arrangements compared with a broadly based yield-neutral alternative, such as a VAT.

"Discriminatory Features of Domestic Factor Tax Systems in a Goods Mobile-Factors Immobile Trade Model: An Empirical General Equilibrium Approach" uses a numerical general equilibrium model of domestic and foreign trade activity for the U.S., the (nine-member) EEC, and Japan to analyze the effects of removing distortions in domestic factor taxes, taking into account international trade flows.

"Foreign Exchange Premia and the Nonneutrality of Monetary Policy in General Equilibrium Models" presents a simple monetized extension of a traditional small-country, real-side, general equilibrium trade model in which premia on foreign exchange occur, with the value of the quota and the quota premium endogenously determined. Monetary policy is nonneutral in the model, and has real effects, illustrated using a small open economy general equilibrium model of the Philippines, which includes foreign exchange premia. Results emphasize the importance of incorporating domestic monetary policy, fixed exchange rates and associated foreign exchange premia when analyzing the trade policy regime in such a country.

"Exploring Policy Options in Joint Intertemporal-Spatial Trade Models Using an Incomplete Markets Approach" discusses the desirability of service trade liberalization in the presence of incompleteness of markets where there is both interspatial and intertemporal trade between countries. It uses numerical simulation methods for insights and relates the discussion to the General Agreement on Trade in Services (GATS) in the WTO.

"Goods Market Responses to Trade Shocks and Trade and Wages Decomposition" uses trade and wages literature to ask whether trade or technology has been the major factor behind increases in wage inequality in OECD countries since the 1980's. Using an Armington heterogeneous goods trade model to capture demand side effects, it shows how trade shocks affecting the price of unskilled-intensive importable goods can be absorbed on the demand side of goods markets, with little or no impact on relative wage rates. No wage impact occurs if the elasticity of substitution in preferences between imports and import substitutes is one. As this elasticity increases, trade plays an ever larger role in explaining wage inequality changes, and as the elasticity goes below one the sign of the effect changes.

"The Choice of Structural Model in Trade-Wages Decompositions" uses a calibrated general equilibrium model to decompose observed wage changes from trade and technology shocks into portions attributable to each source. It highlights some difficulties with the numerical performance of widely used theoretical trade structures. For small economies, a Heckscher–Ohlin model reveals specialization problems unless the price changes accompanying trade shocks are small. It can also yield strikingly different decompositions of the same wage change. A differentiated-goods model removes specialization problems and accommodates large price changes, but introduces demand-side responses greatly reducing the effect of trade on wages, and performs implausibly with sector-biased technical change.

3. The Past and The Future

Today, no one seriously doubts both the significance and role of international trade in the global economy, but there are questions over the usefulness of the computational application of standard trade models in simulation format to contemporary trade problems. Model results often suggest small impacts of policy changes, viewed by the policy community as sometimes implausible. Data is often old and key changes in our rapidly globalizing world not captured. Today, trade patterns are changing fast (China's exports grow at 30% per year, for instance) and most models are not good at either predicting or accommodating these changes. In addition, the world of today is repleat with large global imbalances, and models do not accommodate these in any satisfactory endogenous manner. Also computational models tend to lag theoretical developments (in literature on trade and heterogeneous firms, for instance).

Also there is now a dual evolution of models in policy settings and in more academic research. Large data set based modeling structures, like GTAP, use simple structural models but with great detail in disaggregation since this is what the policy process calls for. Key parameters (elasticities) and elements of structure remain central to results but are less fully analyzed. In academic research, in contrast, variations on structure provide the gist for challenges made repeatedly to current conventional wisdom.

Economics, in my view, like all disciplines is in constant evolution and change in the trade area is a prime example of this. There is now less reliance then in earlier years on analytical results derived from simple structures, and more on numerical analysis in complex structures for which simple analytical results are unobtainable. There is also a move away from theory to large data set empirical econometrics. And the changing focus of world trade debate (the 2008 Financial Crisis, The Rise of China) affects work in the area.

Policy decision making will, again in my view, always provide a demand for policy relevant numerical analysis as an input to decision making. But its imprecision and dependence on structure and parametric specification make policy practitioners cautious; especially if model results (as can too easily happen) are oversold as providing precise forecasts. This will remain true, in my view, in the future for national governments, international agencies, multination negotiation process and other policy discussion processes. The virtue of numerical modeling of the form presented here is that it allows the analytical structures of basic economic theory to be brought into policy debate in a loosely quantified way which gives (often first assessments) of what effects are large and small, and even their sign. But it only gives first guesses which then need to be challenged and carefully scrutinized; which in our modern world of immediacy and sound bites all too often falls a little by the wayside. But the evolution I see in this field shows to me that this demand for quantitative assessment from the policy process can be met, and in the years ahead I look forward to seeing it evolve more.

Part I

Trade Policy and General Equilibrium

Chapter 1

On the Computation of Competitive Equilibrium on International Markets with Tariffs*,†

John B. Shoven
Stanford University, Stanford, California 94305, U.S.A.

John Whalley
University of Western Ontario
National Bureau of Economic Research (NBER)

1. Introduction

In recent years, there has developed a considerable interest in quantitative assessment of the effects of changes in tariff rates. It is becoming accepted that a satisfactory treatment of these issues must necessarily involve a general rather than partial equilibrium analysis. The formal general equilibrium analysis of international trade models with tariffs has a long history going back to Bickerdike (1905) and Edgeworth (1908), and recently nonconstructive proofs of the existence of competitive equilibria in international trade models have been obtained by Sontheimer (1971) and Shoven (1974). This chapter explores the application of a computational procedure due to Scarf (1973) to these problems which is of use in analyzing such questions as the gains or losses from the formation or expansion of customs unions, as well as tariff adjustment questions. This procedure allows a competitive equilibrium on international markets with tariffs to

*Portions of this work form part of the first author's dissertation presented for the degree of Doctor of Philosophy in Yale University. He was supported by a Federal Deposit Insurance Corporation fellowship. We are both indebted to Herbert E. Scarf for guidance and to John S. Chipman and Larry Kimball for comments on an earlier draft. This chapter was presented at the Econometric Society Meetings, New York, December 28, 1973.
†This chapter was first published in (1974). *Journal of International Economics*, **4**(4), 341–354.

be calculated; it is of interest that the procedure also serves to demonstrate the existence of an equilibrium.

2. General Equilibrium on International Markets with Tariffs

It is assumed that there are N commodities in the model (including both outputs and inputs) where a commodity is thought of as a particular good in a particular country.[a] The commodities such as labor and cheese in one country are treated as separate commodities from labor and cheese in another country. Associated with each of the world's N commodities is a price π_1 and thus $\pi = (\pi_1, \ldots, \pi_N)$ is the vector of world prices. These prices are net of any tariffs and may be thought of as sellers' prices. Transport costs are ignored in this model but may be incorporated into a more complex formulation.

A finite number of countries, arbitrarily ordered $1, \ldots, K$, are treated in the model. Commodities are distinguished by their country of origin (the country in which they are produced or initially located) as well as by their physical characteristics. Thus, each country k has associated with it a given number n^k of "domestic commodities" (i.e., domestic outputs and inputs).[b] All other commodities may be imported and the consumers of country k may or may not face tariffs on these items.[c] For notational convenience, let $N^k = \sum_{s=1}^{k-1} n^s$ be the number of domestic commodities of all countries indexed lower than k. The domestic commodities of country k are then those indexed from $N^k + 1$ to $N^k + n^k = N^{k+1}$.

Each country imposes a nonnegative vector of *ad valorem* tariff rates $T^k = (t_1^k, \ldots, t_N^k)$. These tariffs are assumed to be paid by the consumers

[a] Similar goods in different locations are treated as different commodities. This is not uncommon in general equilibrium international trade models, but may result in large dimensional examples for computational purposes. Methods to alleviate this problem to some extent are available. The alternative formulation which treats similar goods in different locations as perfect substitutes is at odds with observed behavior. In most empirical applications countries import, export, and produce domestically goods of roughly the same physical characteristics.

[b] At this level of generality, the assignment of commodities by country must be viewed as somewhat arbitrary. However, in most applications an appropriate procedure will be evident. See, for instance, the treatment of the foreign trade sector in Whalley's (1973) general equilibrium tax model for the U.K.

[c] Only import tariffs are considered for expositional simplicity. However, export tariffs and import and export subsidies could be incorporated into this computational framework.

of country k. While these consumers may not be the persons who actually remit the tariff revenue to the government (customarily the importer), in a competitive model tariffs represent the proportional difference between the price the consumer pays and the amount the producer receives as net of tariffs. Tariff rates applying to domestically used and produced commodities are taken to be zero (i.e., $t^k_{N^k+1}, \ldots, t^k_{N^k+1} = 0$). The purchase (i.e., gross of tariff) prices faced by country k's consumers are given by the N-dimensional vector $\tilde{\pi}^k$, where

$$\tilde{\pi}^k = \pi(1 + T^k). \tag{1}$$

The tariff revenue received by the kth government, R^k, is distributed among the consumers of that country. It is assumed that the consumers of country k pay tariff revenue only to country k. In this formulation, the government acts solely as a redistributive agency. It is possible, however, to extend the model to allow the government to retain for itself some revenue for "social consumption activities". Each individual consumer's distribution is given by an arbitrary continuous function of R^k, with the added constraint that the total of the distributions to consumers just exhaust R^k. The total demands of the consumers of the kth country are assumed to be a function of $\tilde{\pi}^k$ and R^k. That is,

$$\begin{array}{c} \xi^k_1(\tilde{\pi}^k, R^k) \\ \vdots \\ \xi^k_N(\tilde{\pi}^k, R^k), \end{array} \tag{2}$$

where ξ^k_1 is the total demand in country k for commodity i. For a given T^k, it follows that demands are a function of π, R^k. Thus for given T^k, $k = 1, \ldots, K$, total world demands, the sum of the country demands, are a function of (π, R), where $R = (R^1, \ldots, R^K)$. These may be written as

$$\begin{array}{c} \xi_1(\pi, R) \\ \vdots \\ \xi_N(\pi, R). \end{array} \tag{3}$$

The market demands in any country are assumed to be bounded from below by zero. They are assumed to be continuous, homogeneous of degree zero in (π, R) and to be derived from the maximization of a utility function with the property of no satiation for each consumer. The sum of the individual budget constraints for the consumers of country k implies

$$\sum_{i=1}^{N} \pi_i(1+t_i^k)\xi_i^k = \sum_{i=1}^{N} \pi_i w_i^k + R^k, \tag{4}$$

where w_i^k is the total endowment of the ith good in the kth country.[d] These endowments are measured in physical rather than in value units. It is not excluded that consumers of the kth country initially own assets in other countries. Letting E^k, the tariff revenue collected by country k, be defined as

$$E^k \equiv \sum_{i=1}^{N} \pi_i t_i^k \xi_i^k, \tag{5}$$

(4) may be rewritten as

$$\sum_{i=1}^{N} \pi_i \xi_i^k + E^k = \sum_{i=1}^{N} \pi_i w_i^k + R^k. \tag{6}$$

Summing (6) over the K countries gives

$$\sum_{i=1}^{N} \pi_i \xi_i + \sum_{k=1}^{K} E^k = \sum_{i=1}^{N} \pi_i w_i + \sum_{k=1}^{K} R^k, \tag{7}$$

where ξ_i and w_i are the world demands and initial endowments,

$$\xi_i = \sum_{k=1}^{K} \xi_i^k, \quad w_i = \sum_{k=1}^{K} w_i^k.$$

The production possibilities available anywhere in the world are described by an activity analysis matrix

$$A = \begin{bmatrix} -1 & 0\ldots & 0 & a_{1,N+1}\cdots a_{1,M} \\ 0 & -1\cdots & 0 & a_{2,N+1}\cdots a_{2,M} \\ \vdots & \vdots & \vdots & \vdots \qquad \vdots \\ 0 & 0\ldots & -1 & a_{N,N+1}\cdots a_{N,M} \end{bmatrix}, \tag{8}$$

in which each column represents a feasible activity. Outputs are given positive and inputs negative coefficients, and each activity can be operated at any nonnegative level. The first N columns indicate the feasibility of

[d]Equation (4) clearly cannot hold if all N prices equal zero. This case will be excluded as a possible competitive equilibrium later.

free disposal of each commodity. It is assumed that the set of nonnegative vectors x which satisfy $Ax + W \geqq 0$ is bounded, where W is the N-dimensional vector of the w_i's, the world's initial endowments. This condition can be interpreted as implying that the production possibilities frontier is finite in all dimensions.

It is assumed that each activity in the production matrix A uses only commodities located in one country. This implies that A is partitionable into a matrix of disposal activities and a block diagonal sequence of arrays.

Given the notation and formulation presented above, a competitive equilibrium is defined by a vector $P^* = (\pi^*, R^*)$ and a vector of nonnegative activity levels x^* such that

(i) demand equals supply for each commodity, i.e.,

$$\sum_{j=1}^{M} a_{ij}x_j^* + w_i = \xi_i(\pi^*, R^*), \quad \text{for } i = 1, \ldots, N; \tag{9}$$

(ii) profit is maximized at prices π^* with activities in use breaking even, or

$$\sum_{i=1}^{N} x_i^* a_{ij} \leqq 0, \quad j = 1, \ldots, M, \tag{10}$$

with equality if $x_j^* > 0$;

(iii) the tax revenue received by each country is equal to that dispersed by the government of that country, i.e.,

$$\sum_{i=1}^{N} \pi_i^* t_i^k \xi_i^k = R^{k^*}. \tag{11}$$

Such an equilibrium is termed as an International Tariff Competitive Equilibrium.

It follows by substitution of (11) into (4), that at an equilibrium

$$\sum_{i=1}^{N} \pi_i^* \xi_i^k = \sum_{i=1}^{N} \pi_i^* w_i^k. \tag{12}$$

That is, the value of the total demand of the consumers of country k is equal to the value of their initial endowments. This can be written as

$$\sum_{i=N^k+1}^{N^{k+1}} \pi_i^* \xi_i^k + \sum_{i \neq N^k+1}^{N^{k+1}} \pi_i^* \xi_i^k = \sum_{i=N^k+1}^{N^{k+1}} \pi_i^* w_i^k + \sum_{i \neq N^k+1}^{N^{k+1}} \pi_i^* w_i^k. \tag{13}$$

In (13), the first left-hand-side term is the value of domestic purchases by the consumers of country k while the second left-hand-side term is the value of imports purchased by country k's consumers.

Multiplying Eq. (9) by π_i^* and summing for $i = N^{k+1}, \ldots, N^{k+1}$ gives

$$\sum_{i=N^{k+1}}^{N^{k+1}} \pi_i^* \xi_i = \sum_{i=N^{k+1}}^{N^{k+1}} \sum_{j=1}^{M} \pi_i^* a_{ij} x_j^* + \sum_{i=N^{k+1}}^{N^{k+1}} \pi_i^* w_i. \tag{14}$$

By (10) and the fact that activities involve only the commodities located in one country, the first right-hand-side term of (14) is zero. Thus (14) can be written as

$$\sum_{i=N^{k+1}}^{N^{k+1}} \pi_i^* \xi_i^k + \sum_{g\neq k} \sum_{i=N^{k+1}}^{N^{k+1}} \pi_i^* \xi_i^g = \sum_{i=N^{k+1}}^{N^{k+1}} \pi_i^* w_i^k + \sum_{g\neq k} \sum_{i=N^{k+1}}^{N^{k+1}} \pi_i^* w_i^g. \tag{15}$$

In words, (15) can be interpreted as the value of domestic purchases by the consumers of country k plus the value of exports from country k equals the value of domestic ownership of domestic assets plus the value of foreign ownership of domestic assets.

Subtracting (15) from (13) gives

$$\sum_{i\neq N^{k+1}}^{N^{k+1}} \pi_i^* \xi_i^k - \sum_{g\neq k} \sum_{i=N^{k+1}}^{N^{k+1}} \pi_i^* \xi_i^g = \sum_{i\neq N^{k+1}}^{N^{k+1}} \pi_i^* w_i^k - \sum_{g\neq k} \sum_{i=N^{k+1}}^{N^{k+1}} \pi_i^* w_i^g. \tag{16}$$

The interpretation of (16) is that in equilibrium the value of imports into country k minus the value of exports from that country is equal to the value of domestic ownership of foreign resources minus the value of foreign ownership of domestic resources.

3. Computation of an International Tariff Competitive Equilibrium

For the purpose of computing a competitive equilibrium such as described above, we use Scarf's algorithm.[e] As both the production and demand responses are homogeneous of degree zero in $P = (\pi, R)$, only augmented price vectors whose components sum to unity will be considered. That is,

$$\sum_{k=1}^{K} R^k + \sum_{i=1}^{N} \pi_i = 1, \quad R^k \geqq 0, \quad \pi_i \geqq 0. \tag{17}$$

[e]For a full explanation of the algorithm, see Scarf (1973).

The algorithm is essentially a search procedure on this unit simplex for an approximate equilibrium price vector $\hat{P} = (\hat{\pi}, \hat{R})$ and activity levels $\hat{x}$ which approximately meet conditions (9), (10), and (11).

A fine grid of price vectors $P^1, \ldots, P^F$ is defined on the unit simplex, where F may be as large as 10^{30}. Typically we work with all vectors which can be expressed as $(d_1/D, \ldots, d_{N+K}/D)$, where the d_i, $i = 1, \ldots, N+K$, and D are nonnegative integers with $\sum_{i=1}^{N+K} d_i = D$. As the algorithm requires that no two ith components of the vectors $p^1, \ldots, p^F$ be identical, numeric ties between components are broken lexicographically.

The algorithm always works with a subset of $N + K$ of the augmented price vectors $p^1, \ldots, p^F$ which are referred to as a primitive set and which are "close to each other" in a particular sense. Let c_i be the smallest ith component among an arbitrary collection of $N+K$ vectors, $P^{j1}, \ldots, P^{jN+K}$ being considered. If there is no vector P^j among the entire list $P^1, \ldots, P^F$ for which

$$P_i^j \geqq c_i, \quad \text{for all } i = 1, \ldots, N+K, \tag{18}$$

then the vectors $P^{j1}, \ldots, P^{jN+K}$ form a primitive set. When it is desired to remove a vector from a primitive set, then there is a rule which gives a replacement vector such that the new collection of vectors form a primitive set.

Each vector P^j in the list $P^1, \ldots, P^F$ is associated with a specific $(N+K)$-dimensional column vector b^j according to the following rules:

(1) If any of the elements $P_1^j, \ldots, P_{N+K}^j$ are zero, the $(N+K)$-dimensional associated vector contains a one in place of the first zero entry and zero's elsewhere.

(2) If none of the elements $P_1^j, \ldots, P_{N+K}^j$ are zero, the profit of each activity in the technology matrix A is evaluated for the augmented price vector P^j when operated at a unit level. If the maximum profit is positive, then the $(N+K)$-dimensional corresponding column is given by

$$\begin{matrix} -a_{1l} \\ \vdots \\ -a_{Nl} \\ 0 \\ \vdots \\ 0, \end{matrix} \tag{19}$$

where l is the most profitable of the M activities.

(3) If none of the elements $P_1^j, \ldots, P_{N+K}^j$ are zero and if the maximum profit is nonpositive, then the corresponding column is given by

$$\begin{matrix} \xi_1(\pi^j, R_j) + \theta \\ \vdots \\ \xi_N(\pi^j, R^j) + \theta \\ -R^{1j} + E^{1j} + \\ \vdots \\ -R^{Kj} + E^{Kj} + \Delta, \end{matrix} \tag{20}$$

where $\xi^{kj} = \sum_{i=1}^N \pi_i^j t_i^k \xi_1^a(\pi^j, R^j)$ and θ and Δ are arbitrary positive constants.[f]

Thus, each price vector in the list $P^1, \ldots, P^F$ has a $(N+K)$-dimensional corresponding column vector, and these column vectors can be arrayed in an $(N+K) \times F$-dimensional matrix B,

$$B = \begin{bmatrix} P^1 & \ldots P^{N+K} & P^{N+K+1} & \ldots P^F \\ 1 & \ldots 0 & b_{1,N+K+1} & \ldots b_{1,F} \\ 0 & \ldots 0 & b_{2,N+K+1} & \ldots b_{2,F} \\ \vdots & \vdots & \vdots & \vdots \\ 0 & \ldots 1 & b_{N+K,N+K+1} & \ldots b_{N+K,F} \end{bmatrix}. \tag{21}$$

If $\tilde{W}$, the augmented vector of world initial holdings, is defined as

$$\tilde{W} = (w_1, \ldots, w_N, \Delta, \ldots, \Delta)',$$

then the theorem which is the basis of Scarf's algorithm may be stated as the following:

Theorem. There exists a primitive set $P^{j1}, \ldots, P^{jN+K}$ such that

$$By = \tilde{W} \tag{22}$$

has a nonnegative solution, where $y_j = 0$ for $j \neq j_1, \ldots, j_{N+K}$. The proof of this theorem appears in Scarf (1973). Empirically, the algorithm finds such a primitive set very rapidly.

---

[f]In the next section, a specific upper bound for Δ is derived which is necessary to guarantee the existence of a competitive equilibrium. For specific grids of vectors $P^1, \ldots, P^F$ bounds on both Δ and θ can be calculated which both guarantee a solution and effect the degree of approximation.

The remaining task is to show that such a final primitive set describes (or, in the finite grid case, approximates) an international tariff competitive equilibrium. Given that $y_j = 0$ for $j \neq j_1, \ldots, j_{N+K}$ the $N + K$ equations $By = \tilde{W}$ can be written out explicitly as

$$-\sum_j a_{il}x_j + \sum_j \{\xi_i(\pi^j, R^j) + \theta\}z_j = w_i, \qquad i = 1, \ldots, N, \tag{23}$$

$$\sum_j \{-R^{kj} + E^{kj}(\pi^j, R^j) + \Delta\}z_j + y_k = \Delta, \quad k = 1, \ldots, K, \tag{24}$$

where the positive y_j corresponding to augmented demand columns have been renamed z_j, and those corresponding to the negative of activity columns have been replaced by x_j's. The y_k term in (24) is the weight associated with the $(N + k)$th column of B, the matrix of corresponding columns. This weight can be positive only if one of the final primitive set vectors has a zero $(N + k)$th component. As before, the subscript l refers to the activity which maximizes profit at prices π^j.

We may imagine sequentially increasing the list of vectors on the unit simplex (the value of F) until the augmented price vectors become everywhere dense on the $(N + K)$-dimensional unit simplex. Excluding for the present the case where a limit of $\sum_{i=1}^{N} \hat{\pi}_i = 0$, $\sum_{k=1}^{K} \hat{R}^k = 1$, is approached, the vectors of the final primitive set will all approach the vector $(\hat{\pi}, \hat{R})$, the demand functions converge to $\xi(\hat{\pi}, \hat{R})$ and the weights $\{x_j\}$, $\{z_j\}$, and $\{y_k\}$ approach $\{\hat{x}_j\}$, $\{\hat{z}_j\}$, and $\{\hat{y}_k\}$. It follows from the convergence of π, R and $\xi^k(\pi, R)$ that $\{E^{kj}\}$ approaches $\{\hat{E}^k\}$ for $k = 1, \ldots, K$. In the limit (23) and (24) become

$$-\sum_j a_{i1}\hat{x}_j + \sum_j \{\xi_i(\hat{\pi}, \hat{R}) + \theta\}\hat{z}_j = w_i + \theta, \quad i = 1, \ldots, N, \tag{25}$$

$$\sum_j \{-\hat{R}^k + \hat{E}^k + \Delta\}\hat{z}_j + \hat{y}_k = \Delta, \qquad k = 1, \ldots, K. \tag{26}$$

The rules of correspondence imply that if one $\hat{z}_j$ is positive, no activity makes a positive profit, while those with a positive $\hat{x}_j$ break even. Thus, in this case, the second condition of an equilibrium is satisfied.

To show that the other equilibrium conditions are met, it must be argued that the sum of the $\hat{z}_j$ is unity and that $\hat{y}_k = 0$ for all k. First, consider the case where the revenue for one country,[g] say k^* is zero. That

[g]The argument remains unchanged in the case with more than one country with zero revenue, although the notation is more cumbersome.

is, $\hat{R}^{k^*} = 0$ (implying $\hat{y}_k \geqq 0$). The K equations (26), can each be solved for $\sum_j \hat{z}_j$, giving[h]

$$\sum_j \hat{z}_j = \frac{\Delta - \hat{y}_{k^*}}{\Delta + \hat{E}^{k^*}} \leqq 1 \tag{27}$$

$$\sum_j \hat{z}_j = \frac{\Delta}{\Delta + \hat{E}^k - \hat{R}^k}, \quad k \neq k^*. \tag{28}$$

Together (27) and (28) imply that $\hat{E}^k \geqq \hat{R}^k$ for all $k = 1, \ldots, K$.

To show that $\sum \hat{z}_j \geqq 1$, multiply the N equations (25) by $\hat{\pi}_i$ and sum yielding

$$-\sum_{i=1}^{N} \sum_j \hat{\pi}_i a_{il} \hat{x}_j + \sum_j \hat{z}_j \sum_{i=1}^{N} \hat{\pi}_i \{\xi_i(\hat{\pi}, \hat{R}) + \theta\} = \sum_{i=1}^{N} \hat{\pi}_i (w_i + \theta). \tag{29}$$

Solving this for $\sum_j \hat{z}_j$ gives

$$\sum_j \hat{z}_j = \frac{\sum_{i=1}^N \hat{\pi}_i w_i + i \sum_{i=1}^N \hat{\pi}_i + \sum_{i=1}^N \sum_j \hat{\pi}_i a_{il} \hat{x}_j}{\sum_{i=1}^N \hat{\pi}_i \xi_i(\hat{\pi}, \hat{R}) + \theta \sum_{k=1}^N \hat{\pi}_i}. \tag{30}$$

Substituting (7) in the denominator gives

$$\sum_j \hat{z}_j = \frac{\sum_{i=1}^N \hat{\pi}_i w_i + \theta \sum_{i=1}^N \hat{\pi}_i + \sum_{i=1}^N \hat{\pi}_i a_{il} \hat{x}_j}{\sum_{i=1}^N \hat{\pi}_i w_i + \theta \sum_{i=1}^N \hat{\pi}_i + \sum_{k=1}^K (\hat{R}^k - \hat{E}^k)}. \tag{31}$$

The rules of correspondence guarantee that the last term in the numerator, the total production profit, is nonnegative. Since it has been shown that $\hat{E}^k \geqq \hat{R}^k$ for all $k = 1, \ldots, K$, the numerator is at least as large as the denominator which is nonnegative and thus

$$\sum_j \hat{z}_j \geqq 1. \tag{32}$$

Together with (27), this implies

$$\sum_j \hat{z}_j = 1. \tag{33}$$

From (27) this implies both that $\hat{y}_{k^*} = 0$ and that $\hat{E}^{k^*} = 0$.

---

[h] The reader is reminded that $\hat{y}_k^*$ may only be positive, if $\hat{R}^{k^*} = 0$.

Having shown that the weights on the augmented demand columns sum to unity in this case where at least one of the revenue terms is zero, it follows immediately that the second condition of an equilibrium (nonpositive profitability) holds. The first condition, that demand equals supply, is met by substituting $\sum_j \hat{z}_j = 1$ into (25). Likewise, given that this sum is unity, (27) and (28) imply that the third condition of equilibrium (the revenue dispersed equals the revenue collected for each country) is satisfied.

To analyze the situation where none of the countries has zero revenue, sum the K equations (26) and add the result to (26).[i] The result is

$$-\sum_{i=1}^{N}\sum_{j}\hat{\pi}_i a_{il}\hat{x}_j + \sum_j \hat{z}_j \left\{\sum_{i=1}^{N}\hat{\pi}_i\{\xi_i(\hat{\pi},\hat{R})+\theta\} = \sum_{k=1}^{K}(\hat{E}^k - \hat{R}^k) + K\Delta\right\}$$
$$= \sum_{i=1}^{N}\hat{\pi}_i(w_i+\theta) + K\Delta. \tag{34}$$

The first left-hand-side term is the negative of production profits and is zero if one of the $\hat{z}_j > 0$. Thus, in this case we have

$$\sum_j \hat{z}_j = \frac{\sum_{i=1}^{N}\hat{\pi}(w_i+\theta)+K\Delta}{\sum_{i=1}^{N}\hat{\pi}_i\{\xi_i(\hat{\pi},\hat{R})+\theta\}+\sum_{k=1}^{k}(\hat{E}^k-\hat{R}^k)+K\Delta}. \tag{35}$$

By (7), this expression equals unity, and, as before, all of the equilibrium conditions are met as long as one of the $\hat{z}_j$ is positive. However, if all $\hat{z}_j$ are zero, (34) becomes

$$-\sum_{i=1}^{N}\sum_{j}\hat{\pi}_i a_{il}\hat{x}_j = \sum_{i=1}^{N}\hat{\pi}_i(w_i+\theta) = K\Delta, \tag{36}$$

which contradicts the positivity of θ and Δ.

Finally, we must exclude the case where all N prices are zero. That is where $\sum_{i=1}^{N}\hat{\pi}_i = 0$ and $\sum_{k=1}^{K}\hat{R}^k = 1$. For each of a sequence of increasingly fine grids, (23) and (24) must be satisfied. Given that it is assumed that the x satisfying $Ax + W \geqq 0$ form a bounded set, the x satisfying (23) must likewise form a bounded set. Thus $\sum_j a_{il}x_j$ is a finite number. Given that $\{\xi_i(\pi^j, R^j)+\theta\}$ is bounded from below by θ, $\Sigma_j z_j$ are bounded from above. To establish a positive lower bound on $\Sigma_j z_j$ [and, hence, from (23),

[i]The reader is reminded that in this case $y_k = 0$ for all k.

an upper bound on $\xi_i(\pi^j, R^j)$], consider a country, say $\tilde{k}$, for which the limiting revenue $\hat{R}^{\tilde{k}} > 0$. Thus, at some stage in the sequence of finer grids, $y_{\tilde{k}} \to 0$. Walras' Law for country $\tilde{k}$ (6) implies that

$$E^{\tilde{k}j}(\pi^j, R^j) \leqq \sum_{i=1}^{N} \pi_i w_i^{\tilde{k}} + R^{\tilde{k}j}. \tag{37}$$

As $\sum_{i=1}^{N} \pi_i = 0$ is the limit being approached, at some stage

$$E^{\tilde{k}j}(\pi^j, R^j) \leqq R^{\tilde{k}j} \leqq 1, \quad \text{for all } j. \tag{38}$$

Therefore $\{-R^{kj} + E^{kj}(\pi^j, R^j) + \Delta\}$ is bounded from above by Δ, which implies that there exists a c' such that

$$\sum_j \hat{z}_j \geqq c' > 0. \tag{39}$$

Given this, it follows that the demands $\xi_i(\pi^j, R^j)$ are bounded and that $\sum_j z_j E^{\tilde{k}j}(\pi^j, R^j)$ approach zero for all $\tilde{k}$, where the limiting value of $\hat{R}^{\tilde{k}} > 0$. If we apply Eq. (24) for all countries $(1, \ldots, \tilde{K})$ for which the limiting revenue is strictly positive, the resulting equation in the limit is

$$\sum_j (-1 + \tilde{K}\Delta) z_j = \tilde{K}\Delta. \tag{40}$$

This is contradictory, if Δ is chosen such that $0 < \Delta < 1/\tilde{K}$.

4. A Simple Computational Example

In empirical applications of the model presented above, the production technologies and the demands must be explicitly specified. In many cases, a distinction is made between outputs and factors of production. Continuous production functions producing single outputs may be appropriate in these instances and are used in an extensive portion of the international trade literature. This treatment is appropriate if accurate measurement of factor substitution effects is of interest. The example presented in this section will utilize a specific form of these functions to illustrate to international trade practitioners the application of these techniques to problems with which they are continually dealing. The incorporation of continuous production function into the computational procedure is straightforward. For any price vector, the cost minimizing factor inputs for a particular output level, say unity, can be calculated for each production function. The activity which makes the largest profit per unit output may be obtained by a comparison of the cost minimizing activities for each output. The negative of this activity will be entered as the corresponding column should it make a positive profit.

For simplicity of exposition the example presented here involves only two countries with two consumers in each. There are two factors of production, and two domestic outputs in each country. These may be thought of as follows:

Good 1 — Durable output in country 1,
Good 2 — Nondurable output in country 1,
Good 3 — Durable output in country 2,
Good 4 — Nondurable output in country 2,
Good 5 — Labor in country 1,
Good 6 — Labor in country 2,
Good 7 — Capital in country 1,
Good 8 — Capital in country 2.

Each country imposes tariff rates on outputs of the other country, imported for domestic consumption. As demands for factors for consumption purposes are zero, no tariffs are charged on these goods. The tariff rates may be listed as follows:

	Country 1	*Country* 2
Good 1	0.0	0.05
Good 2	0.0	0.07
Good 3	0.10	0.0
Good 4	0.10	0.0

Each consumer is considered to have demand functions of the form

$$X_{ij} = \frac{a_{ij}}{[\pi_i(1+t_i^k)]^{S_j}} \frac{I_j}{\left[\sum_{i=1}^{4} a_{ij}[\pi_i(1+t_i^k)]\right]^{1-S_j}},$$

$i = 1, \ldots, 4$; $j = 1, \ldots, 4$; $k = 1, 2, \ldots,$ where X_{ij} is the amount of the ith commodity demanded by the jth individual of the kth country. These demand functions may be derived from maximization of a C.E.S. utility function[j] subject to a budget constraint. The terms a_{ij} represent the

[j]A utility function of the form:

$$U^j = \left[\sum_{i=1}^{N} a_{ij}^{1/S_j} x_{ij}^{(S_j-1)/S_j}\right] S_j/(S_j-1).$$

weight on the ith commodity in the jth individual's utility function and the term S_j the elasticity of substitution; the term I_j represents the income of individual j. These demand functions are more general than those which may be derived from Cobb–Douglas utility functions in that the portion of income spent on various commodities need not be constant.

In this example, the following parameters are assumed for the demand functions:

Country	*Individual*	S_j	a_{1j}	a_{2j}	a_{3j}	a_{4j}
1	1	1.1	0.4	0.4	0.1	0.1
1	2	0.7	0.6	0.3	0.05	0.05
2	1	0.9	0.1	0.1	0.4	0.4
2	2	1.2	0.15	0.15	0.3	0.4

The individuals are assumed to have the following endowments of factors of production which they sell to obtain income:

Country	*Individual*	w_5	w_6	w_7	w_8
1	1	30.0	0.0	20.0	0.0
1	2	30.0	0.0	40.0	0.0
2	1	0.0	20.0	0.0	30.0
2	2	0.0	40.0	0.0	40.0

Zero endowments of outputs are assumed.

In addition, each individual obtains income from revenue distributed by his government; the following dispersion scheme is used:

Country	*Individual*	*Share of revenue in country* 1	*Share of revenue in country* 2
1	1	0.4	0.0
1	2	0.6	0.0
2	1	0.0	0.4
2	2	0.0	0.6

The production side of the example is described by a series of C.E.S. production functions, one for each output, of the form

$$y_i = A_i[\delta_i(L_i^k)^{-\rho_i} + (1-\delta_i)(K_i^k)^{-\rho_i}]^{-1/\rho i}, \quad i = 1,\dots,4;\ k = 1,2,$$

where y_i is the output, A_i is the normalizing constant which defines units of measurement for outputs δ_i and ρ_i are parameters. Outputs 1 and 2 require the factors of country 1 (K^1, L^1) as inputs and outputs 3 and 4 those of country 2 (K^2, L^2). The following parameters are assumed:

Output	δ_i	ρ_i	A_i
1	0.6	0.9	1.0
2	0.3	1.1	1.0
3	0.5	1.2	1.0
4	0.4	0.8	1.0

To compute a competitive equilibrium for this example the procedure described above was employed using a simplex, where all components sum to 70.[k] A final termination routine was applied to give an improvement in accuracy.[l] The procedure terminated after 1653 iterations.

After applying the termination procedure the following solution was obtained:

Good	*Equilibrium price*	*Total demand*	*Total supply*[m]
1	5.439	36.031	36.031
2	5.434	25.343	25.343
3	2.759	30.295	30.295
4	2.718	35.079	35.079
5	2.710	0.0	−0.00002
6	1.426	0.0	0.0
7	2.910	0.0	−0.00002
8	1.333	0.0	0.00002
R^1	4.237		
R^2	2.519		

The profitabilities of the optimal activities for each output were:

Output	*Profit per unit output*
1	0.0
2	0.0
3	0.000001
4	0.000002

[k] In terms of the notation used earlier, $D = 70$.

[l] This is described in Shoven and Whalley (1972).

[m] The reader is reminded that outputs are represented by positive numbers and inputs by negative numbers. Supplies are thus production plus endowments and are very close to zero for the factors of production.

Corresponding to this solution the consumption of goods by each individual was as follows:

Country	*Individual*	*Output* 1	*Output* 2	*Output* 3	*Output* 4
1	1	10.065	10.279	4.875	4.957
1	2	22.103	11.205	2.805	2.835
2	1	1.269	1.270	9.934	10.070
2	2	2.592	2.593	12.680	17.216

and the usage of factors of production for each output was:

	Output 1	*Output* 2	*Output* 3	*Output* 4	*Total usage*
L^1	40.11	19.89	0.0	0.0	60.0
L^2	0.0	0.0	29.84	30.16	60.0
K^1	31.21	28.79	0.0	0.0	60.0
K^2	0.0	0.0	30.77	39.23	70.0

5. Conclusion

This chapter examines a static general equilibrium international trade model and presents a computational procedure for the calculation of a competitive equilibrium on international markets with tariffs. Using this procedure, a proof of the existence of such equilibrium may be demonstrated. As an illustration of the techniques, a simple numerical example is presented which is chosen to represent the type of formulation that might be adopted in applications by other international trade researchers. For this reason, a distinction between factors of production and outputs is introduced into the example and continuous production functions are used.

This procedure is of relevance in a number of policy problems such as customs union issues. This work may be integrated with methods for domestic tax considerations developed in Shoven–Whalley (1973) and Whalley (1973). These techniques should prove of considerable use in the analysis of fiscal harmonization.

References

Bickerdike, CF (1906). The theory of incipient taxes. *The Economic Journal*, **16**(64), 529–535.

Edgeworth, FY (1908). Appreciations of mathematical theories. *The Economic Journal*, **18**(71), 424–443.

Graff, J de (1949). On optimum tariff structures. *The Review of Economic Studies*, **17**(42), 1949–1950.

Hansen, T (1968). On the approximation of competitive equilibrium. PhD Thesis, Yale University, New Haven, Conn.

Miller, M and J Spencer (1971). The static economic effects of the U.K. joining the EEC and their welfare significance: An attempt at quantification in a general equilibrium framework, mimeo.

Scarf, HE and T Hansen (1973). *The Computation of Economic Equilibrium*. New Haven: Yale University Press.

Shoven, JB (1974). A proof of the existence of a general equilibrium with *ad valorem* commodity taxes. *Journal of Economic Theory*, **8**, 1–25.

Shoven, JB and J Whalley (1972). A general equilibrium calculation of the effects of differential taxation of income from capital in the U.S. *Journal of Public Economics*, **1**(3), 281–321.

Shoven, JB and J Whalley (1973). General equilibrium with taxes: An existence proof and computational procedure. *The Review of Economic Studies*, **40**(4), 475–489.

Sontheimer, KC (1971). The existence of international trade equilibrium with tax-subsidy distortions. *Econometrics*, **39**(6), 1015–1035.

Whalley, J (1973). A numerical assessment of the April 1973 tax changes in the United Kingdom. Unpublished PhD Thesis, Yale University, New Haven, Conn.

Chapter 2

Optimal Tariff Calculations in Alternative Trade Models and Some Possible Implications for Current World Trading Arrangements*

Bob Hamilton and John Whalley[†,‡]
University of Western Ontario,
London, Ontario, Canada N6A 5C2
[†]*National Bureau of Economic Research (NBER)*

In this chapter, we report calculations of optimal tariffs both with and without retaliation in a sequence of 2×2 trade models. We extend the earlier calculations by Johnson (1954, 1961) and Gorman (1957) which assume constant elasticity offer surfaces by using functional forms from the Cobb–Douglas/CES/LES family for utility functions and by also incorporating production into our calculations. Results indicate that the most critical parameters in any such calculations for a 2 × 2 model are the import prices elasticities and we briefly survey the empirical evidence as to their values. Our major conclusion is that these models confirm the suggestion from casual inspection of reported trade elasticities that current levels of tariff protection are some distance from optimal tariffs and that the margin for tariff retaliation in a worldwide trade war is potentially large. Other implications of the results are explored in the text.

1. Introduction

In this chapter, we report results of calculations of optimal tariffs with and without retaliation in a sequence of simplified two-good, two-country trade models. We consider both pure exchange models and models with production; we use conventional functional forms for preferences and production sets and crudely calibrate parameter values to our interpretation of current "empirical" knowledge. We relate our calculations to earlier work

*This chapter was first published in (2010) as Trade Working Papers 2382.
[‡]We are grateful to a referee for helpful comments on an earlier draft, and to the Ford Foundation for their financial support through an award made under their competition in International Economic Order.

by Gorman (1957), Johnson (1954), and Kuga (1973) and discuss their relevance to current world trade policy issues.[a]

We motivate our approach as follows.

(1) In the literature on the optimal tariff, we have been able to find three pieces in which calculations of post-retaliation Nash equilibria are reported. In two of these (Johnson and Gorman), two-country, two-good pure exchange trade models with constant elasticity excess demand functions are used to produce cases in which one country can be better off in a Nash equilibrium compared to free trade. In the other, Kuga (1973) considers a three-country, two-good case and constructs a payoff matrix involving 27 pure strategies and calculates a Nash equilibrium involving nonpure strategies for at least one country. Nowhere in the literature on the optimal tariff, as far as we are aware, has there been any attempt to examine tariff rates associated with Nash equilibria in light of either existing or historical levels of protection among major trading areas. There is discussion of the apparent large size of first step optimal tariffs in Kahn (1947) and de Graaf (1949), but since this exchange, there appears to be no discussion of the relation between optimal tariff calculations and contemporary trade policy issues.[b]

---

[a] A recent paper by Markusen (1981) discusses the distribution of gains from bilateral tariff reductions, a topic closely related to the present chapter.

[b] A key issue in evaluating the policy relevance of optimal tariff calculations is whether or not one believes that tariffs in world trade are the outcome of a cooperative or noncooperative process. If bargaining has driven tariffs down to present low levels among OECD countries one can argue that an explicit model of the bargaining process is needed to analyze current policy issues in the area.

The general consensus at the present time as to the relevance of optimal tariff analysis for the evaluation of protection in the industrialized world would appear to be that (a) for major industrialized countries, post-Kennedy (and eventually post-Tokyo) Round tariffs are low, averaging significantly less than 10% for manufactured products and therefore probably some distance from "optimal" tariffs, (b) for industrialized countries, nontariff barriers (quotas, standards, health and sanitary restrictions, government procurement and the like) are much more important than tariffs as protective devices and while they could correspond to or exceed "optimal" tariff protection they remain largely unquantifiable, and (c) what tariffs exist may well be more appropriately viewed as the political outcome of lobbying efforts by narrowly defined interest groups (textile unions, steel unions and the like) rather than the result of a rational centralized calculation involving maximization of a national welfare function.

We take the view that (i) much of the analytical literature on tariffs is dominated by the same kind of framework we use and (ii) given the relative lack of numerical calculation, some numerical investigation seeking to extend current theory in a quantitative direction may be useful, even if performed with a healthy dose of skepticism.

(2) The two well-known pieces by Johnson and Gormon consider constant elasticity excess demand functions in both countries. These have the property that optimal tariffs for each country are independent of the retaliation of the other country. It is widely acknowledged that constant elasticity excess demand functions imply strong (and, to some, unpalatable) restrictions on preferences and the pattern of endowments.

(3) We are able to compute Nash equilibria for a wider class of models than are used in existing literature. We do not require excess demand functions to be of constant elasticity form and we also incorporate production into some of our calculations. While we maintain the restriction to two-good, two-country models, we explicitly use functional forms for preferences and production sets drawn from the widely used CES/LES family. We determine the changes occurring in elasticities of excess demand functions as our calculations proceed, and for many of our formulations, this takes us some distance from the Johnson–Gorman assumptions.

(4) By varying preference weighting parameters, implicit own price elasticities of demand functions, and the relative size of countries, we are able to loosely characterize alternative representations of various bilateral trade scenarios. We suggest that such bilateral trade cases as U.S.–Canadian, U.S.–EEC, U.S.–Japan, North–South and OPEC–non-OPEC, all differ in one or more of the characteristics of relative size of trading blocs, degree of specialization, and price elasticities in determining trade. We analyze a number of cases in which these characteristics vary and compare free trade, Nash equilibria, and first step optimal tariff outcomes for each country.

(5) In the light of our calculations, we are able to discuss what form a noncooperative outcome in world trade could take if both current multilateral trade agreements under the GATT and bilateral arrangements (such as the U.S.–Canadian auto pact) were to be removed or break down. We explore the relative size of calculated and current levels of protection. We also briefly discuss protection in the 1930s which appears, in the light of our calculations, as possibly being roughly consistent with a noncooperative Nash solution.

(6) Our calculations also provide some indications as to what elements of structure in some of the larger scale "empirical" general equilibrium models of trade are important for the fairly strong terms of trade effects sometimes found, and we suggest that the so-called "Armington" assumption, which implies a form of complete specialization, may be responsible for this.

The extension of our calculations beyond the 2×2 framework, we regard as nontrivial for computational reasons. We are forced to approximate the offer surfaces derived from conventional utility functions by piecewise linear segments and we repeatedly refine these linear approximations in the neighborhood of the Nash equilibria we compute. The determination of the "with tariff" offer surfaces involves a prior assumption as to the direction of trade. More goods complicates matters due to both of these problems; more countries complicates the programing of the retaliatory processes. While these are not insuperable difficulties, it is our current judgment that significant extension in dimensionality considerably extends the complexity of code with no clear enrichment of structure.

2. The Johnson–Gorman–Kuga Discussion of the Optimal Tariff Problem

In two pieces in the 1950s, Johnson (1954) and Gorman (1957) analyze the optimal tariff problem in the two-country, two-good pure exchange case. Johnson's piece was subsequently amended in light of Gorman's paper when it was reprinted in Johnson (1961). Kuga (1973) attempts an extension of the Johnson–Gorman analysis beyond the two-good, two-country case.

The motivation for the original Johnson piece comes from the earlier literature on optimal tariffs. The rediscovery by Kaldor of Bickerdike's earlier argument that a tariff can improve domestic welfare had led to de Scitovsky's (1941) suggestion that repeated retaliation by each country in a two-good model to changes in the other country's tariff would result in a situation where both countries are worse off as a result of a retaliatory trade war. Johnson sets out to demonstrate that this need not be the case. He shows that one country can be better off even after the retaliatory process is completed and attempts to stimulate conditions under which a particular country will gain or lose. This involves the numerical determination of characteristics of a Nash equilibrium associated with the implicit two-person nonzero sum game which characterizes the optimal tariff model.

The simplifying device which Johnson uses to analyze his model is to assume that offer surfaces are of constant elasticity form. The main feature of such an assumption is that the optimal tariff of each country is determined directly from the assumed elasticity of the other country's offer surface. Retaliation by either country leaves the optimum tariff of the other unaffected and so the Nash equilibrium is easy to determine. In his original paper, Johnson suggests that there is only a single functional form for offer surfaces consistent with such an assumption, a proposition which Gorman demonstrates to be false, and in his later revision presents a model incorporating this class of preferences.

Johnson assumes two countries, I and II, each characterized by a social welfare function (or equivalently a single consumer's utility function) defined on the net trades (imports and exports) of the form:

$$U^{\mathrm{I}} = f^{\mathrm{I}}(kX^{a/k} - A^{a/k}Y^a) \quad (1 \leqq a \leqq k), \tag{1}$$

$$U^{\mathrm{II}} = f^{\mathrm{II}}(jY^{b/j} - B^{b/j}X^b) \quad (1 \leqq b \leqq j), \tag{2}$$

where X is the imported good and Y the exported good for country I. The f's are monotonic functions which, for purposes of ranking bundles of goods associated with different equilibrium outcomes, can be ignored. A and B are unit parameters, k and j are parameters which determine the elasticities of the offer surfaces; a and b determine the way the offer surfaces are displaced by any given tariff.[c]

For country I the first-order conditions from maximization of (1) yield the offer curve:

$$X = A(1 + t_1)^{k/a}Yk, \tag{3}$$

where t_{I} is the tariff in country I ($t_{\mathrm{l}} = 0$ if there is free trade). This offer curve is of elasticity k, where its elasticity, following Johnson, is defined by $(dX/dY) \cdot (Y/X)$. It follows directly that the optimal tariff for country II is the elasticity of I's offer curve minus one, or $k - 1$; similarly, the optimal tariff for I is given directly by $j - 1$.

By numerical calculation, Johnson proceeds to determine combinations of values for the import price elasticities in each country[d] such that country I would gain from a tariff war, country II would gain, and both would lose. His conclusion is that a country is only likely to gain in a tariff war if its import price elasticity is significantly higher than that in the other country,

---

[c]Johnson suggests that the parameters a and b may be interpreted as controlling the way in which the offer surfaces in countries I and II will be displaced as each country changes its own tariff. He considers four cases: $a/b = l/j$, $a/b = k/j$, $a/b = 1$, and $a/b = k$, giving an interpretation for each. The case $a/b = k$, for instance, his suggestions corresponds to the situation where imports are a pure luxury and exports a pure necessity in country I, while imports are a pure necessity and exports a pure luxury in country II. These different cases all imply properties of the excess demand functions which can be stated in terms of income elasticities, a notion more completely formalized in Gorman's paper.

[d]$\eta_1 = k/(k-1)$ and $\eta_2 = j/(j-1)$ are the import price elasticities of demand in countries I and II, respectively.

and the scope for this gain is greater and closer to its export good that approximates a pure luxury in world consumption. The cases he considers also show that a country could gain if both import price elasticities are low and the country's exports are a luxury item in world consumption (income elasticity for imports above unity in the foreign country).

Gorman extends Johnson's original paper by formalizing the properties of preference functions implied by the restriction of excess demand functions to constant elasticity form (or equivalently, constant price elasticity of the import demand functions). Gorman obtains the somewhat surprising result that if neither good is inferior nor the demand for each is elastic, then the volume of trade is about three times as great under free trade as in the final tariff equilibrium. As the import price elasticity approaches infinity in both countries this ratio approaches $e(2.72)$. Like Johnson, Gorman also analyzes numerically the issue of conditions under which countries gain from a tariff war, analyzing situations which he characterizes as involving "Europe" and the "Commonwealth".

Kuga (1973) begins by providing a general statement of existence of tariff distorted equilibria which has been missing from earlier literature. He then proceeds to use this result to prove the existence of a Nash equilibrium supported by retaliatory tariffs in an M-country, N-good world. By way of illustration, he considers as a numerical example a two-good, pure exchange model with nested Cobb–Douglas preferences. Using a particular numerical specification assumed solely for illustrative purposes, he constructs a payoff matrix involving 27 pure strategies. He then arithmetically calculates a Nash equilibrium, the main characteristic of which is that it involves nonpure strategies for at least one country. The calculation is neither related to the Johnson–Gorman calculations nor to any set of "realistic" parameters for the model.

We note the following points in connection with these calculations.

(i) Neither in the papers by Johnson and Gorman, nor subsequently, is there substantive discussion of the assumption of constant elasticity offer surfaces. For a simple two-good, pure exchange, general equilibrium model, it is not difficult to construct cases in which the elasticity of each country's offer curve varies substantially, or changes sign, as one moves along the offer curve. We present in Fig. 1, the offer curves generated from CES utility functions for a number of different parameter specifications where the endowment point is in the "corner" of the Edgeworth Box. As is apparent from the diagram, the assumption of constant elasticity offer surfaces is some distance from what is implied by the use of CES utility functions

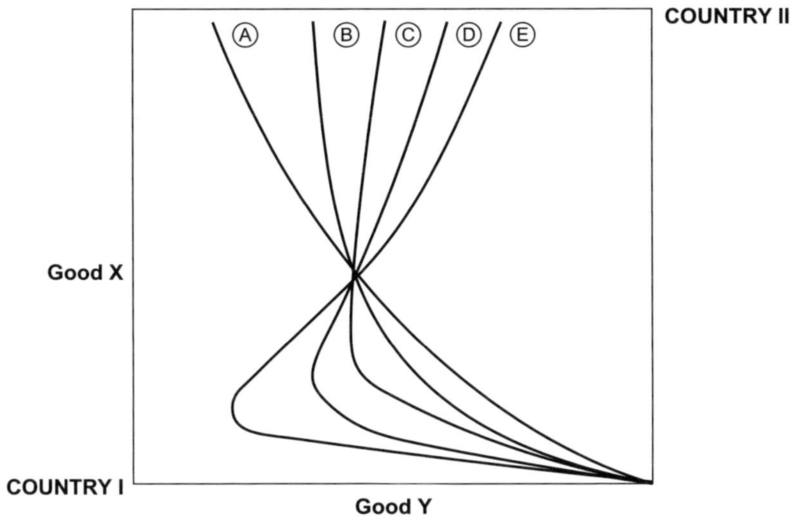

Characteristics of the offer curves

Offer curve	Elasticity of substitution in CES function	Elasticity of the offer curve along ray $2X = Y$ through endowment point	Elasticity of the offer curve along ray $X = Y$ through endowment point	Elasticity of the offer curve along ray $X = 2Y$ through endowment point
A	2.5	0.301	0.511	0.671
B	1.25	0.147	0.218	0.291
C	0.75	−0.090	−0.033	0.014
D	0.5	−0.332	−0.230	−0.171
E	0.25	−0.797	−0.171	−0.395

Fig. 1. Diagrammatic representation of offer curves generated from CES utility functions. Five offer curves for country 1, each generated from CES preference functions to pass through the same initial endowment point (the corner of the box) and constructed to cross a 45° line from the endowment point.

in these cases; and the same would hold for the Cobb–Douglas or LES functions. In the presence of production, it is equally difficult to devise a set of production and utility functions giving constant elasticity excess demand functions which incorporate a production response.

(ii) There is no clear indication given in these parameters as to how some of the more widely recognized "parameters of trade" can be incorporated into the analysis. Characteristics such as the degree of specialization in each country in the presence of trade and the relative sizes of the countries involved will affect the size of optimal tariffs, and yet no obvious way exists of introducing these into the Johnson–Gorman framework except by varying elasticities of offer surfaces.

(iii) There is little discussion in the presentation of these calculations of further characteristics of the Nash equilibria involved except the qualitative welfare comparison to the free trade equilibrium for each country. Optimal tariffs and their relation to existing protection in world trade are not discussed. The specification of realistic values for trade elasticities in the light of current empirical evidence is given little or no attention.

We are able to expand on these earlier calculations here by constructing a sequence of 2×2 numerical general equilibrium trade models in terms of preference parameters, endowments, and production functions and are able to bypass the need to specify offer curve elasticities directly, even though such elasticities are implied by the numerical specifications chosen. We therefore begin from more basic parameters than the offer curve elasticities in the Johnson–Gorman calculations and analyze the optimal tariff problem in terms of parameters with which empirical economists are more familiar. Using conventional CES/LES functional forms, we are able to numerically determine Nash, free trade, and autarky equilibria. We compare these equilibria and calculate optimal tariffs with and without retaliation. We also provide our evaluation as to whether there is anything of significance in these calculations for current discussion of policy issues in the world economy.

3. The Computation of Nash Equilibria

This section describes the sequence of models used, and outlines the methods adopted to numerically solve for the various equilibria reported on below. Two countries, each characterized on the demand side by a single consumer, are assumed. We then consider alternative models with and without a production structure in each economy. General notation is initially used to represent the solution concepts in the models and we later describe the specific functions adopted.

Following Shoven and Whalley (1974), we recognize that market demand functions in the presence of revenue generating trade distortions must be defined as functions of both prices and the revenue assumed generated by the distortion. For given *ad valorem* tariffs in country k on imported goods, denoted by the vector t^k, we write the market demand function for commodity i in country k as $\xi_i^k(\pi, R^k)$, where π denotes the vector of world (net of tariff) prices, R^k denotes the tariff revenue distributed on the demand side of the economy in country k, and the index i denotes the commodity i. Demand functions are assumed to satisfy a domestic version of the Walras Law. In those cases where production enters we assume the domestic production set to be represented by a transformation frontier defined over the vector of domestic outputs X. We write the transformation frontier for each country as $F^k(X)$; the case of a pure exchange economy involves the fixed endowment vector w as the function F^k.

We consider the following alternative solution concepts (in addition to the autarky solution) which are stated for the pure exchange variant of these models.

(1) *Free trade equilibrium* ($t^k = 0, \forall k$; $R^k = 0, \forall k$). Equilibrium is defined by a vector of world market prices π^* such that market demands are less than equal to supplies with strict equalities holding where corresponding prices are strictly positive:

$$\sum_k \xi_i^k(\pi^*) \leqq \sum_k w_i^k, \quad \forall_i (= \textit{if } \pi_i^* > 0).$$

A property of such equilibrium, following from the assumption of the Walras Law holding separately in each country, is that external sector balance prevails for each country.

(2) "*First step*" *optimal tariff for country* k (all countries but k have zero tariffs; $t^l = 0, l \neq k$; $R^l = 0, l \neq k$). Equilibrium is defined by a vector of world market prices π^* such that country k maximizes the social welfare function:

$$U^k(\xi^k(\pi^{k^*}, R^{k^*})),$$

subject to the equilibrium conditions:

$$\xi_i^k(\pi^{k^*}, R^{k^*}) + \sum_{l \neq k} \xi_i^l(\pi*) \leqq \sum_{l \neq k} w_i^l + w_i^k, \quad \forall i \ (= \textit{if } \pi_i^* > 0).$$

π^{k^*} denotes the vector of consumption prices in country k, and equilibrium is supported by the vector of optimal tariffs $(\pi^{k^*} - \pi^*)/\pi^*$. Two properties which will hold in equilibrium are government budget balance, $R^{k^*} = \sum_i (\pi_i^{k^*} - \pi_i^*) \xi_i^k(\pi_i^k(\pi^{k^*}, R^{k^*}))$, and external sector balance $\sum_i \pi_i^*(\xi_i^k(\pi^{k^*}, R^{k^*}) - w_i^k = 0$.

(3) *Post-retaliation (Nash equilibrium) optimal tariff outcome for all countries.* Equilibrium is defined by vector of world market prices π^* such that all countries maximize their social welfare function:

$$U^k(\xi^k(\pi^{k^*}, R^{k^*})), \quad \forall k,$$

subject to the equilibrium conditions:

$$\sum_i \xi_i^l(\pi^{l^*}, R^{l^*}) \leqq \sum_l w_i^l, \quad \forall_i(= \textit{if } \pi_i^* > 0).$$

Here π^{k^*} denotes the vector of consumption prices in country k, and equilibrium is supported by the vector of optimal tariffs $(\pi^{k^*} - \pi^*)/\pi^*$ in each country. Government budget balance and external sector balance both hold in equilibrium.

The interpretation of each of these solution concepts in a two-country model proceeds as follows. In free trade equilibrium, we determine a set of equilibrium prices such that all markets clear. In a "first step" optimal tariff equilibrium, the country imposing the optimal tariff will determine their optimal tariff by maximizing utility subject to the excess demand functions of the other country. In a post-retaliation (Nash) equilibrium each country simultaneously maximizes utility subject to the tariff distorted excess demands of the other country; the optimal tariffs determined for each country are consistent with the values assumed by the other country in determining their optimal tariff.

In order to compute equilibria of these types in a two-good, two-country framework, we consider piecewise linear approximations to the excess demand functions in both countries. In determining the optimal tariff for one country, we derive the excess demand functions for the other country from maximization of conventional CES/LES type preference functions subject to that country's endowment or production constraint. These excess demand functions change as different foreign tariffs are levied and the piecewise linear approximations change accordingly. The next step is to trace out consumption possibilities for the home country using the endowment or production constraint, along with the locus of new trade possibilities of the foreign country. The optimal tariff is that domestic country tariff rate needed to achieve the utility maximizing consumption bundle for the home country through a tariff distorted competitive process.

In order to compute an optimal tariff at any stage in our calculations, we need to assume that the predetermined direction of trade remains unchanged in the face of tariff retaliation. We follow the process of retaliation through which optimal tariffs are calculated by each country, and revised in light of any changes in tariffs adopted by the other country. When no further retaliation occurs, an approximation to the Nash equilibrium is achieved. We determine a Nash equilibrium given the degree of approximation assumed in the linear segments for the excess demand functions, and repeatedly refine the approximation in the neighborhood of our approximate solution until a solution within a satisfactory tolerance is obtained. Convergence appears to be rapid in all the cases we have examined and the amounts of execution time involved are small. A procedure of explicitly using the fixed point mapping in strategy space which characterizes a Nash equilibrium and using a fixed point computational procedure could be followed but is unnecessary for the cases we consider.

The demand functions derived from CES/LES type preference functions[e] can be written in the form:

$$X_i^k = C_i^k + \frac{\alpha_i^k \left(I^k - \sum_j P_j^k C_j^k\right)}{p_i^{kE^k} \cdot \sum_j \alpha_j^k P_j^{k(1-E^k)}}, \quad i = 1, 2; \quad k = 1, 2, \tag{4}$$

where the α_i^k and C_i^k are share and minimum requirement parameters in the preference functions. P_i^k indicates the consumer price for good i in country k, and E^k is the elasticity of substitution in the preference function. Where tariffs operate, the price terms P_i^k are gross of tariffs and the income term I^k includes the tariff revenue.

We choose values for the parameters C_i^k to calibrate to point estimates of income elasticities of demand functions; values of E^k are set to calibrate to point estimates of import price elasticities. Alternative values of the parameters α_i^k affect both the volume of trade in a free trade equilibrium and the extent of specialization.

We also consider variations on pure exchange models in which production enters through constant elasticity transformation surfaces between the two goods for which alternative values for the elasticity of transformation are specified. As this elasticity approaches zero the production model reverts to a pure trade specification. These functions

[e]These are of the form:

$$u^k = \left[\sum_l (\alpha_i^k)^{1/E^k} (X_i^k - C_i^k)^{(E^k-1)/E^k}\right]^{E^k/(E^k-1)}.$$

are written as:

$$Y = \left[\sum_i b_i^k X^{k^{(\sigma^k/(\sigma^k - 1)}} \right] \quad (k = 1, 2), \tag{5}$$

where σ^k is the elasticity of transformation in country k, b_i^k define weighting parameters in country k's transformation function, and Y is a constant. The X_i^k denote the output levels of good i in country k.

We consider a number of different numerical specifications of these functions for which Nash equilibria are computed. These equilibria are compared to free trade and autarky equilibria and values for the associated optimal tariffs reported.

4. Trade Elasticities and the Optimal Tariff Problem

The formulations of the optimal tariff problem by Johnson and Gorman are concerned primarily with the qualitative proposition that it is possible for a country to gain through a retaliatory tariff war. They demonstrate this by numerical examples which are especially easy to solve. Whether such occurrences are likely, depends on trade elasticities (each country's import price and income elasticities), and these elasticities in turn are critical parameters in determining the size of optimal tariffs (either as first step or post-retaliation solutions). Neither Johnson nor Gorman were able to relate their calculations to empirical literature since at the time the literature was sparse. Even though more literature is now available these estimates remain contentious. Nonetheless, to provide more basis for evaluation of our results which follow, we now briefly review this literature.

The most complete set of estimates of trade elasticities is the recent compendium compiled by Stern *et al.* (1976). They briefly summarize the results of approximately 150 empirical studies from the period 1960–1975 which estimate trade elasticities by product and by trading area. They report the main findings of each study and produce central tendency tables from which they extract "best guess" estimates which we reproduce in Table 1. They suggest that there is little basis on which to produce "best guess" estimates on a more detailed product classification than the single digit SITC categories is shown in Table 1 and they also stress the small sample size for estimates for countries other than the U.S.

Table 1. Central Tendency Trade Elasticities Reported by Stern *et al.* (1976).

Uncompensated own price elasticity of import demand						Uncompensated own price elasticity of export demand				
SITC 0 + 1	SITC 2 + 4	SITC 3	SITC 5 − 9	Total (trade weighted average)	Country	SITC 0 + 1	SITC 2 + 4	SITC 3	SITC 5 − 9	Total (trade weighted average)
−0.80	−0.47	−0.96	−1.84	−1.66	U.S.	−0.85	−0.86	n.a.	−1.24	−1.41
−0.80	−0.58	−0.52	−2.06	−1.30	Canada	n.a.	n.a.	n.a	n.a.	−0.79
−0.66	−0.91	−0.57	−1.42	−0.78	Japan	n.a.	n.a.	n.a.	−1.77	−1.25
−0.58	−0.80	−1.11	−2.36	−1.08	France	n.a.	n.a.	n.a.	n.a.	−1.31
−0.78	−0.25	−1.17	−2.53	−0.88	W. Germany	n.a.	n.a.	n.a.	n.a.	−1.11
−0.87	−0.25	−0.44	−1.22	−0.65	U.K.	n.a.	n.a.	n.a.	−2.00	−0.48
−1.06	−0.22	−1.35	−1.34	−0.83	Belgium–Luxembourg	n.a.	n.a	n.a	n.a.	−1.02
−1.52	−0.47	−1.00	−2.61	−1.05	Denmark	n.a.	n.a.	n.a.	n.a.	−1.28
−1.59	−0.93	−0.44	−2.64	−1.37	Ireland	n.a.	n.a.	n.a.	n.a.	−0.86
−0.96	−0.50	−1.16	−1.02	−1.03	Italy	n.a.	n.a.	n.a.	n.a.	−0.93
−0.26	−0.94	−0.01	−0.88	−0.68	Netherlands	n.a.	n.a.	n.a.	n.a.	−0.95
n.a.	−0.27	n.a.	−0.74	−1.32	Austria	n.a.	n.a.	n.a.	n.a.	−0.93
−0.09	−0.50	−0.33	−0.99	−0.50	Finland	n.a.	n.a.	n.a.	n.a.	−0.78
−0.58	−1.15	−1.36	−1.65	−1.19	Norway	n.a.	n.a.	n.a.	n.a.	−0.81
−0.47	−0.52	−0.24	−1.05	−0.79	Sweden	n.a.	n.a.	n.a.	n.a.	−1.96
−0.15	−0.17	−2.78	−1.21	−1.22	Switzerland	n.a.	n.a.	n.a.	n.a.	−1.01
−0.73	n.a.	n.a.	n.a.	−0.42	Australia	n.a.	n.a.	n.a	n.a.	−0.74
−1.12	−0.75	−0.34	−1.23	−1.12	New Zealand	n.a.	n.a.	n.a.	n.a.	−0.70

Source: Stern, Francis and Schumacher (1976, p. 20).
n.a. indicates not available.
SITC 0 + 1 = food, beverages and tobacco.
SITC 2 + 4 = crude materials; oils and fats.
SITC 3 = mineral fuels.
SITC 5 − 9 = manufactured goods.

There are several striking features of these estimates.

(1) The total estimates for both import and export price elasticities strike many people as surprisingly low (in absolute value). Crudely averaging across all countries, numbers in the range of −1 are obtained. There has been extensive discussion of bias in estimates based on time series data following Orcutt's well-known paper (1950) and a further paper by Kemp (1962) has provided an argument as to why trade elasticities might be biased towards −1. Some authors argue for, and use, substantially higher trade elasticities.[f] Some recent literature has suggested that the problems of bias first raised by Orcutt may not be as serious as once supposed and estimates in the range reported by Stern *et al.* remain both widely accepted and widely used.

(2) Reported estimates of export price elasticities do not appear to follow the ranking one would expect from the relative sizes of countries. If one argues that small economies are price takers, they should face export price elasticities which are larger in absolute value than for larger price making countries. Thus, the values of −1.41 for the U.S. versus −0.79 for Canada, and −1.25 for Japan versus −0.70 for New Zealand or −0.74 for Australia seem a little counterintuitive.

(3) The estimates for import price elasticities suggest strongly that current tariffs are not consistent with optimal tariffs. If an optimal tariff is being pursued it must equal one over the foreigner's import demand elasticity minus one.[g] Thus, if one examines U.S.–Canadian trade and treats this as bilateral trade excluding all other countries, optimal tariffs of approximately 300% for the U.S. and 133% for Canada would seem to be consistent with a post-retaliation Nash equilibrium. These tariff levels are dramatically larger than post-Kennedy Round tariffs of less than 10%. Given similar import price elasticities in other U.S. trading partners, this rough calculation is not much altered by aggregating all non-U.S., countries into the "rest of the world" for a U.S.–Rest of the World bilateral calculation.

(4) A number of countries have import price elasticities in absolute value less than one, implying that if a two-country optimal tariff equilibrium was involved the other country's optimal tariff would be negative. Thus, not only are the values for most countries inconsistent with an optimal

[f] Balassa and Kreinin (1967) for instance use higher elasticities (in absolute value).
[g] See Johnson (1961, Appendix to Ch. 2, pp. 56–58); the import price elasticity is used in absolute value terms.

tariff outcome as a description of current tariffs in world trade, they are also inconsistent with a constant elasticity offer curve formulation of the optimal tariff problem since negative tariffs would always result. We argue that this observation gives further weight to the case for calculations of the type we report.

(5) No central tendency tables are provided for import income elasticities by Stern *et al.*, but there are a number of studies summarized in which import income elasticities are greater than unity. Houthakker and Magee (1969), for instance, report an income elasticity of import demand on the U.S. of 1.51.

Our procedure, in light of this evidence, is to incorporate a capability of prespecification of import demand price and income elasticities in our calculations at some chosen point on the offer curve for each country (typically, the free trade equilibrium). Given the nonconstant elasticity nature of the offer curves we use, we are able to work backwards to the implied elasticities of substitution and other parameters in the preference and production frontier functions. We perform calculations for a range of values and then appeal to the estimates reported in Table 1 to provide a guide as to which cases are more plausible than others.

An important point of interpretation with these estimates arises in the case of models which incorporate production. We suggest the appropriate interpretation of estimates of import demand elasticities are as elasticities of excess demand functions (demand less supply) with respect to prices. Thus, low import price elasticities imply a low sum of transformation and demand elasticities in the models with production. The interpretation of such estimates in a general equilibrium trade model with production would be that the production response of the economy would also appear in the data generating the estimated functions. In models incorporating production, we, therefore, suggest the natural interpretation of the Stern, Francis, and Schumacher results is as the composite of demand and supply elasticities, rather than as demand side elasticities alone. It should also be squarely noted that this interpretation is critical for some of our later conclusions.

An important recent paper by Goldstein and Kahn (1978) reports high export supply elasticities for some countries in a simultaneous equations approach to estimation of export demand and supply functions. Effectively infinite supply elasticities for Japan are found, values in the neighborhood of 5.0 are found for the U.S. and West Germany, and values closer to 1.0 for smaller economies such as Belgium. A difficulty in relating such estimates to traditional trade models is that there is not a supply function for exports as such in these models but a supply function for exportables. The market is in the homogeneous product which is consumed in both countries rather than a market in the product consumed abroad. Traditional trade models with linear homogeneous production will yield partial equilibrium supply elasticities of exportables which approach infinity in the sense that profit-maximizing producers who face equilibrium prices for which zero profit conditions hold are indifferent as to what quantity they sell. To the extent that one is willing to interpret estimated supply elasticities in this way, no necessary contradiction exists with low transformation elasticities.

5. Some Numerical Results from a Sequence of Simple Trade Models

In this section, we report calculations from a number of different formulations with alternative numerical specifications for each. All cases involve two goods and two countries. For each we specify an autarky point, preference function parameters, and (for cases involving production) parameters of the production transformation frontier. The specification of our first model may be summarized as follows.

5.1. *Specification* 1

(1) Pure trade only — no production is considered in either country.
(2) CES preference functions have all $C_i^k = 0$; this is equivalent to specifying unitary income elasticities in all demand functions.
(3) Endowment points, are (75, 25) in country 1, (25, 75) in country 2. The dimension of the pure exchange Edgeworth Box is 100×100 in quantity terms.
(4) The α_i — weighting parameters in preference functions — are set at 0.5 in both countries. This places the contract curve (locus of free trade equilibria) along the diagonal of the Edgeworth Box.
(5) Elasticities of substitution in preferences are set so as to calibrate the excess demand functions to specified values of import price elasticities at free trade; import price elasticities vary between cases and thus elasticities of substitution also vary between cases.
(6) By construction; free trade prices are unity; utility levels of each country at free trade are 100.0; free trade is characterized by consumption vectors of (50, 50) in each country and trade of 25 in each commodity.

Table 2 reports results from a sequence of cases which follow Specification 1 and which only deviate one from another in the setting or import price elasticities at free trade. For each case, we report utility levels at free trade, autarky, and post-retaliation (Nash) equilibria. We also report post-retaliation optimal tariffs, first step optimal tariffs in country 1, and the volume of trade at free trade and the post-retaliation equilibrium. While Table 2 contains a substantial amount of detail some of the major features can be highlighted as follows.

(i) The indications from the Johnson–Gorman calculations as to conditions under which one country may gain even after a tariff war appear to be similar between this table and Johnson's original calculations. In Fig. 2, we summarize our results and those of Johnson for a 4×4 grid of cases which differ by the setting of income elasticities, reporting who gains and who loses. The comparison indicates a similarity to the Johnson–Gorman findings although the results are not identical.

(ii) The assumption of constant elasticity of the offer surfaces in the Johnson–Gorman calculations is departed from a number of the cases reported in Table 2. If a constant elasticity offer curve prevailed in both countries the optimal tariff would be the same for the imposing country regardless of retaliation by the other country. With import price elasticities at free trade set at -2 in both countries for instance, country 1 has a first step optimal tariff of 58% but a post-retaliation optimal tariff of 42%. Other cases also confirm the nonconstant elasticity nature of the offer surfaces.

(iii) The level of post-retaliation tariffs calculated for the smaller values of import price elasticities are surprisingly large. For the $(-2, -2)$ case post-retaliation optimal tariffs above 40% are produced. The initial indication is that in light of the available empirical evidence on trade elasticities a worldwide tariff war would produce tariffs significantly above existing tariffs in the world economy. Tariffs in the region of the 50% and higher which prevailed in the 1930's in the U.S. for many (but not all) commodities might thus be realistic as optimal tariffs. We comment below on the relation between the post-retaliation optimal tariffs reported and current protection in world trade.

(iv) Table 2 also provides some findings relevant to the Gorman result that with constant elasticity offer curves the volume of trade in a Nash equilibrium compared to free trade is relevated by the ratio $1/e$. As the import price elasticities increase, the ratio of trade seems to approach a limit of $1/2$, rather than $1/e$ and the approach is far from being monotonic, increasing and then decreasing.

Table 2. Results from Alternative Cases Using Specification 1.[a]

Import price elasticity at free trade		Utility at autarky		Utility at free trade equilibrium		Utility at post-retaliation (Nash) equilibrium		First step optimal tariff in country 1	Post-retaliation (Nash equilibrium) optimal tariffs		Volume of trade at free trade		Volume of trade at Nash equilibrium	
Country 1	Country 2	Country 1	Country 2	Country 1	Country 2	Country 1	Country 2		Country 1	Country 2	Exports of good 1 to country 1	Exports of good 2 to country 2	Exports of good 1 to country 1	Exports of good 2 to country 2
−1.0	−1.0	75.3	75.3	100.0	100.0	91.8	91.8	318.8	222.0	222.0	25.0	25.0	10.6	10.6
−2.0	−1.0[b]	91.2	75.3	100.0	100.0	106.9	84.1	236.6	193.1	40.5	25.0	25.0	16.7	7.7
−3.0	−1.0[b]	94.7	75.3	100.0	100.0	109.5	82.7	219.6	191.9	24.9	25.0	25.0	18.0	7.4
−4.0	−1.0[b]	96.3	75.3	100.0	100.0	110.7	82.0	213.3	185.3	26.2	25.0	25.0	18.7	7.2
−2.0	−2.0	91.2	91.2	100.0	100.0	97.8	97.8	58.4	41.8	41.8	25.0	25.0	12.0	12.0
−3.0	−2.0[b]	94.7	91.2	100.0	100.0	100.5	95.9	53.8	42.4	22.8	25.0	25.0	13.0	11.2
−4.0	−2.0[b]	96.3	91.2	100.0	100.0	101.6	95.2	51.9	42.6	15.0	25.0	25.0	13.4	10.9
−3.0	−3.0	94.7	94.7	100.0	100.0	98.6	98.6	31.4	24.1	24.1	25.0	25.0	11.6	11.6
−4.0	−3.0[b]	96.3	94.7	100.0	100.0	99.8	97.8	30.2	24.3	15.7	25.0	25.0	12.1	11.4
−4.0	−4.0	96.3	96.3	100.0	100.0	99.0	99.0	20.6	16.1	16.1	25.0	25.0	12.1	12.1
−5.0	−5.0	97.1	97.1	100.0	100.0	99.3	99.3	16.4	12.0	12.0	25.0	25.0	12.4	12.4
−6.0	−6.0	97.6	97.6	100.0	100.0	99.4	99.4	12.2	10.0	10.0	25.0	25.0	12.0	12.0
−7.0	−7.0	98.0	98.0	100.0	100.0	99.5	99.5	10.2	8.0	8.0	25.0	25.0	12.6	12.6

[a]The characteristics of this specification are given in the text.

[b]Since the countries are symmetric in all respects cases such as (−2, −1) or (−3, −1) are identical to (−1, −2) and (−1, −3).

Import price elasticity in country 1	Present paper[a]	Johnson[b]	Present paper[a]	Johnson[b]	Present paper[a]	Johnson[b]	Present paper[a]	Johnson[b]
−4.0	1 gains	1 gains	1 gains	1 gains	Both	1 gains	Both	Both
	2 loses	2 loses	2 loses	2 loses	lose	2 loses	lose	lose
−3.0	1 gains	1 gains	1 gains	1 gains	Both	Both	Both	Both
	2 loses	2 loses	2 loses	2 loses	lose	lose	lose	lose
−2.0	1 gains	1 gains	Both	Both	2 gains	Both	2 gains	Both
	2 loses	2 loses	lose	lose	1 loses	lose	1 loses	lose
−1.0	Both	Both	2 gains	Both	2 gains	2 gains	2 gains	2 gains
	lose	lose	1 loses	lose	1 loses	1 loses	1 loses	1 loses
	1.0		−2.0		−3.0		−4.0	
	Import price elasticity in country 2							

[a]See Table 2 which reports results for Specification No. 1.
[b]From case 1 in the diagram in Johnson (1961, p. 52).

Fig. 2. Representation of gainers and losers between Nash equilibrium and free trade in Table 2. Comparison to the calculations by Johnson.

The cases from Table 2 are explored further through a number of further calculations. We first examine cases incorporating production.

5.2. *Specification* 2

As for Specification 1, except for the following.

(a) Rather than a pure trade case, we consider production possibilities in each country to be given by constant elasticity transformation frontiers. The transformation elasticities differ between cases and are listed in Table 3. In each variant the production possibility frontier is constructed to pass through the endowment point from the corresponding pure exchange case and have a slope of minus one at this point. Because of the use of 0.5 weighting parameters in each country and the (25, 75), (75, 25) endowment points used in Table 2, the free trade equilibrium prices and utilities are the same in all cases in Table 3 and equal to those of the corresponding pure exchange variant.

(b) We fix the free trade import price elasticities at $(-2, -2)$ and $(-2, -4)$, respectively, in the two blocs of results we report.

In Table 3, we report results from these cases. The cases in Table 3 differ in the values which are specified for elasticities of transformation for the production possibility frontier in each country. In each reported case both countries have identical transformation elasticities, although this is not necessary for the computations performed.

As might be expected, results in Table 3 indicate that as the elasticity of transformation gets smaller the results from the corresponding pure exchange case are approached. As the elasticity of transformation approaches infinity optimal tariffs approach zero since no terms of trade effects from tariffs are possible because the production surfaces are linear. With transformation elasticities at one-half the demand side elasticities, optimal tariffs in a post-retaliation equilibrium are approximately one-half of the pure exchange case values. A noticeable result is that the $(1.0, 1.0)$ production case result using $(-2.0, -2.0)$ as import price elasticities is approximately the same as the $(-3.0, -3.0)$ pure exchange case. This suggests a plausible approximation that the sum (in absolute value) of the final import demand and transformation elasticities gives a total import demand elasticity which in turn can be approximated by a pure exchange variant. Given that estimated import demand elasticities are total elasticities incorporating both demand side and production side responses, a given "estimated" import demand elasticity can be calibrated to in these

Table 3. Results from Cases Using Specification 2[a] (Specification 1[a] but with Production).

Elasticity of transformation in production in each country		Utility at free trade equilibrium		Utility at post-retaliation (Nash) equilibrium		First step optimal tariff in	Post-retaliation (Nash equilibrium) optimal tariffs	
Country 1	Country 2	Country 1	Country 2	Country 1	Country 2	Country 1	Country 1	Country 2
(A) *Import price elasticities at free trade set at −2 in both countries*								
0.25	0.25	100.0	100.0	98.0	98.0	60.2	35.9	35.9
0.33	0.33	100.0	100.0	98.1	98.1	37.5	34.1	34.1
0.5	0.5	100.0	100.0	98.3	98.3	32.3	31.1	31.1
1.0	1.0	100.0	100.0	98.6	98.6	36.3	24.4	24.4
3.0	3.0	100.0	100.0	99.2	99.2	17.9	13.4	13.0
5.0	5.0	100.0	100.0	99.5	99.5	12.9	9.0	9.0
10.0	10.0	100.0	100.0	99.7	99.7	6.9	5.0	5.0
(Comparable pure exchange case from Table 2)		100.0	100.0	97.8	97.8	58.4	41.8	41.8
(B) *Import price elasticities at free trade set at −2 in country 1 but −4 in country 2*								
0.25	0.25	100.0	100.0	96.0	101.2	25.2	15.1	35.8
0.33	0.33	100.0	100.0	96.2	101.1	2.4	14.9	34.0
0.5	0.5	100.0	100.0	96.6	100.9	22.2	14.3	30.9
1.0	1.0	100.0	100.0	97.4	100.5	22.4	12.8	24.2
3.0	3.0	100.0	100.0	98.7	100.0	14.6	8.9	13.0
5.0	5.0	100.0	100.0	99.2	99.9	8.3	6.8	6.8
10.0	10.0	100.0	100.0	99.6	99.8	5.5	4.3	5.0
(Comparable pure exchange case from Table 2)		100.0	100.2	95.2	101.6	24.8	15.5	42.6

[a]These specifications are described more fully in the text.

models either through implied demand side substitution elasticity alone or through demand and production side elasticities whose sum meets the specified condition.

Table 3 also provides some indications as to the quantitative impact of increasing values of supply side elasticities on compound optimal tariffs. With transformation elasticities of 10.0, optimal tariffs in the $(-2, -2)$ case fall from over 40% in the pure exchange case (or zero transformation elasticity) to around 5%. Five percent tariffs are approximately the range in which post-Tokyo Round tariffs[h] will lie after 1987 for major industrialized countries. An argument can be made that these tariffs do not differ too sharply from optimal tariffs because of a high elasticity of the production side response. As already noted, this is not the interpretation of empirical evidence on trade elasticities which seems to us most natural.

In Specification 3, we consider the effects of allowing income elasticities to depart from unity for the $(-2, -2)$ case considered in Table 2 and we report our results in Table 4. We vary the values of the C_i^k in the LES/CES demand functions and determine the income elasticities of import demand at the free trade equilibrium in each case.

5.3. *Specification* 3

As for Specification 1, except for the following.

(a) Values for the C_i^k are set at nonzero values by product and by country and the implied point estimates of income elasticities for imports at free trade calculated (these differ from unity as in earlier specifications).

(b) The C_i^k and the weighting parameters in demands are set so that the free trade equilibrium is the same in each case. The autarky equilibria differ between cases.

(c) To restrict the number of possible cases, we only consider cases in which the free trade import price elasticities are -2 in each country.

Results from Table 4 indicate that relatively small differences in income elasticities do not produce a situation where one country gains when this is not the case in a unit income elasticity environment. In fact, computed post-retaliation optimal tariffs are largely insensitive to variations in income elasticities except when these elasticities become small. With income elasticities of 0.7 and 1.7 in countries 1 and 2, respectively, country 2 does not gain at a Nash equilibrium compared to free trade, the same outcome

[h]But not the *ad valorem* equivalents of NTBs.

Table 4. Results from Cases Using Specification 3[a] (Specification 1[a] but with Import Income Elasticities Displaced from Unity.) Import Price Elasticities at Free Trade Set at −2 in Both Countries.

Income elasticity of demand for imports		Minimum requirements				Autarky utilities		Free trade utilities		Post-retaliation Nash equilibrium utilities		First step optimal tariff in	Post-retaliation Nash equilibrium tariffs		Elasticity substitution in demand		Volume of trade at Nash equilibrium		Preference weighting parameters constructed to yield the same free trade outcome in each case			
		Country 1		Country 2															Country 1		Country 2	
Country 1	Country 2	Good 1	Good 2	Good 1	Good 2	Country 1	Country 2	Country 1	Country 2	Country 1	Country 2	Country 1	Country 1	Country 2	Country 1	Country 2	Good 1	Good 2	Good 1	Good 2	Good 1	Good 2
0.5	0.5	25.0	−25.0	−25.0	25.0	81.1	100.0	100.0	95.3	95.3	86.4		77.8	77.8	2.4	2.4	7.0	7.9	0.25	0.75	0.75	0.25
0.6	0.6	20.0	−20.0	−20.0	20.0	88.3	88.3	100.0	100.0	96.7	96.7	70.3	55.5	55.5	2.1	2.1	9.8	9.8	0.3	0.7	0.7	0.3
0.7	0.7	15.0	−15.0	−15.0	15.0	89.7	89.7	100.0	100.0	97.2	97.2	64.1	47.8	47.8	1.8	1.8	10.8	10.8	0.35	0.65	0.65	0.35
0.8	0.8	10.0	−10.0	−10.0	10.0	90.4	90.4	100.0	100.0	97.4	97.4	61.7	45.5	45.5	1.7	1.7	11.1	11.1	0.4	0.6	0.6	0.4
1.0	1.0	0.0	0.0	0.0	0.0	91.2	91.2	100.0	100.0	97.7	97.7	58.4	41.9	41.9	1.5	1.5	12.0	12.0	0.5	0.5	0.5	0.5
1.1	1.1	−5.0	5.0	5.0	−5.0	91.4	91.4	100.0	100.0	97.8	97.8	57.6	41.0	41.0	1.5	1.5	12.3	12.3	0.55	0.45	0.45	0.55
1.2	1.2	−10.0	10.0	10.0	−10.0	91.6	91.6	100.0	100.0	97.9	97.9	58.5	41.1	40.8	1.5	1.5	12.4	12.4	0.6	0.4	0.4	0.6
1.4	1.4	−20.0	20.0	20.0	−20.0	92.0	92.0	100.0	100.0	98.0	98.0	57.4	40.2	40.2	1.6	1.6	12.8	12.8	0.7	0.3	0.3	0.7
1.5	1.5	−25.0	25.0	25.0	−25.0	92.2	92.2	100.0	100.0	98.1	98.1	58.9	38.6	38.6	1.7	1.7	13.3	13.3	0.75	0.25	0.25	0.75
1.7	1.7	−35.0	35.0	35.0	−35.0	92.9	92.9	100.0	100.0	98.4	98.4	54.4	34.9	34.9	2.3	2.3	14.1	14.1	0.85	0.15	0.15	0.85
1.5	1.1	−25.0	25.0	5.0	−5.0	92.2	91.4	100.0	100.0	98.1	97.7	60.6	44.3	37.4	1.7	1.5	12.7	12.4	0.75	0.25	0.45	0.65
1.5	1.3	−25.0	25.0	10.0	−10.0	92.2	91.8	100.0	100.0	98.1	97.9	58.5	41.7	38.4	1.7	1.5	12.9	12.8	0.75	0.25	0.4	0.6
1.7	1.1	−35.0	35.0	5.0	−5.0	92.9	91.4	100.0	100.0	98.8	97.4	61.7	46.5	30.1	2.3	1.5	13.6	12.8	0.85	0.15	0.45	0.55
1.7	1.2	−35.0	35.0	10.0	−10.0	97.9	91.6	100.0	100.0	98.8	97.6	59.4	44.0	30.5	2.3	1.5	12.3	13.2	0.85	0.15	0.4	0.6
1.5	0.9	−25.0	25.0	−5.0	5.0	92.2	90.6	100.0	100.0	98.1	97.5	62.6	46.8	36.7	1.7	1.6	12.5	12.1	0.75	0.25	0.55	0.45
1.7	0.7	−35.0	35.0	−15.0	15.0	92.9	89.7	100.0	100.0	99.2	96.5	67.3	55.7	26.9	2.3	1.8	13.3	12.0	0.85	0.15	0.65	0.35

as with unit income elasticities. Post-retaliation tariffs vary from 47% to 35% as income elasticities in both countries vary between 0.7 and 1.7. As elasticities change from 0.7 to 0.5 in both countries, optimal tariffs rise to 78%.

The sensitivity of optimal tariff rates to further changes in specification is investigated in cases in which the endowment point in a pure trade case is systematically varied. These cases are represented by Specification 4.

5.4. *Specification* 4

As for Specification 1 except that the endowment point (75, 25), (25, 75) is varied as described. We examine cases in which import price elasticities are preserved at $(-2, -2)$ in both countries and income elasticities are unity.

Results in Table 5 indicate that the relative size of the two countries makes a substantial difference as to whether a country will gain from a retaliatory tariff war and also to the size of calculated optimal tariffs.

In the first set of results in Table 5, we systematically vary the relative size and endowment mix of the two countries. As we move from a situation of equal size to dominance by country 1 for unchanged point estimates of import price elasticities at free trade, 1 becomes a gainer in a trade war. Interestingly, the post-retaliation optimal tariffs in 1 first rise and then fall as the relative size of country 1 increases. In the second set of results, we move the endowment point in our pure trade example along a diagonal of the Edgeworth box towards the contract curve. As we approach the contract curve optimal tariffs fall, and on this basis we are able to relate optimal tariffs to the degree of specialization which trade produces. Thus, with the value of trade being 10% of the value of endowments optimal tariffs of 8% result, but with trade being 90% of the value of endowments optimal tariffs of 130% result.

Table 5 also indicates that with increasing degrees of specialization in free trade larger post-retaliation optimal tariffs are involved which, in turn, reflect progressively stronger terms of trade effects. The "Armington" assumption of treating products as heterogeneous by trading area which is common in empirically based general equilibrium trade models involves an implicit assumption of complete specialization. These results suggest that these models may incorporate stronger terms of trade effects than may be the case in practice. Applied models use this assumption due to the empirical observation of cross-hauling in trade data, and an assumed complete specialization is involved.

Table 5. Results from cases using Specification 4[a] (Variations in the Endowment Point of Pure Exchange Case). Import Price Elasticities at Free Trade Equal −2 in Both Countries, Unit Import Income Elasticities.

Endowment configuration				Utility at free trade		Utility at post-retaliation (Nash equilibrium)		First step optimal tariff in	Post-retaliation (Nash equilibrium) optimal tariffs	
Country 1		Country 2								
Good 1	Good 2	Good 1	Good 2	Country 1	Country 2	Country 1	Country 2	Country 1	Country 1	Country 2
99	1	1	99	100.0	100.0	82.3	82.3	281.6	200.0	200.0
99	5	1	95	104.0	96.0	94.9	76.0	277.5	205.8	131.9
99	10	1	90	109.0	91.0	105.6	69.7	270.8	209.4	96.3
99	15	1	85	114.0	86.0	114.3	64.2	266.7	213.2	74.8
99	20	1	80	119.0	81.0	121.6	59.4	261.2	213.4	61.9
99	25	1	75	124.0	76.0	128.3	54.9	256.2	212.3	51.8
99	50	1	50	149.0	51.0	155.6	35.5	222.9	198.2	23.7
99	75	1	25	174.0	26.0	178.1	18.6	172.3	168.2	8.6
95	5	5	95	100	100	88.4	88.4	191.7	133.3	133.3
85	15	15	85	100	100	94.6	94.6	103.0	74.5	74.5
75	25	25	75	100	100	97.6	97.6	60.7	44.1	44.1
65	35	35	65	100	100	99.3	99.3	31.7	22.0	22.0
55	45	45	55	100	100	99.9	99.9	10.2	8.1	8.1

[a]This specification is described more fully in the text.

Using a further variation in specification (Specification 5), we report additional results from cases in which the relative sizes of the two countries vary in Table 6. In these cases the size of country 1 is systematically increased while 2 remain unchanged.

5.5. *Specification* 5

As for Specification 1 except we vary the sizes of the countries by varying their endowments one to another while preserving their relative endowments across commodities.

Table 6 confirms the importance of relative country size in the determination of optimal tariffs, as suggested by Table 5. With countries both of equal size, both lose through a trade war. Where country 1 is double the size (all other parameters unchanged) country 1 gains from a trade war. Post-retaliation tariffs change from (44%, 44%) in the equal size cases to (61%, 28%) where one country is double the size, to (89% to 9%) in the 10 to 1 size case. The ratio of optimal tariffs is approximately equal to the relative sizes of countries of all other parameters (including import price elasticities) being the same across countries.

6. Synthesis and Interpretation of Results

It would be unrealistic to claim a precise set of policy conclusions on the basis of the calculations reported in Section 5, but the implications of these results for trade policy evaluation are nonetheless worth exploring. We list our synthesis of results in point form but emphasize that these should be construed as approximate working hypotheses from current analytics and empirical evidence, rather than definitely proven findings.

(1) Given current empirical evidence on import price elasticities, and interpreting this as evidence on elasticities of excess demand functions, the indications from our calculations are that in a post-retaliation trade war environment tariffs among major world trading areas (U.S., EEC, Japan) could be significantly higher than is currently the case. One could argue that existing nontariff barriers by industrialized countries substitute for these high retaliatory optimal tariffs, but the lack of reliable estimates of *ad valorem* equivalents for NTBs causes us to hesitate in advocating this position too strongly.

(2) We feel that a "best guess" set of post-retaliation tariffs are indicated to be in excess of 50% (and possibly significantly higher) for the

Table 6. Results from Cases Using Specification 5[a] (Changes in Relative Country Size). Import Price Elasticities at Free Trade in Both Countries at −2, Unitary Import Income Elasticities.

Endowments				Utility of autarky		Utility at free trade		Utility at post-retaliation (Nash) equilibrium		First step optimal tariff in	Post-retaliation optimal tariffs		Volume of trade at free trade		Volume of trade at post-retaliation (Nash equilibrium)	
Country 1		Country 2		Country 1	Country 2	Country 1	Country 2	Country 1	Country 2	Country 1	Country 1	Country 2	Country 1 imports	Country 2 imports	Country 1 imports	Country 2 imports
25	75	75	25	91.0	91.0	100.0	100.0	97.6	97.6	60.7	44.1	44.1	25.0	25.0	11.6	11.6
30	90	75	25	109.3	91.0	118.3	101.6	116.7	98.0	63.7	47.8	38.9	26.4	28.1	12.9	12.9
35	105	75	25	127.5	91.0	136.3	103.2	135.7	98.4	68.8	50.9	34.5	27.8	31.2	14.1	14.1
40	120	75	25	145.7	91.0	154.6	104.2	154.5	98.6	69.8	54.9	32.3	28.9	33.6	14.6	14.6
45	135	75	25	163.9	91.0	172.8	105.3	173.0	98.8	74.1	56.9	31.9	29.9	36.0	15.0	15.2
50	150	75	25	182.1	91.0	190.7	106.5	192.0	98.9	75.1	60.7	28.1	30.3	37.8	15.8	15.8
125	375	75	25	455.2	91.0	461.2	115.9	468.9	100.1	88.7	77.7	15.5	34.8	55.3	20.1	20.5
250	750	75	25	910.4	91.0	914.3	121.5	926.3	100.4	95.1	88.7	9.1	36.9	65.9	22.3	22.3

[a]This specification is described more fully in the text.

U.S. and the EEC, while being somewhat less for Japan due to its relative size. We also suggest that tariffs of 50% plus which occurred in the early 1930s might not be too far out of line with post-retaliation optimal tariffs.

(3) We suggest that if a sequence of 2×2 trade models were constructed in which each country traded with a "Rest of the World" treated as a single cooperating coalition, the size of any country's optimal tariff would be proportional to their relative size to the "rest of the world". This involves calibrating parameters of excess demand functions to estimated import price elasticities as point estimates at free trade. This calculation would suggest that, for instance, Canada's tariff would be one-tenth of that of the U.S., other things being equal.

(4) We do not believe that incorporation of income elasticities for imports other than unity into these calculations dramatically changes this overall picture. Our calculations indicate that income elasticities for imports have to be considerably dissimilar to significantly change results, more disparate than seems to be indicated by currently available evidence.

(5) Results suggest that a worldwide tariff war between major trading areas could result in a significant loss in worldwide welfare even assuming that full employment were to apply throughout the trade war and no short-run adjustment costs were generated during the retaliatory process.

(6) A possible view of world protection suggested by our calculations would be that tariff rates in the mid-1930's following the depression were of the order of magnitude suggested by our post-retaliation tariff calculations. International agreements since that date, and in particular under the GATT, have successfully exploited cooperative reductions in the level of protection since this period and thus current protection is significantly below post-retaliation tariffs. This suggests that the major role of GATT negotiations such as the Kennedy and Tokyo Rounds is the preservation of cooperative arrangements in the setting of world trade policies.

7. Conclusion

In this chapter, we report calculations of optimal tariffs both with and without retaliation in a sequence of 2×2 trade models. We extend the earlier calculations by Johnson (1954, 1961) and Gorman (1957) which assume constant elasticity offer surfaces by using functional forms from the Cobb–Douglas/CES/LES family of utility functions and by also incorporating production into our calculations. Results indicate that the most critical parameters in any such calculations for a 2×2 model are the import price elasticities and we briefly survey the empirical evidence as to their values. Our major conclusion is that these models confirm the suggestion from casual inspection of reported trade elasticities that current levels of tariff protection are some distance from optimal tariffs and that the margin for tariff retaliation in a worldwide trade war is potentially large. Our interpretation of the calculation suggests that such a trade war could yield a significant worldwide welfare loss even assuming full employment were to be maintained in all trading areas. Other implications of the results are explored in the text.

References

Balassa, B and ME Kreinen (1967). Trade liberalization under the "Kennedy Round": The static effects. *The Review of Economics and Statistics*, **49**, 125–137.

Goldstein, M and MS Kahn (1978). The supply and demand for exports: A simultaneous approach. *Review of Economics and Statistics*, **60**, 275–286.

Gorman, WM (1957) Tariffs, retaliation, and the elasticity of demand for imports. *Review of Economic Studies*, **25**, 133–162.

de Graff, J (1949). On optimum tariff structures. *Review of Economic Studies*, **17**, 47–59.

Houthakker, HS and SP Magee (1969). Income and price elasticities in world trade. *Review of Economics and Statistics*, **51**, 111–125.

Johnson, HG (1954). Optimim tariffs and retaliation. *Review of Economic Studies*, **21**, 142–153; reprinted with amendments HG Johnson (ed.), International trade and economic growth (George Allen and Unwin, 1961).

Kahn, RF (1947). Tariffs and the terms of trade. *Review of Economic Studies*, **15** (1), 14–19.

Kemp, MC (1962). Errors of measurement and bias in estimates of import demand parameters. *Economic Record*, **38**, 369–372.

Kuga, K (1973). Tariff retaliation and policy equilibrium. *Journal of International Economics*, **3**, 351–366.

Markusen, James R (1981). The distribution of gains from bilateral tariff reduction. *Journal of International Economics*, **11**, 553–572.

Orcutt, GH (1950). Measurement of price elasticities in international trade. *Review of Economics and Statistics*, **32**, 117–132.

de Scitovsky, T (1941). A reconsideration of the theory of tariffs. *Review of Economic Studies*, **9**, 89–110.

Shoven, JB and J Whalley (1974). On the computation of competitive equilibria on international markets with tariffs. *Journal of International Economics*, **4**, 341–354.

Stern, RM, J Francis and B Schumacher (1976). Price elasticities in international trade: An armored bibliography. Macmillan, for the Trade Policy Research Centre.

Chapter 3

Interactions Between Trade Policies and Domestic Distortions in a Small Open Developing Country*

Ramon L. Clarete and John Whalley[†,‡]
University of Western Ontario,
London, Canada, N6A 5C2
[†]*National Bureau of Economic Research (NBER)*

This chapter reports results from a price-taking open economy numerical general equilibrium model of the Philippines whose purpose is to explore the ways in which trade policies and other domestic distortions interact in a small open developing economy. The trade policies featured in the model include tariffs, export taxes, and import quotas, while the domestic distortions considered are rent seeking, and Harris–Todaro labor market dualism. Results clearly indicate that interactions between trade policies and other domestic distortions are significant, and need to be more fully considered in numerical economic policy analyses for developing countries.

1. Introduction

In this chapter, we explore the interaction of trade policies with other domestic distortions in a numerical general equilibrium small open economy model of the Philippines. Its purpose is to highlight the ways in which domestic distortions in developing countries can change the traditional analysis of trade policies, such as tariffs. The domestic distortions that we focus on are rent-seeking activities associated with import quotas, and sector-specific minimum wages which induce rural–urban migration. While the impacts of these distortions have been explored in the theoretical literature (Harris and Todaro, 1970; Krueger, 1974), the quantitative dimensions of their links to trade policies have not been

*This chapter was first published in (1988). *Journal of International Economics*, **24**(3), 345–358.
[‡]We wish to thank two referees for helpful comments. We are responsible for any remaining errors.

explored in numerical general equilibrium models. Our results suggest that existing numerical models need to incorporate such domestic institutional arrangements when analyzing trade policy issues in developing countries since they can change the perceptions on what constitutes an appropriate trade policy stance.

We describe the structure of the basic model in Section 2, and incorporate import quotas, rent seeking, and a Harris–Todaro labor market distortion into the model in Section 3. In Section 4, we describe how the model is calibrated to Philippine data for 1978. The interactions explored in this study are discussed in Section 5. Section 6 concludes the chapter.

2. The Basic Model

The model of the Philippines used here is a basic Arrow–Debreu model with production, into which domestic distortions and trade policies are incorporated. Following Shoven and Whalley (see Shoven and Whalley, 1984), the model is calibrated to a benchmark equilibrium data set and a fixed-point algorithm (e.g., Broadie, 1983; Merrill, 1972) is then used to solve equilibrium prices under various counterfactual assumptions.

The main point of departure relative to earlier applied general equilibrium modeling efforts is the explicit modeling of a small open economy. Several features make this approach especially suitable for analyzing trade and other policies in small developing countries. As in theoretical trade models, we treat imports as perfect substitutes for comparable domestic products, and the model thus avoids using the Armington (1969) assumption, common in other applied general equilibrium trade models. The model specification also explicitly introduces parameters which directly determine output supply elasticities which enter here through share parameters on industry specific factors of production in industry production functions. Finally, the price-taking behavior of these countries which has hitherto been assumed only for imports (e.g., see Dervis, de Melo and Robinson, 1983) is broadened here to include exports as well.

The model includes N sectors producing T traded goods and NT nontraded goods; $N = T + NT$. Each industry uses K variable factors and an industry-specific fixed factor in production. There is one aggregate consumer, and world prices are given for traded goods.[a]

[a]The structure of the basic model was described in Clarete and Roumasset (1987). However, tariff policies were the only policy distortions incorporated in this earlier work.

More specifically, production in each industry is represented by a Cobb–Douglas value-added function defined over both variable and sector-specific factors. Denoting X_j as the output of sector j, F_{ij} as sector j's use of the variable factor i, and $\overline{Z}_j$ as the fixed factor in sector j,

$$X_j = B_j \prod_{i=1}^{K} F_{ij}^{\alpha_{ij}} \overline{Z}_j^{(1-\theta_j)}, \quad \forall j, \tag{1}$$

where $\theta_j = \sum_{i=1}^{K} \alpha_{ij}$, and $\theta_j \geq 0$. θ_j and α_{ij} are Cobb–Douglas exponents, and B_j is a units parameter.

Intermediate production enters the model through fixed intermediate coefficients, $a_{ij}, i, j = 1, 2, \ldots, N$, defining the use of good i in production of one unit of good j. Thus, the demand for input i in sector j, ID_{ij}, equals $a_{ij}X_j$.

Given these production functions, industry supply functions from profit maximization are:

$$X_j = \left[B_j p_j^{\theta_j} \prod_{i=1}^{K} (\alpha_{ij}/w_i)^{\alpha_{ij}} \right]^{[1/(1-\theta_j)]}, \quad \forall j, \tag{2}$$

where p_j and w_i are domestic prices of good j and factor i, respectively. The price elasticity of supply for good j is $\theta_j/(1-\theta_j)$. Since θ_j is the total share of variable factors in value added in sector j, it follows that the supply of a good j is more elastic the larger the weight on variable factors relative to the fixed factor. From a modeling perspective, supply elasticities introduced through sector-specific factors provide a natural strategy for avoiding the well-known problems of specialization in production when modeling the effects of policy changes in small open price-taking economies.

Given any set of world commodity and domestic factor prices, the total return to all sector-specific factors, M, in the model is obtained by deducting intermediate and factor costs from the value of total output, i.e.,

$$M = \sum_{j=1}^{N} p_j X_j - \sum_{j=1}^{N} \sum_{i=1}^{K} w_i F_{ij} - \sum_{j=1}^{N} \sum_{i=1}^{N} p_i a_{ij} X_j. \tag{3}$$

Since the consumer sector owns these sector-specific factors, the rent accruing to factor owners appears as part of household income.

For simplicity, consumer demands are assumed to be Cobb–Douglas, with the demand for good j given by:

$$C_i = \gamma_j Y / p_j, \quad \forall j, \tag{4}$$

where Y is the total household income, and γ_j is the share of commodity j in total expenditure.

In a small open economy with no nontraded goods, the given world prices fully characterize a domestic equilibrium. Any excess demands are absorbed by the rest of the world, and trade balance is satisfied by Walras' Law. But in the presence of nontraded goods, the prices of nontradables are endogenously determined, since in equilibrium excess demands for each home good must be zero.

To solve this model for an equilibrium, we therefore utilize the Hicks composite commodity theorem (Diewert, 1978; Hicks, 1936), which states that if the prices of a group of commodities are fixed, these goods can be treated as one composite commodity with its own price. Tradables can thus be aggregated using their fixed world prices to form a Hicksian composite good. The domestic demand, C_T, and supply, X_T, of this good are

$$C_T = \sum_{j=1}^{T} \bar{p}_j (C_j + ID_j) \tag{5}$$

and

$$X_T = \sum_{j=1}^{T} \bar{p}_j X_j,$$

where $\bar{p}_j$ represents the given world prices, and ID_j is the domestic intermediate demand for good j, i.e., $ID_j = \sum_{i=1}^{N} a_{ji} X_i$.

This treatment of tradables as a Hicksian composite good closes the external sector of the model. The excess demand function for this aggregate commodity is, by definition, the total net imports of domestic residents. Since no international flows of financial assets enter the model, when the market for this commodity clears trade balance holds, i.e., residents sell enough goods and services to non-residents at the given world prices to pay for their own imports.

Because relative domestic prices of traded commodities are based directly on the given relative world prices, larger impacts of changes in trade policies tend to this type of model compared to those produced by Armington (1969) models which treat imports and domestic products as imperfect substitutes for each other. The latter approach fails to fully transmit trade-related disturbances to domestic prices, resulting in smaller impacts on domestic consumption and production.

In the following section, we expand on this basic model and describe how we incorporate tariffs, quotas, rent-seeking activities, and a Harris–Todaro fixed rural–urban wage differential into the model. As we add each of these distortions to the model, we indicate how the system of excess demand functions, associated with it, is solved to obtain a general equilibrium.

3. Trade and Domestic Distortions in the Model

To incorporate trade taxes into the model described above, we introduce a government which collects both tariffs and export taxes and redistributes the revenues to consumers in a lump-sum fashion. We denote the *ad valorem* trade tax rates as t, where $t_j > (<)\, 0$ if j is an importable (exportable), and E_j as the net import good j.[b] The combined tariff and export tax revenues, R, of the government are given by:

$$R = \sum_{j=1}^{T} p_j t_j E_j. \tag{6}$$

A common feature of all general equilibrium models of distortions is the simultaneity between the revenues generated by distortions and demands originally pointed out in Shoven and Whalley (1972). In order to deal with this in the present model, we assume the expected trade tax revenues, L, are distributed to the household sector in lump-sum form and we treat them as endogenous in the model. Thus, in any evaluation of consumer demands, the government distributes L to the consumer sector, who then calculates income as the value of endowments of variable and sector-specific factors, plus transfers from the public sector. Given this income, the consumer sector then evaluates demands, based on which R can be computed. In full equilibrium, the lump-sum transfers received by the consumer sector from the government exactly match the trade tax revenues actually collected.

Denoting Y as income and $\overline{F}_j$ as the endowment of variable factor i,

$$Y = \sum_{i=1}^{K} w_i \overline{F}_i + M + L = \sum_{j=1}^{N} p_j C_j. \tag{7}$$

The second equality implies that the consumer sector spends its entire income, implying that the relevant version of Walras' Law holds.

[b] E_j is positive if good j is imported, and is negative if good j is exported.

The excess demand system associated with this extension of the model involves:

(i) excess demand functions for each nontraded good, i.e., $(C_j + ID_j - X_j)$;
(ii) excess demand functions for each variable factor, i.e., $(F_i - \overline{F}_i)$;
(iii) an excess demand function for the composite traded good, i.e., $(C_T - X_T)$; and
(iv) a government budget imbalance function, i.e., $(R - L)$.

If a zero for all of these functions occur simultaneously at a set of endogenously determined prices for factors and nontradables (and tariff revenues), then an equilibrium for the model will be found. Such equilibrium prices can be computed using a fixed-point or other algorithm.

3.1. *Import quotas*

Besides tariffs, import quotas can also be incorporated into the model. Quantitative import restrictions are commonly imposed in developing countries both as a short-term response to current account deficits, and as a further way of protecting domestic industries from foreign competition to allow import substitution to occur.

To enforce restrictions, we assume that the government imposes an imports licensing system. Under the licensing scheme, importers are required to purchase a license from the government for every unit of quota-restricted imports they bring into the country. Importers demand licenses for restricted importables, while the government fixes the supply of licenses at the permitted quota. The cost of a license reflects the scarcity premium on restricted importables induced by the quota policies.

In the one consumer model we use, we assume that the government sells licenses and returns the proceeds in lump-sum fashion to consumers. Denoting $\overline{Q}_j$ as the import quota for good j, and T' as the set of importables with quotas, the total quota premium value, QR (in the presence of tariffs), is given by:

$$QR = \sum_{j \in T'} [p_j - \bar{p}_j(1 + t_j)]\overline{Q}_j, \tag{8}$$

where the difference inside the bracket is the per unit premium value of the quota on importable j.

The four excess demand functions listed above for the tariff case still hold in this model variant, except that the public sector budget in balance becomes $R + QR - L$. Besides these functions, including import quotas introduce one additional excess demand function into the model for each restricted importable. Excess demands for restricted importables are accommodated by the rest of the world only to the extent permitted by the quota. Thus, domestic prices of quota-restricted imports adjust until the domestic supply plus the quota matches domestic demand. Equivalently, given that one license is required to bring in one unit of import, the domestic prices of licenses (the premium values of imports) adjust such that the market for licenses clear. Thus, for all tradables with binding quotas, $(C_j + ID_j - X_j - \overline{Q}_j)$ will be equal to zero in equilibrium.

3.2. *Rent seeking*

Our modeling approach also allows us to incorporate rent-seeking activities into the case where import licenses are allocated by administrative discretion. Competitive rent-seeking activities are widely thought to be a major source of economic inefficiency [Krueger (1974)] since these activities use real resources to seek out rights to quotas and other rent-bestowing licenses. Under perfectly competitive rent seeking, agents will invest resources to acquire licenses until the value of rents equals the cost of rent seeking. Resources used in rent seeking produce no incremental output and are thus wasted.[c]

In practice, the amount of waste associated with rent seeking depends upon how rent seeking activities are specified. Little is known about the extent of rent seeking in practice, and not all economies that use quotas necessarily exhibit large degrees of rent seeking. The popular perception seems to be that rent seeking is common in the Indian subcontinent and in some Pacific Rim countries, but is less prevalent in Latin America. The claim sometimes made is that Latin American countries have monopoly importers, and so competition for licenses is largely excluded.

Following Hamilton, Mohammad, and Whalley (1984), the variant of our model which incorporates rent seeking assumes that the value of resources used in rent seeking equals the value of rents created by import

[c]Tariff-revenue seeking, as analyzed by Bhagwati and Srinivasan (1980), is not included in our analysis, since with revenue seeking the process of assignment of a rent-accruing device to a particular firm or agent is not the same, and the assumption of a rent dissipation process, at least in the Philippines case, seems to us to be weaker.

licenses. The proportion of each factor used in rent seeking is assumed to reflect the relative economy-wide endowments of each factor input. Factor demands thus include both the amounts of factors used productively, and those employed in rent seeking.

Denoting FRS_i as the amount of variable factor $i$used in rent seeking,

$$FRS_i = \left(\overline{F}i \Big/ \sum_{j=1}^{K} w_j \overline{F}_j \right) QR. \tag{9}$$

Thus, in the presence of rent seeking, the excess demand function for variable factor i becomes $(F_i + FRS_i - \overline{F}_i)$. In calculating consumer income, rents from quotas are excluded since these are effectively lost through resources used up in rent seeking. With these modifications, the model is the same as the quota variant described above.

3.3. *Rural–urban wage gap*

We can also extend our basic model to incorporate a fixed rural–urban wage differential inducing rural–urban migration and urban unemployment. As in Harris and Todaro (1970), labor migrates from rural areas to the cities in response to a higher wage in urban sectors until the expected urban wage (i.e., the urban wage multiplied by the probability of being employed) is equal to the free-market wage in rural sectors.

In this model variant, the total labor endowment of the economy (including those employed) is valued at the free-market wage in the rural sector, since all migrants expect to receive the rural wage when they migrate to the urban sector. Letting ρ be the urban employment rate, $(1/\rho)$ workers will move and compete for each job offered in urban areas. Denoting UR and RL as the sets of industries in urban and rural sectors, respectively, the superscripts U and R as urban and rural, and L as labor, the wage bill of employed labor is given by:

$$\sum_{i \in UR} w_L^U L_i + \sum_{i \in RL} w_L^R L_i. \tag{10}$$

Since $w_L^U = w_L^R / \rho$, and

$$\rho = \sum_{i \in UR} L_i \Big/ \left(\sum_{i \in UR} L_i + UE \right),$$

the total wage bill can be restated as:

$$w_L^R\left(\sum_{i\in UR} L_i + \sum_{i\in R} L_i + UE\right) = w_L^R\overline{L},$$

where UE denotes unemployed labor in the urban areas. The excess demand function for labor in this model extension becomes $(LD + UE - \overline{L})$, where LD is total productively employed labor. In determining an equilibrium in this model extension, the rural wage is adjusted until $(LD + UE - \overline{L}) = 0$.

With this series of modifications, the basic model outlined in Section 2 can incorporate a series of institutional arrangements common in developing countries, each of which is potentially important to the evaluation of impacts of trade policy changes. These extensions allow us to consider how these features, either singly or in combination, interact with traditionally analyzed trade policies (such as *ad valorem* tariffs and export taxes) and either modify or amplify the effects usually associated with these distortions.

4. Applying the Approach Using Philippine Data

We have applied the model outlined in the previous two sections to Philippine data, calibrating the model to a Philippine benchmark equilibrium data set for 1978 following the procedures described in Mansur and Whalley (1984), and performed counterfactual equilibrium analysis for a range of policy changes. In doing so, we treat the Philippines as a small open, price-taking economy in both its exports and imports.[d]

The main thrust of Philippine post-war trade policy has been to promote import-competing industries at the expense of agriculture-based, export-oriented industries. Under the Philippine Tariff Code, a basic revenue tariff of 10% applies to all imports. In addition, further tariffs up to a maximum of 100% are imposed on certain imports to protect domestic industries. On exports, a basic 4% tax is collected. Additional taxes up to 10% are added to the basic rate for some exports to promote domestic processing of primary products, such as copra. In combination, tariffs and export taxes accounted for a quarter of the total public revenue in 1978.

[d]Although the Philippines is the world's largest exporter of coconut products, it has little monopoly power in coconut trade because of several coconut substitutes (see Clarete and Roumasset, 1983).

Import licensing applies to most nonessential consumer goods, with the prior approval of the Philippine Central Bank being required to import these items. Goods falling under this category of licensing account for about 1,300 out of approximately 3,500 items listed in the country's tariff schedule in 1978. A few intermediate goods are subject to import licensing, but most are also inputs into export production.[e] There are no studies estimating the import premium values created by the import licensing system in the Philippines, and few for other developing countries. As a result, we assume alternative values of import premia in our benchmark data, and conduct sensitivity analysis around these.

Following Clarete (1984), the model we use specifies seven productive sectors: three are exportables and two importables in the 1978 benchmark data, and two are nontraded goods. Exportables are commercial crops, agricultural food industries, and industrial exportables. The importables include industrial importables, which consist mainly of producer goods, and import substitutes. Other agricultural products and services are nontraded. Two variable factors are specified: labor and capital. The aggregate supply of each is assumed to be fixed.

The tariff and export tax rates are trade-weighted averages of respective industry rates which, in turn, are averages over commodity-specific rates listed in the Tariff Code. Industrial importables have an *ad valorem* tariff rate equal to 23%, and import substitutes face a rate of 62%. Export tax rates for commercial crops, agricultural food industries, and industrial exportables are set at 5, 3, and 3%, respectively.

We have assembled a series of benchmark equilibrium data sets for 1978, for each of the model variants used in our analyses. In variant I, quotas, rent seeking and Harris–Todaro features in labor markets are excluded, but tariffs and export taxes are present. Variants II and III introduce rent seeking associated with import licensing; variant II assumes binding quotas on all imports, and variant III only on import substitutes. Variants IV and V correspond to II and III, but exclude rent seeking. Both rent seeking and Harris–Todaro features are included in variants VI and VII.

Under the model variants incorporating quotas, we assume the quotas are binding in the benchmark equilibrium and are equal to the observed 1978 net imports; namely 16,216 million pesos of industrial importables

[e]The tariff and import licensing structures were applicable in 1978, the benchmark year we use. From 1981 to 1985, however, Philippine tariff rates were lowered, and over a thousand imports were liberalized under a structural adjustment program.

and 2,187 million pesos of import substitutes. The assumed import premium values are 20 and 5%, respectively, for these importables. Where rent seeking activities for quotas are incorporated, they are assumed to completely dissipate all the rents associated with the import licensing system.

We use Philippine employment data reported in de Dios (1984) to specify the rural–urban wage differential for model variants VI and VIII, which has a Harris–Todaro labor market structure. In 1978, 0.8 million people, or 5.2% of the country's labor force were unemployed and another 1.5 million individuals were estimated to be underemployed. Of those employed in 1978, 52.9% were in agriculture, 19% were in industry, and 28.1% in the service sectors.

Using these data, we estimate the benchmark urban employment rate to be 72%. This calculation assumes that both unemployed and underemployed labor are all in the urban areas and that industry and services are exclusively urban activities. In calibrating the relevant model variants, the rural–urban wage differential parameter in the model is given by the estimated urban-employment rate. The urban sectors in the model are assumed to be industrial exportables, industrial importables, import substitutes, and services.

In applying these model variants, the policy parameters listed above are combined with other data from Clarete (1984) to assemble corresponding benchmark equilibrium data sets. We use these data in calibration to determine the parameters for the production and demand functions in our model. These, in turn, are used in a series of counterfactual equilibrium analyses.

5. Empirical Results

We have performed a series of policy experiments using the model variants described above. These include the separate removal of tariffs on industrial importables, on import substitutes, and on both imports; the removal of export taxes; the removal of both tariffs and export taxes taken together; of import quotas; of all trade distortions (tariffs, export taxes, and quotas); and of both trade and Harris–Todaro labor market distortions. The resulting counterfactual equilibria are then compared with the benchmark equilibrium data for the relevant model variant. Welfare impacts associated with each policy change are then calculated using a Hicksian equivalent income variation.

Table 1. Welfare Effects of Trade Policy Changes in the Philippines in 1978 Using Various Model Variants (Equivalent Variation as a Percentage of Benchmark Income).

	Model variants						
Policy change	I	II	III	IV	V	VI	VII
Remove tariff on industrial importables	−0.25	−1.1	0.51	0.0	0.43	−1.1	0.51
Remove tariff on import substitutes	2.86	−0.4	−0.45	0.0	0.00	−0.4	−0.45
All tariffs removed	3.30	−1.5	0.02	0.0	0.43	−1.5	0.02
Export taxes removed	0.30	−0.2	0.08	+0.0	0.11	−0.2	0.08
All trade taxes removed (export taxes and tariffs)	3.40	−1.6	0.04	+0.0	0.46	−1.6	0.04
All quotas removed	—	1.7	1.50	1.3	1.3	1.7	1.5
Trade taxes and quotas removed	—	5.2	5.00	4.8	4.8	5.2	5.0
Harris–Todaro labor market distortion removed	—	—	—	—	—	5.1	5.3
Trade taxes/quotas/Harris–Todaro labor market distortion removed	—	—	—	—	—	10.3	10.1

Note: The distortions included in each model variant are as follows:
I: tariffs and export taxes
II: tariffs, export taxes, quotas on all imports and rent seeking
III: tariffs, export taxes, quotas only on import substitutes, and rent seeking
IV: variant II without rent seeking
V: variant III without rent seeking
VI: variant II with Harris–Todaro labor market distortion
VII: variant III with Harris–Todaro labor market distortion.

In Table 1, we report the equivalent variation expressed as a percentage of benchmark national income for this series of policy changes using the model variants. These results clearly suggest that interactions of trade policies with other domestic distortions can change estimates of the welfare impacts of trade policies significantly.

Tariffs and export taxes in model variant I cause a deadweight loss of 3.4% of national income. The same trade distortions interacting with import quotas and rent seeking activities cost 5.2% of total income in model variant II. If the Harris–Todaro labor market distortion is also taken into account, the resulting economic inefficiency from these distortions taken together is 10.3% percent of national income in model variant VI.

A further example is the result that in the model variants II and VI, the equivalent variation from removing tariffs in the presence of rent seeking is −1.5% of national income, i.e., the economy is worse off. Removing tariffs in the presence of rent seeking increases the economic rents associated with import quotas, which in turn are wasted in rent seeking. Without tariffs, the premium values of import quotas increase, and consequently, the economic rents competed away through unproductive rent seeking are larger. In the case where quotas are binding only on import substitutes, a similar result prevails, but reducing tariffs on non-quota restricted imports is welfare improving, in large part due to the reduction in premium values (and hence rent seeking) for quota-restricted imports. Based on these results, the net effect of removing tariffs if quotas with associated rent seeking are unchanged, seems to be to make the economy worse off.

An example of interactions on the export side is that removing export taxes increases the premium values associated with import quotas and, in the presence of rent seeking, reduces overall welfare. In model variants II and VI, the equivalent variation changes from −1.5 to −1.6% of national income as export taxes are also removed along with tariffs, while rent seeking associated with quotas remains in place. Removing export taxes alone gives a welfare loss of −0.2% of national income. However, in model variants III and VII with only one binding quota in place, lifting export taxes improves welfare (although by an amount less than that in variant I). In this case the surge in exports is accompanied by an increase in the non-quota-restricted import.

Results using model variants incorporating labor market distortions (model variants VI and VII) yield similar results except when the Harris–Todaro distortion is also removed. Because these model variants are calibrated to the same benchmark equilibrium data on production and prices as the other model variants, the rural–urban wage differential used in model variants VI and VII implies that labor employed in urban-based sectors will be productive, displacing surplus urban labor to maintain the same level of production as in other model variants. Thus, given the wage data to which these model variants are calibrated, their results will be similar unless idle labor is productively re-employed.

The extent to which these various domestic distortions affect measures of the deadweight losses of tariffs and export taxes clearly depends on the assumed prices of the import premium rates among other parameter values. To explore this, we have also performed sensitivity analysis around the import premium parameter values assumed for model variant II. We have increased the benchmark quota premium values on import substitutes first from 20% to 50%, and then to 100%, holding the premium value for industrial importables constant at 5%. Variants II, II-A, and II-B referred to in Table 2 correspond to these different import premium assumptions.

Table 2. Sensitivity of Welfare Effects of Trade Policy Experiments to Alternative Benchmark Import Premium Values (Philippine Data for 1978 Equivalent Variations as a Percent of Benchmark Income).[a]

	II	II-A	II-B
All tariffs removed	−1.5	−1.4	−1.3
Tariffs/export taxes removed	−1.6	−1.6	−1.5
Import quotas removed	1.7	4.1	8.6
Tariffs/export taxes/import quotas removed	5.2	7.7	12.4

[a]The values of import premia associated with quotas on import substitutes assumed in the benchmark data are 20% for variant II; 50% for variant II-A; and 100% for variant II-B. The premium value for industrial importables is 5% in all three cases.

In Table 2, the equivalent variation from removing tariffs and import quotas from model variant II of 5.2% of national income is repeated, but this gain becomes progressively larger in model variants II-A and II-B. However, the loss from removing tariffs falls as the assumed quota premium values increase in the benchmark data. The explanation seems to be that the marginal increase in economic rents from import quotas following the lifting of tariffs is smaller, the larger is the base case import premium, largely because tariff revenues are lower on account of smaller import volumes. The negative equivalent variations in Table 2, as in Table 1, emphasize that the net effect of removing tariffs in the presence of quotas and rent seeking is likely to leave the economy worse off.

Table 2 also confirms the welfare-worsening effects of removing export taxes in the presence of import licensing and rent seeking. Estimates of the associated equivalent variations are also all negative in this table, implying a welfare loss. As discussed above for Table 1, lifting export taxes increases the import premia.

These results therefore suggest not only that trade policies interact strongly with domestic distortions in this model of the Philippines, but these interactions produce important sensitivity behavior of results with respect to key parameter values.

6. Summary and Conclusion

This chapter reports results from a price-taking open economy numerical general equilibrium model of the Philippines whose purpose is to explore the ways in which trade policies and other domestic distortions interact in a small open developing economy. We use a small economy model of the Philippines similar to that in Clarete (1984) and incorporate quotas, rent seeking, and Harris–Todaro labor market distortions with urban unemployment, in addition to tariffs and export taxes.

This model differs from trade models reported elsewhere in the applied general equilibrium literature in featuring explicit price-taking behavior, rather than making all prices fully endogenous. The model also specifies homogeneous rather than heterogeneous products across countries (as under the Armington assumption). Sector-specific factors in each sector are incorporated in order to bound production responses, and the Hicks composite commodity theorem is used in closing the external sector of the model. We believe that this not only yields a more realistic modeling approach for small developing countries, but also one which is easier to implement than most existing approaches.

The results clearly indicate that interactions between trade policies and other domestic distortions are significant. A particularly interesting result is that in the presence of import quotas and rent seeking, removing tariffs (even for a small open price-taking economy) is typically welfare worsening. This is because in the presence of quotas, tariffs serve to reduce quota values and lower the social costs of rent seeking. Thus, removing tariffs is typically undesirable if quotas with associated rent seeking remain in place. Even the lifting of export taxes has the same effect since the premium value from quotas increases. However, where one import is quota restricted and the other is not, and rent seeking is present, lifting the tariffs of the quota-free imports enhances economic efficiency because of substitution away from the restricted import, reducing rents, and waste due to rent seeking. The social cost of trade distortions (including quotas) in the presence of rent seeking and the Harris–Todaro labor market distortions is approximately double their cost when these labor distortions are ignored. The lesson would seem to be that these interactions need to be considered more fully in numerical economic policy analyses for developing countries.

References

Armington, PS (1969). A theory of demand for products distinguished by place of production. *IMF Staff Papers*, **16**, 159–176.

Bhagwati, J and TN Srinivasan (1980). Revenue seeking: A generalization of the theory of tariffs. *Journal of Political Economy*, **88**, 1069–1087.

Broadie, M (1983). OCTASOLV User's Guide, Systems Optimization Laboratory Technical Report 83-9. Stanford University, Department of Operations Research.

Clarete, RL (1984). The cost and consequences of trade distortions in a small-open economy: A general equilibrium model of the Philippines. PhD dissertation, University of Hawaii, Economics Department.

Clarete, RL and JA Roumasset (1983). An analysis of the economic policies affecting the Philippine coconut industry. Working paper 83-08, Philippine Institute for Development Studies.

Clarete, RL and JA Roumasset (1987). A Shoven–Whalley model of a small open economy: An illustration with Philippine tariffs. *Journal of Public Economics*, **32**, 247–261.

De Dios, N (1984). *An Analysis of the Philippine Economic Crisis*. Philippines: University of the Philippines Press.

Dervis, K, J de Melo and S Robinson (1982). *General Equilibrium Models for Development Policy*. New York: Cambridge University Press.

Diewert, E (1978). Hicks' aggregation theorem and the existence of a real value-added function. In *Production Economics: A Dual Approach to Theory and Applications*, M Fuss and D McFadden (eds.), Vol. 2, pp. 17–43. Amsterdam: North-Holland.

Hamilton, B, S Mohammed and J Whalley (1984). Rent seeking and the north–south terms of trade. *Journal of Policy Modeling*, **6**, 485–511.

Harris, T and M Todaro (1970). Migration unemployment and development: A two-sector analysis. *The American Economic Review*, **60**, 126–142.

Hicks, JR (1936). *Value and Capital*. Oxford: Clarendon Press.

Krueger, AO (1974). The political economy of the rent-seeking society. *The American Economic Review*, **64**, 291–303.

Mansur, A and J Whalley (1984). Numerical Specification of Applied General Equilibrium Models: Estimation, Calibration, and Data, HE Scarf and JB Shoven (eds.), Applied general equilibrium analysis. New York: Cambridge University Press.

Merrill, OH (1972). Applications and extensions of an algorithm that computes fixed points of certain upper semi-continuous point to set mappings. PhD dissertation, University of Michigan, Department of Industrial Engineering.

Shoven JB and J Whalley (1972). A general equilibrium calculation of the effects of differential taxation of income from capital in the U.S. *Journal of Public Economics*, **1**, 281–321.

Shoven, JB and J Whalley (1984). Applied general equilibrium models of taxation and international trade. *Journal of Economic Literature*, **22**, 1007–1051.

Chapter 4

General Equilibrium Evaluations of Tariff-Cutting Proposals in the Tokyo Round and Comparisons with More Extensive Liberalization of World Trade*,†

Fred Brown and John Whalley[‡]
University of Western Ontario, Canada
[‡] *National Bureau of Economic Research (NBER)*

In this chapter, a numerical general equilibrium model of international trade involving major world trading blocs (the U.S., Japan, the EEC, and the Rest of the World) is used to analyze the effects of alternative tariff-cutting formulae proposed by the major participants in the Tokyo Round negotiations under the GATT at an earlier stage preceding the recent agreement which was initialled in April 1979. We also compare our findings with model experiments involving more extensive forms of world trade liberalization. Multilateral tariff reductions corresponding to individual country proposals are considered along with a sequence of more wide-ranging trade liberalization measures on multilateral, bilateral and unilateral bases. The model used is described elsewhere (Whalley, 1978a) and only a brief verbal summary is given here so as to keep the main focus of the chapter on results.

We use a Heckscher–Ohlin type trade model incorporating the Armington assumption of product heterogeneity by trading area. The model assumes constant returns to scale production and no scale economies are considered. We solve this model numerically for alternative world trade equilibria associated with different policy regimes and thus are able to capture the terms of trade effects associated with variations in tariffs since we use a price endogenous general equilibrium framework.

---

*We are grateful to Jon Fuller and Bob Hamilton for research assistance, to a seminar group at Western Ontario for comments and to Jan Tumlir at GATT for help with data. This work has been supported by the Ford Foundation under their Program of Research on International Economic Order.
†This chapter was first published in (1980). *The Economic Journal*, **90**(363), 838–866.

This contrasts with some of the calculations of possible impacts made from trade liberalization under the GATT. In the recent Brookings study of the impact of the Tokyo Round multilateral tariff negotiations on participating countries (Cline *et al.*, 1978), static welfare gains are calculated from tariff reductions on a country-by-country basis assuming that relative producer prices of traded products remain constant. Under these calculations, all countries gain from tariff cuts through the reduction in price distortions between imported and domestically produced goods. An important characteristic of our results is that we show terms-of-trade effects to be significant, and for some trading areas losses may result. While our aggregate welfare gains from the various proposals are not too different from those reported in the Brookings study, their distribution by trading area is because of the role of terms-of-trade effects. Our findings for the three industrialized trading areas are approximately consistent with those reported by Deardorff and Stern (1979) who also note differences between their findings by trade area and those in the Brookings study.

In the past Heckscher–Ohlin trade models have not been used extensively in empirical work due to the difficulties of assembly and computational solution. We have overcome these problems by using a model of limited dimensionality[a] which is able to capture the terms-of-trade effects between major categories of traded items. The model is solved using general equilibrium computational methods for international trade general equilibrium models.

In an Armington[b] variant of a Heckscher–Ohlin model, unlike a traditional model, products by country are treated as heterogeneous. This rules out cases of complete specialization and accommodates the empirical phenomenon of "cross-hauling"[c] appearing in the trade statistics used. This

[a]We consider an aggregated five product variant of a more disaggregated 33 product model described in Whalley (1978a). The Brookings study is able to disaggregate to a tariff line basis for their calculations; detail at a tariff line basis can involve as many as 20,000 line items. Some recent modifications to our computational procedures suggest that repeated solutions of larger-dimensional models should prove somewhat easier than in the past and in future work with this model larger-scale variants will, in all probability be used.

[b]See Armington (1969).

[c]There are, of course, a whole range of explanations which can be offered for the phenomenon of "cross-hauling" in addition to that of qualitative difference. One illustration of this is provided by U.S.–Canadian trade. In U.S.–Canadian trade statistics the same product can be observed to be exported by British Columbia to the Western States of the U.S., and to be imported by Eastern Canada from the Eastern U.S. due to the saving in transportation costs.

modeling also enables us to integrate empirical estimates of import price elasticities by trading area into our calculations. In contrast to traditional models, however, no autarky solution exists with conventional preferences since domestic production of foreign goods is not possible; also trade does not arise from differences in factor endowments as in a "pure" Heckscher–Ohlin model. There are also grounds for arguing that the implicit complete specialization in Armington models will result in stronger terms-of-trade effects than in a comparable model with incomplete specialization, an observation which should be borne in mind in evaluating our findings. The model used incorporates a higher degree of substitution in demand between comparable products (e.g., Japanese and U.S. cars) than between general product groups (e.g., cars and food). This is accomplished by using nested CES preference function as a basis for demand patterns. As the elasticity of substitution between comparable products by area becomes large, a traditional Heckscher–Ohlin model is more closely approximated.

We examine three major trading blocs: the U.S., the nine-member EEC, and Japan, and also consider the rest of the world as an independent entity. Each of these countries trades with each other in a list of designated products; some trade occurs in intermediate products and some in products for final demand. Productive factors are immobile between countries. Due to our use of data to estimate our model, we have different production coefficients in each of our trading blocs and trade does not originate from differences in factor endowments alone. Differences in production technologies are a further factor determining comparative advantage. As already mentioned, the Armington approach enables empirical estimates of price elasticities of demand for imports and exports to be incorporated through the utility function parameters used and we discuss our estimation procedures and these production technology differences later. The majority of the parameter estimates relate as far as is possible to the single year 1973.[d]

Our major findings are that the worldwide gains from any of the multilateral tariff reductions proposed are small but the role of terms-of-trade effects in determining the allocation of gains by trading area is

---

[d]A single year's data is needed due to the methods used to estimate the model. 1973 is chosen as a recent year for which the major portion of the required data is available. At first sight it may appear a bad choice due to the Middle East War during the year; however the war occurred at the end of the year and major disruptions from the war occurred in subsequent years.

significant. The three major trading areas of the EEC, the U.S., and Japan gain, while the rest of the world loses. Under an exclusion of agriculture and textiles from formula proposals less-developed countries have most to lose, and the U.S. does not gain nearly as much as the EEC, which is the largest gainer. We report a perhaps surprising result that countries gain more from other country proposals than from their own and vice versa. We are able to rationalize these results in terms of the existing tariff structures in the trading areas. Compared to the potential gains from more extensive trade liberalization involving quantifiable nontariff barriers our results indicate the effects from any of the tariff-cutting formulae are minor. This, in turn, suggests that recent negotiations under the GATT have been concerned with relatively small changes in trade policies and larger potential gains are being forgone through the exclusion of nontariff barriers and the limitations on formula cuts within the recent negotiations. Since we use a long-run equilibrium model, we do not incorporate short-run adjustment problems in our analysis and this caveat to our findings should be kept in mind.

1. The Structure of the Model[e]

The general equilibrium model used incorporates four trading blocs reflecting major participants in world trade: the (nine-member) EEC, the U.S., Japan, and the rest of the world. The sizes of these blocs in the model reflect relative GNP for these areas for 1973.[f] The EEC, the U.S. and Japan between them account for some 60% of world production and a substantial fraction of world trade.[g] In setting their tariff policies each of these areas can therefore be expected to have some impact on the terms of trade which they face.

---

[e]A more detailed description of, an earlier version of the model is given in Whalley (1978a). An appendix describing the present model in equation form appears in Whalley (1978b). The differences in structure between the current version used here and the earlier version are that the earlier version uses a fixed coefficient technology to describe intermediate production while the version used here embodies substitutability between intermediate products.

[f]GNP for the rest of the world is obtained from the World Bank Atlas (1975).

[g]For each of the trading blocs there is a trading area considered in the model as part of the rest of the world which is important for that bloc while relatively unimportant for the others. For the U.S., Canada fills this role; for the EEC, it is EFTA; for Japan, Taiwan, Hong Kong, and South Korea. Tariff policy towards each of these areas is important for the major blocs concerned while relatively unimportant for the others. These additional areas are not separately identified in the model.

The model considers a number of products each of which is treated as being produced solely in one of the trading blocs. Products are differentiated on the basis of geographical point of production as well as their physical characteristics with "similar" products being close substitutes in demand. As already noted, this "Armington type" Heckscher–Ohlin model is used to accommodate the statistical phenomenon of "cross-hauling" in international trade and to exclude complete specialization in production.

The model used is an aggregated variant of that described in Whalley (1978a) with a richer specification of behavioral functions. The products considered both here and in Whalley (1978a) for each trading bloc are listed in Table 1. The more detailed variant clearly enables a richer treatment of discriminatory aspects of commercial policies to be considered at a computational cost. The differences in functional forms involved are discussed later.

Even the 33 product classification considers broad groups of commodities which are much coarser than the finely divided categories which are the subject of detailed tariff negotiations. Tariff negotiations under the Tokyo Round involved negotiations on a tariff-line basis which covered as many as 20,000 commodity items in certain cases. We have not been able to use a tariff-line basis in our model as this produces a general equilibrium structure which can be neither formulated nor solved. Our model, therefore, gives indications of general equilibrium impacts in terms of the broad product categories which are the subject of tariff cuts. Important aspects of tariff policies, capable of consideration by our model, are the treatment of agricultural products (which are excluded from the original formula proposals in the GATT negotiations), the treatment of textiles (which are excluded in the original U.S. tariff-cutting proposal), and the relative size of tariffs on heavy and light manufactured items.

An outline of the model is given in Table 2. Production and demand patterns in each of the trading blocs revolve around the domestic and world price system. Producers maximize profits and competitive forces operate such that in equilibrium all supernormal profits are competed away. Explicit demand functions are used which are derived from utility maximization. Demand functions have conventional downward-sloping properties and also have cross-price effects incorporated.

For each product the market price is the price at point of production. Sellers receive these prices, purchasers (both intermediate and final demands) pay these prices gross of tariffs and domestic taxes. Financial investment flows enter the world market system and are treated as

Table 1. Product and Industrial Classifications Used in the General Equilibrium Trade Models Adopted Here by Whalley (1978a).

Product classification used in Whalley (1978a)	Aggregated product classification used in the chapter
Agriculture	(1) Agriculture and Food (1)–(4) + (8)–(11)
(1) Meats and dairy products	(2) Raw materials and extractive products (5)–(7)
(2) Cereals	(3) Nondurable manufactures (12)–(17)
(3) Other agricultural products	(4) Durable manufactures (18)–(24)
(4) Forestry and fisheries	(5) Services (25)–(33)
Mining	
(5) Coal	
(6) Oil, natural gas	
(7) Metallic, non-metallic and other	
Manufacturing nondurable goods, prepared food and kindred products	
(8) Tea, sugar, coffee, spices, cocoa	
(9) Alcoholic drinks	
(10) Other foods	
(11) Tobacco	
(12) Apparel and textile products	
(13) Paper, printing, publishing	
(14) Pharmaceuticals and toiletries	
(15) Other chemical and allied products	
(16) Petroleum and coal products	
(17) Rubber and plastics	
Durable goods	
(18) Lumber, wood and furniture	
(19) Primary and fabricated metals, stone, glass	
(20) Machinery except electrical	
(21) Electrical machinery	
(22) Transport vehicles	
(23) Scientific and precision instruments	
(24) Miscellaneous manufacturing	
Services	
(25) Construction*	
(26) Water transportation	
(27) Other transportation and communications	
(28) Housing services*	
(29) Electricity and sanitary services	
(30) Wholesale and retail trade*	
(31) Finance, insurance and real estate	
(32) Other services	
(33) Government*	

*Denotes a nontraded good.

Table 2. The General Equilibrium Model of U.S.–EEC–Japanese Trade — A Structural Outline.

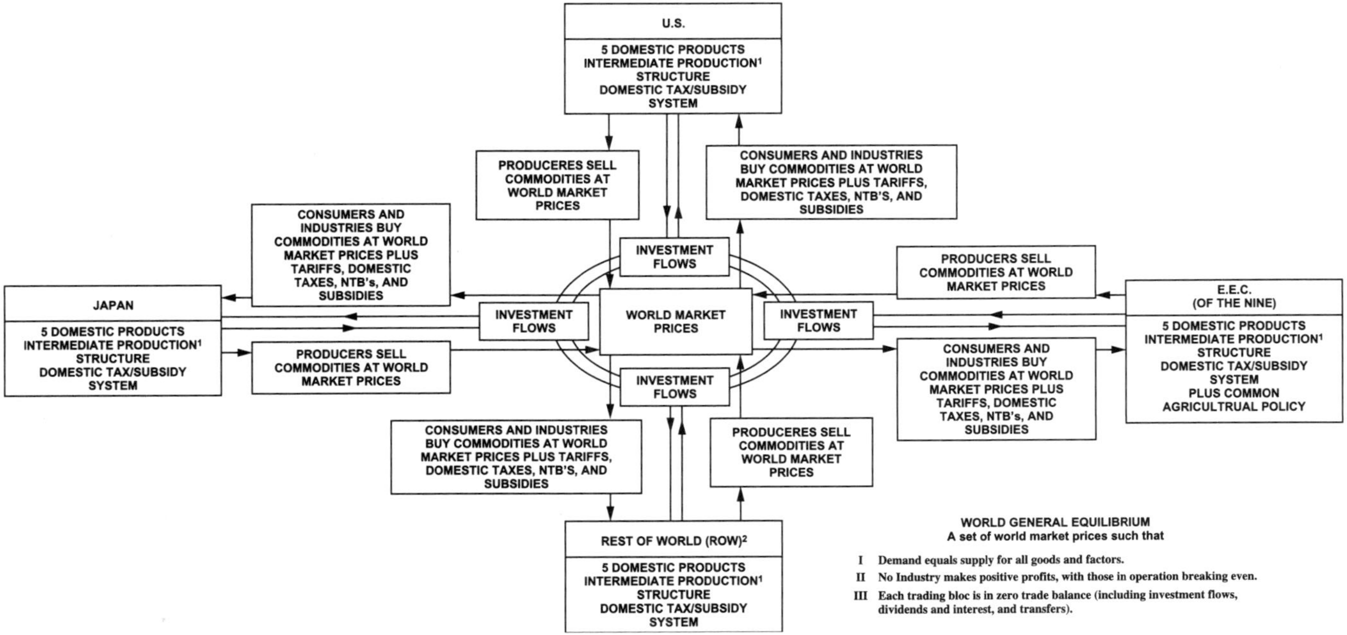

[1]This incorporates intermediate substitution between similar inputs differentiated by country of origin; e.g., a fixed steel requirement per car produced in the U.S. might be specified but this can be met by a substitutable mix of domestically produced steel and steel imported from the various trading blocs.

[2]The rest of the world is specified "schematically" and no strong claims to realism are made. An arithmetic average of comparable parameters in the three major trading areas is used. The factor endowments in the rest of the world are, however, selected to reflect the relative capital abundance of the three major trading areas. The capital to labor ratio in the rest of the world is considered to be in aggregate 1/5 of that in the combination of the three major trading areas with a ratio of 1:10 for manufacturing.

components of foreign trade. These are treated as purchases of capital goods by agents located in the country of source of the capital funds. The difference between capital movements and merchandise trade is that the capital goods acquired are not repatriated to the country of location of the purchaser, but remain in the source country to generate income in future time periods.

An equilibrium in the model is a situation where demands equal supplies for all products and in each industry a zero-profit condition is satisfied representing the absence of supernormal profits. A zero foreign trade balance condition applies to each country. The effect of a tariff change in any country is to alter the relative prices of imported and domestically produced goods and affect the volume of imports. This, in turn, changes the pattern of domestic demands and, indirectly, prices of products. Alterations in tariff policies will affect the equilibrium achieved, resulting in new equilibrium prices and quantities. Measures of worldwide gains or losses and the distribution by trading bloc can be obtained through a comparison of equilibria.

1.1. *Production Side of the Model*

On the production side of the model, each industry in each trading bloc has a number of possible methods of production. Each production process uses two different sets of inputs. The first are substitutable capital and labor inputs located in that country; each industry has a value-added production function of CES form which specifies the substitution possibilities between the inputs, capital services, and labor services. No technical change is incorporated and it is thus assumed that no changes in technology will result from adoption of alternative tariff policies. This specification also excludes the possibility of relocation by industries in response to tariff changes.

In addition to the CES value-added functions, each industry uses the outputs of other industries as inputs (both domestic and imported). In the detailed version of this model described in Whalley (1978a), it is assumed that input–output coefficients are fixed and cannot change. This is somewhat unrealistic in that it specifies, for example, fixed amounts of both Japanese and U.S. steel as required to produce a car in the U.S. These intermediate requirements operate independently of the relative prices of Japanese and U.S. steel. In the version of the model used here, substitution between intermediate products is considered and fixed coefficients in terms of composite goods only are assumed. Thus, the fixed amount of steel required to make a car can be met by a substitutable mix of Japanese and U.S. steel. Each fixed coefficient in terms of composite goods is a CES function with types of composite goods (products identified by geographical point of production) entering as arguments. This more complex formulation requires more substantial amounts of execution time to solve than the fixed coefficient version and is thus used for the aggregated variant of the model. The data which are used to estimate these equations are discussed later.

1.2. *Demand side*

On the demand side of the model a single household consumer group is considered in each of the trading blocs. Each of these groups has demand functions defined over the various products available. Government expenditures and investment are separately incorporated through price endogenous demand patterns. These demand functions are obtained by maximizing a nested CES utility function for each household group. Within this form, a fixed elasticity of substitution is assumed between products imported from the various trading areas and domestic products of a similar type, along with a different elasticity of substitution between the composite products. This approach enables empirical estimates of price elasticities in world trade to be incorporated into the model; these values are used to guide parameter choice for elasticity values in the CES forms in a manner to be discussed later. Since each group generates demands from utility maximization, the market demand functions satisfy Walras' Law. This specifies that at any set of prices the total value of demands equals the total value of incomes. The incomes of consumer groups are derived from the ownership of primary factors located in each trading bloc (which can be sold at the set of factor prices which each consumer faces) plus transfers received from the government. The government in each trading bloc collects taxes from households and also disperses transfer incomes. Government expenditures enter as a separate demand category and are financed by tax collections. A separate demand category is incorporated for investment expenditures.

1.3. *Policies considered in the model*

A number of different components of commercial policy are considered since the model has been constructed to yield a multi-purpose capability of analyzing the price-distorting effects of a number of policy interventions in world trade. Tariffs, nontariff barriers, and domestic tax policies are all

Table 3. Summary of Average 1973 Tariff Rates* by Broad Category and by Trading Bloc.†

Product category from Table 1	Percentage rate on U.S. imports	Percentage rate on EEC imports	Percentage rate on Japanese imports
(1) Agriculture and food products	5.3	30.0	72.9††
(2) Raw materials	2.5	2.3	3.3
(3) Nondurable manufactures	16.9	10.2	11.0
(4) Durable manufactures	6.6	9.0	10.1
(5) Services	0	0	0

*All rates are calculated to apply to imports valued on an f.o.b. basis; this involves data adjustments for the EEC and Japan.
†The sources used are GATT (1974), Yeats (1976, 1977), and authors' own calculations.
††This rate is upward biased due to inclusion of tariffs on tobacco. In Japan, high tobacco tariffs operate in place of the domestic taxes on tobacco products common in many countries. Tariffs on agriculture and food products are not considered to be part of possible negotiated tariff cuts and no reduction in this rate is considered in the application of formula proposals in the model.

incorporated in *ad valorem* form. These change the pattern and structure of world trade between the trade blocs from a no-policy regime. The motivation for considering policies additional to tariffs is that the tariff-cutting formulae examined can then be compared to more extensive forms of liberalization of world trade. This approach is followed even though there are difficulties in quantifying the nontariff barriers as described below.

Tariffs are considered to apply in *ad valorem* form to imports of products for both final and intermediate uses valued at f.o.b. prices.[h] Tariff collections become part of the general government revenues for financing government expenditures. As is well known there is substantial difficulty in obtaining average tariff rates in *ad valorem* form for aggregated classification of the form presented in Table 1. The procedure used has been to adopt the 1974 GATT study averaged rates for manufactured and mining products which use 1973 MFN tariff schedules. The GATT averaging procedure of using world imports for 1970 and 1971 has been extended in arriving at estimates consistent with the classifications in Table 1. Estimates for agricultural and food items are taken from Yeats (1976, 1977).

The broad pattern of tariff rates is given in Table 3 where average rates for the five broad categories considered in the aggregated variant are

[h]This approximates the customs clearance basis in the U.S.; in Japan and the EEC tariffs apply to valuations much closer to a c.i.f. price.

reported by trading bloc. A notable feature of Table 3 is that average tariff rates across all manufactured products do not differ sharply between the U.S., the EEC, and Japan with perhaps slightly higher rates prevailing in Japan. The dispersion in tariff rates between nondurable and durable manufacturing is, however, more pronounced in the U.S. case. The tariff rates corresponding to the tariff-cut proposals are more fully discussed later.

Nontariff barriers include an assortment of policies which either deliberately or coincidently affect trading patterns in addition to those effects induced through tariff policy. In recent years, they have attracted increasing attention due to the view of many people that they serve in practice as a more severe impediment to trade than conventional tariff policy. A number of studies (Baldwin, 1970; UNCTAD, 1969, 1970; Walter, 1972) have attempted to classify and describe these barriers, although numerical estimates are somewhat sparse. A recent study by Roningen and Yeats (1976) drawing on UNCTAD documentation provides estimates for France, Japan, Sweden, and the U.S., and a related study by Yeats (1976) contains estimates of the role of nontariff barriers on agricultural products in the EEC. A descriptive list of nontariff barriers would include government purchasing policies, quotas, seasonal restrictions, specific licensing regulations, valuation procedures for tariff purposes, voluntary export restraints, special import charges (including such items as variable levies in the European Community Agricultural Policy), and health and sanitary regulations. Clearly, some of these are more important than others and some can be quantified more satisfactorily than others. The major nontariff barriers by trading bloc and by product are outlined in Table 4 which also reports *ad valorem* equivalents used for these barriers. These have been primarily derived from estimates reported by Roningen and Yeats (1976), although other sources including Baldwin (1970) have been used. The relative size of these nontariff barriers, as modeled to the tariffs is apparent from Tables 3 and 4.

Domestic taxation and subsidy policies also enter the model and affect trade patterns. The model incorporates the domestic taxation and subsidy systems of each of the trading blocs by treating corporate and property taxes as taxes on profit-type returns by industry, social and security taxes on labor use by industry, value-added and sales taxes as production-type taxes, specific duties as consumption taxes, and income taxes as charges on income receipts by consumer groups.

Table 4. Summary[1] of Major Nontariff Barriers by Category and by Trading Bloc.

	Nontariff barriers on U.S. imports		Nontariff barriers on Japanese imports		Nontariff barriers on EEC imports	
Category	Description	*Ad valorem* equivalent used	Description	*Ad valorem* equivalent used	Description	*Ad valorem* equivalent used
Agricultural and food products	Quotas on meat and dairy products, international agreements on coffee, sugar, cocoa	31.9	Health and sanitary restrictions; subsidies (primarily to rice producers); international agreements on coffee, sugar, cocoa; state trading in alcohol and tobacco	97.0	Common agricultural policy (meat, dairy, and grains); international agreements on coffee, sugar, cocoa	45.4
Raw materials	License fee system on petroleum imports quotas (petroleum, and metallic and nonmetallic ores) Depletion allowances	Effects small; value of o used	Subsidies to coal; quotas on petroleum, natural gas	65.6	Subsidies to coal; quotas on coal; state trading in coal, petroleum, natural gas	88.6
Nondurable manufactures	Quotas on petroleum and oil products, textile quotas	28.0	Quotas on chemical and petroleum products	17.9	Quotas on chemical products, petroleum and coal products, rubber, textiles	22.9

(*Continued*)

Table 4. (*Continued*)

	Nontariff barriers on U.S. imports		Nontariff barriers on Japanese imports		Nontariff barriers on EEC imports	
Category	Description	*Ad valorem* equivalent used	Description	*Ad valorem* equivalent used	Description	*Ad valorem* equivalent used
Durable manufactures	Subsidies via government research expenditures, steel restrictions	Effects small in 1973: value of o used	Quotas (computers, transistors, communications equipment) subsidies (shipbuilding)	9.0	Quotas (steel, electrical machinery, transport equipment); subsidies; restrictive standards	16.8
Service items and other	Merchant marine flag discrimination	No estimates available — assumed small: value of o used	—	No estimates available — assumed small: value of o used	—	No estimates available — assumed small: value of o used
General nontariff barriers	Government procurement policies	—	"Buy National" policies; voluntary export restraints; government procurement policies	—	"Buy National" policies; government procurement policies	—

[1]Summary and rates apply as far as possible to the period immediately prior to 1973 and take no account of subsequent changes in policies, especially to raw materials, since the events of late 1973.

Sources: for description, various GATT and UNCTAD documents, U.S. Tariff Commission Reports (1974); for estimates of rates, Yeats and Roningen (1976), Baldwin (1970) and authors' own calculations.

Quotas and other nontariff barriers are represented in the model in *ad valorem* equivalent form rather than as restrictions on quantities imported. A distinguishing characteristic of both quotas and nontariff barriers is that, in practice, they generate no tax revenue for the government. This is accommodated by returning receipts from these charges in lump sum form to consumer groups; the lump sum payments being determined by ratios of consumer incomes in basic data.

The effects of quotas are more realistically captured in a general equilibrium model not as equivalent *ad valorem* charges but directly as quantity restrictions. From a computational point of view it is straightforward to incorporate the quantity restrictions implied by quotas by considering an additional fictitious commodity which must be purchased when a good involved is imported. The endowment of this commodity can be made equal to the value of the quota involved and owned by the recipient of the rents which quotas create. If a quota is not binding in equilibrium, the corresponding artificial commodity will have a zero price. While this approach can be implemented in small dimensions, the extra dimensions created raise computational difficulties which are avoided here by considering quotas in equivalent *ad valorem* form.

2. Estimation of the Model

The model as specified contains a large number of parameter values which must be estimated prior to the model being used to evaluate the effects of alternative tariff cuts. A model on such a scale cannot be easily estimated in its entirety using conventional econometric methods and resort is therefore made to a sequence of procedures which have been developed in recent years for large-scale general equilibrium models. The procedure is to assemble a set of data for a given period of time in a form which is consistent with the equilibrium conditions of the model. Once assembled, parameter values for equations can be directly estimated from the equilibrium conditions. This data set is termed a benchmark equilibrium data set and has the properties of a worldwide competitive equilibrium that demands and supplies for products will balance, that no profits will be made in any of the domestic industries, and that each country will be in zero balance in its trading relations with all other countries.

The adoption of this overall approach implies the need to construct an equilibrium data set involving both the domestic and trading activity of each of the trading blocs. Many divergent source materials need to be assembled and corrected for inconsistent classifications and definitions and, even when this is complete, further corrections are necessary to adjust the data mutually so that the equilibrium conditions of the model are satisfied. A complete description of sources used in the assembly of this data set for the year 1973 appears in Appendix B of Whalley (1978a). 1973 is chosen as a recent year for which much of the data is available[i] and for which the disruptions stemming from the Middle East war towards the end of 1973 are largely absent. Even so, there are substantial problems of inconsistent classifications and definitions, gaps in data availability, and differences in dates of basic sources, and the data set produced must therefore be considered only as a first approximation to an ideal data set for the model.

The estimation procedure uses the model equilibrium conditions as a set of identifying restrictions. A nonstochastic estimation procedure is used for determining parameter values which are consistent with both benchmark data and the equilibrium conditions. On the demand side, demand functions are solved for parameters consistent with both equilibrium prices and quantities. On the supply side, cost functions derived from the production structures assumed are used to solve for parameter values consistent with equilibrium prices and input use by industry. Depending upon the complexity of functional forms this procedure may require additional identifying restrictions beyond those represented by the benchmark equilibrium data set. These identifying restrictions, where needed, take the form of the specification of unit-free parameters represented by the elasticities of substitution in the functional forms.[j] On the production side the elasticities of substitution are obtained from a literature search.[k] On the demand side no empirical evidence is

[i]The GATT tariff study used is available only for 1973 tariff data; the data used for the U.S. draws heavily on the data set constructed by Fullerton, Shoven and Whalley (1978) for 1973; certain of the data used for Japan and the EEC have 1973 as the latest year of availability.

[j]The ease with which estimation of parameters from the equilibrium data set can proceed depends upon the complexity of the behavioral equations used in the model. If Cobb–Douglas functional forms are used for demand functions, the exponents in the Cobb–Douglas functions are given directly by the expenditure shares in basic data. With CES functions more information is needed and extraneous values of substitution elasticities are needed prior to the use of this procedure.

[k]The recent survey by Caddy (1976) provides the main source for these estimates. An average over the estimates reported by Caddy is used for each industry in the model; the values adopted, the same for each trading area, are: agriculture and food 0.64; raw materials 0.50; nondurable manufactures 0.93; durable manufactures 0.74; services 0.97.

directly available and a procedure is used of relating the substitution elasticities in preference functions to estimate price elasticities in world trade.

At the benchmark equilibrium given by the consistent data set, it is possible to calculate the implied point estimates of the price elasticities of demand for imports in each of the trading blocs. These values can be compared to estimates obtained from literature searches and on that basis modifications made to the estimates of the substitution elasticities in preferences. The substitution elasticities derived from import price elasticities are critical parameters for the model as their value substantially affects trade responses to tariff cuts in the model, and not surprisingly changes in the values used affect results. We have relied heavily on the recent compendium of elasticity values produced by Stern, Francis, and Schumacher (SFS) (1977). These authors suggest that the empirical evidence on price elasticities in world trade is not conclusive and argue that limited reliability can be placed in elasticity values available for detailed product classifications. They produce "best guess" estimates for price elasticities for total imports by country and conclude that the majority of these are approximately in the range of −1.0. This is somewhat larger than the region suggested by Houthakker and Magee (1969) in their earlier survey although some authors, such as Balassa and Kreinin (1967), have argued for and used higher values on the grounds of a downward bias associated with time series estimation procedures.

We use two specifications of the substitution elasticities derived from import demand function estimates. One has the substitution elasticities in demand functions to be the same value for substitution between products designated by area. This gives import price elasticities with limited variation for all products. We also set different values by product type to calibrate approximately to the best guess SFS estimates by product.

For comparability to elasticity values used in other international trade studies of a nongeneral equilibrium nature, we have listed the point estimates of import price elasticities by trading area from our first approach in Table 5.

These can be seen to approximate the SFS "best-guess" values and the values used in the Brooking study. Balassa and Kreinin, as mentioned, used higher values. Because of the importance of these values to our results we have performed sensitivity analysis around our substitution elasticity values and the implied variation in aggregate price elasticities are reported in Section IV, where these results are discussed. Our model also incorporates

Table 5. Implied Point Estimates of Uncompensated Own Price Elasticities of Import Demand Functions in the Model and Comparison to Values Used or Reported in Other Studies.

	EEC	U.S.	Japan
Point estimates of import price elasticities for final demand functions at the benchmark equilibrium in the model	−0.91	−1.63	−0.77
Central value import price easticities suggested by Stern, Francis and Schumacher (1976)	−0.78 (average over EEC country estimates in SFS)	−1.66	−0.78
Weighted average import price elasticities reported by Cline *et al.* (Brookings study) (1978)	−0.92	−1.85	−1.39
Import price elasticities for finished manufactures used by Balassa/Kreinin (1967)	−3.09	−4.12	−3.09

substitution between domestic and imported products in intermediate use and we have used a value of 1.15 for this substitution elasticity in all trading areas. This is an approximate average over the import price elasticities in all trading areas.

Once fully specified, the model is solved for a general equilibrium by using a Newton method which has been modified from earlier computer programs originally designed to refine the approximation obtained from the application of Scarf's algorithm.[1] These Newton methods work swiftly and, although there is no *ex ante* argument of convergence which is built into the procedures, they have been successful in implementation. Because of the complexity of the model no statement of uniqueness of equilibrium is obtained, although with other variants of the model some experimentation has been done in displacing equilibria once found and then checking that these are returned to and also approaching equilibria from different points and at different speeds. None of these tests has yet revealed a situation of nonuniqueness of equilibria in these complex environments, although nonuniqueness is certainly not excluded. The structure of the computer programs used in the set of analyses is outlined in Table 6.

[1]See Scarf (1973) and the extension to international trade models with tariffs by Shoven and Whalley (1974).

Table 6. Structure of Computer Programs Used in the General Equilibrium Model of World Trade.

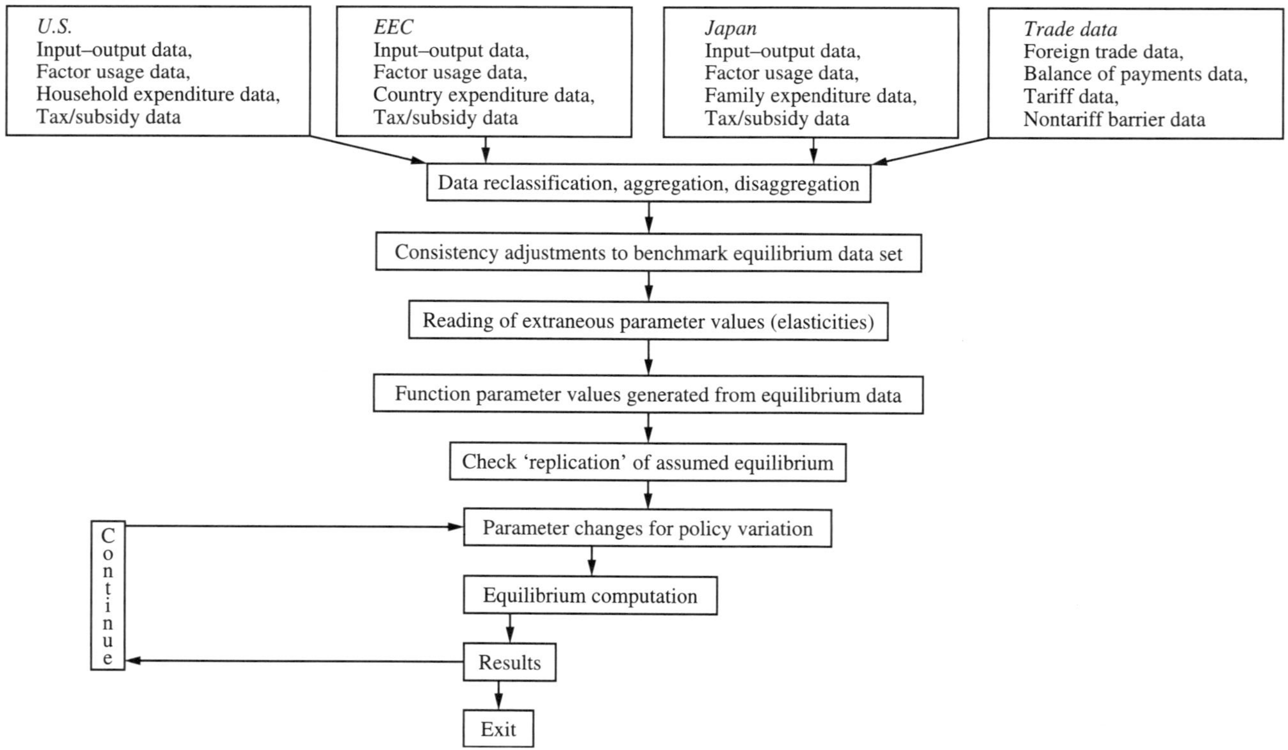

Machine and Program Features

Machine: Cyber 73 (slower than a CDC 7,600 by a factor of, perhaps, 16; slower than an IBM 370/168 by a factor of, perhaps, 8).

Table 6. (*Continued*)

Notes: (*For Table* 6 *continued*)
Program length in number of statements: (approx.) equilibrium computation 4,000; data classification and adjustments 3,000; parameter value generation 2,000; print format and results 3,000.
Execution time: Depending on parameter values and nature of policy change in the region 1/2 hour.
Compilation time: Approx. 40–50 seconds for the code of the main program.
Space requirement: Main frame (49K), plus most of an extended core facility (88K) plus 250K of a mass storage device. Space requirements arise mainly in the work with basic data.
Data requirements: "Crude" data usage around 60,000 numbers; "model" data requirement 1,000 parameter values.
Behavioral function evaluations: To calculate one excess demand correspondence for a given price vector requires evaluation of around 500 derived demand functions (by product and agent). A run of 1/2 hour would evaluate 240–300 excess demand correspondences.[1]

[1]An important development since these calculations were made has been the construction of a solution method which substantially reduces the number of these evaluations to around 20 or less. This offers the possibility of solving the model in the full dimensionality of 33 products by area while also incorporating the richer functional forms used in this chapter in somewhat less than 1/2 hour.

3. Tariff-Cutting Proposals and their Representation in Model Equivalent Forms

Five proposals for multilateral cuts in tariffs by participating countries of the GATT are considered and are each represented in model equivalent form. These proposals correspond to those made by the U.S., the EEC, Japan, Canada, and Switzerland in the recent Tokyo round of negotiations concluded in April 1979. These may be thought of as the first round of offers (made at the general formulae stage of negotiations around the end of 1977) and after this time the negotiations became more complex with counter offers, exclusions proposed, modifications to tariff valuation procedures suggested, and other departures from the general formulae. These first round formula proposals are what are analyzed in this chapter and are listed in Table 7.

Table 7. Tariff-Cutting Formulae Proposed by Country Participants in the Tokyo Round.

U.S. Proposal (T_N = post-cut tariff, T_0 = pre-cut tariff)

$$T_N = 0.4T_0 \quad \text{if } T_0 > 0.067,$$
$$T_N = 0.5T_0 - 1.5T_0^2 \quad \text{if } T_0 \leq 0.067.$$

EEC Proposal (Four iterative cuts)

$$T_N = T_0 - 2T_0^2 + 2T_0^3 - T_0^4 - (T_0 - 2T_0^2 + 2T_0^3 - T_0^4)^2 - [T_0 - 2T_0^2 + 2T_0^3 - T_0^4 - (T_0 - 2T_0^2 + 2T_0^3 - T_0^4)^2]^2.$$

Japanese Proposal[1] (applied to Post-Kennedy Round and not current tariffs)

$$T_N = 0.3T_0 + 0.035 \quad \text{if } T_0 > 0.05,$$
$$T_N = 0.3T_0 \quad \text{if } T_0 \leq 0.05.$$

Canadian Proposal[1] (cut on the basis of U.S. tariffs and all countries adopt reduced U.S. tariffs)

$$T_N = 0.4T_0^{U.S.} \quad \text{if } T_0 > 0.05,$$
$$T_N = 0.0 \quad \text{if } T_0 \leq 0.05.$$

Swiss Proposal (compromise formula)

$$T_N = \frac{AT_0}{A + T_0}, \quad A \text{ is a constant (a realistic value is 0.14).}$$

[1]The Canadian proposal was in fact restricted to the sector by sector negotiations and was proposed primarily in the context of tariffs on pulp and paper, but we have considered it here as an alternative general formula.

Putting differences in the structures of the formulae on one side, there are some important common characteristics to all of these proposals. The first is that they apply only to manufactured products and raw materials; raw materials for the most part have small tariffs currently applying to them. The exclusion of agricultural products is obviously of substantial consequence to the U.S. Second, certain product groups besides agriculture are excluded from some of the proposals. Textiles are excluded by the U.S. (which has higher textile tariffs than the EEC or Japan) but included in the EEC and Japanese formulae. In our calculations, we have assumed that the tariff-cutting formulae apply to all products considered in the model with the exclusion of agricultural products and textiles. Textiles appear as a component of nondurable manufacturing product. The effect of these exclusions combined with existing low tariffs on raw materials is that less developed countries, which export mainly these products are likely to suffer terms-of-trade losses from negotiated cuts using formulae irrespective of which specific formula is adopted. This is a prominent feature of our results, as is the result that the U.S. gains proportionately less than other trading blocs given larger U.S. agricultural exports. The EEC as the major exporter of manufactured products is a major gainer.

A further point to note is that these formulae contain features which are clearly included due to the perceived national interest. The Japanese proposal, for instance, bases cuts on post-Kennedy round tariffs rather than current tariffs. The fact that Japan has had unilateral tariff cuts since the Kennedy round whereas other blocs have not, means that implementation of the Japanese formula would produce larger cuts outside Japan. For this reason, we consider two variants of the Japanese proposal, one applied to current tariffs and the other with allowance for smaller cuts by Japan due to this feature. The Canadian formula explicitly cuts all small tariffs to zero. A substantial portion of Canadian exports are of raw materials to the U.S., where these tariffs are already small, and this provision is clearly aimed in this direction.

Other features of these proposals are a little mysterious and appear to run counter to perceived national interest. The EEC iterative cut is a nonlinear cut which cuts high tariffs more than proportionately compared to low tariffs. This proposal stems from the EEC desire to "harmonize". Our results suggest that the EEC gains more from the U.S. proposal, and the U.S. more from the EEC proposal; this result is mainly explained by the average depth of the cutting proposals rather than the nonlinearities of the formulae. For Canada to suggest all countries adopt the U.S. tariff also seems counter to perceived national interest[m] since Canadian tariff protection is higher than most of the industrialized world and Canada would suffer a deeper cut than other countries through the proposal.

The compromise Swiss formula ultimately accepted as the general formula in the negotiations may have been acceptable primarily because subtle features interpreted by opposing negotiators as in the national advantage of other blocs are missing. The value of the constant term in the Swiss formula seemed likely to be in the region of 11–17% at the time of our model assembly and the mid-range value of 14% has been assumed in our calculations.

Figures are given in Table 8 of what each of the proposed formulae in Table 7 would involve for tariff rates of 5%, 10%, 15% and 20%. As can be seen, the U.S. proposal is a deeper cut on average than the EEC proposal. The Canadian proposal turns out to be the most severe cut of all in practice since the adoption of the U.S. tariff means that EEC and Japan tariffs would be cut further on a product-by-product basis than under a simple U.S. formula.

Our representation of the tariff cut proposals in model equivalent form uses the tariff data from the GATT tariff study (1974) referred to earlier. This study formed the basis for much of the current negotiations on the tariff cuts which took place in Geneva. It converts all MFN tariffs onto a comparable *ad valorem* equivalent basis for the detailed product line basis

Table 8. Application of Tariff-Cutting Formulae Listed in Table 7 to Illustrative Tariff Rates.

	Ad valorem rate before formula applied			
Tariff cutting formula	5%	10%	15%	20%
U.S. proposal	2.1	4	6	8
EEC proposal	4.1	7.0	8.9	10.3
Japanese proposal	5	6.5	8	9.5
Canadian proposal	0	4	6	8
Swiss proposal	3.7	5.8	7.2	8.2

[m]Although some would argue that Canada as a small country cannot substantially affect its terms of trade through a tariff and the major effect of the domestic tariff is a welfare loss in Canada.

corresponding to the GATT tariff nomenclature.[n] This has been done for a detailed seven digit level, and the *ad valorem* equivalent tariffs have then been averaged onto a more aggregated classification of some 200 products.

A number of different averaging procedures are used in the summary GATT tariff rates and the choice of average clearly makes a difference to the perceived effect of any cutting proposals. We calculate the "post-cut" rates from our own average of the summary tariff rates and for this reason the choice of GATT average is worth of some discussion.

In the GATT summary tariff study, eight different averaged estimates for each product group are reported for each trading area. Arithmetic averages are reported along with weighted averages where the weights involve both the own imports by any country and a composite bundle representing world imports. The difficulties of deciding on quantity weights for averaging are well known; the use of own imports to average is unsatisfactory since those products which are protected have reduced inward trade flows and a low weighting is given to high tariffs; the use of a "typical" import bundle for all trade areas may not reflect trade preferences. Averages using both of these approaches to weighting are reported in the GATT study. Because of the difficulties of using detailed data on own imports, a dual procedure was used in the GATT study of first averaging to a four-digit GATT classification by two different methods. There are, therefore, four different averaging procedures which are used: arithmetic, weighting by "world" imports, and weighting by own imports using two different procedures. For each of these there is an additional difference in the treatment of duty-free items. Depending upon whether a zero tariff is included in the average for all items which have no tariff, a substantial difference results in the tariff estimates used, and both inclusion and exclusion of duty-free items is used in the GATT averages.

We have selected the averages calculated using own imports as weights including the zero tariff applied to duty-free items. We have then averaged

[n]There is, however, no explicit correction for differences in valuation procedures by country. In certain countries administered rather than market prices form the basis for assessment and the nominal tariff rate underestimates the tariff on a market price basis. This is especially true in the U.S., where the American Selling Price (ASP) system is used for chemicals and footwear which substantially increases the tariff on a market price basis. (See Grubel and Johnson (1967).) In addition U.S., Canadian, and Australian tariffs are on a f.o.b. basis while all others are on a c.i.f. basis. This gives the appearance of higher tariffs in these countries. In our use of Japanese and EEC tariff data, we attempt to correct for this feature.

from the GATT summary tariff classification to the classification in the detailed variant of the model of 33 products used by Whalley (1978a) following the same averaging procedures as used by Whalley. The tariff rates on the classification of 33 products form the basis for the application of the tariff-cutting proposals. We have mechanically applied the formulae described in Table 7 to the tariff rates on the 33 products, which are then further averaged for use in the aggregated variant of the model adopted here. For the Japanese formulae, we do not have detailed information on the differences between current and post-Kennedy round tariffs and have applied the formula to Japan, initially ignoring this difference (Japan 1). We then consider special cases where Japan only has one half the cut to their own tariff calculated by the Japanese formula in order to evaluate crudely the use of post-Kennedy round rather than current tariffs in this formula.

The average tariffs for each trading bloc which result from these cuts are represented in Table 9 where for each of the formulae the new and old tariffs of each of the trading blocs are represented. Because of the tariff-averaging procedure of using imports as weights and the model treatment of imports by country as separate products, different composite tariffs by aggregated product for each trading bloc result. Tariffs for the rest of the world are crudely calculated as an average over the tariffs for the three major blocs (which may well be an underestimate). Cuts are not reported for this trading area but enter the calculations.

The pre-cut tariffs on manufactured products average in the region of 9–11% with the U.S. slightly lower in aggregate than the EEC, which in turn is somewhat lower than Japan. The effect of the tariff-cutting proposals is to cut these average tariffs on all manufactured products to a region of 4–5% (U.S. cut) to 7–8% (Japanese cut). With these proposals represented in model equivalent form, we apply the new tariff rates as inputs to the basic data set of the model and compute a new equilibrium solution of our model; old and new equilibria are then compared.[o] Results from these calculations are presented in the next section.

---

[o]A point which has been raised in the policy discussion of the tariff cut proposals is the revenue effect which tariff cuts may induce. There is a revenue loss for each of the trading blocs involved, and although this may seem relatively small compared to total tax revenues it is of some potential significance in terms of the overall evaluation of the tariff cuts in a macro-framework. We employ a full employment general equilibrium model and the stabilization effects associated with tariff-cutting proposals are not satisfactorily analyzed through our approach. In our results, we focus on welfare results on a country-wide basis and the different intersectoral transfers associated with varying tariff collections are of little consequence.

Table 9. Calculated Pre- and Post-Cut Tariff Rates by Product by Area in the Model.

	1. Pre-cut imported by			2. U.S. formula imported by			3. EEC formula imported by			4. Japanese (Japan 1) formula imported by		
	EEC	U.S.	Japan	EEC	U.S.	Japan	EEC	U.S.	Japan	EEC	U.S.	Japan
Produced in the EEC												
goods* 1	0	6.3	53.7†	0	6.3	53.7	0	6.3	53.7	0	6.3	53.7
goods* 2	0	3.0	4.0	0	1.4	1.8	0	2.7	3.4	0	3.0	4.0
goods* 3	0	14.5	11.4	0	13.4	8.8	0	14.1	10.0	0	14.3	9.8
goods* 4	0	6.5	11.4	0	2.6	4.6	0	5.0	7.5	0	5.4	6.9
goods* 5	0	0	0	0	0	0	0	0	0	0	0	0
Produced in the U.S.												
goods* 1	38.2	0	92.7†	38.2	0	92.2	38.2	0	92.2	38.2	0	92.2
goods* 2	2.6	0	2.5	1.2	0	1.1	2.4	0	2.0	2.6	0	2.0
goods* 3	9.7	0	10.7	4.9	0	7.8	7.3	0	9.2	7.0	0	8.9
goods* 4	8.6	0	8.9	3.4	0	3.6	6.2	0	6.2	6.1	0	6.2
goods* 5	0	0	0	0	0	0	0	0	0	0	0	0
Produced in Japan												
goods* 1	21.8	4.4	0	21.8	4.4	0	21.8	4.4	0	21.8	4.4	0
goods* 2	2.0	2.0	0	0.9	0.9	0	1.8	1.8	0	2.0	2.0	0
goods* 3	10.5	19.3	0	6.4	18.8	0	8.3	19.2	0	8.0	19.2	0
goods* 4	9.4	6.8	0	3.8	2.8	0	6.6	5.2	0	6.3	5.5	0
goods* 5	0	0	0	0	0	0	0	0	0	0	0	0
Produced in the rest of the world												
goods* 1	24.3	7.0	26.9	24.3	7.0	26.9	24.3	7.0	26.9	24.3	7.0	26.9
goods* 2	0.3	3.9	9.3	0.1	1.7	3.7	0.3	3.4	6.4	0.3	3.9	6.0
goods* 3	8.9	12.3	11.9	6.0	11.2	8.3	7.6	12.0	9.7	7.6	12.3	9.3
goods* 4	7.4	6.7	7.9	3.0	2.7	3.2	5.5	5.1	5.6	5.6	5.4	5.9
goods* 5	0	0	0	0	0	0	0	0	0	0	0	0

(Continued)

Table 9. (*Continued*)

		5. Japanese (Japan 2) formula imported by			6. Canadian formula imported by			7. Swiss formula imported by		
		EEC	U.S.	Japan	EEC	U.S.	Japan	EEC	U.S.	Japan
Produced in the EEC										
goods*	1	0	6.3	53.7	0	6.3	53.7	0	6.3	53.7
	2	0	3.0	4.0	0	0	0	0	2.4	3.1
	3	0	14.3	11.1	0	13.2	7.5	0	14.0	9.6
	4	0	5.4	10.3	0	2.2	0.8	0	4.4	6.3
	5	0	0	0	0	0	0	0	0	0
Produced in the U.S.										
goods*	1	38.2	0	92.2	38.2	0	92.2	38.2	0	92.2
	2	2.6	0	2.4	0	0	0	2.2	0	1.8
	3	7.0	0	10.4	1.7	0	6.2	6.4	0	8.6
	4	6.1	0	8.2	0	0	0.4	5.3	0	5.2
	5	0	0	0	0	0	0	0	0	0
Produced in Japan										
goods*	1	21.8	4.4	0	21.8	4.4	0	21.8	4.4	0
	2	2.0	2.0	0	0	0	0	1.7	1.7	0
	3	8.0	19.2	0	4.2	18.5	0	7.6	19.1	0
	4	6.3	5.5	0	1.1	1.0	0	5.6	4.5	0
	5	0	0	0	0	0	0	0	0	0
Produced in the rest of the world										
goods*	1	24.3	7.0	26.9	24.3	7.0	26.9	24.3	7.0	26.9
	2	0.3	3.9	8.6	0	0	0	0.2	3.1	5.4
	3	7.6	12.3	11.1	4.3	10.4	6.0	7.1	11.9	9.0
	4	5.6	5.4	7.3	0.8	0.9	0.6	4.7	4.5	4.8
	5	0	0	0	0	0	0	0	0	0

*This classification is the same as in Table 1; 1, Agriculture and food, 2, Raw materials, 3, Nondurable manufacturing, 4, Durable manufacturing, 5, Services.

†See Footnote 3 to Table 3.

4. Results of Alternative Tariff-Cutting Formulae and More Extensive Trade Liberalization

In this section, we present our results of the general equilibrium impacts of alternative tariff-cutting formulae that we have obtained from our model and compare our findings with cases of more extensive trade liberalizations. The main summary statistic which we used to appraise the effects of the tariff cuts is a measure of the effect on national welfare of any given tariff-cutting proposal. We have calculated the compensating and equivalent variation for each of the trading blocs. The compensating variation is the change in income needed to compensate a consumer for a price change which has occurred. The equivalent variation is the income change which is equivalent to the price change. These are dollar measures of the real income change associated with the movement between the equilibrium situations but the measures differ because of the changes which take place in relative prices between equilibria. These measures are opposite in sign; an improvement being indicated by a positive equivalent variation and a negative compensating variation. We, however, adopt a convention of reporting positive numbers for welfare-improving changes for both measures. Because of the separate demand patterns for households, investment, and government, an aggregation is required over the welfare measures of each group in each trading area.

In Table 10, we summarize the welfare effects of the tariff-cutting proposals for the central case specification of the model incorporating the trade elasticity values appearing in Table 5. It can be seen in Table 10 that the aggregate worldwide effects involved for the tariff-cutting proposals range from 2.2 billion dollars under the Canadian proposal to 0.7 billion dollars under the EEC proposal. These are within the range of the figures produced by the Brookings study mentioned earlier. U.S. GNP for 1973 is in the region of 1,200 billion dollars and the calculated gains are thus small compared to the total value of production in each trading area.[p]

What is striking about these results, however, is not so much the similarity in aggregate size of the gains to earlier studies but their division

[p]Scaling up these figures to reflect the recent Tokyo Round agreement is difficult due to the departures in the agreement from general formulae and the lack of detail in the present calculation. The suggestion from these calculations would seem to be that the static welfare gains are likely to be small compared to GNP, a conclusion which is perhaps predictable from other exercises of this type (see especially the calculations of Miller and Spencer (1977) on British entry into the EEC).

Table 10. Welfare Effects of Tariff-Cut Proposals, by Trading Bloc.

1973 U.S. $ billion

Tariff-cutting formula considered	Trading bloc									
	EEC		U.S.		Japan		Rest of world		World total	
	CV[1]	EV[1]	CV	EV	CV	EV	CV	EV	CV	EV
(1) U.S. proposal	2.27	2.24	0.78	0.77	0.91	0.89	−2.48	−2.52	1.48	1.38
(2) EEC proposal	1.06	1.05	0.64	0.64	0.34	0.34	−1.32	−1.33	0.72	0.70
(3) Japanese proposal (Japan 1)	1.10	1.10	0.91	0.90	0.31	0.31	−1.57	−1.58	0.75	0.73
(4) Japanese proposal (Japan 2)	1.08	1.07	0.85	0.85	0.51	0.50	−1.74	−1.76	0.70	0.66
(5) Canadian proposal	3.15	3.10	1.36	1.35	1.23	1.21	−3.58	−3.66	2.16	2.00
(6) Swiss proposal	1.45	1.44	0.79	0.78	0.49	0.49	−1.75	−1.77	0.98	0.94

[1] CV denotes "compensating variation" and EV denotes "equivalent variation"; these are explained more fully in the text.

by trading bloc. The gains by trading bloc clearly indicate that the major loser is the rest of the world and the major gainer is the EEC. This contrasts with the calculations reported in the Brookings study, since the relative price effects across the trading blocs cannot be taken into account. We show that these terms-of-trade effects are significant. The rest of the world always appears as a loser because of the exclusion of agricultural products from the tariffs negotiations. This is reinforced by the fact that low tariffs already exist on raw materials so small cuts only occur on these items. The difference in aggregate effects between the U.S., EEC, and Japanese proposals is in the region of a factor of two.

A further interesting finding is that the gains to each trading bloc across the proposals do not vary in a uniform manner, between the U.S. proposal and the Japanese proposal there is a reduction of one-half in the total worldwide gain. The U.S. gains more, however, under the Japanese proposal than they do under their own. In contrast, the gains for the EEC fall sharply and for Japan even more. In fact, a striking characteristic is that between the three proposals from the three major trading blocs the EEC appears to do worse under their own proposal than all other proposals.

The Japanese also appear to do worse under their own proposal (Japan 1) compared to all other proposals. Only in the case of the U.S. does this extreme result not hold; the U.S. proposal, however, is dominated from the U.S. perspective by the Japanese and Canadian proposals.

The Swiss formula (compromise proposal) comes out as a compromise in terms of its results. The gains for each of the trading blocs are in the range of the potential gains under each of the proposals considered and this is also true for the aggregate gains. As with all of the proposals the rest of the world is a substantial loser. Under a Swiss proposal, it is reasonable to summarize the likely impacts as follows: The major gainer is the EEC; effects for the U.S. are positive although not as large as has been suggested in some of the political statements supporting the trade negotiations. For Japan gains in absolute terms are smaller although in proportional terms are comparable to the U.S. Although Japan gains from reduction in foreign tariffs on manufactured products, Japan is the most protectionist of the three major trading blocs. The significant loser is the rest of the world.

The terms-of-trade effects associated with the tariff-cutting proposals are reported in Table 11. These are expressed in terms of the percentage change in relative prices for a composite bundle of goods purchased both at home and abroad. A positive movement in terms of this percentage change indicates a terms-of-trade gain to the importing country and a negative movement indicates a terms-of-trade loss. The movements against the rest of the world and the U.S. are particularly important and illustrate the importance of the exclusion of agricultural products from the tariff negotiations.

Under all of the proposals, the rest of the world is a substantial loser in its terms of trade. The EEC is unambiguously a gainer in its terms of trade with all other trading blocs under all proposals. While these terms-of-trade movements might appear small, it has to be remembered that the average cut in tariffs associated with these proposals may be no more than 2–3% points. For certain pairwise combinations, these cuts result in movements of relative prices advantageous to one of the trading partners in the order of $1\frac{1}{2}\%$. These are significant movements and indicate that for the parameter values used here terms-of-trade effects associated with tariff-cutting proposals are strong enough that they should be taken account of in any calculation of the division of gains from the tariff-cutting formulae.

The terms-of-trade effects do not always correspond exactly with the results in Table 10 as terms-of-trade effects have to be offset against the domestic welfare gains from the removal of distortions associated with

Table 11. Terms-of-Trade Effects Associated with Tariff-Cut Proposals.

(% change in relative price of a composite bundle of goods[1] purchased abroad and at home; + indicates terms-of-trade gain to the importing country.)

Tariff-cutting formula	Importing country	Trade with			
		EEC	U.S.	Japan	Rest of world
(1) U.S. proposal	EEC	–	0.8	0.6	2.0
	U.S.	−0.8	—	−0.2	1.2
	Japan	−0.6	0.2	—	1.4
	Rest of the world	−2.0	−1.2	−1.4	—
(2) EEC proposal	EEC	—	0.2	0.4	1.0
	U.S.	−0.2	—	0.2	0.8
	Japan	−0.4	−0.2	—	0.6
	Rest of the world	−1.0	−0.8	−0.6	—
(3) Japanese proposal (Japan 1)	EEC	—	0	0.5	1.1
	U.S.	0	—	0.5	1.1
	Japan	−0.5	−0.5	0	0.6
	Rest of the world	−1.1	−1.1	−0.6	0.0
(4) Japanese proposal (Japan 2)	EEC	—	—	0.1	1.1
	U.S.	0	—	0.1	1.1
	Japan	−0.1	−0.1	—	0.9
	Rest of the world	−1.1	−1.1	−0.8	—
(5) Canadian proposal	EEC	—	0.9	0.9	2.8
	U.S.	−1.0	—	−0.1	1.9
	Japan	−0.9	0.1	—	2.0
	Rest of the world	−2.8	−1.9	−1.8	—
(6) Swiss proposal	EEC	—	0.3	0.5	1.3
	U.S.	−0.3	—	0.2	1.0
	Japan	−0.5	−0.2	—	0.9
	Rest of the world	−1.3	−1.0	−0.8	—

[1]Figures reported are percentage change in producer (world) prices and own production levels are used as weights in the construction of the composite commodity.

tariffs. An example is the set of results for the Japanese proposal. In this case, Japan is a terms-of-trade loser suffering $1\frac{1}{2}$% disadvantageous movement in its terms of trade with both the EEC and the U.S. Yet the effect of the tariff-cutting proposal on the domestic welfare level in Japan is still positive. This suggests that domestic welfare gain from the removal of the distortions, more than offsets these terms-of-trade losses in this case. A further calculation involves applying the terms-of-trade changes to benchmark equilibrium trade flows to give a monetary measure of the terms-of-trade movements. Doing this for the case of the U.S. proposal gives monetary measures of +1.7 billion dollars, +0.5 billion dollars, +0.4 billion dollars, and −2.6 billion dollars for the EEC, U.S., Japan, and ROW respectively. Comparing these figures to the welfare effects reported in Table 10 indicates that the dominant component of the gain or loss for any trading area is the terms-of-trade effect.

Table 12 reports the impacts of the tariff-cutting proposals on the level and pattern of world trade. From examination of the trade shares reported, the effect of any of the tariff-cutting proposals on the trade share matrix, in value terms, is extremely small even though the aggregate volume of trade changes and relative prices change. In all cases, there is an expansion of world trade and the expansion is related to the depth of the cut. The U.S. proposal represents a deeper cut than either the EEC or Japanese proposal and the 2% expansion of world trade associated with the U.S. proposal contrasts with an expansion in the region of 1% for the EEC and Japanese proposals. The Swiss proposal produces a result somewhat intermediate.

In Table 13, the sensitivity of estimates is explored. A number of different specifications of the model are considered for the Swiss proposal (Table 9, Case 6) and the welfare estimates are reported. For this case, a surprisingly limited sensitivity is obtained and suggests that other estimates could also be reasonably robust.

In Table 14, the results obtained for the tariff-cutting proposals are compared to more extensive trade liberalization experiments. The first evident feature is that the effects of the tariff-cutting proposals are small compared to the potential gains from more extensive trade liberalization. The abolition of nontariff barriers in all trading blocs leads to a gain in the region of 14 billion dollars per year. The abolition of all tariff and nontariff barriers in all trading blocs would yield a gain of around 20 billion dollars per year. This contrasts with the gains under the tariff-cutting proposals in the region of one-and-a-half billion dollars per year. Thus the limitation of the negotiations under the Tokyo Round first to tariffs, secondly to non-agricultural products, and lastly to cuts rather than total abolition means that the world forgoes a substantial potential welfare gain. The current tariff negotiations in Geneva have to be seen as dealing with a relatively limited part of all interferences to world trade and the overall gains which are potentially realizable as a result of these negotiations are small.

As with the tariff-cutting proposals the results in Table 14 also reveal the importance of terms-of-trade effects in all of these potential liberalization processes. The unilateral abolition of tariffs by the EEC yields a world gain which is larger than the gains realized by formula tariff cuts

Table 12. Impacts on Level and Pattern of World Trade of Tariff-Cut Proposals.

	Importing country	% of trade (imports) with[1] EEC	U.S.	Japan	Rest of world	$% change in total imports
(1) No policy change dituation (1973 fata)	EEC	0.0	20.5	5.3	74.2	—
	U.S.	24.6	0.0	13.8	61.5	—
	Japan	9.8	25.8	0.0	64.4	—
	Rest of the world	51.0	33.6	15.4	0.0	—
(2) U.S. proposal	EEC	0.0	20.5	5.4	74.1	2.6
	U.S.	24.3	0.0	14.0	61.7	2.4
	Japan	9.8	25.6	0.0	64.6	1.5
	Rest of the world	50.8	33.7	15.5	0.0	2.0
(3) EEC proposal	EEC	0.0	20.4	5.4	74.2	1.2
	U.S.	24.5	0.0	13.9	61.6	1.2
	Japan	9.8	25.7	0.0	64.5	0.6
	Rest of the world	50.9	33.6	15.5	0.0	0.9
(4) Japanese proposal (Japan 1)	EEC	0.0	20.4	5.4	74.2	1.2
	U.S.	24.5	0.0	13.9	61.6	1.3
	Japan	9.8	25.6	0.0	65.4	0.6
	Rest of the world	50.9	33.6	5.4	0.0	0.8
(5) Modified Japanese proposal (Japan 2)	EEC	0.0	20.4	5.4	74.2	1.2
	U.S.	24.4	0.0	13.9	61.7	1.3
	Japan	9.8	25.6	0.0	64.6	0.9
	Rest of the world	51.0	33.6	15.4	0.0	0.6
(6) Canadian proposal	EEC	0.0	20.4	5.4	74.2	4.0
	U.S.	24.0	0.0	13.9	62.1	3.8
	Japan	9.8	25.5	0.0	64.7	3.1
	Rest of the world	50.8	33.8	15.4	0.0	2.4
(7) Swiss proposal	EEC	0.0	20.4	5.4	74.2	1.6
	U.S.	24.4	0.0	14.0	61.6	1.6
	Japan	9.8	25.6	0.0	64.6	0.9
	Rest of the world	30.9	33.7	15.5	0.0	1.2

[1]Both old and changed trade levels are calculated at original (old) equilibrium prices.

with the EEC having a welfare loss of 32 billion dollars per year because of the adverse movement in the terms of trade. Similarly, an abolition of the U.S. tariff would result in a worldwide gain but at a substantial cost to the U.S. These results suggest that from the standpoint of national

Table 13. Sensitivity of Welfare Estimates for Swiss Proposal to Model Parameters.

1973 U.S. $ billion

Experiment considered	EEC		U.S.		Japan		Rest of the world		World total	
	CV[1]	*EV*[1]	*CV*	*EV*	*CV*	*EV*	*CV*	*EV*	*CV*	*EV*
(1) Central case analysis of Swiss formula (Table 10, Case 6)	1.45	1.44	0.79	0.78	0.49	0.49	−1.75	−1.77	0.98	0.94
(2) Central case with all substitution elasticities in preference functions between domestic and imported products equalling 0.75 in all trading areas[2]	1.52	1.51	1.05	1.04	0.42	0.41	−2.07	−2.09	0.92	0.87
(3) As in 2, but with a value 3.0 instead of 0.75	1.10	1.10	1.05	1.04	0.50	0.49	−1.25	−1.27	1.40	1.36
(4) As in 2, but with a value of 6.0 instead of 0.75	1.13	1.12	1.21	1.20	0.58	0.57	−0.90	−0.91	2.02	1.98
(5) Different elasticities of substitution by product[3] in final demands	0.99	0.99	1.12	1.11	0.57	0.57	−1.52	−1.54	1.16	1.13

[1] *CV* denotes "compensating variation" and *EV* "equivalent variation". These are explained in the text.
[2] Values used in the central case are given in Table 5.
[3] Corresponding approximately to estimates by product reported by "SFS". The values used are as follows:

	EEC	U.S.	Japan
Agriculture and food	0.78	0.80	0.66
Raw materials	1.17	0.96	0.57
Nondurable manufacturing	2.53	1.84	1.42
Durable manufacturing	2.53	1.84	1.42
Services	0.88	1.66	0.78

For the test of the world an arithmetic average by product is used.

Table 14. Tariff-Cut Proposals Compared to More Extensive Trade Liberalizations (Welfare Effects).

1973 U.S. $ billion

	Trading bloc									
	EEC		U.S.		Japan		Rest of world		World total	
Experiment considered	*CV*[1]	*EV*[1]	*CV*	*EV*	*CV*	*EV*	*CV*	*EV*	*CV*	*EV*
(1) U.S. proposal (Table 10, Case 1)	2.27	2.24	0.78	0.77	0.91	0.89	−2.48	−2.52	1.48	1.38
(2) Swiss proposal (Table 10, Case 6)	1.45	1.44	0.79	0.78	0.49	0.49	−1.75	−1.77	0.98	0.94
(3) Unilateral abolition of tariffs by EEC	−3.64	−3.85	0.86	0.85	−0.44	−0.43	5.51	5.38	2.29	1.95
(4) Unilateral abolition of tariffs by U.S.	1.07	1.06	−3.19	−3.31	0.63	0.62	2.40	2.37	0.91	0.74
(5) Unilateral abolition of tariffs by Japan	0.24	0.23	1.63	1.60	−0.97	−1.12	0.55	0.54	1.45	1.25
(6) Multilateral abolition of tariffs	4.84	4.67	2.77	2.69	1.48	1.37	−2.15	−2.22	6.94	6.51
(7) Abolition of tariffs by U.S. and EEC on bilateral trade	0.62	0.62	1.47	1.46	−0.01	−0.01	−1.44	−1.45	0.64	0.62
(8) Abolition of tariffs by U.S. and Japan on bilateral trade	0.12	0.12	1.78	1.75	0.35	0.32	−1.48	−1.49	0.77	0.70
(9) Abolition of tariffs by Japan and EEC on bilateral trade	0.27	0.27	0.11	0.11	0.41	0.41	−0.57	−0.57	0.22	0.22
(10) Abolition of all nontariff barriers in all blocs	3.73	2.74	−1.49	−1.55	−0.08	−0.73	12.64	11.70	14.80	12.16
(11) Abolition of all tariff and nontariff barriers in all blocs	8.08	6.11	2.32	2.04	−0.15	−1.66	9.28	8.30	19.53	18.11

[1] *CV* denotes "compensating variation" and *EV* denotes "equivalent variation". These are explained in the text.

interest tariffs in these trading blocs should be increased to more closely approximate to an optimal tariff.

In the case of the abolition of all tariffs and nontariff barriers, large gains accrue to the rest of the world. Some care is needed in interpreting this result since the rest of the world is only schematically modeled and trade-restrictive policies in third world and other countries are not captured in the model. The model does suggest, however, that the rest of the world is a significant loser from current trade policies pursued in the major trading blocs especially because of the restrictive tariff and nontariff barriers applied to agricultural products and raw materials. Removal of these results in significant gains for these countries and their stake in the trade negotiation processes which should be large has been effectively curtailed as a result of the limitation of the negotiations to tariffs and within the tariffs to nonagricultural products.

Table 14 also contains some findings of interest for the abolition of tariffs on a bilateral basis (customs union cases). Experiments are considered where the U.S., the EEC, and Japan abolish tariffs on a bilateral basis. Bilaterally, substantial gains can occur (e.g., the U.S. and the EEC) and these gains outweigh the losses imposed on the other trading blocs.

5. Conclusions

In this chapter, a recently constructed general equilibrium model of world trade between major trading blocs has been used to evaluate various general formulae proposed in the Tokyo Round Negotiations under the General Agreement on Tariffs and Trade. These have also been compared with more extensive forms of liberalization of world trade. The model is described fully elsewhere (Whalley, 1978a) and only a summary is given in this chapter, which aims to give the major focus to results.

It is found that the aggregate welfare gains obtained from comparing equilibria achieved as a result of the application of these tariff-cutting formulae to the pre-cut situation are in the region of 0.8 to 3 billion U.S. dollars per year using 1973 data. These aggregate effects constitute very small fractions of world GNP and are within the same range produced by other studies including the recent Brookings study (Cline *et al.*, 1978). It is shown that the terms-of-trade effects result in a country-wide allocation of gains which is somewhat different from what has previously been projected. The EEC is portrayed as, relatively, the main gainer, while the U.S. is a more modest gainer. The Rest of the World loses. It is suggested that these findings are due to the exclusion of agriculture from the general formulae coupled with the fact that the rest of the world, in particular, is an exporter of raw materials which already have low tariff rates associated with them.

Inconsistencies occur between the various national proposals; the U.S. gain more from the Japanese than their own proposal, and Japan and the EEC gain least from their own proposals of all proposals considered. The aggregate effects of the tariff cuts are described as relatively small and the potential effects on the level of world trade under any of the tariff-cutting proposals are no more than 2%.

Comparison of the results obtained from the tariff-cut proposals to more extensive forms of world trade liberalization is made. Although these other schemes cannot be politically implemented at the present time they do demonstrate that the gains on a worldwide basis accruing under any of the tariff-cutting proposals are small compared to the potential gains from the removal of all distortions of world trade. It is shown that the abolition of all tariff and nontariff barriers in all major world trading blocs could result in a potential gain in the region of 20 billion dollars per year in contrast to an upper bound of 3 billion dollars resulting from any tariff cuts as proposed in the national formulae. The majority of this gain accrues in the model to the rest of the world due to the restrictive policies modeled in the major industrialized trading blocs. Trade policies in third world and less developed countries are not realistically modeled and some care is needed in interpreting this result. However, the suggestion remains that the potential gains for less developed and developing countries in liberalization of world trade is significant but the means to realize these gains are excluded under current GATT negotiations.

References

Armington, PS (1969). A theory of demand for products distinguished by place of production. *I.M.F. Staff Papers*, 159–176.

Balassa, B and ME Kreinin (1967). Trade liberalization under the "Kennedy Round": The static effects. *Review of Economics and Statistics*, **49**, 125–137.

Baldwin, RA (1970). *Non-Tariff Distortions of International Trade*. Brookings Institution.

Caddy, V (1976). Empirical estimation of the elasticity of substitution: A review (mimeo). *Industries Assistance Commission*, Melbourne, Australia.

Cline, WR, N Kawanabe, TOM Kronsjö and T Williams (1978). *Trade Negotiations in the Tokyo Round: A Quantitative Assessment.* Brookings Institution.

Deardorff, AV and RM Stern (1979). An economic analysis of the effects of the Tokyo Round of multilateral trade negotiations on the United States and the other major industrialized countries. MTM Studies No. 5, prepared for Subcommittee on International Trade, Committee on Finance, U.S. Senate, 96th Congress, Washington, D.C.

Fullerton, D, JB Shoven and J Whalley (1978). General equilibrium analysis of U.S. taxation policy. In *1978 Compendium of Tax Research.* Washington, D.C.: Office of Tax Analysis, Department of the Treasury.

GATT (1974). *Basic Documentation of the Tariff Study.* Geneva.

Grubel, HG and HG Johnson (1967). Nominal tariff rates and United States valuation practices: Two case studies. *Review of Economics and Statistics*, 138–143.

Houthakker, HS and SP Magee (1969). Income and price elasticities in world trade. *Review of Economics and Statistics*, **51**, 111–125.

Miller, MH and J Spencer (1977). A static general equilibrium evaluation of the gains from British entry into the EEC. *Review of Economic Studies.*

Roningen, V and AJ Yeats (1976). Non-tariff distortions of international trade: Some preliminary empirical evidence. *Weltwirtschaftliches Archiv*, **112**, 613–625.

Scarf, HE (1973) (in collaboration with T. Hansen). *The Computation of Economic Equilibria.* Yale University Press.

Shoven, JB and J Whalley (1974). On the computation of competitive equilibria on international markets with tariffs. *Journal of International Economics*, **4**, 341–354.

Stern, RM, J Francis and B Schumacher (1976). *Price Elasticities in International Trade: An Annotated Bibliography.* Macmillan, for the Trade Policy Research Centre.

UNCTAD (1969, 1970). *Liberalization of Tariffs and Non-Tariff Barriers.* UNCTAD documents TD/B/C.2/83, 1969; TD/B/C.2/R.I., 1969 and TD/B/C.2/R.3, 1970 Geneva.

U.S. Tariff Commission (1974), Trade Barriers, II Volume report to the U.S. Senate Committee on Finance and its Subcommittee on International Trade on Investigations, 332–366 and 332–367 under Section 332 of the Tariff Act of 1930, T. C. Publication 665, Washington, D.C.

Walter, I (1972). Non-tariff protection among industrialized countries: Some preliminary evidence. *Economia Internazionale*, **25**, 335–354.

Whalley, J (1978a). General equilibrium analysis of U.S.–EEC–Japanese trade and trade distorting policies. To appear in *Economie Appliqué* in a Symposium issue on international trade general equilibrium models.

Whalley, J (1978b). Discriminatory features of domestic taxation policies and their impact on world trade: A general equilibrium approach. Paper presented to the Econometric Society Meetings, Chicago, Illinois (August). Revised version to appear in the *Journal of Political Economy.*

World Bank (1975). World Bank Atlas. Washington, D.C.

Yeats, AJ (1976). Effective protection for processed agricultural commodities: A comparison of industrial countries. *Journal of Economics and Business*, **29**, 31–40.

Yeats, AJ (1977). An evaluation of the common agricultural policy as a barrier facing agricultural exports to the EEC. *American Journal of Agricultural Economics*, **59**, 99.

Chapter 5

How Reasonable are Assumptions Used in Theoretical Models? Computational Evidence on the Likelihood of Trade Pattern Changes*

Lisandro Abrego
International Monetary Fund

Raymond Riezman
Department of Economics, University of Iowa, U.S.A.

John Whalley†
Department of Economics, University of Western Ontario, Canada
National Bureau of Economic Research (NBER)

In theoretical literature, it is common to make the assumption that in a multi-country, multi-good world, the direction of trade (import and export by commodity) is predetermined and fixed for each good for each country. We consider a simple three-country, three-good, pure-exchange model with CES preferences. We compute free trade competitive equilibria, three-country noncooperative Nash equilibria, and customs union equilibria for randomized parametrizations, and find that trade pattern changes between free trade and customs union equilibria in around 35% of cases.

1. Introduction

This chapter reports computational evidence that suggests that, despite assumptions made in theoretical analysis to the contrary, changes in the

---

*This chapter was first published in (2006). *Canadian Journal of Economics*, **39**(3), 781–789. New York: John Wiley and Sons.

†John Whalley is also affiliated with NBER, CESifo, and CIGI. We are grateful to the Centre for the Study of Globalisation and Regionalisation at the University of Warwick and the Henry B. Tippie College of Business at the University of Iowa for support; and to Scott Page, Carsten Kowalczyk, Carlo Perroni, Ben Zissimos, Ben Lockwood, and Ted To for discussions. An earlier version of this chapter was presented at a seminar at Warwick in March 2000. Views expressed are not necessarily those of the International Monetary Fund. Email: jwhalley@uwo.ca

pattern of trade are surprisingly likely to occur in three or more country trade models that compare various tariff equilibria and free trade. Early customs unions models (Berglas, 1979; Lipsey, 1970; Lloyd, 1982; Meade, 1955; Viner, 1950) assumed fixed trade patterns, sometimes implicitly rather than explicitly. Berglas (1979) is explicit when he states on page 329, "*We deliberately ignored the possibility that the formation of a customs union would extinguish or reverse the flow of trade.*" The more modern regional trade agreements literature, which focuses on general equilibrium and optimal tariffs, restricts model structures in ways that effectively rule out changing trade patterns. Kennan and Riezman (1990), Kose and Riezman (2000) and Syropoulos (1999), all assume symmetry and have fixed trade patterns as a result. Krugman (1991) uses symmetry and monopolistic competition (which ensures complete specialization), with the result that trade patterns also will not change across equilibria. The assumption of fixed trade patterns also is pervasive in the tariff retaliation literature (Johnson, 1953–1954; Kennan and Riezman, 1988). Our analysis suggests that in environments with three or more countries and three or more goods and where asymmetries of size and/or preference patterns enter, trade patterns can frequently change across equilibria.

This finding brings into question, the robustness of some of the results in the theoretical literature on both regional trade agreements and optimal tariffs, since these are based on the assumption that trade flows by commodity and by country remain unchanged in direction as different equilibria are compared. The wider implications are both that it is possible to assess the reasonableness of their assumptions using the methods we outline and that in extending two-country results in the literature to models with three or more countries and three or more goods, one has to deal with the possibility that a move from free trade to tariff equilibrium involves changing trade patterns.

In making our computations, we consider a simple three-country, three-good, pure-exchange economy[a] with CES preferences, since it is a parsimonious, transparent structure within which to conduct our

[a]Models with production add more parameters to the model specification but do not change the basic feature that country behavior towards each other in terms of optimal tariff setting is determined by elasticities of excess demand functions. These, particularly in turn, reflect underlying demand and supply functions. If supply functions are perfectly inelastic, demand functions determine excess demand elasticities. Randomizing over preference, function parameters is thus sufficient to generate an implicit randomization over excess demand function elasticities.

analysis. The strategic variables we consider in the noncooperative games are country tariff rates. We consider random draws on possible model parametrizations. For each generated parametrization, we compute a free trade equilibrium; a customs union equilibrium in which the two member countries play noncooperatively against the third country; and a three-country, noncooperative Nash equilibrium.[b] Instead of imposing a trade pattern on any equilibrium considered in the model, as is usually done in the literature, we allow it to be endogenously determined as part of each equilibrium computation.

We find trade pattern changes in about 35% of cases when free trade and customs union equilibria are compared and around 40% of cases for comparisons between three-country Nash equilibria and customs unions. We believe that these frequencies would increase as more goods and countries are added, but we have not considered such cases because of the computational complexities involved. We conclude that, while assumptions of unchanged directions of trade in theoretical models may be convenient or even necessary for analytical tractability, they are not supported by computational experience for the models and functional forms we consider here.

2. The Computational Model

To analyze the likelihood of trade pattern changes, we specify functional forms, parameter values, and endowments and use numerical simulation techniques applied to a three-country trade model. We use a procedure of random selection of parameter values; randomly drawing preference share parameters, elasticity parameters, and endowments from pre-specified admissible ranges. For each model specification generated in this way, we compute three types of equilibria: free trade equilibrium, a three-country noncooperative Nash equilibrium, and a two-country customs union equilibrium with the member countries jointly playing Nash against the third country. For each parametrization, we determine whether or not trade patterns change in comparisons across these equilibria and on this basis compute sample frequencies for trade pattern changes.

[b]We assume uniqueness of these equilibria. We have not encountered any instances of multiplicity in our model solutions, although there are no guarantees, even with the simple structures we use, that this will be so (see Kehoe, 1980).

2.1. *Model structure*

In the three-country, three-good, pure-exchange general equilibrium model, each country has a single representative consumer who has endowments of the three goods and a utility function of the form

$$U^i = U^i(X_1^i, X_2^i, X_3^i) \quad (i = 1, \dots, 3). \tag{1}$$

For any good j, we define the seller's price (i.e., net of tariff prices) as P_j and allow each country to impose tariffs at rate t_j^i on good j imported by country i. Tariffs are set to zero on any good exported by country i. This implies that internal costs (gross of tariff prices) for good j in any other country i are

$$P_j^i = (1 + t_j^i)P_j. \tag{2}$$

Tariff revenues collected by country i are given by

$$T^i = \sum_{i=1}^{3} t_j^i P_j[\max((X_j^i - \bar{E}_j^i), 0)], \tag{3}$$

and the income of the country i is given by

$$I^i = \sum_j P_j \bar{E}_j^i + T^i. \tag{4}$$

Maximizing (1) subject to (2), (3), and (4) implies that a zero trade balance condition holds for each country.

In the customs union case, the two union members will jointly set an optimal tariff, and the third country will do so unilaterally. In the three-country Nash case, countries set optimal tariffs on all imported goods. The model we use assumes nothing about the direction of trade, since this is endogenously determined as part of the equilibrium structure, and so only after trade directions are known do the pricing relationships in (2) apply.

In our computations, we use CES preferences for the utility functions (1), for which (in the CES case) utility-maximizing demands are given by

$$X_j^i = \frac{a_j^i I}{(P_j^i)^{\sigma^i} \sum_{j=1}^{3} \alpha_j^i P_j^{i(1-\sigma^i)}} \quad (i = 1, \dots, 3) \quad (j = 1, \dots, 3). \tag{5}$$

2.2. *Free trade competitive equilibria*

In free trade equilibria, tariff rates are zero on all products in all countries. Given that only relative prices matter in such a structure, we can normalize prices to sum to unity in computing such equilibria; that is,

$$\sum_{j=1}^{3} P_j = 1, \quad P_j \geq 0. \tag{6}$$

Equilibrium prices clear markets globally; that is, equilibrium prices (P_1^*, P_2^*, P_3^*) are determined such that

$$\sum_{j=1}^{3} X_j^i(P_1^*, P_2^*, P_3^*) - \sum_{j=1}^{3} \bar{E}_j^i = 0 \quad (i = 1, \ldots, 3), \tag{7}$$

and global excess demand are zero for each good.

2.3. *Three-country noncooperative Nash equilibria*

We also compute three-country, noncooperative Nash equilibria. In these, each country reacts to the other two countries' tariff setting and computes its own optimal tariffs. In the Nash equilibrium, country computations of optimal tariffs are mutually consistent.[c]

Specifically, in these cases each country determines its own optimal tariffs (t_j^i) by maximizing U^i subject to the constraint that global equilibrium in the three goods markets occurs. Each country maximizes U^i subject to (2), (3), and (4), with the (t_j^i) being endogenously determined. In these optimization problems, each country treats the other countries, tariffs as fixed, so that in the optimization the values of (t_j^i) for $i \neq j$ are taken as given. These are denoted by $\hat{t}_j^i$.

In a Nash equilibrium, optimal-tariff rates $t_j^{i*}$are such that

$$t_j^{i*} = \hat{t}_j^i, \quad \forall i, j \tag{8}$$

and market-clearing conditions hold:

$$\sum_{j=1}^{3} X_i^j(P_1^*, P_2^*, P_3^*, T^{*1}, T^{*2}, T^{*3}) - \sum_{j=1}^{3} \bar{E}_i^j = 0 \quad \forall i. \tag{9}$$

A Nash equilibrium occurs in this structure when each country charges its optimal tariffs on imports given the tariffs set by other countries,

[c]See Johnson (1953–1954) for computation of Nash equilibria for the two-country case where each country's best reply is independent of the other country's actions (constant elasticity offer surfaces) and Hamilton and Whalley (1983) for the two-country CES/Cobb–Douglas case.

country optimization is mutually consistent, and global markets clear. Market-clearing, trade balance, and optimizing behavior on tariffs in each country thus define equilibria. Tariff revenues, T^i, also enter this version of the model and affect demands, since they are redistributed to the country's representative consumer in lump-sum fashion. As above, no prior assignment of trade directions by product and by country is made.

2.4. *Customs union equilibria*

We also compute customs union equilibria using this structure. These are constrained Nash equilibria in which two of the three countries play cooperatively. Thus, if countries 1 and 2 form a customs union, they have zero tariffs between them and set a common external tariff against country 3. We constrain the intra-CU tariffs to be zero and allow countries 1 and 2 to jointly set an optimal tariff against country 3. Country 3 also sets an optimal tariff against the two-country customs union. Countries 1 and 2 have a conflict of interest as to how their joint external tariff is set, and how they might best resolve this conflict has been the subject of previous research (see Kennan and Riezman, 1990). Here, we simply assume that the joint external tariff is set to maximize the sum of country 1 and 2's utilities. Once again, the pattern of trade is not pre-specified.

The optimization problem for the members of the customs union (countries 1 and 2) is thus given as

$$\max U^1 + U^2, \tag{10}$$

subject to (2), (3), and (4) for each country and the constraints on t_j^i set out above.

In this mixed cooperative, noncooperative structure, countries 1 and 2 set zero tariffs against each other; that is, if the supplying country is 1 or 2 then

$$t_j^1 = t_j^2 = 0. \tag{11}$$

Implicit in this formulation is the assumption that members of the union receive the tariff revenues collected on their own imports from the third country. When a member country imports a good from both the member and non-member country, tariffs are applied only to the portion of imports coming from the non-member country. For example, suppose countries 1 and 2 form a customs union, and in equilibrium country 1 imports good 2 from both country 2 and country 3, in this case

$$P_2^1 = P_2^2 = (1 + t_2^1)P_2.$$

The tariff t_2^1 is directly applied not to imports from country 2, in this case, only to imports from country 3. In computation, we therefore need to determine bilateral trade flows.

3. Implementation and Model Results

To assess the frequency of trade pattern changes in comparisons across these equilibria for this model, we use a procedure of random draws on parametrizations of the model for preferences and endowments. Table 1 outlines the model structure, we use in our calculations and other details of our procedures. These apply for pre-specified ranges of share parameters and elasticities in preferences and also for endowments.[d] We consider 2,000 model parametrizations in our central case, and later we do sensitivity analysis to allow for different numbers of random draws of parameter specifications and restrictions on the coverage of randomization (say, only for endowments).

In these model formulations, in contrast to theoretical work, the direction of trade in goods can change across equilibria, say, between free trade and customs union equilibria. We endogenize trade direction changes in our computational analysis by modifying directional assumptions

Table 1. Model Structure and Other Details of Experiments Used to Assess the Frequency of Trade Pattern Changes.

Dimensionality:	Three countries, three goods
Preferences:	CES, with parameter values generated by random draws
Endowments:	Preference parameters and endowments are randomly drawn from a unit interval
Number of cases:	We consider 2,000 different model specifications in our central case, with an equilibrium computed for each
Equilibria computed for each case:	Competitive equilibria, three-country Nash equilibria, customs union equilibria (the sum of member utilities is maximized)

[d]These ranges are between 0 and 1 for share parameters, with shares normalized to sum to one across goods for any country; between 0 and 1 for endowments of goods by country, since relative endowments are what matter; and between 0.5 and 1.5 for substitution elasticities so as to yield a central tendency value of 1.0 (Cobb–Douglas).

made in successive country optimization problems on the basis of what computed equilibria actually reveal. Specifically, any computation made as part of a sequence of calculations resulting in an equilibrium uses the last computation to yield the trade pattern assumption to be used in the next calculation. As computation progresses, the trade pattern is allowed to change, and full equilibrium requires that the trade pattern does not change from one iteration to the next. In the competitive equilibrium case, all that is required is that trade patterns be consistent from one calculation to the next, and markets clear. In the customs union and three-country Nash cases, equilibrium requires that, in addition to trade pattern consistency, assumed and optimal tariffs must be the same for each country.

For free trade and customs union cases, we are able to compute all equilibria for all model parametrizations generated by randomizations over the parameter space using these methods. We are unable, however, to compute three country Nash equilibria for approximately 17% of the model parametrizations, we consider. In these cases, solutions to country optimization problems settle on local rather than global optima and cycling occurs between such local solutions. In these cases, it is not possible to easily determine points on country reaction functions. There is no prior literature, to our knowledge, on computation of three-person Nash equilibria, and hence previous discussion of the problem does not seem to exist. No problems of the type outlined above are encountered in the two-country case using our model solution code for Nash equilibria. Such cases are ignored in our calculation of frequency of trade direction changes.

Our results are shown in Table 2. They reveal significant sample frequencies for trade direction changes between free trade and customs union equilibria, as well as between three-country Nash outcomes and these two equilibrium solutions. In 35% of the cases that we consider, at least one element of inter-country trade changes sign between customs unions and free trade equilibria, and 40% of cases show similar changes between Nash and customs union equilibria. Between free trade and Nash equilibria, the direction of trade changes in about 21% of computed cases.

Table 2. Percentage Sample Frequencies for Trade Pattern Changes.

Equilibrium comparisons	Sample frequencies for trade pattern changes
1. Free trade and customs union	35.6
2. Noncooperative Nash and customs unions	41.1
3. Free trade and noncooperative Nash	21.0

Table 3. Sensitivity Analysis of Percentage Sample Frequencies for Trade Direction Changes.

	Percentage of sample frequencies for which trade reversals occur		
	Free trade and CU	Between Nash and CU	Free trade and Nash
Central case	35.6	41.1	21.0
Reducing the numbers of randomizations to 500	35.3	41.9	18.8
Reducing the numbers of randomizations to 1,000	37.3	40.8	21.7
Increasing the numbers of randomizations to 3,000	36.0	40.6	20.2

Table 3 reports on the sensitivity of our results to both different numbers of randomizations and restrictions on the coverage of randomizations. These indicate only small changes in the sample frequencies for changes in trade patterns.

Taken as a set, these results suggest that assumptions on pre-specified and unchanging trade directions usually made in theoretical analyses are difficult to justify for the model specifications, we consider here. Trade direction changes seem to occur surprisingly frequently and extensively, and these can potentially undermine theoretical results generated by theoretical trade models analyzed with fixed directional assumptions.

4. Conclusion

In this chapter, we present computational evidence on the reliability of the assumption widely used in the trade theory literature that the direction of trade by commodity and country remains unchanged as various comparative static exercises are undertaken. In a three-country, three-good model, we compute free trade, customs union, and three-country Nash equilibria for a pure-exchange model for a series of randomly generated parametrizations of the model. We find that in around 35% of free trade-customs union cases and in around 40% of customs union three-country Nash cases trade patterns change, with comparisons showing trade pattern changes in about 20% of free trade three-country Nash cases. Our conclusion is that the assumption of unchanged trade patterns, widely used in theoretical literature on geographically discriminatory trade agreements, has only weak computational support.

References

Berglas, E (1979). Preferential trading theory: The n commodity case. *Journal of Political Economy*, **87**, 315–331.

Hamilton, B and J Whalley (1983). Optimal tariff computations in alternative trade models and some possible implications for current world trading arrangements. *Journal of International Economics*, **15**, 323–348.

Johnson, HG (1953–1954). Optimum tariff retaliation. *Review of Economic Studies*, **21**, 142–153.

Kehoe, T (1980). An index theorem for general equilibrium models with production. *Econometrica*, **48**, 1211–1232.

Kennan, J and R Riezman (1988). Do big countries win tariff wars? *International Economic Review*, **29**, 81–85.

_____ (1990). Optimal tariff equilibria with customs unions. *Canadian Journal of Economics*, **23**, 70–83.

Kose, A and R Riezman (2000). Understanding the welfare implications of preferential trade agreements. *Review of International Economics*, forthcoming.

Krugman, P (1991). Is bilateralism bad? In *International Trade and Trade Policy*, E Helpman and E Razin (ed.). Cambridge, M.A.: MIT Press.

Lipsey, RG (1957). The theory of customs unions: Trade diversion and welfare. *Economica*, **24**, 40–46.

_____ (1970). *The Theory of Customs Unions: A General Equilibrium Analysis.* London: Weidenfeld and Nicholson.

Lloyd, PJ (1982). A 3 × 3 theory of customs unions. *Journal of International Economics*, **12**, 41–63.

Meade, JE (1955). *The Theory of Customs Unions.* Amsterdam: North-Holland.

Riezman, R (1979). A 3 × 3 model of customs unions. *Journal of International Economics*, **9**, 341–354.

_____ (1985). Customs unions and the core. *Journal of International Economics*, **19**, 355–365.

Syropoulos, C (1999). Customs unions and comparative advantage. *Oxford Economic Papers*, **51**, 239–266.

Viner, J (1950). *The Customs Union Issue.* New York: Carnegie Endowment for International Peace.

Chapter 6

External Sector "Closing" Rules in Applied General Equilibrium Models*

John Whalley
University of Western Ontario
National Bureau of Economic Research (NBER)

Bernard Yeung†
University of Chicago, Chicago, IL 60637, U.S.A.

This chapter examines formulations of external sector behavior adopted in some of the recent applied general equilibrium models. In many cases, these models are constructed for single economies and the model-builder attempts to use a convenient external sector specification to close the model. Issues and difficulties with export demand and import supply functions for foreigners which satisfy trade balance and the modeling of small economy price taking behavior are explored.

1. Introduction

In a number of recent empirically oriented general equilibrium policy models (such as Boadway and Treddenick, 1978; Dervis and Robinson, 1978; Deardorff and Stern, 1981; Dixon *et al.*, 1982; Fullerton *et al.*, 1978) a system of simple export demand and import supply functions is used along with a trade balance condition to represent external sector behavior so as to "close" the model. Usually a number of commodity classes (perhaps in the region of 10–30) are separately identified in these models with the focus of the

*This chapter was first published in (1984). *Journal of International Economics*, **16**(1), 123–138.
†We are grateful to the Social Sciences and Humanities Research Council, Ottawa, for financial support for a project on general equilibrium analysis of taxation policy from which the ideas for this chapter developed. Extensive and extremely helpful comments made on an earlier draft by Don Fullerton have markedly improved the chapter, as have comments from Sverre Munk and Serena Ng. We are grateful to both, but neither should in any way be held accountable for remaining errors.

modeling being on a price endogenous equilibrium framework, thus allowing the analysis of detailed impacts of policy or other variations. In some cases, these models are constructed for single economies and the model-builder attempts to use a relatively simple external sector specification to "close" the model; in other cases external sector policies are investigated and more attention is therefore given to the closure equations. Most models separately identify traded and nontraded goods and use the so-called "Armington" procedure which treats similar domestically produced and imported goods as qualitatively different. The procedure is used primarily to account for the phenomenon of "cross hauling" which appears in the international trade data to which these models are calibrated. This chapter explores some issues in the use of these external sector closure rules and argues that some of the simple closure rules used can be easily misinterpreted.

2. External Sector Closure Rules in Recent Applied General Equilibrium Models

The precise structure of the external sector in the empirically oriented general equilibrium models tend to vary somewhat from model to model, although the broad characteristics are similar. While it is impossible to reproduce exactly all of these specifications here, we note that the models reported in Boadway and Treddenick (1978), Dervis and Robinson (1978), Deardorff and Stern (1981), and Dixon *et al.* (1982) all have exchange rate variables appearing in the external sector of what are presented as otherwise largely conventional general equilibrium models. It is common in these models, for results to be presented from policy or other experiments in which changes in exchange rates are reported as if financial variables have real effects. All of these models also separately incorporate traded and nontraded goods and use the "Armington" assumption of product heterogeneity across countries. The model used by Fullerton *et al.* (1978) has no exchange rate term in the external sector formulation and does not adopt the Armington assumption but uses an assumption that the real value of net trade in each commodity is constant. This treatment has been changed in later versions of this model.[a]

Boadway and Treddenick (1978) present an especially clear explanation of their external sector closure procedure, and it is useful to use their discussion to illustrate some issues common to all these models. Their focus

[a]See Goulder *et al.* (1983).

is on the domestic impacts of variations in Canadian tariff policy and they construct a model for Canada with substantial industrial and commodity detail involving either Cobb–Douglas or CES functions for both primary and intermediate production. The data base for the model is provided by the Canadian input–output tables. Boadway and Treddenick comment on the need for a simple way of closing their domestic economy model by incorporating the external sector, and outline a partial equilibrium system which can be appended to the more elaborate general equilibrium specification of the domestic economy.

They first describe a closure system for a model in which homogeneous products appear, presenting a subsystem in which foreigners are assumed to have constant price elasticity import supply and export demand functions, and a zero trade balance condition applies. They suggest that this is an especially convenient system since these elasticities can be chosen either to correspond to empirical estimates, or to allow for polar cases such as pricetaking behavior. Due to the cross hauling in trade data, however, their computations use the "Armington" assumption of product heterogeneity and the external sector specification differs from that discussed in the earlier part of their paper. They assume foreign demand functions of constant price elasticity form and treat Canada as a taker of world prices for imported goods. This assumes a perfectly elastic foreign import supply function, although foreign and domestic goods are not perfect substitutes. The elasticity of substitution between comparable domestic and foreign goods controls the degree to which the Canadian price system is governed by world prices. An external sector balance condition involving an exchange rate variable closes the system.

Somewhat similar subsystems to that used by Boadway and Treddenick appear in the models of Dervis and Robinson (1978) and Dixon *et al.* (1982). In all cases the "Armington" product heterogeneity assumption is used along with constant price elasticity foreign export demand functions, domestic price taking behavior with respect to world import prices and an external sector balance condition. In all these models, an exchange rate variable also appears. Deardorff and Stern's (1981) model differs from the above models in that the submodels of the separate economies are linked through an international price system. Each country's export demand function is given by the sum of import demands for the country exports across all other countries. The "Armington" product heterogeneity assumption is used and exchange rate variables affect domestic currency import and export prices.

These external sector closure procedures thus have a number of common features. First, an exchange rate variable frequently appears giving the impression of a financial magnitude affecting real variables of the system in long-run equilibrium, even though real models are used with no monetary sector specified. Second, external sector equation systems are described in some models as giving a capability of separately incorporating foreign export demand and import supply elasticities while simultaneously meeting an external sector balance condition. Third, the common procedure is to use the "Armington" assumption of product heterogeneity by country to model price taking behavior with respect to all or some of the imported goods while foreigners' demand functions for domestic exports incorporate some degree of price elasticity. An external sector balance condition also applies in this case.

A number of points involving these procedures are made here.

(i) Systems of equations for behavior of foreigners which also satisfy a trade balance condition are, by construction, complete systems of excess demand functions for foreigners and should not be viewed as a sequence of independent equations. While these systems may conveniently close the model, there is no currency exchange rate in the conventional use of the term as a financial magnitude determined from financial sector activity. This terminology can thus be misleading in the presentation of these models in that it creates the appearance of a financial variable having real long-run equilibrium effects when nonneutralities of monetary variables are not present. The exchange rate variable appearing in the specifications used can, in some cases, be removed by substitution, and computation of international trade equilibria is both simplified and clarified by such a procedure.

(ii) Export demand elasticities and import supply elasticities for the foreign sector are strictly speaking not independent parameters in these equation systems because of the trade balance condition. In a classical two-good trade model, the elasticity of the foreign offer curve is simultaneously related to both foreign export demand and import supply elasticities suggesting difficulties in separately specifying both of these elasticities. Parameters that are specified in the belief that they represent export demand and import supply price elasticities in these equation systems may not accurately represent these elasticities and general equilibrium calculations for models using specifications could therefore be misinterpreted.

(iii) Similar difficulties are encountered in models which follow the "Armington" procedure and attempt simultaneously to incorporate pricetaking behavior for imports, a constant price elasticity of foreign export demand, and a zero trade balance condition. The algebra of these systems rapidly becomes intractable, but we suggest that this construction for the external sector in the two-good case typically involves both domestic and foreign offer curves lying one on top of the other. Foreign import supply passively adapts to domestic import demands, guaranteeing that the external sector is in equilibrium at any set of prices generated by the domestic portion of such models. This is difficult to reconcile with conventional trade analysis as it also implies in the two-good case that the foreign offer curve is of opposite shape to that conventionally drawn.

(iv) If models involving homogeneous goods were to be used to specify pricetaking behavior for all of the traded goods, then a general equilibrium for the pricetaking economy would involve a single parameter in addition to the endogenous nontraded goods prices. This parameter can be interpreted as the price of a composite traded good, relative to a composite of nontraded goods, since the pricetaking economy formulation specifies only relative and not absolute prices of traded goods. The fixed relative prices of the traded goods can be used as weights in the construction of the composite traded good, and we outline below a formulation of equilibrium in a small open pricetaking economy with both traded and nontraded goods. This equilibrium formulation indicates the need for the additional parameter mentioned above in model solution, and we suggest that this parameter could be equated with the exchange rate variable appearing in some of the empirically oriented general equilibrium models even though no financial variables appear in the model. A similar interpretation of the exchange rate variable appears in Srinivasan's comments (1979) on the Deardorff and Stern model (1981).

(v) The external sector specification can considerably affect the perceived impact of policy changes, even when trade accounts for only a relatively small fraction of total activity in the economy. We report equilibrium calculations from a simple numerical example in which the domestic effects of a distorting factor tax are evaluated. We consider alternative external sector formulations and show the quantitative differences involved.

The first three points listed above are illustrated here by a simplified two-good trade model in which no nontraded goods appear. We devote separate sections to formulations with and without the "Armington" assumption. We then consider an equilibrium formulation for a small open pricetaking economy where we separately identify traded and nontraded goods. We explore the interpretation of the additional parameter mentioned under point (iv), and show the potential quantitative significance of the external sector specification.

3. A Simple Two-Commodity Formulation of External Sector Closure

A simple system of external sector closure suggested by Boadway and Treddenick for a general equilibrium model in which no "Armington" assumption appears (products are homogeneous between countries) can be used to illustrate some of the issues in design of closure rules. Their suggestion can be represented by the following system of simple foreign export demand and import supply functions:

$$E = E_0 \left(\frac{P_E}{e}\right)^{\eta}, \quad -\infty < \eta < 0, \tag{1}$$

$$M = M_0 \left(\frac{P_M}{e}\right)^{\mu}, \quad 0 < \mu < \infty, \tag{2}$$

where P_E and P_M are the home country prices paid for exports and received for imports. E and M are vectors of exports and imports, respectively, and E_0 and M_0 are "base year" imports and exports, η and μ are described as export demand and import supply price elasticities, respectively, explaining the restrictions on η and μ in (1) and (2). e is described as the exchange rate between domestic and foreign currency. (P_E/e) and (P_M/e) are foreign country (world) prices and thus enter the functions (1) and (2). A balance of payments condition:

$$P_M M = P_E E, \tag{3}$$

closes the system.

In computing an equilibrium for a larger general equilibrium model of a domestic economy with this form of external sector closure, domestic prices are determined as cost covering prices from zero profit conditions. Using the equation system (1), (2), and (3), and some form of solution for e (iterative or otherwise), M, and E are determined and hence market excess demands for all commodities in the model can be calculated. The equilibrium vectors P_M and P_E are calculated as those guaranteeing excess demands equal to zero for all commodities.

The external sector system actually used by Boadway and Treddenick in their analysis of Canadian tariff policy differs from the above specification as indicated earlier. However, with the system they adopt, they perform different calculations on the effects of policy changes in their model for alternative values of η, which they interpret as the export price elasticity. In each case, impacts on the exchange rate are reported and interpreted.

Two issues arising immediately with this specification are the role of the exchange rate term in this formulation since it can be removed by simple substitution, and the interpretation of the parameters μ and η which have an alternative elasticity interpretation to that which the system above might appear to offer. These points derive from the fact that the system of Eqs. (1), (2), and (3) is a system of three equations which, in the two-good case where M and E are scalars, specify a foreign offer curve of constant elasticity. This single elasticity parameter determines both the import supply and export demand elasticities. Since a real trade model does not involve an exchange rate term, the system of equations is overidentified.

This can be illustrated by substituting (1) and (2) into (3), and e can be solved for as:

$$e = \left(\frac{M_0}{E_0}\right)^{1/(\mu-\eta)} \cdot \frac{P_M^{(\mu+1)/(\mu-\eta)}}{P_E^{(\eta+1)/(\mu-\eta)}}. \tag{4}$$

Using this solution for e enables (1) and (2) to be rewritten as:

$$E = E_0 P_E^{-1} \cdot \left(\frac{M_0}{E_0}\right)^{-\eta/(\mu-\eta)} P_M^{-(\mu+1)\eta/(\mu-\eta)} \cdot P_E^{\mu(\eta+1)/(\mu-\eta)}, \tag{5}$$

$$M = M_0 P_M^{-1} \cdot \left(\frac{M_0}{E_0}\right)^{-\mu/(\mu-\eta)} \cdot P_M^{-(\mu+1)\eta/(\mu-\eta)} \cdot P_E^{\mu(\eta+1)/(\mu-\eta)}. \tag{6}$$

Equations (5) and (6) describe a system of excess demand functions in which the prices P_M and P_E appear but the exchange rate e is absent. It should be noted that unlike conventional excess demand functions the sign of E and M cannot change; the direction of trade assumed by choice of E_0 and M_0 remains unaltered irrespective of the equilibrium prices determined by the remainder of the model to which the subsystem (1)–(3) is appended.

More importantly, the system (5) and (6) does not have the same properties as those suggested by Eqs. (1), (2), and (3). The export demand elasticity (ξ_E^{FD}) with respect to the endogenously determined home country export price P_E is not η as suggested by (1), but:

$$\xi_E^{FD} = \frac{\partial E}{\partial P_E} \cdot \frac{P_E}{E} = \frac{\eta(1+\mu)}{(\mu - \eta)}, \tag{7}$$

and the import supply price elasticity in the respect to the home country import price (ξ_M^{FS}) is not μ but:

$$\xi_M^{FS} = \frac{\partial M}{\partial P_M} \cdot \frac{P_M}{M} = \frac{-\mu(1+\eta)}{(\mu - \eta)}. \tag{8}$$

For this import supply elasticity to have the appropriate sign, the restriction should be $\eta \leqq -1$ rather than $\eta \leqq 0$ as in (1). This difference in interpretation arises because the elasticities in (7) and (3) are measured with respect to the home country's prices rather than world prices.

The values of two elasticities in (7) and (8) are constrained by the trade balance condition (3).[b] These are not independent parameters but are jointly determined by the single elasticity of the offer surface. For the case where E and M are scalars, we can define the elasticity of the foreign offer curve, ξ^{OC}, as

$$\xi^{OC} = \frac{M}{E} \cdot \frac{dE}{dM}, \tag{9}$$

which implies that

$$\xi^{OC} = \frac{\xi_E^{FD}}{\xi_E^{FD} + 1} = \frac{\xi_M^{FS} + 1}{\xi_M^{FS}}, \tag{10}$$

and it follows from both (7) and (8) that

$$\xi^{OC} = \frac{\eta}{1+\eta} \cdot \frac{1+\mu}{\mu}. \tag{11}$$

Thus, specifying an equation subsystem (1), (2), and (3) is equivalent in the two-good case to the specification of a foreign offer curve of constant elasticity. The elasticities of export demand and import supply functions with respect to home country prices are derived from the elasticity of the

[b]Econometricians do not typically incorporate the restrictions implied by trade balance when they estimate export demand and import supply elasticities. This issue is explored in Mansur (1982).

Table 1. Home Country Price Elasticity of Foreign Export Demand.

η	μ	ξ_E^{FD} (home country price elasticity of foreign export demand)
−10	1	−1.8
−10	10	−5.5
−10	50	−10.2
−25	1	−1.9
−25	10	−7.8
−25	25	−13
−25	50	−17

offer curve as shown in Eq. (10). The critical parameter in this case is neither μ nor η taken alone, but the product $[\eta/(1+\eta)] \cdot [(1+\mu)/\mu]$. If $\eta < -1$ and $\mu > 0$, it follows that $1 < \xi^{OC} < \infty$, and if η is specified close to -1, then ξ^{OC} approaches ∞ independently of μ. A large positive value of μ and a large negative value of η causes ξ^{OC} to approach 1. An offer curve with elasticity 1 is a straight line through the origin, i.e., the case of a small pricetaking economy.

In their calculations, Boadway and Treddenick specify three values of η as 1, 10, and 25 and interpret these values as export price elasticities. For the system of Eqs. (1), (2), and (3) these values are not the home price elasticities since the values of η can have this interpretation only if μ and η are both 1. In other cases, solutions using (7) and (8) are obtained, as shown in Table 1.

Thus, if a system of the form described by Eqs. (1), (2), and (3) were to be used to represent the external sector for a two-good general equilibrium model, the equation system can be misleading both in creating an appearance of monetary nonneutralities, and in potentially leading to misspecification of intended elasticity values. For the n good case, trade balance also implies similar cross equation restrictions. Although the algebra is not as simple as in the presentation above, the general point that trade balance needs to be explicitly recognized in specifying combinations of export demand and import supply elasticities still applies.

4. External Sector Closure Using a Mixed Price Endogenous/Fixed Price Formulation

While the system outlined in Section 3 has the virtue of simplicity, the more common formulation in the applied general equilibrium models referenced above is to model the economy under investigation as facing fixed world prices for imports while simultaneously facing a foreign demand function for exports with constant own price elasticity. Domestic and foreign goods are imperfect substitutes in domestic demand functions. An external sector balance condition completes the system. Unlike the specification in Section 3, prices of imports are not endogenously determined in the larger model but given from outside the model as data. The "Armington" assumption commonly used in these models treats imports as different from goods produced domestically, to account for "cross hauling" in trade data.[c]

We can extend the equation system presented in Section 3 to capture such a formulation. The foreign export demand equation is as in Section 3:

$$E = E_0(P_E/e)^{\eta}, \quad -\infty < \eta < 0, \tag{12}$$

where P_E is the home country price of exports.

The foreign import supply function is constructed to guarantee that any amount will be supplied at a fixed (exogenously determined) world price. To close the system we therefore need to consider the domestic import demand function which for now, is of constant elasticity form. It should be noted that this specification is typically a part of a more complex domestic general equilibrium system which contains specific substitution parameters to capture the fact that domestic and foreign goods are imperfect substitutes.

This formulation gives an external sector equation subsystem as (12) plus

$$M = M^S = M^D, \tag{13}$$

$$M^D = M_0(e \cdot P_M)^{\mu}, \quad -\infty < \mu < 0, \tag{14}$$

$$P_M = \bar{P}_M, \tag{15}$$

where M^S and M^D denote foreign import supply and domestic import demand, respectively, and P_M denotes the world price of imports which is fixed at $\bar{P}_M$. We note that P_M has a different interpretation to Section 3 since it denotes a world rather than a domestic price. Also, μ is now elasticity of the domestic import demand function rather than the foreign import supply function as in Section 3, and a different sign restriction on μ from the previous section applies.

[c]This specification is used by Boadway and Treddenick in the calculations they report and is common to the other models referenced.

The system is completed by a balance of payments condition as in Section 3 but changes slightly due to the fact that P_M denotes a world price

$$\bar{P}_M M = \frac{P_E}{e} \cdot E. \tag{16}$$

By substitution in this system, e can be removed as in Section 2

$$e = \left(\frac{E_0}{M_0}\right)^{1/(\mu+\eta+1)} \cdot P_E^{(\eta+1)/(\mu+\eta+1)} \bar{P}_M^{-(\mu+1)/(\mu+\eta+1)}, \tag{17}$$

giving the reduced forms

$$M = M_0 \left(\frac{E_0}{M_0}\right)^{\mu/(\mu+\eta+1)} \cdot P_E^{\mu(\eta+1)/(\mu+\eta+1)} \cdot \bar{P}_M^{(\mu\cdot\eta)/(\mu+\eta+1)}, \tag{18}$$

$$E = E_0 \left(\frac{E_0}{M_0}\right)^{-\eta/(\mu+\eta+1)} \cdot P_E^{(\mu\cdot\eta)/(\mu+\eta+1)} \cdot \bar{P}_M^{(\mu+1)\eta/(\mu+\eta+1)}, \tag{19}$$

and the reduced form elasticities which are identical to each other

$$\frac{\partial E}{\partial P_E} \cdot \frac{P_E}{E} = \frac{\mu \cdot \eta}{(\mu+\eta+1)} \tag{20}$$

and

$$\frac{\partial M}{\partial \bar{P}_M} \cdot \frac{\bar{P}_M}{M} = \frac{\mu \cdot \eta}{(\mu+\eta+1)}. \tag{21}$$

Thus, in a similar vein to the argument in Section 3, the specification of parameters for Eqs. (12) and (14) could be misleading, since it creates the impression of specifying separate export and import demand elasticities, η, and μ, whereas (20) and (21) involve a single elasticity parameter. It should be noted that the import elasticity (21) is not an independent supply elasticity as in Section 3, but is a reduced form elasticity reflecting domestic import demands and the trade balance condition. Also, as in Section 3, no real effects of exchange rates enter the system.

A further characteristic of this system is that, in the two-good case, a complete foreign offer curve is not specified by the equation system (12)–(15). The reduced form system (18) and (19) determines the equilibrium values of M and E for both domestic and foreign sectors of the model, provided the export prices are consistent with zero profit conditions in the model. Equations (18) and (19) passively meet the equilibrium conditions necessary for both domestic and foreign economies for any set of prices specified. Unlike the formulation in Section 3, the equation system (12)–(15) does not define a foreign offer curve but a locus of external sector equilibria. Instead of two intersecting offer curves as in traditional trade theory, offer curves of both domestic and foreign countries are constructed so as to satisfy external sector equilibrium conditions at any set of prices, i.e., lie one on top of the other. This formulation thus seems to run counter to conventional trade theory.

In the applied general equilibrium models referenced above, the domestic portion of the general equilibrium system usually does not contain constant elasticity import demand functions, but uses other functions for complete domestic demand systems. Cobb–Douglas and CES forms are particularly common. Even in these cases, the same problems arise as with the above formulation.

Suppose we consider the foreign export demand function to be as in (12), namely

$$E = E_0(P_E/e)^{\eta}, \quad -\infty < \eta < 0, \tag{22}$$

but allow the domestic import demand function to be part of a system of Cobb–Douglas demand functions for domestic and foreign goods, derived from utility maximization. For simplicity we may assume a pure trade formulation with no production where the only source of domestic income is the sale of a fixed endowment $\bar{E}$ of the exportable commodity. This gives an import demand function

$$M^D = \frac{\alpha(P_E\bar{E})}{\bar{P}_M \cdot e}, \tag{23}$$

where α is the Cobb–Douglas weight on the imported good in the utility function. Use of the balance of payments condition (16) yields

$$e = \left(\frac{E_0}{\alpha\bar{E}}\right)^{I/\eta} \cdot P_E, \tag{24}$$

from which we obtain

$$E = \alpha\bar{E} \quad \text{and} \quad M = \frac{(\alpha\bar{E})^{(\eta+1)/\eta} \cdot E_0^{-1/\eta}}{\bar{P}_M}. \tag{25}$$

As a reduced form, this system differs sharply from the specification intended. The notable characteristic of (25) is that η from (22) does not appear in the export function. The reason is that the Cobb–Douglas demand functions must satisfy a domestic version of the Walras' Law, and this together with the balance of payments condition yields (25) independently of the value of η in (22).

5. External Sector Closure Using a Pricetaking Formulation for all Tradables

An alternative procedure to the external sector closure systems outlined in Sections 3 and 4 is to assume that the domestic economy faces fixed world prices for all traded goods. This involves abandonment of the "Armington" assumption of product heterogeneity and adoption of an assumption of product homogeneity among countries. Domestic prices are endogenously determined in this system with an "exchange rate" variable determined to give external sector balance. The exchange rate variable is in fact the relative price between a composite of traded and nontraded goods.

The role of the exchange rate in this formulation can be seen most simply by considering a price taking pure exchange economy engaging in international trade. To present this model, more than two goods are required and our notation and presentation differ somewhat from the preceding two sections.

We consider N commodities, where the first η_0 are traded goods and the remainder, $\eta_0 + 1, \ldots, N$, are nontraded goods; $\eta_0 \leqq N$. The economy faces fixed world prices for the traded goods. We define the vector of prices $P = (P_1, \ldots, P_N)$ to the vector of domestic prices, and we define a set of domestic market demand functions $D_i(P)$ $(i = 1, \ldots, N)$ which are nonnegative, continuous, homogeneous of degree zero in the domestic prices P, and satisfy a domestic version of the Walras' Law:

$$\sum_{i=1}^{N} P_i D_i(P) = \sum_{i=1}^{N} P_i Z_i,$$

where the vector $Z = Z_1, \ldots, Z_N$ defines the economy-wide endowments of the N commodities.

We suppose the world prices of traded goods $P^W = (P_1^W, \ldots, P_{\eta_0}^W)$ to be given and fixed. For convenience we consider this to be a unit vector, i.e., $\Sigma_{i=1}^{\eta_0} P_i^W = 1$. Equilibrium is characterized in this model by a vector of domestic prices P^* such that demand-supply equalities hold for each nontraded good, where relative domestic prices of traded goods are the same as the fixed relative world prices and a zero trade balance condition applies.

From the homogeneity of degree zero of domestic demand functions, we can arbitrarily normalize domestic prices to sum to an arbitrary constant such as unity: $\Sigma_{i=1}^{N} P_i = 1$. Furthermore, we can impose the restrictions implied by the fixed relative world prices of traded goods by only considering domestic price vectors $(\lambda P_1^W, \ldots, \lambda P_{\eta_0}^W, P_{\eta_0+1}, \ldots, P_N)$, where $P_1^W, \ldots, P_{\eta_0}^W$ are the given world prices of traded goods. The normalization rule on P is satisfied if we consider vectors $(\lambda P_{\eta_0+1}, \ldots, P_N)$ whose elements sum to unity. The notation $P(\lambda)$ denotes the vector $(\lambda P_1^W, \ldots, \lambda P_{\eta_0}^W, P_{\eta_0+1}, \ldots, P_N)$.

An equilibrium may be formally characterized by a vector $P^*(\lambda^*) = (\lambda^*, P_{\eta_0+1}^*, \ldots, P_N^*)$ such that

(1) demands equal supplies for nontraded goods:

$$D_i(P^*(\lambda^*)) - Z_i \leqq 0 \ (= 0 \ if \ P_i^* > 0), \quad i = \eta_0 + 1, \ldots, N;$$

(2) zero trade balance holds for traded goods:

$$\sum_{i=1}^{\eta_0} P_i^W (D_i(P^*(\lambda^*)) - Z_i) = 0.$$

In such a formulation, λ plays the role of a relative price between traded and nontraded goods. Existence of an equilibrium in such a model follows directly from a small modification to the Gale Nikaido mapping used in conventional proofs which follow Brouwer's Theorem.[d] The relevance of this model to the discussion here, however, is that in some of the formulations adopted in the applied models mentioned above, a parameter such as λ implicitly appears. The implication of the above discussion is that in using these models the "real" exchange rate should not be equated with a financial exchange rate.

An external sector formulation using this approach clearly differs from the formulations presented in Sections 3 and 4 and some comments on their relative merits are in order. A simplifying feature of the closure procedure outlined in this section is that no specification of elasticities in the rest of the world is involved since the external sector closure involves a single parameter which sets the relative prices of traded and nontraded goods. In a two-good case, the foreign offer curve is a straight line with a slope given by the world prices of traded goods. The domestic offer curve will have some

[d]See Mansur and Whalley (1982) in which this proof is given as part of a decomposition computational algorithm for international trade general equilibrium models.

elasticity to it, depending on the specification of the domestic portion of the model constructed. Their intersection will determine equilibrium quantities traded. An obvious disadvantage of this procedure is that the pricetaking assumption will be unpalatable for work on large countries (e.g., the U.S.). Also, the formulation of the present section is unable to accommodate "cross hauling" in trade statistics. Thus, the simplicity of this formulation in all probability makes it unpalatable for applied work since trade elasticities usually play a critical role.

6. A Simple Numerical Example

To highlight the potential quantitative significance of the choice of the external sector specification in applied models, we briefly report some calculations of alternative equilibria under different external sector closure specifications for a simple numerical example. We examine cases in which the same distorting factor tax is abolished, and we report large differences in the perceived impact of the tax change under different external sector specifications. While these differences may not be unexpected, they serve to emphasize the potential quantitative significance of some of the points made in earlier sections.

We consider a domestic economy with four commodities, where the first two are tradables and the second two are nontradables. Each commodity is produced according to a CES two-factor (capital and labor) production function with substitution elasticities all set somewhat arbitrarily at 0.8. We consider an equilibrium in the presence of a distorting tax, characterized by prices of unity for all goods and factors. Output 1 is exported and output 2 is imported. The configuration of factor use in the tax distorted equilibrium is as shown in Table 2. The trade flows involve export of 150 of good 1 and imports of 150 of good 2. Taxes on capital in sector 1 are 200 (giving a tax rate on a net of tax basis of 111%).

Following the calibration procedure common in many of the applied models, we construct parameters for production and a single Cobb–Douglas

Table 2. Configuration of Factor Use in the Tax Distorted Equilibrium.

	(Export) Sector 1	(Import competing) Sector 2	(Nontraded goods) Sector 3	Sector 4
Capital	180	20	100	100
Labor	20	180	100	100

demand function so that all equilibrium prices in the presence of the tax are reproduced as unity. The output value of each good[e] is (400, 200, 200, 200), giving a national income of 1,000.

Our example is deliberately constructed so that the distorting tax falls heavily on the factor intensive in the export industry to illustrate the importance of the external sector specification. In this constructed example, any attempt to analyze the impact of removal of the distorting tax cannot help but be highly dependent on the specification of the external sector. If the country has any influence over its terms of trade, the distorting tax may result in a gain for the country since the terms of trade gain could outweigh the domestic distortionary cost. If, however, the country is a price taker on world markets there can be no terms of trade gain from such a tax and distorting losses are all that are involved.

We represent the difference between these cases by constructing a sequence of foreign offer curves of increasing curvature, all of which are consistent with the same tax equilibrium. Increasing curvature also corresponds to decreasing elasticities of offer surfaces. The foreign offer curves (of increasing curvature) all intersect the origin and the (150, 150) trade flow point characterizing the tax distorted equilibrium. The initial equilibrium before the tax is abolished is thus the same in all cases. To represent the foreign offer curves we consider a sequence of circles, all of which pass through the points (0, 0) and (150, 150). As we increase the radii of these circles, the foreign offer curve becomes flatter, and we move closer to a small country formulation; as we reduce the radius we move closer to a large country formulation in which the country has substantial influence over its terms of trade. An alternative procedure which would demonstrate the same point is to vary the elasticity of the foreign offer curve while preserving the tax distorted equilibrium. In each case, we abolish the distorting tax and measure the welfare gains to the domestic economy in terms of compensating and equivalent variations.[f]

The alternative cases we consider, differ in terms of the value which determines the radius of the circle. In Table 3, we report welfare gains as a percentage of national income in the pre-change equilibrium.

The calculations in Table 3 reveal the critical importance of the external sector specification. The estimates of "loss" from the tax range all the way from +7% of national income to almost −1.5%. The 7% case is the domestic

[e]Total costs including taxes.

[f]Calculated for the single national agent with Cobb–Douglas preferences.

Table 3. Alternative Calculations of Welfare Gains from Removal of Distorting Capital Tax in Sector 1 in the Numerical Example.

Radius of foreign offer curve	Hicksian compensating variation as % of national income	Hicksian equivalent variation as % of national income
1,000,000	+5.58	+7.02
10,000	+5.08	+6.32
1,000	+2.35	+2.73
150	−1.36	−1.40

gain from the removal of a distorting tax; the −1.5% case incorporates a strong terms of trade loss which offsets the gain since the foreign offer curve has low elasticity. While such sensitivity may not appear surprising in an artificial numerical example, it nonetheless highlights the critical importance of the external sector specification in models of this form.

7. Conclusion

In this chapter, we have discussed the external sector closure procedures implicit in a number of recently constructed applied general equilibrium models. We argue that some of the systems currently used can be deceptive. There is neither financial exchange rate variable as model descriptions sometimes suggest, nor are the trade elasticities as simply characterized as the models sometimes imply. We suggest that any closure system in these models must inevitably involve a complete system of foreign excess demands and this could perhaps be more widely recognized in discussing these models. Substantial sensitivity of numerical findings from such models to external sector specification can easily arise. We illustrate this with a simple numerical example.

References

Boadway, R and JM Treddenick (1978). A general equilibrium computation of the effects of the Canadian tariff structure. *Canadian Journal of Economics*, **11**(3), 424–446.

Deardorff, A and RM Stern (1981). A disaggregated model of world production and trade: An estimate of the impact of the Tokyo Round. *Journal of Policy Modeling*, **3**, 127–152.

Dervis, K and S Robinson (1978). The foreign exchange gap, growth, and industrial strategy in Turkey. World Bank Staff Working Paper 306, 1973–1983.

Dixon, P, B Parmenter, J Sutton and D Vincent (1982). *ORANI: A multisectoral model of the Australian economy.* (Amsterdam: North-Holland).

Fullerton, D, JB Shoven and J Whalley (1978). General equilibrium analysis of U.S. taxation policy. 1978 Compendium of tax research, Office of Tax Analysis, U.S. Treasury Department, Washington.

Goulder, LH, JB Shoven and J Whalley (forthcoming). *Domestic Tax Policy and the Foreign Sector: The Importance of Alternative External Sector Formulations to Results from a General Equilibrium Tax Analysis Model.* M. Feldstein (ed.), Behavioral simulation methods in tax policy analysis, University of Chicago Press for the National Bureau of Economic Research.

Mansur, AH (1982). On the estimation of import and export demand elasticities and elasticity pessimism. Working Paper No. 8207, Center for the Study of International Economic Relations, University of Western Ontario, London, Canada.

Mansur, AH and J Whalley (1982). A decomposition algorithm for general equilibrium computation with application to international trade models. *Econometrica*, **50**, 1547–1557.

Srinivasan, TN (1979). Comments on "A disaggregated model of world production". World Bank Office Memorandum No. 8, Unpublished.

Part II

World Trade Liberalization, Terms of Trade and Patterns of Trade

Chapter 7

The North–South Debate and the Terms of Trade: An Applied General Equilibrium Approach*,†

John Whalley
University of Western Ontario, Canada
National Bureau of Economic Research (NBER)

A price endogenous numerical general equilibrium model of world trade is used to analyze terms of trade issues in the North–South debate. Seven regions are identified, the U.S., EEC, Japan, Other Developed, OPEC, New Industrialized, and Less Developed Countries. The model is benchmarked to a global 1977 micro-consistent data set. In the central case analysis, protectionist trade policies in the North inflict an annual welfare loss on the South of around 30 billion dollars per year with an associated terms of trade deterioration of around 9%. The annual welfare cost to the South from northern trade restrictions is somewhat larger than annual North–South aid flows. Protection in the South, and the potential terms of trade impacts of differential growth, are also analyzed.

1. Introduction

In this chapter, results of general equilibrium computations on the North–South terms of trade are reported from an extended version of an earlier world trade model due to Whalley (1980) and used by Brown and Whalley (1980) in their analysis of the Tokyo Round trade negotiations under the GATT. The present model uses data from 1977 and incorporates seven trading areas; the U.S., the European Economic Community (EEC), Japan,

*This is a revised version of a paper presented at the Latin American Meetings of the Econometric Society, Mexico City, July 22–26, 1982. Financial support from the Ford Foundation under their research program in International Economic Order is gratefully acknowledged, as is fine research assistance by Bob Hamilton, Jon Fuller, and Randy Wigle. Helpful comments have been received from seminar groups at Southern Illinois, Western Ontario, Toronto, Yale, and the Marga Institute, Sri Lanka.
†This chapter was first published in (1984). *The Review of Economics and Statistics*, **66**(2), 224–234.

Other Developed, OPEC, Newly Industrialized Countries (NICs), and Less Developed Countries (LDCs). A more detailed presentation of the structure of both models appears in Whalley (1985).

The approach adopted parallels that used in other recent applied general equilibrium models, in that counterfactual equilibrium analysis is performed around a benchmark equilibrium data set to which the model specification is calibrated. The model incorporates demand and production functions by region with trade policies modeled in *ad valorem* equivalent form. The model uses the "Armington" assumption of product heterogeneity by region to accommodate "cross hauling" in observed trade data. Also, preferences and production function parameters are separately specified for each region. As a result, trade is determined by more than differences in factor endowment ratios, as in traditional Hecksher–Ohlin models, since technology and preferences differ across regions. Results indicate the size of annual welfare losses inflicted on the South through northern trade policies. The North, however, also loses from protection in the South. Additional results are reported for the effects of differential growth rates in the world economy.

Results obtained for the effects of global trade protection are mainly accounted for by the combination of levels of protection and the relative sizes of trading areas. Protection in the North (which impacts most harshly on the South through agricultural nontariff barriers (NTBs) and textile restrictions) is milder in terms of *ad valorem* equivalents than protection in the South, where import substitution policies frequently produce large *ad valorem* equivalent protection. However, the South (in Gross National Product (GNP) terms] is much smaller than the North, and North–North trade in manufactures is a dominant feature of world trade. Thus, *ad valorem* protection at the same rate in both the North and the South would produce different effects because the South is small relative to the North. In the data used, the larger protection in the small region and the smaller protection in the large region produce comparable worldwide losses, but with a different geographical composition.

While these findings contain important messages for the emerging North–South debate, they also need careful qualification. The data used are, in places, of poor quality, and several key parameters (especially *ad valorem* equivalents of protection policies in the South) are little more than stylized best guesses. Income and price elasticities in trade are other key parameters and heavy reliance is placed on a literature search in selecting values. The *ad valorem* equivalents used to represent protectionist policies are presented in Whalley (1985) where the main features of the 1977 "benchmark" data are also presented. Trade elasticities are discussed in the text.

2. A General Equilibrium Model of North–South Trade[a]

The general equilibrium model used to analyze North–South trade incorporates seven trading areas reflecting major participants in world trade. The grouping of individual countries involved is given in Table 1 along with the corresponding population and U.S. dollar GNP per capita in 1977. The size of these regions in the model reflects the relative U.S. dollar GNP for these areas for 1977 in the World Bank Atlas. The conversion of country GNP data into U.S. dollars using the same exchange rates as in the World Bank Atlas should be noted as an important feature which neglects differences between purchasing power parity and official exchange rates. As noted by Kravis *et al.* (1975), these differences are particularly significant for LDCs.

The model incorporates six products produced in each region: (1) Agriculture and Food, (2) Mineral Products and Extractive Ores, (3) Energy Products (including oil), (4) Nonmechanical Manufacturing, (5) Machinery and Transport Equipment (including vehicles), (6) Construction, Services, and other Nontraded Goods. Each of the first five goods is internationally traded with an assumed heterogeneity by region prevailing across production sources. The sixth commodity is nontraded for all regions.

The same commodity classification is used for trade, domestic production, and final demand data, with an approximate concordance adopted between the different classification systems appearing in the basic data. The model incorporates less disaggregation by product than the full version of the four-region model (Whalley, 1980), which identifies 33 commodities in each region. Problems of data availability for all regions on this more detailed classification, plus the large dimensionalities involved in obtaining a general equilibrium solution for a seven-region model have limited the dimensionality to six products and seven regions; 42 products in total.

[a]A more detailed description of earlier versions of the model incorporating only the EEC, the U.S., Japan, and a residual rest of the world is given in Brown and Whalley (1980), and Whalley (1980).

Table 1. Classification of Countries Into Regions.

	Countries included			
Region 1: (EEC)	Belgium Denmark France	Ireland Italy	Luxemburg Netherlands	U.K. West Germany
Region 2: (U.S.)	U.S.			
Region 3: (Japan)	Japan			
Region 4: (Other Developed)	Albania Australia Austria Bahamas Barbados Bermuda Bulgaria Canada	Czechoslovakia East Germany Finland Fr. Polynesia Gilbralter Greece Greenland Guam	Hungary Israel Malta New Zealand Norway Poland Portugal Puerto Rico	Romania Samoa Spain Sweden Switzerland U.S.S.R. Virgin Islands Yugoslavia
Region 5: (OPEC)	Bahrain Brunei Kuwait	Indonesia Iran Iraq Libya	Nigeria Oman Qatar	Saudi Arabia Un Arab Em Venezuela
Region 6: (NIC)	Argentina Brazil Chile Costa Rica Cyprus Ecuador Fiji	Fr. Guiana Hong Kong Jamaica S. Korea Lebanon Macao Malaysia	Martinique Mexico N. Caledonia Pacific Island Panama Singapore	Surinam Taiwan Trinidad Turkey Uruguay
Region 7: (LDC)	Afghanistan Algeria Angola Antigua Bangladesh Belize Benin Bhutan Bolivia Botswana Burma Burundi Cameroon Cape Verde Ce. Africa Chad China Colombia	El Salvador Ethiopia Gabon Gambia Ghana Grenada Guadeloupe Guatemala Guinea Guinea-Bis Guyana Haiti Honduras India Ivory Coast Jordan Kenya Kiribati	Mali Mauritania Mauritius Mongolia Morocco Mozambique Namibia Nepal New Hebrides N. Guinea Nicaragua Niger Pakistan Paraguay Peru Philippines Reunion Rodesia	Solomon Is. Somalia S. Africa Sri Lanka Sudan Swaziland Syrian A R Tanzania Thailand Togo Tonga Tunisia Uganda Upp Volta Vietnam Yemen A R Yemen PDR Zaire

(*Continued*)

Table 1. (*Continued*)

Comoros	N. Korea	Rwanda	Zambia
Congo	Laos Fdr	St. Kitts	
Cuba	Lesotho	St. Lucia	
Djibouti	Liberia	St. Vincent	
Dominica	Madagascar	Sao Tome	
Dominion Rp	Malawi	Senegal	
Dm Kampuch	Maldives	Seychelles	
Egypt		Sierra Leone	

	1977 GNP/Capita in billion U.S. dollar	1977 Population in billions	1977 GNP in billion U.S. dollar
Region 1 (EEC Countries)	6283	0.3	1629
Region 2 (U.S.)	8751	0.2	1897
Region 3 (Japan)	6511	0.1	737
Region 4 (Other Developed)	3848	0.5	2024
Region 5 (OPEC)	1000.3[a]	0.3	303
Region 6 (NIC)	1306	0.4	461
Region 7 (LDC)	325.1	2.4	773
TOTAL	1863	4.2	7824

Note: All figures used are taken from the World Bank Atlas for 1977. Conversions of country GNP into U.S. dollar in the World Bank Atlas are at market or official exchange rates, and there is a widespread view that relative to "purchasing power parity" calculations this substantially underestimates U.S. dollar GNP/capita in most LDCs. The most widely quoted estimates of "purchasing power parity: premia are in Kravis *et al.* (1975).
[a]This seemingly low figure for OPEC arises from the inclusion of Nigeria and Indonesia as large population members of OPEC.

The "Armington" assumption of product heterogeneity by trading area is used both to accommodate the statistical phenomenon of cross hauling in international trade data, and to exclude complete specialization in production as a behavioral response in the model. This structure also enables empirically based import demand elasticities to be incorporated into the model specification. Thus, products are differentiated on the basis of geographical point of production as well as by their physical characteristics with "similar" products being close substitutes in demand; i.e., Japanese manufactures are treated as qualitatively different products from U.S. or EEC manufactures.

Production and demand patterns in each of the trading areas revolve around the domestic and world price systems. For each product in the model the market price is the price at point of production. Sellers receive these prices, purchasers (of both intermediate and final products) pay these prices gross of tariffs, NTB tariff equivalents, and domestic taxes; no transportation costs are considered. Explicit demand functions are used which are derived from hierarchical CES/LES preference functions, and CES functions characterize production sets. Producers maximize profits and competitive forces operate such that in equilibrium all supernormal profits are competed away.

Investment flows, interest and dividends, and foreign aid also enter the model, with the second two of these being treated as income transfers. Foreign investment is treated as purchases of capital goods by agents located in the country of source of capital funds. The difference between investment flows and merchandise trade is that the capital goods acquired are not repatriated to the country of location of the purchaser, but remain in the source country to generate income in future time periods.

An international trade equilibrium in the model is a situation where demands equal supplies for all products, and in each industry a zero-profit condition is satisfied representing the absence of supernormal profits. In equilibrium, a zero external sector balance condition (including investment flows, dividends, interest and transfers) holds for each region.

An important feature of the model is the structure of substitution possibilities on both the demand and production sides, represented by the CES and CES/LES functions. The elasticities of substitution in these functions determine price elasticities in goods and factor demand functions. Because of the Armington product heterogeneity assumption these elasticities also control import and export demand elasticities for each region.

This is outlined in Table 2. In production, each industry has a CES value-added production function which specifies substitution possibilities between the primary factor inputs, capital and labor services. No technical change is incorporated and factors are immobile between regions. In addition to the CES value-added functions, each industry uses the outputs of other industries (both domestic and imported) as inputs in its own production process. Substitution between intermediate products is allowed while fixed coefficients in terms of composite goods are assumed. Each fixed coefficient requirement is specified in terms of a composite good, which itself is represented by a nested CES function with elements of the composite (e.g., products identified by geographical point of production) entering as arguments. Substitution occurs between comparable domestic and composite imported commodities at the top level of nesting, with further substitution taking place between import types differentiated by location of production.

Table 2. Hierarchy of Substitution Possibilities in the World Trade Model.

DEMAND

Final Demand Functions

In each region, a 4 level CES/LES functional form is used.

CES Hierarchy

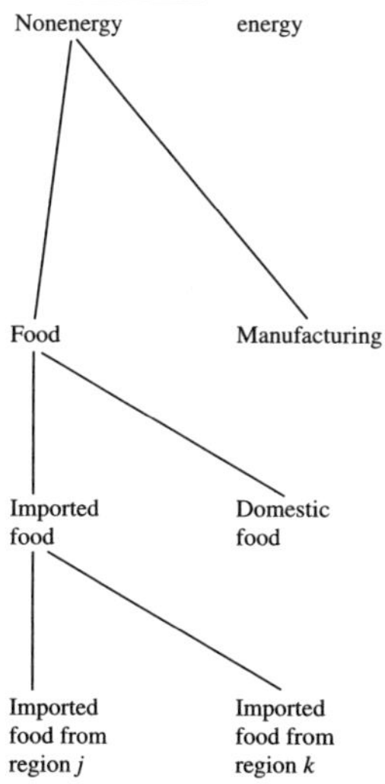

Level 1

Substitution between categories (e.g., energy/nonenergy

Level 2

Substitution within categories among composite goods (e.g., among composite of nonenergy)

Level 3

Substitution between domestic and import composite (e.g., between domestic and imported food)

Level 4

Substitution between import types in import composites (e.g., between imported food from regions *k* and *j*)

LES Hierarchy

Minimum requirements for each import composite at level 3 used. These allow income elasticities for import demands to be different from unity.

PRODUCTION

Value added Functions

Each industry in each region has a CES value added function with capital and labor services as primary inputs.

Intermediate Substitution

Fixed coefficient intermediate requirements technology, but with each fixed coefficient expressed in terms of composites only (i.e., a fixed machinery requirement per unit of manufacturing).

Each fixed coefficient input requirement met by cost minimizing bundle of domestic and import composites obtained from CES substitute functions.

CES hierarchy (For each fixed coefficient in terms of composites, e.g., machinery requirement per unit of manufacture).

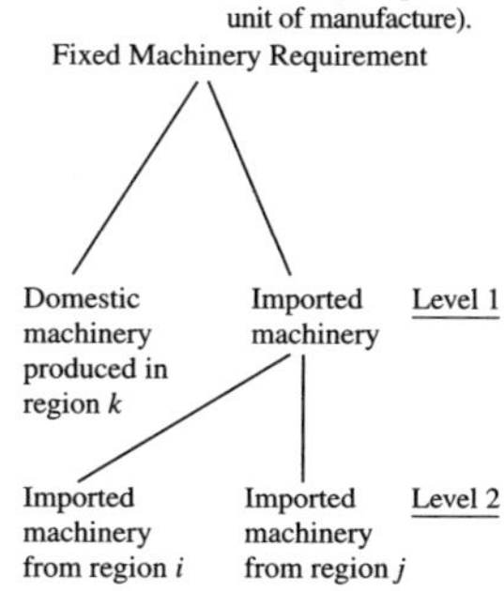

By way of example, were the model to separately identify steel as a commodity, this technology would specify a fixed requirement of steel in the production of a car. The fixed steel requirement could be met by a substitutable mix of domestic and imported steel. Imported steel, in turn, would be a composite of the various types of steel available (differentiated by location of production) with substitution between each. The substitution elasticity between domestic and imported steel would be the major determinant of the price elasticity of demand for steel imports. Substitution between types of steel would affect the price elasticity of the demand function facing exporters to the region.

On the demand side a single set of final demand functions is obtained for each region by maximizing a nested CES/LES utility function. Within this functional form, a hierarchy of substitution possibilities applies between similar products imported from the various trading areas, and between composites of imports across sources and comparable domestic products. Two sets of elasticity values determine substitution among the composite domestic-import products.[b] The LES feature of the demand functions specifies minimum requirements for commodities appearing in the third level of the nesting structure. These four level functions differ from the two level functions used in Brown and Whalley (1980) both in allowing separate substitution between import types as well as between imports and domestic products and in incorporating an LES specification.

Use of these nested functions enables empirical estimates of price elasticities in world trade to be incorporated into the model. These values guide parameter choice for inter-nest elasticity values in the CES functions (i.e., between "similar" products subscripted by location and production). The LES features in the hierarchy allow income elasticities in import demand functions to differ from unity.

Since each region generates demands from utility maximization, the market demand functions in the model satisfy Walras' Law. This is the condition that at any set of prices the total value of demands equals the total value of incomes. The incomes of trading areas are derived from the sale of primary factors owned by each region, plus transfers received (including foreign aid).

Finally, the model incorporates trade protection policies in each region in *ad valorem* equivalent form. These policies comprise tariff protection and NTBs,[c] along with certain features of domestic tax policies in the

[b]The use of two rather than one level nesting above the import substitution stage reflects a purpose of model design not exploited in the chapter. A future application of the model to world energy trade is planned, and the price elasticity of energy demand would become a key parameter. The need to separately treat energy in such an analysis explains this additional flexibility in nesting.

[c]Nontariff barriers include an assortment of policies which either deliberately or coincidently affect trade beyond those effects resulting from tariffs. Natural barriers to trade, including transportation costs, are excluded from NTBs. In the North, NTBs would include government purchasing policies, quotas, seasonal restrictions, specific licensing regulations, voluntary export restraints, special import charges (variable levies in the EEC common Agricultural Policies), and health and sanitary regulations. The estimates used for the North calculate NTBs in *ad valorem* form by a residual method using differences in domestic and world prices net of transport costs and tariffs. In addition to conceptual difficulties with this approach noted in Whalley (1985), it is

North. Protection in the North is milder than protection in the South although substantial variation occurs among the countries which make up the region. In the North, post Tokyo Round tariffs on manufactures will average between 6% and 8% by 1987, with important NTBs on agricultural products, textiles and footwear. In contrast, LDCs and NICs frequently have extremely protective tariffs and restrictive import licensing reflecting import substitution policies. Data, especially on *ad valorem* equivalents of NTBs are limited. The parameter values used along with sources are given in Whalley (1985).

In the South, *ad valorem* protection both through tariffs and quantitative restrictions (import licensing) applies. In many developing countries quantitative restrictions are the binding constraint on imports, with rationing allocating imports in the presence of the excess demands. In this case, tariffs are nonmarginal distortions which only redistribute income. The procedure employed to represent protection in the South is to use estimates of nominal tariff rates for a sample of developing countries along with estimates of the additional import premia caused by import licensing. Separate attribution of protective effects to tariffs and NTBs in the South is thus a little hazardous due to this compounding feature.

3. Benchmark Calibration, Elasticities, and Equilibrium Solution of the Model

A flow chart outlining the procedures used in applying the model is given in Table 3. A worldwide general equilibrium constructed from 1977 data is assumed to hold in the presence of existing trade policies. The model is calibrated to this data set through a procedure which determines parameter values for the model functions consistent with the equilibrium observation. Counterfactual analysis then proceeds for any specified change; such as changes in protection, or differential growth of factor inputs by region.

The calibration procedure involves first constructing a data set for a given year in a form which is consistent with the equilibrium solution concept of the model; a so-called benchmark equilibrium data set. Once assembled, parameter values for equations can be directly calculated from the equilibrium conditions using the calibration procedure described in Mansur and Whalley (1984). The model specification is then capable of

important to note that this treatment assumes all revenues from NTBs, including voluntary export restraints, accrue to the importing country.

Table 3. Model Flow Chart for World Trade General Equilibrium Model.

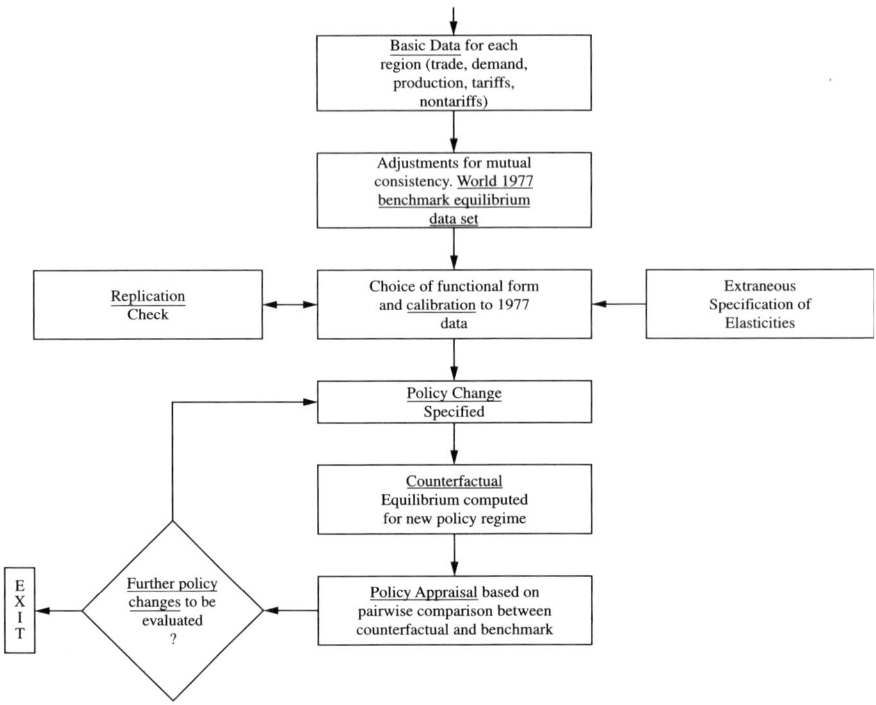

reproducing the benchmark data as an equilibrium solution to the model, and comparative statics can be performed with the model by computing new equilibria for alternative regimes, and comparing new and benchmark equilibrium data. The benchmark equilibrium data set constructed for this purpose has the properties of a worldwide competitive equilibrium in that demands equal supplies for all products, no profits are made in any of the domestic industries and each region is in zero external sector balance.

The micro-consistent benchmark data set involves both the domestic and trading activity of each of the regions. Many divergent source materials are required for this purpose and need adjustment for inconsistent classifications and definitions. A description of the sources and methods used in assembling the 1977 data set used appears in Whalley (1985).

Parameter values, consistent with the equilibrium observation, are found by solving the model equilibrium conditions using the benchmark data. Because of the CES/LES functional forms used, this procedure requires more information than that contained in the benchmark equilibrium data set.[d] This information requirement is met by specifying elasticities of substitution and minimum requirements in the functional forms. Once these are chosen, demand functions are solved for share parameters consistent with both equilibrium prices and quantities. On the supply side, cost functions are similarly solved for share and unit parameters consistent with equilibrium prices and input use by industry.

As might be expected, the values chosen for substitution elasticities have a substantial impact on the results produced by the model and the procedure followed is to adopt a central case model specification around which sensitivity analysis is performed. Given the present focus on trade policies, an important set of parameters is the substitution elasticities which determine implicit trade elasticities. Import price elasticities for developed countries in the model reflect the Stern *et al.* (1976) compendium of trade elasticities, and estimates for developing countries are due to Khan (1974). Recent estimates for the U.S., EEC, and Japan by Stone (1979) provide detailed estimates by product and are also approximately consistent with the values used in the model. The low values (in absolute terms) of import price elasticities produced by these and other studies have been extensively commented in the literature, but in the present model these produce strong terms of trade effects from trade policy changes and their role should thus be highlighted.

The substitution elasticities between comparable domestic and foreign goods in both final demands and intermediate production are based on own price elasticities of import demands by region from literature sources. For any region, the same values are used for all products in the central case specification of the model. Elasticities between import types in both final demand and intermediate substitution functions are all set at 1.5. This parameter determines export price elasticities for exporting regions. No simple method is available to relate estimates for export price elasticities for each region to the substitution elasticities in importing regions in the model,

[d]If, for example, Cobb–Douglas functional forms are used for demand functions, then the exponents in the Cobb–Douglas functions are given directly by the expenditure shares in benchmark data. With CES/LES functions, more information is needed and extraneous values of substitution elasticities and minimum requirements are needed prior to the application of this procedure.

since regions typically import from all (or most) sources. The common value of 1.5 is close to literature estimates and sensitivity analysis can be used around this value. Import income elasticities are all set at unity in the central case, with sensitivity analysis in later cases to reflect the suggestion from some literature of values above unity. Unitary income elasticities correspond to the case of homothetic preferences. Other elasticities are (i) Cobb–Douglas at higher levels for substitution between composite goods in demand; and (ii) literature-based estimates for capital-labor substitution in the CES value-added functions.

Once specified, the model is solved for a new general equilibrium for a policy or other change using a Newton method involving an estimate of the Jacobian matrix of excess factor demands and government budget imbalances. Although there is no *ex ante* argument of convergence with the Newton method used, it has been successful in implementation.

4. Results from Counterfactual Equilibrium Calculations

In this section, results are reported on impacts of changes in trade protection in the North and South and other variations in model specification. Two types of results are highlighted: the impact on the terms of trade by region and the annual welfare gain or loss to each region from the policy or model change.

For each experiment, changes in the net barter terms of trade are calculated for each region in its trade with all other regions. The net barter terms of trade is simply a quantity weighted price index giving the relative price between a composite of imports and a composite of domestic products (exports). Two alternative sets of quantity weights are available, involving those associated with the benchmark equilibrium or the new equilibrium. Both of these terms of trade measures are calculated although in later tables only those using benchmark quantities are reported to economize on space.

Annual welfare impacts of trade policy changes are measured as equivalent income variations (EVs) by region, with the arithmetic sum of EVs reported as the worldwide welfare gain or loss. Aggregation difficulties arise with such a measure, but in the absence of other simple alternatives, this is nonetheless used. Primary stress is placed on equivalent variations since they use old period prices and pairwise comparisons between new and benchmark equilibria produce estimates of welfare effects which all use the same prices.

In Table 4, computations using the central case specification of the model are reported for three policy variations: The abolition of tariff and NTBs in the North (regions 1–4); the South (regions 5–7), and the world (all regions), respectively. In the case where the abolition of tariff and NTBs occurs in the North, a significant annual welfare gain is produced for LDCs and NICs of 30 billion dollar, with these two regions accounting for the majority of the worldwide welfare gain displayed. These welfare changes are collinear with terms of trade effects, with the terms of trade of NICs and LDCs improving by around 9%. Terms of trade measures are affected by the choice of quantity weights, but the broad picture remains the same.

An interesting implication is that the annual gain to the South from removing protection in the North is somewhat larger than the annual aid flow from the North to the South. A "cynical" view of the North–South aid mechanism would therefore be that the North gives approximately 20 billion dollar per year to the South which is then more than offset by terms of trade loss inflicted through protectionist policies in the North. Such a finding clearly supports the contention raised in North–South debates that significant gains are available to the South from the removal of protection in the North. This annual gain of 30 billion dollar is in the region of $2\frac{1}{2}\%$ of GNP for the NIC/LDC group.

The effects of trade protection in the North, however, must be considered along with trade protection in the South where *ad valorem* equivalent protection is significantly higher. Removal of protection in the South yields substantial gains to the North and losses to the South. The worldwide gain from removal of southern tariff and NTBs is in the region of 24 billion dollar but an approximately 60 billion dollar loss is inflicted on the South along with an annual gain to the North of over 80 billion dollar. An especially strong terms of trade gain occurs for Japan.

These results dramatize the feature that the focus of the North–South debate has been almost exclusively on ways of improving the position of the South. It would seem on the basis of the results presented here that a possible response by the North to pressure from the South to liberalize is that trade liberalization in the North should be accompanied by some liberalization in the South.

These results also argue that as a region the South will not gain by liberalizing trade policies in spite of the arguments often made by development economists that trade liberalization is a desirable policy option for many, if not most, LDCs. While individual countries in the South may well gain from trade liberalization if the region as a whole does

Table 4. Annual Welfare Impacts of Trade Policy Variations in the Model (Central Case Specification).

	(i) *Annual Welfare Impacts — EVs in $ bill 1977*		
	Abolition of Tariff and Nontariff Barriers in North (regions 1–4)	Abolition of Tariff and Nontariff Barriers in South (regions 5–7)	Abolition of Tariff And Nontariff Barriers in all Regions
EEC	−0.8	38.2	35.5
U.S.	−1.6	12.9	9.8
Japan	−1.4	21.4	20.8
Other Dev.	−4.1	4.7	−1.8
OPEC	5.7	7.0	8.3
NIC	13.2	−31.8	−21.0
LDC	17.0	−28.4	−18.7
TOTAL	28.0	24.1	33.1

(*Continued*)

Table 4. *(Continued)*

(ii) *% Change in Terms of Trade for the Same Cases (+ve indicates improvement)*

	Abolition of Tariff and Nontariff Barriers in North (regions 1–4)		Abolition of Tariff and Nontariff Barriers in South (regions 5–7)		Abolition of Tariff and Nontariff Barriers in all Regions	
	Using Benchmark Equilibrium Quantity Weights	Using New Equilibrium Quantity Weights	Using Benchmark Equilibrium Quantity Weights	Using New Equilibrium Quantity Weights	Using Benchmark Equilibrium Quantity Weights	Using New Equilibrium Quantity Weights
EEC	−3.1	−2.8	14.9	18.5	12.7	14.9
U.S.	−2.2	−1.9	2.5	6.8	1.5	5.0
Japan	−5.1	−4.9	24.0	27.9	23.1	25.1
Other Dev.	−3.7	−3.6	−2.0	1.0	−4.7	−2.6
OPEC	4.8	5.0	−0.1	3.0	1.7	3.9
NIC	8.5	8.7	−29.6	−28.7	−23.0	−22.6
LDC	9.5	9.7	−33.6	−33.9	−29.3	−29.6

not liberalize, simultaneous moves by all countries to liberalize will be detrimental to the South because of the adverse terms of trade impacts.

The last case reported in Table 4 involves the joint abolition of all tariff and NTBs in all regions. Here the worldwide gain of 33 billion dollar is smaller than the sum of the gains reported in the subcases in Table 4. The finding is thus that in terms of worldwide protection, the South is the significant gainer in terms of trade impacts due to the higher protection which prevails in their region. This more than offsets the size differential between regions.

Because of the key role played by elasticities in the calculations reported in Table 4, a number of sensitivity analyses on these cases have been performed. Due to space constraints these are not reported here in detail, but can be summarized nonetheless. As might be expected, variations in elasticity values significantly affect the estimated impacts of policies. Terms of trade effects associated with the abolition of tariff and NTBs in the North are substantially strengthened by raising import price elasticities in all regions. Terms of trade effects are weakened by raising export price elasticities, and gains from the removal of protection in the North accrue more heavily to the North rather than to the South. Variations resulting from varying income elasticities are less significant, as are changes in the relative sizes of regions resulting from attempts to correct intercountry GNP calculations for differences between purchasing power parity and official exchange rates.

Table 5 reports cases where the terms of trade effects associated with differential growth rates in North–South trade are analysed using the model. These analyses are motivated by the literature on immiserizing growth (Bhagwati, 1958). The annual growth rates by region taken from the World Bank Atlas are reported, with the North on average being slower growing in GNP terms than the South. The rate of growth of GNP in the South does not, however, imply higher growth of GNP per capita since population growth in the South is significantly higher. These data are used as rates of growth of both factor endowments in each region, even though growth may not in practice be balanced. This treatment of factor endowment growth corresponds to that used in theoretical literature on immiserizing growth.

As is to be expected from the literature discussion of this issue, the regions which are relatively fast growing suffer a deterioration in their terms of trade. In the homothetic preference cases, after ten years the EEC and the U.S. have a 7% appreciation of their terms of trade with deterioration in the terms of trade of the South of 7–8%. This ten-year deterioration

Table 5. Differential Growth Rates and North–South Terms of Trade.

(A) *Annual GNP Growth by Bloc Computed from World Bank Atlas (10 year averages — 1968–78)*

EEC	U.S.	Japan	Other Dev.	OPEC	NIC	LDC
3.3%	2.8%	4.8%	4.1%	3.5%	5.2%	4.5%

(B) *Terms of Trade Impacts of Differential Growth (homothetic case, central case specification, benchmark equilibrium quantity weights)*

	After 5 Years	After 10 Years	After 20 Years
EEC	3.4	6.9	14.0
U.S.	3.5	7.0	14.0
Japan	−3.3	−6.7	−13.0
Other Dev.	−2.9	−5.7	−11.1
OPEC	0.9	1.8	3.5
NIC	−4.4	−9.0	−17.2
LDC	−3.1	−6.1	−12.1

(C) *Nonhomothetic Cases (terms of trade impacts after 10 years using benchmark equilibrium quantity weights)*

Import Income	Regions 1 – 4 (North)	1.5	0.5	0.75
Elasticities[a]	Regions 5 – 7 (South)	1.5	1.5	1.25
EEC		6.4	6.7	6.8
U.S.		6.6	6.9	6.7
Japan		−5.9	−6.4	−6.2
Other Dev.		−5.4	−5.6	−5.5
OPEC		1.8	1.8	1.7
NIC		−8.8	−9.0	−8.9
LDC		−5.9	−6.0	−6.1

[a]The income elasticity in OPEC is left at unity; the same as for the homothetic case.

is approximately equal to the adverse move in southern terms of trade resulting from protectionist trade policies in the North. Thus ten years differential North–South growth appears roughly comparable in significance for the North–South terms of trade to the annual terms of trade effects of protection in the North.

Results from nonhomothetic cases are also reported. These are partially motivated by the literature indications that income elasticities in world trade exceed unity and partially by the rationalization for the "Prebisch–Singer" thesis that with differential income elasticities in import demands there will be an inevitable deterioration in the terms of trade of the South. The results produced from these cases are little different from the homothetic case, although the seemingly counter-intuitive finding is reported that with higher import income elasticities in all regions in terms of trade effects from continuing differential growth are weaker. This result is due to the Engel aggregation condition that demand functions satisfy. Since the weighted sum of income elasticities across domestic and imported goods must be unity in all regions, the smaller import expenditure share in the South produces higher income elasticities for own products than in the North.

5. Conclusion

In this chapter, the role of trade protection policies and other features of current world trading arrangements on the North–South terms of trade are explored using a numerical general equilibrium model involving seven major world trading areas.

Results from the central case model specification suggest that a significant annual term of trade loss is inflicted on the South through trade protection policies in the North. The annual welfare cost to the South is a somewhat larger order of magnitude than the annual aid flow from the North to the South. However, trade protection in the South at much higher *ad valorem* equivalent rates than in the North has larger impacts on worldwide terms of trade and trade flows. A combined assessment of trade protection in the North and the South suggests that the North are net losers from worldwide trade protection and the South net gainers.

Results are also reported on the extent to which higher growth rates of GNP (although not of GNP per capita) in the South lead to deterioration in the southern terms of trade. Results suggest that after ten years of differential growth at current annual rates, the deterioration in the terms of trade of the South will be approximately equal to the current annual terms of trade loss from protection in the North. Thus, continued differential growth performance will have long-run adverse impacts on the terms of trade of the South, which could be partially or wholly offset by continued reduction of trade protection in the North.

References

Bhagwati, J (1958). Immiserizing growth: A geometrical note. *Review of Economic Studies*, **25**, 201–205.

Brown, F and J Whalley (1980). General equilibrium evaluations of tariff-cutting proposals in the Tokyo Round and comparisons with more extensive liberalization of world trade. *Economic Journal*, **90**, 838–866.

Khan, MS (1974). Import and export demand in developing countries. *IMF Staff Papers*, 678–693.

Kravis, IB, Z Kennessey, A Heston and R Summers (1975). *A System of International Comparisons of Gross National Product and Purchasing Power.* Baltimore: Johns Hopkins University Press for the World Bank.

Mansur, AH and J Whalley (1984). Numerical specification of applied general equilibrium models: Estimation, calibration, and data. In *Applied General Equilibrium Analysis*, H Scarf and J Shoven (eds.). New York: Cambridge University Press.

Stern, RM, J Francis and B Schumacher (1976). *Price Elasticities in International Trade: An Annotated Bibliography.* London: Macmillan, for the Trade Policy Research Centre.

Stone, JA (1979). Price Elasticities of Demand for Imports and Exports: Industry Estimates for the U.S., the EEC, and Japan. *Review of Economics and Statistics*, **60**, 306–312.

Whalley, J (1980). General Equilibrium Analysis of U.S.–EEC–Japanese Trade and Trade Distorting Policies. *Economie Appliqué*, Symposium issue on International Trade General Equilibrium Models.

_____ (1985). *Trade Liberalization Among Major World Trading Areas: A General Equilibrium Approach.* Cambridge, M.A.: MIT Press.

Chapter 8

Trade and Environment: Bargaining Outcomes from Linked Negotiations*

Lisandro Abrego and Carlo Perroni
University of Warwick, Coventry CV4 7AL, U.K.
lisandro.abrego@warwick.ac.uk

John Whalley
University of Warwick and Western Ontario,
London, Ontario, Canada N6A 5C2.
National Bureau of Economic Research (NBER)

Randall M. Wigle†
Wilfrid Laurier University, 75 University Ave W.,
Waterloo, Ontario, Canada N2L 3C5.

Some recent literature has explored physical and policy linkages between trade and the environment. This chapter explores linkage through leverage in bargaining, whereby developed countries can use trade threats to achieve improved developing-country environmental management, while developing countries can use environmental concessions to achieve trade discipline in developed countries. A global numerical simulation model is used to compute bargaining outcomes from linked trade and environment negotiations. Results indicate joint gains from expanding the trade bargaining set to include the environment. However, compared with bargaining with cash side-payments, linked negotiations on policy instruments provide significantly inferior outcomes for developing countries.

1. Introduction

Since the early 1990s, trade and the environment has been a high-profile issue, with environmental groups arguing that restrictions are needed on

*This chapter was first published in (1999). CSGR Working Paper Series 27/99.
†We acknowledge comments, advice, and suggestions from Don Fullerton, Larry Goulder, Geoff Heal, Bill Nordhaus, and V. Kerry Smith, and from an anonymous referee. We are grateful to the ESRC for financial support under an award on fiscal policies and the environment. Concluding stages of the work have drawn on support from the John D. and Catherine T. MacArthur Foundation.

certain types of trade (e.g., species, tropical lumber, pollution-intensive manufactures), and less-developed countries (LDCs) opposing what they see as a new threat of trade restrictions against their exports. Where countries fail to institute policies which internalize global or cross-border environmental externalities, environmental groups argue that appropriate trade restrictions can improve resource allocation. Trade liberalization advocates, on the other hand, see trade measures as very much second-best environmental policy and worry over new trade restrictions.

This chapter discusses possible LDC participation in linked trade and environment negotiations in the World Trade Organization (WTO), which we suggest would largely break down on North–South lines. The South we see as the custodian of environmental assets yet to be used (such as forests) and the North as having a high dependence on the use of these assets.

Whether or not environmental issues should be part of any future (post-Uruguay Round) trade negotiations is now central to the debate. Developed countries (DCs), responding to pressures from their own nongovernmental environmental organizations, have supported their inclusion, while LDCs have appeared more reluctant to do so. They instead seek direct compensation for implementing growth-slowing policies.

We argue here that global (and cross-border) environmental externalities provide LDCs with strategic leverage over the use of trade restrictions by DCs. Although GATT/WTO tariff barriers in OECD countries are now low, sectoral barriers in textiles, apparel, footwear, steel, and other areas are still significant, as are voluntary export restraints, regulatory restrictions in services, and the use of antidumping and countervailing-duty measures. Linking environmental and trade negotiations thus provides opportunities to developing countries restrain adverse trade policies in DCs, with environmental concessions being available to bargain for lower trade barriers. Linkage expands the bargaining set, which can result in more trade and lowered barriers. Seemingly, negotiations that link trade and the environment should be embraced by both the developing and developed world.

The literature on this has focused primarily on two related questions: whether international trade contributes to lowered environmental quality (e.g., Anderson, 1992a,b; Dean, 1992; Rauscher, 1992); and whether trade liberalization is desirable, both in terms of global efficiency and individual-country interest, when environmental emissions are not internalized (e.g., Dean, 1992; Pearce, 1992). The policy debate has also often been interpreted as reflecting concerns over these forms of linkage. There seems to be a presumption that linkage between trade and environmental policies is weak, and that trade policies are ineffective instruments of environmental protection — a conjecture confirmed by model-based estimates (Perroni and Wigle, 1994). As Blackhurst and Subramanian (1992) have pointed out, there are also strategic reasons for linking trade and environmental policies in multilateral negotiations; global cooperation should be easier to sustain when pursued through linked negotiations.

However, this strategic linkage does not seem to have been addressed directly in the literature. Barrett (1994) and Ulph (1996a,b), among others, have studied the matter theoretically, but define the strategic element from the standpoint of the market structure in which firms operate. Copeland and Taylor (1995) examine environmental policy games between open economies; they mention the possibility of a linkage between North–South trade and environmental policies, but do not explore it in detail. The papers that are most closely related to the analysis, we present here, are Cesar and Zeeuw (1994), Ludema and Wooton (1994), Nordhaus and Yang (1996), and Spagnolo (1996). The first of these builds a general framework linking environmental cooperation with cooperation in some other, nonspecified area, and shows that cooperation in both areas is sustainable provided that the two games roughly offset each other. Spagnolo's paper models linked international negotiations within a repeated-game framework. In both these papers, however, the policy games examined are fully independent, which is not the case for trade and environmental policies. Ludema and Wooton use a partial-equilibrium model to examine a noncooperative policy game between two countries in the presence of a cross-border externality, but do not explore the possibility of environmental policy cooperation; although they point out that a linkage between trade and the environment could be implicitly present in some free trade agreements involving countries of different size. Nordhaus and Yang use a multi-region dynamic general-equilibrium model to compute noncooperative Nash equilibria in environmental policies as well as cooperative equilibria where countries adopt globally efficient policies to reduce emissions. In their model, however, bargaining solutions are not examined and no interaction between trade and the environment is considered.

Here, we explore this negotiation linkage using a two-region (North–South) numerical simulation model of world trade and the environment, benchmarked to 1990 data and projected over a 100 year time horizon. We compute noncooperative Nash equilibria (disagreement outcomes for bargaining), and bargaining outcomes (Nash bargaining) for trade negotiations only and joint negotiations over trade and the environment. The trade side of the model is a conventional heterogeneous-products (Armington) model, in which trade elasticities play a key role. The environmental structure of the model involves environmental assets in the South which are depleted more rapidly when used in trade-related production activities, and whose existence value enters North's preferences considerably more strongly than is the case for Southern preferences. The calibration of the model involves some strong assumptions and adjustments of data for model admissibility, but generates a specification with sharply asymmetric North–South preference weightings on environmental asset depletion.

The central case results we generate show that, relative to free trade, the South (as the smaller region) loses in a trade war. A trade-only negotiation helps both the North and South in lowering trade barriers, but leaves large barriers in the North. A joint trade and environment negotiation allows the North to generate welfare gains from Southern environmental management and the South to lower Northern trade barriers. The main theme is that LDCs should embrace a trade and environment negotiation as it provides them with more leverage over trade. However, in a negotiation with side-payments the South does considerably better than in a constrained negotiation, suggesting that a trade-environmental policy negotiation may be an inferior option; that is, a negotiation of cash compensation is better for them.

In our concluding section, we also note that bargaining is constrained by trade rules — in which existing rules (such as MFN) are taken to imply restrictions on the bargaining set — may yield a different picture. If we consider a trade and environment linkage as a proposal under which MFN trade rules would also be relaxed where environmental effects are an issue, and if an initial weakening of MFN could lead to further system-wide weakening in other areas, then LDCs' concerns over a trade and environment negotiation may be more firmly based. In such cases, gains from expanded bargaining could be more than offset by losses from the weakening of prior agreed restraints on trade policy.

2. A Two-Region North–South Trade and Environment Model

We consider a world consisting of two regions, which we refer to as "North" (N) and "South" (S). Focusing on a two-region structure avoids the numerical complexities associated with computation of noncooperative equilibria in higher dimensions, and allows us to focus on two-player cooperative solution concepts. Computational limitations in working with noncooperative and cooperative game-theoretic solution concepts, rather than more traditional competitive equilibria, thus severely restrict dimensionality in the numerical analysis.

We consider an environmental asset, E, which is entirely owned by the South, and can be viewed as a stock reflecting available tropical habitat. Each region produces two goods, a tradable good X and a nontradable good Y. Region S uses two factors in production, value-added V, and the natural resource asset. Production in region N only uses value-added. Each region views tradables produced domestically and abroad as imperfect substitutes and consumes both domestic and imported traded goods, along with own-region nontradables. The environment is depleted by its use in production and enters the utility function of each region. Depletion occurs more heavily from use in production of the traded good. The endowment of value-added is constant in each region, and equal to $G^i (i = N, S)$.

2.1. *Production*

The structure of production in the model is set out in Fig. 1. CES functions are used, in which value-added and the environmental asset can be transformed into an environment-using input at the lower level of nesting. At the higher level of nesting, the environment-using input and value-added are transformed into tradable and nontradable output. We use substitution elasticities of zero at the lower level and of unity at the higher level. Value-added used in the two levels of nest can be transformed at a constant marginal rate of transformation, which we assume to be equal to unity. The rationale for using this construction is that it implies a nonzero cost for the environment-using input even when pollution taxes are zero; this, in turn, prevents infinite substitution away from other inputs. The main difference between the tradable and nontradable goods sectors lies in the share parameters on the environment-using input.

2.2. *Prices and environmental taxes*

Net-of-tax prices for value-added and the environment-using input are denoted as $p^i (i = N, S)$ and are the same within each region. Each unit of environment-using input employed in production in region S reduces

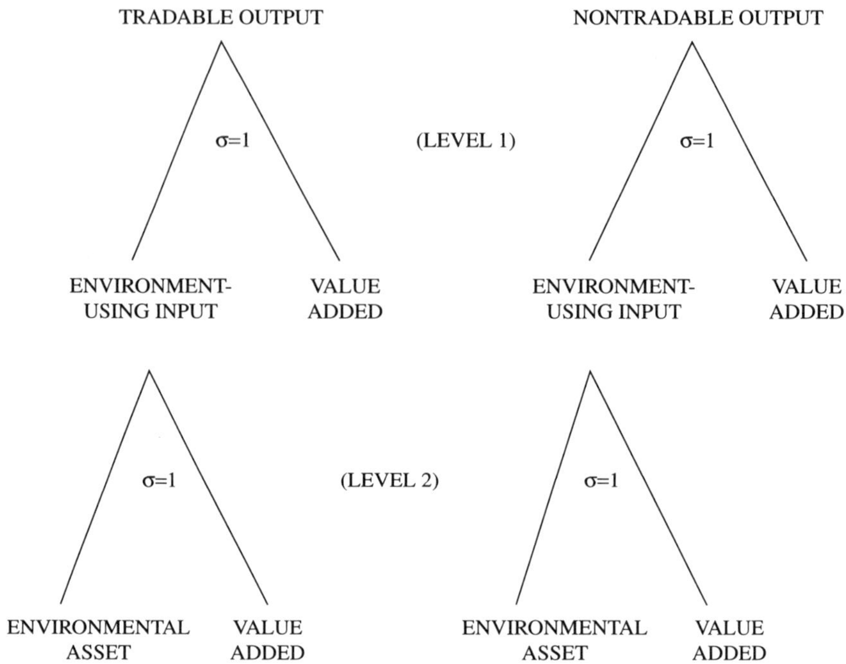

Fig. 1. CES production structure in the model (South region).

global environmental quality by an amount ε. We consider taxes on the use of the environmental asset at rate τ^S, and hence the gross-of-tax price of the environment-using input in the South is

$$p_E^S = p^S + \varepsilon\tau^S. \tag{1}$$

Value-added and the environment-using input are both used in the production of tradables and nontradables through unitary substitution elasticity, constant-returns-to-scale technologies. Thus, domestic prices of domestically produced goods are equal to unit costs.

$$p_j^N = c_j^N(p^N); \quad p_j^S = c_j^S(p^S, p_E^S); \quad j = X, Y. \tag{2}$$

For given output levels $L_j^i (i = N, S, j = X, Y)$, we can write aggregate domestic demands for the environment-using input (using Shephard's Lemma) as

$$D_E^S = \sum_j L_j^S \frac{\partial c_j^S}{\partial p_E^S}, \quad j = X, Y. \tag{3}$$

2.3. *Environmental quality*

Environmental quality enters the preferences of both the North and the South, but with a substantially higher share parameter in the North, reflecting the differential existence value placed on environmental assets by region. The quantity of environmental assets entering preferences as existence value equals the initial stock of assets less that amount used up in production (through deforestation, for instance). The period used for the model is a number of years or decades, during which significant depletion can occur depending upon the policy regime. For given demands for the environment-using input, environmental quality is then given as

$$Q = \bar{Q} - \varepsilon(D_E^S), \tag{4}$$

where $\bar{Q}$ denotes the initial endowment of the environmental asset (before use in production).

2.4. *Trade and demand*

Each region levies *ad valorem* import tariffs at rates t^i, where superscripts refer to the importing region. The gross-of-tariff price of imported tradables is thus

$$q^N = (1 + t^N)p_X^S; \quad q^S = (1 + t^S)p_X^N. \tag{5}$$

Given preferences, a level of environmental quality Q, commodity prices p_j^i, q^i, and incomes I^i, utility maximization yields uncompensated demands for domestic goods, D_j^i, and uncompensated import demands, M^i. The marginal valuation for environmental quality in each country, v^i, is also a function of the same variables.

Expanded income in each region is written as the value of resource endowments, plus tariff revenue, plus revenues from environmental levies, plus the (shadow) value of environmental quality (note that the latter is a function of income itself, which makes the definition of I^i implicit)[a]

$$I^N = p^N G^N + t^N p_X^S M^N + v^N Q; \tag{6}$$

$$I^S = p^S G^S + t^S p_X^N M^S + \tau^S \varepsilon D_E^S + v^S Q. \tag{7}$$

[a]This is added to income since environmental quality is purchased at its shadow price, but this price is not actually paid between countries; i.e., the North makes no actual payment to the South for the existence value of environmental quality they enjoy.

2.5. *Market equilibrium*

Market clearing for competitive equilibrium in which use of the environmental asset is charged only through environmental levies requires the following.

$$L_X^N = D_X^N + M^S; \quad L_X^S = D_X^S + M^N; \tag{8}$$

$$L_Y^i = D_Y^i; \quad i = N, S; \tag{9}$$

$$D_E^i + \sum_j L_j^i \frac{\partial c_j^i}{\partial p^i} = G^i; \quad i = N, S, \quad j = X, Y, \tag{10}$$

where $D_E^N = 0$.

2.6. *Choice of functional form*

In the numerical implementation of the model, unit cost functions for tradables and nontradables production are a constant-elasticity-of-substitution (CES) aggregation of the environment-using input and value-added prices in the South region

$$c_j^S(p^S, p_E^S) \equiv \left[(1-\alpha_j^S)(p^S)^{1-\beta^S} + \alpha_j^S(p_E^S)^{1-\beta^S}\right]^{\frac{1}{1-\beta^S}}; \quad j = X, Y, \tag{11}$$

where the β are the elasticities of substitution between the environment-using input and value-added, and the α are share parameters. Note that, since the environment-using input is not utilized by the North, the corresponding cost function is simply

$$c_j^N = p^N, \quad j = X, Y.$$

Preferences for domestic goods and imports in each region are represented by a two-level nested Cobb–Douglas/CES aggregation of the form

$$\begin{aligned} &H^i(D_Y^i, D_X^i, M_A^i, M_B^i) \\ &\equiv (D_Y^i)^{\theta^i}\left[\delta^i(D_X^i)\frac{\sigma^i-1}{\sigma^i} + (1-\delta^i)(M^i)^{\frac{\sigma^i-1}{\sigma^i}}\right]^{\frac{(1-\theta^i)\sigma^i}{\sigma^i-1}}; \quad i = N, S, \end{aligned} \tag{12}$$

where θ^i is a share parameter for nontradables demand; δ^i refers to the share of domestic goods in total tradables demand; and σ^i is the elasticity of substitution between same-region tradables and tradables produced in the other region.

Preferences for consumption and environmental quality are represented by a Cobb–Douglas utility function[b]

$$U^i(Q, H^i) \equiv Q^{\eta^i}(H^i)^{1-\eta^i}; \quad i = N, S, \tag{13}$$

where η^i is the Cobb–Douglas share parameter on environmental quality.

2.7. *Policy games in the model*

The model incorporates trade policy parameters in the form of tariffs and environmental policy parameters in the form of environmental charges. A traditional tariff game can be analyzed (as in Johnson, 1953–1954) in which regions play strategically against one another in tariffs. With the North being large and the South small, the presumption is that the North will gain from such a retaliatory game while the South will gain little or more likely lose. There is also an environmental game that can be analyzed in terms of environmental charges associated with the use of the environmental asset. Since the South owns the environmental asset and the North places a high existence value on it, the South can use a policy instrument jointly with trade policy in a linked trade and environment game which can result in lower Northern trade protection.[c]

In using the model, therefore, we go beyond conventional numerical simulation work which mainly focuses on Walrasian competitive equilibria, by computing noncooperative equilibria and bargaining outcomes. To do this, we iterate over calculations of optimal policy responses by individual regions, subject to a full set of general equilibrium constraints (as set out above) until convergence to a Nash equilibrium is achieved. We are able to do this separately for the tariff game and for the linked trade and environment game. We also compute cooperative bargaining solutions associated with these games, adopting Nash's (1950) bargaining solution. This is the most widely used cooperative solution concept in the literature,

[b]For this specification, the marginal valuation for environmental quality is proportional to (nonexpanded) income.

[c]Throughout our analysis we maintain the assumption that countries in each bloc are able to coordinate policies among themselves in an interbloc noncooperative equilibrium. Even though the necessary environmental institutional arrangements are not currently in place for such interbloc coordination to take place, they could well emerge in the future as has been the case in the trade arena. In UNCTAD, for instance, the G77 emerged as the common developing country demand for special and differential treatment in GATT gained momentum in the 1970's.

although others, such as Kalai–Smorodinsky (1975), could alternatively be used. In computing bargaining solutions, we take the noncooperative Nash equilibrium solution utilities as representing the disagreement point, simulate the utilities possibilities frontier under cooperation and apply the Nash criterion to the product of the differences in region utilities along the frontier and disagreement utilities.

In our central case, with trade or trade and environment games, no side-payments are considered, and thus the resulting outcomes remain second-best allocations. Typically in such equilibria, there will be less than full internalization of the environmental externality. We also compute bargaining with side-payments. This realizes a full Pareto-optimal allocation, and allows us to assess how far towards Pareto optimality a joint trade and environment policy-based negotiation could move.[d] Note that side-payments should not be interpreted as implying lack of negotiation linkage: if there were no environmental agreement, zero tariffs would not be optimal even with side-payments. Thus, the side-payments we compute here represent net compensation for environmental restraint by the South in conjunction with trade policy cooperation.

3. Data and Model Parametrization

We have calibrated the model to a 1990 base case projected forward over a period of 100 years. The economies of the North and the South are both assumed to lie on a growth path on which value-added, production, and consumption grow at a constant rate, reflecting average growth rates over the period 1985–93. Data for this period imply rates of growth of 2.5% and 4% for the North and South, respectively. We assume a discount rate of 5%.

The production and consumption (and hence trade) data we use are based on information taken from World Bank (1992), World Bank (1995), and IMF (1995). Production activities are disaggregated in two

[d]Alternatively, one could view cooperation as reflecting a subgame-perfect equilibrium of an infinitely repeated game, supported by the threat of future punishment in response to unilateral deviations from a coordinated strategy (trigger strategies). In such a formulation, it would be possible to explore whether a linked trade-environmental policy game makes cooperation in both areas easier to sustain in comparison with a scenario where the trade and environment dimensions of strategic interaction are examined in isolation.

parts: traded and nontraded production.[e] This implies a very high degree of aggregation, but, as indicated earlier, limitations associated with the computation of noncooperative and cooperative equilibria severely restricts numerical analysis dimensionality. Furthermore, given the highly conjectural nature of some of the environment data we use, moving to a more detailed sectoral disaggregation would not significantly improve the reliability of numerical estimates obtained from the model.

In representing the regions, we include countries for the South which account for a significant portion of key global environmental assets, such as tropical forest and biological diversity. Table 1 identifies these countries

Table 1. Countries in the "S" Region in the Model and Their Tropical Forest Cover.

	Hectares 1990 (thousands)	Proportion of world tropical forests (%)
Angola	24,074	1.37
Bolivia	49,317	2.81
Brazil	561,107	31.95
Cameroon	20,350	1.16
Central African Republic	30,562	1.74
Colombia	54,064	3.08
Congo	19,865	1.13
Gabon	18,235	1.04
Guyana	18,416	1.05
India	51,729	2.95
Indonesia	109,549	6.24
Malaysia	17,583	1.00
Mexico	48,586	2.77
Mozambique	17,329	0.99
Myanmar	28,856	1.64
Papua New Guinea	36,000	2.05
Peru	67,906	3.87
Tanzania	33,555	1.91
Sudan	42,976	2.45
Venezuela	45,690	2.60
Zaïre	113,275	6.45
Zambia	32,301	1.84
Total "S" region	1,441,325	82.07
World	1,756,299	100.00

Source: World Resources Institute (1994).

[e] The nontraded-goods sector contains all distribution, transportation, construction, utilities, and government services. This corresponds roughly to 68% and 47% of GDP for the North and South, respectively.

and illustrates their importance in the ownership of the tropical rain forest asset. The countries included in the South region jointly control more than 80% of tropical forest and provide habitat for an unknown but presumed considerable proportion of species.[f] The North we take to be represented by OECD countries — who jointly reflect the environmental concern over depletion of environmental assets and would be the lead players in any eventual trade and environment negotiation in the WTO — and the rest of the world.

Table 2 reports the base-year 1990 data on production by region and the corresponding 1990–2090 discounted data. Table 3 gives share, elasticity, and other parameters. In calibrating the model, we select a value of 2 for Armington substitution elasticities, a choice which is consistent with most

Table 2. Production Data Used in the Model.

	North	South
1990 GDP (billion U.S. dollars)	20,942	1,387
Discounted 1990–2090 GDP (billion U.S. dollars)	800,551	92,954

Table 3. Model Parameters.

	North	South
Goods submodel		
Calibrated share parameters		
Imports in tradables demand	0.037	0.246
Nontradables in aggregate demand	0.681	0.473
Intraregional trade in total trade	0.941	0.046
Substitution elasticities		
Armington trade elasticities (σ)	2.0	2.0
Tradables-nontradables substitution in consumption	1.0	1.0
Environment-using input-value-added substitution	1.0	1.0
Environment submodel		
Overall environmental damage[a]	NA[b]	
Damage coefficients		
Tradables	NA	0.22
Nontradables	NA	0.06
Elasticity of marginal valuation with respect to income	1.25	1.25

[a]As a proportion of North's GDP.
[b]NA, not applicable.

[f]As is well known, tropical ecosystems have a higher and more diverse number of species in a given area than temperate ecosystems. It is estimated that between 40% and 90% of all species live in tropical region habitats (World Resources Institute, 1994).

model-based studies (e.g., Perroni and Wigle, 1994); we subsequently vary this value for sensitivity analysis.

Parameters for the environmental portion of the model are obtained as follows. The environment-using input coefficients by region have been computed from input–output data for selected OECD countries.[g] We make the strong assumption that LDCs use the environment-using input in the two sectors in the same ratio as they are used in OECD countries. We consider the following sectors as providing environment-using inputs: agriculture, forestry and fishing, mining and quarrying; petroleum and coal products; electricity, gas and water; and construction.

The initial (1990) endowment of the environmental assets in the South, relative to which depletion occurs, is set to be half of the North's GDP.[h] The value of base-case environmental damage, in terms of depletion of the endowment of the South's environmental asset, as valued by the North, is set to be equal to 10% of income in discounted value terms. This is admittedly highly conjectural, but could be rationalized as follows. The annual average depletion rate of tropical forests during the period 1981–1990 was 0.6% (World Resources Institute, 1994).

Assuming that this depletion rate remains constant throughout a 100-year period and assuming a quadratic damage function, the estimate of physical damage for our period of analysis would amount to approximately a 60% depletion of Southern environmental assets.

To impute a valuation for this damage, we can take Kramer and Mercer's (1997) estimate for the U.S. of willingness to pay (WTP) to avoid the destruction of a certain area of tropical rainforest. We assume that this WTP changes with income growth (assumed to be 2.5% a year) throughout our period and use an income elasticity of 1.25 (consistent with estimates obtained by Kramer and Mercer) to obtain an estimate for the stream of environmental damage for the 100-year period. Using a 5% discount rate, the present value of this stream is just above 10% of the North's GDP. These calculations are sensitive to parameter assumptions and in particular to the assumed damage function; at the same time, there exist other important

[g] The countries are Germany, U.K., and U.S. The input-output data are taken from OECD (1995).

[h] Although this assumption is largely arbitrary, it has only second-order implications for the behavior of the model; specifically, it affects only the *elasticity* of the marginal valuation of environmental quality, not its level (i.e., the model's behavior for marginal policy changes is unaffected). Nevertheless, we perform sensitivity analysis on this parameter.

aspects of environmental damage (such as loss of biodiversity) which are omitted from the calculation.

By choice of units we are able to set the marginal existence value of the North (v^N) equal to unity. The South's existence value of the environmental asset is calculated on the basis of the difference of per capita income between the two regions and using again an elasticity of marginal valuation with respect to income of 1.25 (again, consistently with Kramer and Mercer's findings). This gives an estimate of approximately 0.04 (relative to the North) for v^S.

We stress the fact that the calibration of the environmental side of the model relies on very strong assumptions on some key parameters. This is especially the case with the initial value for the environmental asset and the shape of the damage function, which crucially affects the elasticity of marginal valuation with respect to damage and the share of the environmental asset in preferences. Although we carry out sensitivity analyses on some key parameters — including the size of both the environmental asset and damage — we emphasize that our data constraints necessarily give our calculations a highly conjectural and illustrative nature, at least from a quantitative standpoint.

4. Simulations and Results

Our parametrized model has been used to analyze the implications for LDCs of a linked trade and environment negotiation. We employ this structure to first compute noncooperative Nash equilibria of a tariff game (the disagreement point). Because of their relatively small size, LDCs are at disadvantage relative to the North in this noncooperative equilibrium. A bargained trade outcome improves the developing country situation a little relative to the disagreement point, but significant trade barriers remain against LDCs. In contrast, a linked trade and environment bargained outcome, where bargaining involves both trade and environmental policies, helps LDCs since they can use their leverage in environmental policy (given the relatively high existence value in the North) to help reduce Northern trade barriers against them. These features emerge strongly from our central-case set of model results summarized in Table 4.[i] Here we have

[i]In our tables, we adopt the zero tariffs and taxes scenario as a benchmark, with which all other simulation results are compared. The idea is that such a scenario reflects the state of affairs at the beginning of the 1990s, when significant trade cooperation had

Table 4. Central-Case Model Results.

	Noncooperative equilibrium	Bargaining over trade	Bargaining over trade and environment
Tariff rates (%)			
North	500.00	253.63	0.0
South	101.03	0.0	47.68
Environmental internalization rate (%)[a]			
North	0.0	0.0	0.0
South	0.41	0.41	54.10
Hicksian equivalent variation (% of GDP)			
A. With respect to disagreement point			
North	0.0	0.57	6.53
South	0.0	2.54	6.87
B. With respect to zero taxes and tariffs			
North	0.27	0.84	6.79
South	−8.89	−6.35	−2.02

[a]Ratio of emission tax to marginal emission damage.

taken the central-case model specification summarized above and computed noncooperative Nash equilibria in tariffs, bargained outcomes in trade (tariffs), and joint bargained outcomes covering both trade and environment policies. Trade elasticities are critical parameters in determining outcomes, and in this specification we have used a value of 2 for both North and South. As is well known, as these values approach unity, in a symmetric case both regions' optimal tariffs would become large, and values significantly in excess of unity need to be used to avoid numerical problems. Because the asymmetries in size in our model can lead to large tariffs and associated numerical problems, we use an upper bound of 500% for tariffs in both regions in computing model solutions.[j] However, this is not of great importance since, well before tariffs reach such a high level, trade between the two regions has virtually ceased.

In the central-case noncooperative equilibrium (first column of Table 4), the South's internalization rate is close to zero, consistent with most of the utility loss from lowered environmental quality being borne by the

been achieved but tensions over global environmental problems were relatively new. One could argue that a scenario featuring optimal taxes from the South's point of view would provide a more natural benchmark; however, since noncooperative taxes are close to zero on our simulations, the difference between the two scenarios is negligible.

[j]We also rule out negative tariffs which, given our model structure, would never be used as an optimal response.

North. The North's trade barriers reach the upper bound of 500%, while the South's noncooperative tariff rate is around 100%. This difference in noncooperative tariff levels reflects both differences in country size and the fact that, under zero environmental internalization in the South, the North employs tariffs as a second-best environmental policy instrument.[k]

The South's loss from a trade war is close to 9% of GDP, whereas the North gains a little relative to a free-trade zero-internalization scenario.

Bargaining over trade policies in the absence of side-payments (column two of Table 4) leads to an elimination of tariffs in the South and lowers tariffs in the North to around 250%. This generates substantial gains in the South (2.54% of GDP), which are significantly smaller than the almost 9.0% loss experienced by the South under tariff retaliation.[l]

In contrast, combining trade and environmental policies in a joint negotiation makes it possible to sustain a level of internalization in excess of 50% and leads to the total elimination of tariffs in the North. Some trade barriers remain in the South, as a "concession" by the North in exchange for the higher internalization rate. In this outcome the South's gains in relation to a noncooperative outcome are considerable — almost 7% of GDP — and a linked trade and environment negotiation is an attractive proposition to them.

As pointed out earlier, we can alternatively think of cooperation as reflecting tacit collusion in an infinitely repeated game,[m] where players maintain a cooperative stance if the gains from unilateral defection are less than the discounted gains from cooperation. By computing payoffs for the various players under cooperation, noncooperation, and for unilateral deviations from cooperation, we could characterize the maximum discount rate for which the threat of future punishment is effective as an inducement to cooperate. To explore how linkage of trade and environment dimensions affects the viability of cooperation, we could compare the maximum discount values obtained for scenarios where dimensions of strategic interaction are considered in isolation and where they are examined jointly.

[k]This also contributes to the high level of tariffs, although the finding of high noncooperative tariffs is, more fundamentally, a feature of Armington models featuring constant substitution elasticities.

[l]Although we allow the noncooperative level of internalization to adjust endogenously, it remains effectively unchanged (to the second decimal digit).

[m]For an application of this approach to trade cooperation, see, for example, Bagwell and Staiger (1993).

Table 5. Trade and Environment Bargaining With and Without Side-Payments.

	Hicksian equivalent variations relative to Zero taxes and tariffs (% of GDP)	
	Central case	Bargaining with side-payments[a]
North	6.79	6.89
South	−2.02	5.11

[a]With side payments, tariff rates are equal to zero, and the environmental internalization rate is equal to 100%.

Given the regional asymmetries in trade and environmental costs and benefits, without side-payments it would never be possible to sustain any form of cooperation in this model that is consistent with Pareto optimality, either in environmental policies or in trade policies, independently of whether they are combined.

With explicit bargaining and lump-sum side-payments (Table 5), on the other hand, it is possible to achieve a first-best outcome with zero tariffs and 100% internalization. Introducing side-payments overwhelmingly benefits the South, whose gains more than double as a result. Compared with a situation with no intervention, with cash transfers the South ends up with welfare gains which are high and not much different from those of the North, even though Southern preferences for environmental quality are much weaker than Northern ones. Thus, compared to a negotiation involving cash compensation for environmental restraint, the South gains far less from a linked trade and environment negotiation. A linked trade and environment negotiation with no side-payments may be preferred to a trade-only negotiation, but may still be the wrong negotiation so far as the South is concerned. In reality, side-payments are not often used; and without side-payments it could be difficult to achieve free trade even abstracting from environmental concerns. Thus, one might interpret our results as showing that linkage can induce freer trade by providing an imperfect substitute for income transfers.

We have performed sensitivity analysis of our central-case results to the Armington elasticities, the size of damage, the North's existence value, and the size of the environmental asset. This shows that varying key parameters have mainly quantitative effects, leaving most of our results qualitatively unaltered. Increasing trade elasticities weakens opportunities for negotiation linkage, resulting in a lower level of internalization through linkage. It can also make the linked negotiation outcome for the South inferior to the trade policy-only bargained outcome — a finding not inconsistent with the comparative statics properties of Nash bargaining solutions: a change which makes the utilities possibilities frontier more "skewed" in favor of one region, can benefit both parties, but it can conceivably also result in a lower level of utility for the other party. Intuitively, if there is more to be gained by one party from moving policies in the direction it favors, the affected party will become a "more concerned" negotiator.

A reduction in trade elasticities strengthens the potential for linked negotiations and makes it possible to achieve a level of internalization close to 100% even in the absence of side payments. On the other hand, decreasing (increasing) the level of damage reduces (increases) the noncooperative level of tariffs in the North since the presence of environmental externalities in tradables production in the South generates an additional incentive for the North to curtail trade beyond the standard terms-of-trade large-country motive. Negotiation linkage, however, becomes weaker (stronger). Lowering the Northern existence value has effects qualitatively similar to those of reducing the assumed level of damage. Finally, reducing the size of the environmental asset lowers noncooperative tariffs, raises internalization levels, and makes the negotiation linkage weaker.

5. Concluding Remarks

This chapter has addressed the issue of whether LDCs should participate in linked trade and environment negotiations in the WTO over the next few decades. We have developed a small-dimensional global simulation model capturing both North–South trade, and Southern use of environmental assets in trade-related production when there is a high Northern existence value on such assets. We calibrated our model to data over a projected 100-year period from 1990 to 2090, in which Southern countries are identified as those accounting for 80% of tropical assets (forest, species). We computed various model solutions for alternative scenarios, principally noncooperative Nash equilibria for tariff games which serve as threat points for cooperative bargaining (Nash) solutions, and similar solutions for linked trade (tariffs) and environmental (taxes) policy games.

In our central-case analysis, linking trade and environmental policies in a joint negotiation expands the bargaining set and offers Southern LDCs an opportunity to exert discipline over Northern trade measures by making environmental concessions. The South thus benefits from a linked negotiation compared with a stand-alone trade negotiation. However, in a negotiation with side-payments, the South gains considerably more, suggesting that LDCs should negotiate over cash for environmental restraint rather than indirectly on trade and environmental policy instruments. Sensitivity analysis suggests that as trade elasticities increase, and optimal stand-alone tariffs fall, the benefits of linkage fall to the point that Southern countries benefit from being shielded from a trade and environment negotiation. Indeed, we report cases where linked negotiations can be detrimental to the South, but this is crucially dependent on the (axiomatic) bargaining solution concept adopted and is not true in our central case.

While model results are suggestive, our model parametrization is heroic, and there are missing features, reflecting developing country concerns over trade and environment linkage, which are not captured here. Trade and environment linkage could become the precedent for further wider linkage in trade negotiations, should developing countries agree to participate (trade and employment standards, for instance). Agreeing to the use of trade measures on environmental grounds would weaken the MFN principle in GATT/WTO, so central to developing-country interests. There is also ambiguity as to whether a cohesive Southern coalition can really be formed to participate in such a negotiation. Furthermore, cooperation in the GATT/WTO may not reflect a bargained agreement (which in the absence of a supranational authority would effectively not be enforceable) but rather a noncooperative equilibrium supported by implicit triggered retaliation threats, which the agreement only serves to ratify *ex post.* Under this interpretation, introducing an environmental dimension alongside trade negotiations may inject instability into the system, especially if policies are not observable (Riezman, 1991), and make retaliatory episodes more likely.

References

Anderson, K (1992a). The standard welfare economics of policies affecting trade and the environment. In *The Greening of World Trade Issues.* K Anderson and R Blackhurst (eds.). London: Harvester-Wheatsheaf.

Anderson, K (1992b). Effects on the environment and welfare of liberalizing world trade: The cases of coal and food. In *The Greening of World Trade Issues.* K Anderson and R Blackhurst (eds.). London: Harvester-Wheatsheaf.

Bagwell, K and RW Staiger (1993). Multilateral tariff cooperation during the formation of regional free trade areas. NBER Working Paper 4364.

Barrett, S (1994). Strategic environmental policy and international trade. *Journal of Public Economics*, **54**, 325–338.

Blackhurst, R and A Subramanian (1992). Promoting multilateral cooperation on the environment. In *The Greening of World Trade Issues*. K Anderson and R Blackhurst (eds.). London: Harvester-Wheatsheaf.

Cesar, H and AD Zeeuw (1994). Issue linkage in global environmental problems. *Nota di Lavoro*, **56.94**, Fondazione ENI Enrico Mattei.

Copeland, B and MS Taylor (1995). Trade and transboundary pollution. *American Economic Review*, **85**, 716–737.

Dean, J (1992). Trade and environment: A survey of the literature. In *International Trade and the Environment*. P. Low (ed.). Washington, D.C.: World Bank.

International Monetary Fund (1995). *Direction of Trade Statistics Yearbook* 1995. Washington: IMF.

Johnson, HG (1953–1954). Optimum tariffs and retaliation. *Review of Economic Studies*, **21**, 142–153.

Kalai, E and M Smorodinsky (1975). Other solutions to bargaining situations: Interpersonal utility comparison. *Econometrica*, **43**, 513–518.

Ludema, R and I Wooton (1994). Cross-border externalities and trade liberalization: The strategic control of pollution. *Canadian Journal of Economics*, **27**, 950–966.

Nash, J (1950). The bargaining problem. *Econometrica*, **18**, 298–346.

Nordhaus, W and Z Yang (1996). A regional dynamic general-equilibrium model of alternative climate-change strategies. *American Economic Review*, **86**, 741–765.

OECD (1995). *The OECD Input–Output Database*. Paris: OECD.

Pearce, D (1992). Should the GATT be reformed for environmental reasons? CSERGE Working Paper GEC 92-06.

Perroni, C and RM Wigle (1994). International trade and environmental quality: How important are the linkages. *Canadian Journal of Economics*, **27**, 551–567.

Rauscher, M (1992). International economic integration and the environment: The case of Europe. In *The Greening of World Trade Issues*. K Anderson and R Blackhurst (eds.). London: Harvester-Wheatsheaf.

Riezman, RG (1991). Dynamic tariffs with asymmetric information. *Journal of International Economics*, **30**, 267–283.

Spagnolo, G (1996). Issue linkage, delegration and international policy cooperation. *Nota di Lavoro* **49-96**, Fondazione ENI Enrico Mattei.

Ulph, A (1996a). Strategic environmental policy and international trade. In *Environmental Policy, International Agreements and International Trade*. C. Carraro, M. Hoel, A. Ulph and A. Ingham (eds.). Cheltenham: Elgar (1996a).

Ulph, A (1996b). Environmental policy and international trade when governments and producers act strategically. *Journal of Environmental Economics and Management*, **30**, 265–281.

World Bank (1992). *World Development Report 1992: Development and the Environment.* New York: Oxford University Press.

World Bank (1994). *World Tables 1995.* Baltimore: Johns Hopkins University Press.

World Resources Institute (1994). *World Resources* 1994–1995. New York: Oxford University Press.

Chapter 9

Global Effects of Developed Country Trade Restrictions on Textiles and Apparel*,†

Irene Trela and John Whalley
University of Western Ontario and
National Bureau of Economic Research

This chapter reports general equilibrium estimates of national and global welfare costs of both developed country tariffs and bilateral quotas on textiles and apparel using an applied general equilibrium model. It covers quotas negotiated between three major developed importing countries (the U.S., Canada, and the EC) and 34 supplying developing countries under the provisions of the Multi-Fiber Arrangement (MFA) applying in mid-1980's (MFA III).

Our results,[a] based on 1986 data, suggest annual global gains from elimination of quotas and tariffs on developed country textile and apparel imports of around 23 billion dollar. Gains to the U.S., Canada, and the EC are respectively, 12.3 billion dollar, 0.8 billion dollar, and 2.2 billion dollar, the first which is considerably higher than existing partial equilibrium estimates for reasons which are discussed in the text. In aggregate, developing countries gain around 8 billion dollar.

These results also suggest that, despite foregone rent transfers, the vast majority of developing countries would gain from removal of restrictions on trade on their textiles and apparel exports, with some gaining proportionately more than others. This is because, contrary to popular belief, all developing country suppliers (including Hong Kong, South Korea, and Taiwan) are

*This is a revised and shortened version of NBER Working Paper No. 26I8, "Do Developing Countries Lose from the MFA?" This work has been presented to seminars at Western Ontario and Guelph, and to a NBER Symposium on Applied General Equilibrium Analysis, held at Stanford, March 5–6, 1988. We are grateful to participants in all these sessions for comments, as well as to Carl Hamilton and Kiichiro Fukasaku.

†This chapter was first published in (1990). *The Economic Journal*, **100**(403), 1190–1205.

[a]These are different than those reported in earlier versions, and in Trela and Whalley (1990), due to adjustments to the imports data used, revised quota premium data, and a new allocation of interdeveloped country trade across quota restricted and unrestricted products. The differences are most pronounced for the U.S. and Canada, due to the different treatment of interdeveloped country trade; results for individual developing countries are more similar.

relatively small compared to developed countries, even in apparel production. Thus, rather than losing share to other developing countries in previously trade restricted textile and apparel items under an MFA elimination, higher income developing countries (like other developing countries) gain market share due to increased developed country consumption, reduced developed country production, and reduced inter-developed country trade. Sensitivity analyses suggest that a number of model features are important for results, but the main themes of results appear to be preserved under the sensitivity analyses we have performed.

1. A General Equilibrium Model for Analyzing the Effects of Restrictions on Global Trade in Textiles and Apparel

Imports of textiles and apparel have been restricted by the major developed countries, including the U.S., Canada, and the EC, since 1974 by a series of international agreements among exporting and importing countries, commonly known as the MFAs (of which there have now been four). The result is a series of discriminatory bilateral quotas that now restrict exports by most lower cost developing countries to the major developed countries.[b]

Under these agreements, licenses to export are issued to exporting countries, who then allocate them to firms within their country. These quotas restrict trade by limiting imports, and further distort the pattern of trade because of their bilateral nature. Since the quotas are specified in physical terms, they also have the effect of encouraging upgrading of quality by exporters. Thus, protected producers in importing countries tend to produce lower quality items than they otherwise would, since the relative price of these increases in the protected domestic market.

We use an applied general equilibrium model to analyze the trade effects of these arrangements, along with the effects of developed country tariffs. The model covers three major developed country importers, the U.S., Canada, and the EC, 34 developing country exporters,[c] 14 specific

[b]Most developed countries continue to impose tariffs on textile imports. Over the years GATT negotiations have slightly reduced these tariffs, but not to the same degree as for other manufactured products.

[c]These are: Bangladesh, Brazil, Bulgaria, China, Columbia, Czechoslovakia, Costa Rica, Dominican Republic, Egypt, Guatemala, Haiti, Hong Kong, Hungary, India, Indonesia, Republic of Korea, Macau, Malaysia, Mauritius, Mexico, Nepal, Pakistan, Panama, Peru, Philippines, Poland, Romania, Singapore, Sri Lanka, Taiwan, Thailand, Turkey, Uruguay, and Yugoslavia.

textile and apparel product categories,[d] and one composite other good.[e] The 14 product categories reflect the constraints implied by generating a cross country data set covering trade under the different MFA quota categories used by the major importing countries (the U.S., Canada, and the EC).[f]

In the model, production in each country involves nested constant elasticity of transformation (CET) production possibilities frontiers involving the 14 textile and apparel products and composite other good (residual GDP). Consumer demands in each region reflect utility maximizing behavior, with a single demand side agent assumed in each country; nested constant elasticity of substitution (CES) functions are used. Details of these functions and how they are used in the model are given in a technical model appendix available on request to interested readers.

All developed countries are treated as net importers of textiles and apparel (and exporters of the other good), while all developing countries are modeled as exporters of textiles and apparel (and importers of the other good). Trade in textiles and apparel among developing countries does not take place in the model; otherwise differences in supply prices between these countries would be arbitraged away. Interdeveloped country trade is quota (although not tariff) free. Thus, the model captures trade diversion effects between developed countries due to their joint bilateral quotas on exports by developing countries and domestic prices in the

[d]The 14 textile and apparel products in the model involve seven restricted and seven comparable unrestricted products. This approach is employed because despite the MFA, significant volumes of trade in textiles and apparel take place in unrestricted quota categories. If products in unrestricted categories are treated as perfect substitutes for quota restricted products, then in a competitive model countries would substitute costlessly into products not subject to quota. In practice, there are differences below the level of aggregation in what is restricted and what is unrestricted and, in addition, a number of bilateral agreements include provisions for consultations that can result in unrestricted products being brought under restraint. An assumption of qualitative differences between comparable restricted and unrestricted categories is the way we treat this difficulty in the model.

[e]We define the composite other good to be residual GDP in the basic variant of our model; "other manufactures" are used in our sensitivity analysis reported on later.

[f]We are unable to include all the MFA quota categories in each country since they include products which belong to more than one of the 14 specific product categories we identify in our model. The categories not included are: handkerchiefs (categories 330 and 630), gloves (331, 431, and 631) and other apparel (359, 459, 659) in the U.S.; work gloves (31) and swimwear (44) in Canada; and handkerchiefs (19), knitted gloves (10), swimwear (72), shawls and scarves (84), woven ties (85), and other clothing accessories (88) in the EC.

various developed countries, therefore, depend on the quota policies of all developed countries.

Importantly, the model treats traded goods as homogeneous between countries, rather than heterogeneous (the "Armington" assumption) as is commonly done in other applied general equilibrium trade models (see the discussion of the "Armington" assumption in Shoven and Whalley, 1984). This is because it greatly reduces both the dimensionality of the equilibrium problem to be solved relative to an Armington type treatment and the difficulties in separating out data by country so as to incorporate product quality differences across countries. Also, the need to deal with cross hauling (countries both importing and exporting the same product), which is part motivates the use of the "Armington" assumption, does not arise here in the same way as in other models since little two-way trade between developed and developing countries occurs in textiles and clothing. In addition, the "Armington" assumption is well known (Brown, 1987) for the strong and often artificial terms of trade effects it induces in results.

The model is calibrated to a 1986 multi-country microconsistent data set involving production, consumption, and trade in 14 major textile and apparel product categories and one other good (residual GDP) for each of the 37 countries captured. This provides the benchmark equilibrium around which counterfactual equilibrium analysis is done for various possible policy changes in the model. In equilibrium, markets clear and external sector balance condition by country holds. Quota restrictions have the effect of segmenting national from global markets, so that in the presence of quota restrictions separate market clearing prices for each quota restricted product in each country are determined in the model. In counterfactual equilibria where restrictions are removed, producer prices in developing countries increase, stimulating both production and exports, while consumption increases and production falls in developed countries. Comparing counterfactual and benchmark equilibria provides the basis for policy evaluation with the model.

Constructing the benchmark set requires information on supply prices by product by country and estimates of key elasticity parameters. The data available for estimating supply prices are not free of problems. For example, while there are some (albeit limited) quota price data for Hong Kong, there is little direct information on supply prices for other supplying countries, and an indirect method related to that recently used by Hamilton (1988) has to be employed. Also, because of incompatibilities among the various quota categories used in the major developed country MFA participants (the U.S.,

Canada, and the EC), capturing effects of quotas on interdeveloped country trade in textiles and apparel is difficult. Below, we discuss in more detail how some of these difficulties are accommodated in the data we use.

2. Data, Model Parametrization, and Elasticity Parameter Values

To determine parameter values for the demand and production functions in this model, we use calibration procedures similar to those used in other applied general equilibrium models (see Mansur and Whalley (1984)). We use a multicountry microconsistent equilibrium data set we have constructed for 1986, which we augment by values of elasticities of transformation and substitution.

Several data sources are used in assembling the microconsistent data set for 1986 on which model calibration is based. Data on the value of imports, by MFA product category and country of origin, are from the U.S. Department of Commerce (1987a,b,c), Canadian Department of External Affairs (unpublished data, 1987), and the European Commission (1987).[g] The major problem with these data is that it is difficult to make comparisons across countries because of the different textile and apparel categories used in administering quotas in each country or region. Since no such cross country data set currently exists, we have constructed as close as comparable 14-good cross country data set as possible to produce

[g]In using these data, we assume that all bilateral quotas were fully binding in the year in question. Whether textile quotas are or are not binding has been a source of controversy for some time. For some exporting countries not all the allocated (category-specific) quotas are fully utilized in any given year (see GATT (1984) and USITC (1987)). Thus it appears, at first sight, that the cost to the U.S. of imposing these restraints may be overestimated by the model. However, there are many reasons why data for export countries can seem to indicate nonbinding quotas and yet in fact be binding. Quotas assigned to firms within an exporting country may not be fully utilized due to capacity constraints within firms and the unwillingness of firms to reassign or reallocate quota (or sell if there are legal markets) for fear of losing their quota allocation in future years. Other reasons can lie in the way quota is allocated among importers. Textile quotas in the EC, for instance, are often allocated between importing countries on the basis of historical market shares with no trading of quota across countries, so that quotas for, say, coats can be binding in Northern Europe but not in Southern Europe. Also sub-aggregate quotas, say for types of shirts, may be greater than an aggregate quota for shirts and hence not appear to be binding at subaggregate level while be binding at aggregate level.

trade data under the different aggregated MFA quota categories used in the model.[h]

Data on the value of production in the U.S. for textiles and apparel in separate aggregate categories are taken from the U.S. Department of Commerce (1987d), while data in Canada, the EC and the developing countries are from the United Nations (1986).[i] These data are disaggregated in order to provide estimates of production for the 14 product categories in the model using the ratios of trade in the individual categories to total trade in the corresponding broad category (textiles or apparel) by country. For each model product in each country, the value of consumption is determined as the residual between value of production and imports, on the one hand, and value of exports on the other.

As noted in the introduction, data on unit costs of production of individual textile and apparel products (supply prices) in the various developing countries are not currently available. While the unit costs of quota unrestricted products can be approximated by the U.S. price minus the tariff, the problem with data arises when we try to estimate supply prices of quota restricted products. These are central to any calculation of the impacts of developed country textile quotas, since they affect estimates of rent transfer per unit export.

Although quotas are freely traded in several exporting countries, comprehensive quota price data are only readily available for Hong Kong, and only limited quota price data are available for Taiwan. Hence, quota price data in a range of countries cannot be used. Also quotas are not necessarily allocated to the most efficient producers within countries, and so even if actual costs of current producers were known, the minimum potential unit cost for each textile and apparel product in the various

[h]In order to capture trade diversion effects between developed countries due to their joint bilateral quotas on exports by developing countries, we have had to allocate interdeveloped country trade between quota restricted and unrestricted products. Otherwise, based on the level of aggregation used in our model, all interdeveloped country trade would be in unrestricted products, and trade diversion effects would not be properly captured by the model. We assume that for each developed country the distribution between quota restricted and unrestricted products in interdeveloped country trade is the same as the distribution of the developed country's trade with the developing countries in these products.

[i]We were unable to obtain production data for some of the developing countries. In these cases trade data, along with estimates of mill consumption to export ratios obtained from FAO (1985) were used to calculate the value of production of each of the 14 product categories in each country.

countries remains unknown. We, therefore, use an indirect method of estimating supply prices of quota restricted items in developing countries closely related to that used by Hamilton (1988).

We take a simple average of Hong Kong quota prices in 1983 and the first five months of 1984, for each of 15 apparel product categories exported by Hong Kong to the U.S., based on calculations made by Hamilton (1986), and assume them to reflect the quota prices for the 15 categories in 1984; 1982 quota prices also from Hamilton (1986), are used in model sensitivity analyses reported on later. Both of these sets of price data are given in Table 1. Hong Kong quota prices of the other MFA apparel products exported to the U.S. are calculated on the basis of an average of the quota prices given in Table 1. In aggregating the MFA apparel products in the

Table 1. Hong Kong Quota Prices* for Selected Apparel Items Exported to the U.S.

		%	
Category description	Category number	1982	1984†
Men's cotton jacket	333/334	10	19
Ladies' cotton jacket	335	20	27
Cotton knit shirt and blouse	338/339	49	50
Men's cotton woven shirt	340	6	38
Ladies cotton woven shirt	341	11	36
Ladies cotton woven skirt	342	n.a.	37
Cotton knit sweater	345	n.a.	59§
Men's cotton pant	347	8	50
Ladies cotton pant	348	10	63
Ladies wool knit blouse	438	1	19
Wool knit sweater	445/446	21	120
Men's MMF jacket‡	633/634	n.a.	23§
Ladies' MMF shirt‡	635	n.a.	15§
MMF knit shirt and blouse‡	638/639	2	27
Men's MMF woven shirt‡	640	n.a.	65§
Ladies' MMF woven blouse‡	641	6	58□□
Ladies' MMF pant	648	8	34□□
Average**	—	10	42

n.a., Not available.
*As a percent of export price.
†Average over the period January 1983 to May 1984.
‡MMF, man-made fibers.
§January to May 1984 only.
□□January to December 1983 only.
**From the proportion of total rent to total export value inclusive of total rent.
[Derived from: Hamilton (1986).]

U.S. into the six restricted apparel product categories used in the model, new quota prices are calculated by taking trade weighted averages of quota prices using the Hamilton data that fall within the categories used in the model.

Quota prices for textile products from Hong Kong would appear to be significantly lower than for apparel, as quota restrictions are less severe. Since no data are available, we assume quota prices on textile products to be one-half the average of quota prices for apparel products given in Table 1.[j]

The calculated quota prices, expressed as export tax equivalents, are then converted into import tariff equivalents[k] and used, along with data on tariff rates on U.S. imports of textiles and apparel obtained from GATT (1984), to calculate unit production costs in Hong Kong of each of the seven restricted product categories used in the model. Our method of calculating production costs of quota restricted items in other supplying countries is to assume that for each product category, the unit cost can be approximated by the unit cost in Hong Kong multiplied by the ratio of the supplying country's relative wage rate in textiles and apparel compared to Hong Kong. We apply a further correction for the relative efficiency of labor and product quality across countries by also multiplying by each country's relative value of gross output per worker in textiles and apparel compared to Hong Kong. This makes a large difference to estimated supply prices.[l] Value of gross output per worker is given by dividing wages per employee by wages in value added, and then dividing by value added in gross output. Data on wages per employee, value added in gross output and wages in value added, for textiles and apparel are from UNIDO (1985). The resulting average supply prices of quota restricted products by country, both adjusted and unadjusted for differences in labor productivity and product quality, for both 1982 and 1984, are presented in Table 2. As can be seen the correction for labor productivity and product quality makes a very large difference to

[j]This is consistent with Cline (1987) who assumes that the tariff-equivalent of textile quotas has averaged 15% increment beyond tariff protection since 1981, and some 25% on apparel.

[k]U.S. export tax equivalents are converted into import tariff equivalents by multiplying by the ratio of f.o.b. and c.i.f. values of clothing imported from Hong Kong. (The f.o.b./c.i.f. ratio is approximately 0.93.) See Hamilton (1986).

[l]Hamilton (I988) analyzes these differences between Hong Kong, Taiwan, and South Korea and concludes they are small and can be ignored. Here, with 34 supplying countries, these factors become considerably more important.

Table 2. Calculated Average Supply Prices of Quota Restricted Textiles and Apparel by Country, 1982 and 1984.

	Adjusted for differences in labor productivity and product quality		Unadjusted for differences in labor productivity and product quality	
Exporting country	1982	1984	1982	1984
Bangladesh	0.41	0.31	0.05	0.04
Brazil	0.35	0.25	0.34	0.25
Bulgaria	0.76	0.55	0.42	0.31
China	0.62	0.46	0.12	0.09
Colombia	0.53	0.39	0.35	0.26
Czechoslovakia	0.76	0.56	0.42	0.31
Costa Rica	0.70	0.51	0.60	0.44
Dominican Republic	0.76	0.56	0.36	0.26
Egypt	0.67	0.49	0.18	0.13
Guatemala	0.67	0.49	0.34	0.25
Haiti	0.62	0.46	0.15	0.11
Hong Kong	0.76	0.56	0.76	0.56
Hungary	0.60	0.44	0.23	0.17
India	0.62	0.46	0.10	0.07
Indonesia	0.58	0.42	0.09	0.07
Korea	0.55	0.41	0.43	0.32
Macau	0.67	0.49	0.68	0.50
Malaysia	0.52	0.38	0.22	0.16
Mauritius	0.58	0.42	0.18	0.13
Mexico	0.67	0.49	0.71	0.52
Nepal	0.62	0.46	0.60	0.04
Pakistan	0.62	0.46	0.12	0.09
Panama	0.76	0.56	0.53	0.39
Peru	0.67	0.49	0.34	0.25
Philippines	0.69	0.51	0.14	0.10
Poland	0.76	0.55	0.42	0.31
Romania	0.67	0.49	0.76	0.55
Singapore	0.70	0.52	0.62	0.45
Sri Lanka	0.62	0.46	0.13	0.10
Taiwan	0.67	0.49	0.67	0.49
Thailand	0.67	0.49	0.22	0.16
Turkey	0.36	0.27	0.40	0.30
Uruguay	0.71	0.52	0.73	0.53
Yugoslavia	0.65	0.48	0.52	0.38

Source: Based on data from Hamilton (1986) and methods described in the text.
All prices are expressed relative to U.S. supply prices of unity.

these estimates; as large as a factor of ten in some cases. The value of quota rents received by each of the developing countries is calculated by using the supply prices of quota restricted products by country and the trade data by model product category by country.[m]

The value of production of other goods in all countries is given by subtracting the value of production of textile and apparel products from GDP in each country. Data on GDP by country are from the World Bank (1986) and from Europa (1987). External sector balance conditions are then used to calculate the value of trade in other goods in each country.

The model also requires elasticity values for transformation surfaces and preferences in each country. For the bottom level of nesting, assumed values of -0.50 and 5.0 are used for all pairwise nests between comparable restricted and unrestricted commodities and in all countries. Given there are no literature estimates to the choice of these values, we justify our specification as follows. An assumption of smooth substitutability in production between comparable restricted and unrestricted commodities would not be appropriate, since there would be no effect of the quotas. Therefore, a low elasticity value is used for all countries, implying a limited ability to substitute products on the supply side. In contrast, a high degree of substitutability is assumed on the demand side of the model. This has some claim to plausibility since from the consumers point of view the relative difference in product characteristics is small.

---

[m]Our estimate of quota rents accuring to developing countries from textile trade restrictions in developed countries is about 8.7 billion dollar. In a recent related general equilibrium model, Tarr (1989) estimates that quota rents transferred just from the U.S. to developing countries are about 7.1 billion dollar. Moreover, Tarr also uses Hamilton's quota price data. These differences in estimates are explained mainly by two factors. First, by differences in supply prices used. For example, in calculating supply prices of quota restricted items in developing countries we incorporate the bilateralism in the quotas, whereas Tarr treats the rest of the world as a single supplying region and calculates a single quota premium rate on textile and apparel equal to the weighted average of Hamilton's (1988) quota premium rate for Hong Kong apparel products in the U.S. in the first five months of 1984 of 47% and an assumed quota premium rate on textiles of 5%. On this score, Tarr's estimate of quota rents will be downward-biased. Second, and perhaps dominant, there are important differences in the trade data used for calculating quota rents. For example, in calculating our quota rents we use data on quota restricted imports of MFA categories. On the other hand, Tarr uses data on U.S. imports of all textile and apparel categories, ignoring the fact that not all categories are MFA categories, and that due to bilateralism in the quotas, not all imports of MFA categories are quota restrained. This procedure will apply a quota premium to imports from other developed countries, which are not quota restrained. Consequently, on this score, Tarr's quota rent estimate will overstate the true quota rents involved.

Elasticity values at the top two levels are calculated as follows. For the developed countries, we base our selection of these values on estimates of U.S. total demand elasticities and assumed supply elasticities of 1.0. For the developing countries, we assume a Cobb–Douglas specification for both transformation and preference functions, which is equivalent to setting all these elasticities to unity.[n] Because of the potentially crucial nature of these elasticity values for model behavior, we use a central set of elasticity values around which sensitivity analyses are performed.

The U.S. total demand elasticity of −0.60 is based on estimates of this elasticity for textiles and apparel, reported in Cline (1987). Since no comparable information on supply elasticities is available, we use a value of 1.0, which is an assumed value used by other researchers (see, for instance, Cline, 1989; Jenkins, 1980; and Hufbauer *et al.*, 1986). We calculate implied elasticities of transformation and substitution for the top two levels of nesting in the developed countries[o] consistent with these estimates. These values are, however, not necessarily consistent with literature estimates of import demand elasticities for textiles and apparel,[p] reflecting the well known incompatibilities between literature estimates of demand and supply elasticities on the one hand and import demand elasticities on the other.

The calibration procedures used to generate the parameter values for the model involve first decomposing the data represented in value terms into separate price and quantity data. This is done through a units convention which defines physical units for all commodities as those amounts which in equilibrium, sell in the U.S. for $1. Hence domestic prices in developing countries for quota restricted items are less than one, and domestic prices in Canada and the EC are less than, greater than, or equal to one, depending upon the direction of trade. Once elasticity values have been selected, share parameters for the CES and CET functions in the model are given from the price and quantity data and the assumption of agent optimization in each country (see Mansur and Whalley, 1984).

---

[n]The reason for making this assumption is because there are currently no estimates of import or export demand elasticities for the developing countries from which implied transformation and substitution elasticities can be calculated.
[o]We assume common values across nests.
[p]Hufbauer *et al.* (1986) believe a conservative estimate of import elasticity of demand for imported textiles and apparel in the U.S. to be about −1.8. We estimate import elasticity of demand in the U.S. at −6.4.

3. Results

The general equilibrium model described above has been used to analyze a variety of possible changes in quota and tariff restrictions used by developed countries towards imports of textiles and apparel. In these analyses major focus is on welfare effects, reported as Hicksian equivalent variations (EVs)[q] by country in billions of 1986 dollars, but trade volume and production effects are also reported. Table 3 presents the welfare, production, and trade effects of removing both developed country bilateral quotas and tariffs on the 14 textile and apparel products covered by the model.

Results clearly show that the vast majority of developing countries gain from the removal of restrictions on trade in textiles and apparel, with some gaining proportionately more than others. The effects by country reflect improvements in each country's market share in developed country markets, as well as the rent transfer effect of the bilateral quotas. The percentage changes in the values of production and consumption (and trade) in developed countries may appear slightly inconsistent with the elasticity configuration used. This discrepancy is accounted for by differences in the percentage changes in producer and consumer prices because of the different aggregation function implied by the assumptions on technology and preferences of the composite textile product.

In aggregate, developing countries gain around 8 billion dollar, suggesting that gains to developing countries from improved access more than offset losses from forgone rent transfers as quotas and tariffs are abolished. This is even the case for relatively larger holders of quotas such as South Korea and Taiwan, whom it has always been argued, have a protected market niche against lower cost competition under the MFA. In the presence of quotas (and tariffs) they, along with other developing countries, are nonmarginal suppliers to developed country markets. Removing protection improves all supplying developing country market shares in developed country markets in previously trade restricted textile and clothing items rather than reallocating shares among them.[r]

[q]Welfare estimates under Hicksian equivalent and compensating measures are very close, and so only EVs are reported

[r]Most supplying developing countries, however, lose market share in unrestricted textile and apparel items under an MFA elimination. Therefore, whether a developing country's market share in developed country markets increases or decreases depends on the combined effect of an increase in the country's market share in the previously quota restricted textile and apparel categories and an increase or decrease in its market share in the unrestricted categories.

Table 3. General Equilibrium Effects of Removing Bilateral MFA Quotas and Tariffs on Textiles and Apparel in all Developed Countries.*

	Hicksian EV's ($billions 1986)	Change in value of production of textiles and apparel at benchmark prices %	Change in value of imports and exports of textiles and apparel at benchmark prices %
U.S.	12.309	−25.14	305.49
Canada	0.831	−18.58	200.17
EC	2.215	−12.42	190.16
Exporting countries			
Bangladesh	0.237	38.19	141.00
Brazil	1.133	79.90	474.12
Bulgaria	0.006	7.21	41.12
China	1.827	11.26	433.57
Colombia	0.477	39.43	1045.00
Czechoslovakia	0.091	12.34	431.06
Costa Rica	0.014	4.04	6.61
Dominican Republic	−0.006	−1.48	−6.15
Egypt	0.022	9.48	532.23
Guatemala	0.006	8.14	120.79
Haiti	−0.002	9.78	20.13
Hong Kong	−0.519	15.86	66.15
Hungary	0.124	22.01	197.38
India	0.077	8.20	197.78
Indonesia	0.610	54.19	461.01
Korea	1.579	34.60	314.88
Macau	−0.030	3.29	25.60
Malaysia	0.217	53.13	274.82
Mauritius	0.021	24.11	101.48
Mexico	0.137	8.96	342.56
Nepal	0.028	12.24	161.13
Pakistan	0.008	13.24	23.29
Panama	0.003	18.48	74.18
Peru	0.061	11.88	309.14
Philippines	0.127	25.83	183.14
Poland	0.176	12.16	418.41
Romania	0.208	25.44	137.69
Singapore	−0.012	37.82	122.30
Sri Lanka	0.048	44.92	105.34
Taiwan	1.193	27.59	223.97
Thailand	0.025	24.74	54.01
Turkey	0.129	5.44	25.82

(*Continued*)

Table 3. (*Continued*)

	Hicksian EV's ($billions 1986)	Change in value of production of textiles and apparel at benchmark prices %	Change in value of imports and exports of textiles and apparel at benchmark prices %
Uruguay	0.010	11.24	77.36
Yugoslavia	0.043	11.01	67.04
All developing countries	8.078	—	—
All countries	23.435	—	—

*Transformation and substitution elasticities set equal to −0.5 and 5.0 in the bottom level of nesting for all countries in the model. In the top two levels, elasticities of transformation and substitution in all developed countries reflect literature estimates of U.S. total demand elasticities and assumed supply elasticities of 1.0. The elasticities are −0.01 and 0.61 in all developed countries. Cobb–Douglas specifications are used at the top two levels in all developing countries.

The global welfare gain is 23.4 billion dollar with gains to the U.S. of 12.3 billion dollar. This estimate is significantly higher than that of Cline (1987) who places the net welfare cost of textile and apparel protection in the U.S. at around 8 billion dollar using 1986 data. Importantly, this divergence in results occurs even though Cline uses a partial equilibrium approach which tends to overstate the welfare costs of protection to the U.S. This is because under a partial equilibrium approach, the U.S. is modeled as a marginal importing country, and so if textile and apparel protection is abolished the world market supply price to the U.S. market would be unchanged, thus implying full rent transfer. But the reason why our results are higher than Cline's is because our model captures the added costs of bilateralism in these trade restrictions, while Cline does not. In addition, our model considers the tariff-equivalent of quota protection in textiles and apparel to be higher than the estimates used by Cline.

In Table 4, we report results where bilateral quotas alone are removed, leaving tariffs in place. In this case, all developing countries are worse off compared to the case in Table 3, because their market access is reduced by developed country tariffs. Even larger gains result for the developed countries. This reflects their more advantageous terms of trade as a result of not also eliminating their tariffs, indicating that in the nonsmall open economy case, optimal tariffs for developed countries are nonzero and that

Table 4. Welfare, Production and Trade Effects of Removing Bilateral Textile and Apparel Quotas, but not Tariffs.*

	Hicksian EV's ($billions 1986)	Change in value of production of textiles and apparel at benchmark prices %	Change in value of imports and exports of textiles and apparel at benchmark prices %
U.S.	15.038	−19.64	235.80
Canada	0.928	−10.26	115.66
EC	3.039	−7.19	117.21
Exporting countries			
Bangladesh	0.188	30.31	90.25
Brazil	0.963	70.74	396.82
Bulgaria	−0.001	1.30	−7.81
China	0.944	6.23	210.78
Colombia	0.368	31.35	774.97
Czechoslovakia	0.021	6.09	211.81
Costa Rica	−0.002	−2.02	−13.94
Dominican Republic	−0.020	−6.25	−21.20
Egypt	0.007	4.55	245.62
Guatemala	0.002	1.37	7.03
Haiti	−0.011	4.75	5.44
Hong Kong	−1.080	10.07	44.63
Hungary	0.075	15.92	128.44
India	−0.071	2.00	31.73
Indonesia	0.361	41.84	355.55
Korea	0.779	28.18	254.41
Macau	−0.089	2.66	26.33
Malaysia	0.143	44.79	220.99
Mauritius	0.004	18.38	68.98
Mexico	0.047	2.66	73.13
Nepal	0.017	7.47	72.88
Pakistan	−0.036	6.72	10.78
Panama	0.000	9.46	44.91
Peru	0.032	6.17	143.25
Philippines	0.003	17.41	118.87
Poland	0.072	6.29	200.82
Romania	0.078	16.37	84.63
Singapore	−0.084	26.97	88.52
Sri Lanka	−0.015	34.00	80.03
Taiwan	0.308	20.77	175.28
Thailand	−0.048	16.49	35.14
Turkey	0.028	0.02	−4.93

(Continued)

Table 4. (*Continued*)

	Hicksian EV's ($billions 1986)	Change in value of production of textiles and apparel at benchmark prices %	Change in value of imports and exports of textiles and apparel at benchmark prices %
Uruguay	0.001	5.32	32.43
Yugoslavia	−0.055	5.36	30.05
All developing countries	2.934	—	—
All countries	21.941	—	—

*Transformation and substitution elasticities set equal to −0.5 and 5.0 in the bottom level of nesting for all countries in the model. In the top two levels, elasticities of transformation and substitution in all developed countries reflect literature estimates of U.S. total demand elasticities and assumed supply elasticities of 1.0. The elasticities are −0.01 and 0.61 in all developed countries. Cobb–Douglas specifications are used at the top two levels in all developing countries.

1986 tariff levels are below optimal tariffs. This again emphasizes the difference in the analysis from the small open economy case.

The sensitivity of these results has been tested through a series of experiments reported on in Table 5. Cases 1, 2, and 3 report the impact on results of various changes in elasticity values for transformation surfaces and preferences in each country. Cases 4 and 5 provide an indication of the magnitudes involved as assumptions on supply prices by country are changed. Case 6 reports the effects on results if the composite other good is defined to be other manufactures instead of residual GDP.[s]

Results in Cases 1, 2, and 3 of Table 5 suggest that for some of the countries the results are highly sensitive to changes in elasticities, while results for others are less. The degree of sensitivity seems to be collinear with the size of the country price effects, and corresponding quantity effects, which are produced when tariffs and quotas are eliminated. If supply prices

[s]The value of production of other manufactures in all countries is calculated by subtracting the value of production of textiles and apparel from total manufacturing production. Data on total manufacturing production by country are taken from the same sources as production data for textiles and apparel. However, data are unavailable for some developing countries. In these cases, production data for textiles and apparel along with estimates of the share of textiles and apparel in manufacturing production from GATT (1984) were used to calculate the value of total manufacturing production in each country.

Table 5. Sensitivity Analyses on Results from Table 3 (Hicksian Equivalent Variations in billions of 1986 dollars).

	Case 1	Case 2	Case 3	Case 4	Case 5	Case 6
U.S.	11.860	8.614	14.578	3.424	49.328	12.179
Canada	0.830	0.582	0.984	0.242	3.529	0.825
EC	1.582	0.952	3.130	−0.160	21.950	2.160
Exporting countries						
Bangladesh	0.292	0.266	0.553	0.218	1.229	0.218
Brazil	1.255	0.995	1.609	1.047	−0.076	1.044
Bulgaria	0.014	0.012	0.007	0.006	0.021	0.006
China	2.557	2.031	2.099	0.907	33.404	1.810
Colombia	0.596	0.462	0.574	0.204	0.124	0.459
Czechoslovakia	0.139	0.109	0.085	0.026	0.211	0.092
Costa Rica	0.026	0.030	0.024	0.008	−0.011	0.015
Dominican Republic	0.007	0.016	−0.004	0.007	−0.035	−0.005
Egypt	0.033	0.028	0.024	0.007	1.090	0.020
Guatemala	0.009	0.009	0.008	0.002	0.008	0.006
Haiti	0.007	0.009	0.009	0.004	0.006	−0.001
Hong Kong	−0.062	−0.119	−0.694	0.043	−2.060	−0.464
Hungary	0.161	0.138	0.176	0.087	0.238	0.127
India	0.187	0.159	0.092	0.203	2.784	0.007
Indonesia	0.837	0.647	0.686	0.192	8.429	0.542
Korea	2.156	1.480	1.605	0.779	−0.955	1.569
Macau	0.012	0.010	−0.038	0.061	−0.285	0.024
Malaysia	0.275	0.206	0.275	0.159	0.283	0.213
Mauritius	0.037	0.031	0.033	0.016	0.043	0.018
Mexico	0.235	0.190	0.158	0.058	0.681	0.140
Nepal	0.039	0.033	0.035	0.014	1.599	0.028
Pakistan	0.034	0.037	0.017	0.034	0.034	0.007
Panama	0.007	0.007	0.004	0.001	0.004	0.003
Peru	0.086	0.072	0.072	0.018	0.081	0.061
Philippines	0.217	0.164	0.144	0.091	5.147	0.119
Poland	0.252	0.222	0.210	0.040	0.264	0.177
Romania	0.293	0.253	0.254	0.111	−0.031	0.199
Singapore	0.055	0.028	−0.028	0.001	−0.229	−0.010
Sri Lanka	0.097	0.069	0.052	0.043	0.111	0.025
Taiwan	1.929	1.350	1.111	0.502	−1.141	1.192
Thailand	0.081	0.067	0.031	0.047	0.021	0.018
Turkey	0.204	0.235	0.617	0.194	−0.181	0.134
Uruguay	0.017	0.016	0.013	0.005	0.025	0.009
Yugoslavia	0.120	0.115	0.063	0.094	−0.206	0.048

(*Continued*)

Table 5. (*Continued*)

	Case 1	Case 2	Case 3	Case 4	Case 5	Case 6
All developing countries	12.218	9.395	9.889	5.245	50.584	7.934
All countries	26.491	19.543	28.583	8.751	125.393	23.100

Case 1. As in Table 3, but with Cobb–Douglas specifications used at the top two levels of nesting of transformation and preference functions in all developed countries.
Case 2. As in Table 3, but with both transformation and substitution elasticities set equal to 0.61 in the top two levels of nesting in all developing countries in the model.
Case 3. As in Table 3, but with transformation and substitution elasticities set equal to −2.5 and 7.0 in the bottom level of nesting in all countries in the model.
Case 4. As in Table 3, except that supply prices in Hong Kong are based on 1982 quota prices.
Case 5. As in Table 3, except that for each developing country the ratio of their relative wage rate (compared to the Hong Kong base) is used as an indicator of relative product price at international values. No account is taken for differences in labor productivity or product quality.
Case 6. As in Table 3, except that the composite other good is defined to be other manufactures instead of residual GDP.

for quota restricted products in Hong Kong are calculated using 1982 rather than 1984 quota prices (Case 4), supply prices in all developing countries for these products rise. Both the welfare estimates and the size of quota rents transferred to foreigners are reduced when this happens. A loss results for the EC. This is due to the high volume of export trade of the EC with other developed countries in MFA products which are quota restrained from developing countries. Thus, under an MFA elimination, the EC loses share to other developing countries in these products, which in this case, more than offsets the gains from removing protection on its import trade.

Case 5 of Table 5 shows that if relative wage rates (compared to Hong Kong) are used as an indicator of relative product supply prices, this has a significant impact on our welfare measures. Prices of quota restricted products decrease considerably in all developing countries, except Macau, Mexico, Romania, Turkey, and Uruguay where prices increase. The effect of decreasing supply prices is to expand the differentials between foreign production costs and the price paid by importers. As a result, developed countries gain even more from elimination of textile and apparel protection. Some developing countries are worse off, while others are better off. In aggregate they gain more, despite greater forgone rent transfers. Finally, results in Case 6 of Table 5 show that using an alternative definition of the composite other good to cover only other manufactures rather than residual GDP does not have large effects on results.

4. Concluding Remarks

In this chapter, we report results from an applied general equilibrium model we have used to analyze the impacts of textile and apparel restrictions used by three major developed countries against textile and clothing imports from developing countries. The model captures trade in 14 key textile and apparel categories involving three developed and 34 developing countries. In the model, countries are represented by their actual size in terms of GDP, weakening rent transfer effects compared to partial equilibrium analysis.

We evaluate both the national and global welfare costs of the bilateral quotas and tariffs captured by the model. Using data for 1986, results suggest global gains from elimination of quotas and tariffs of around 23 billion dollar. In aggregate, developing countries gain around 8 billion dollar. This suggests that despite foregone rent transfers, the vast majority of developing countries would receive gains from eliminating textile and apparel protection through improved access to developed country markets.

Results also show most developing countries gaining in the central variant of the model from an elimination of the MFA only, leaving tariffs on textile and apparel products in place. This is contrary to popular belief which suggests that higher income large quota recipient countries (such as South Korea and Taiwan) would lose. In the model, since all of the developing country suppliers are quota constrained and relatively small compared to large developed countries, they increase their market share in previously trade restricted textile and apparel items at the expense of developed country producers rather than lose share to other developing countries.

Estimates of the gains to the U.S. from the model for the removal of tariffs and quotas are significantly higher than those of other partial equilibrium studies, such as Cline (1987), who places the net welfare cost of textile and apparel protection in the U.S. at around 8 billion dollar, rather than the 12.3 billion dollar reported here. This divergence in results occurs even though the partial equilibrium assumptions of price taking behavior for large developed countries will tend to cause the costs of textile and apparel protection to be overstated. The difference stems mainly from the added cost of bilateralism which our model captures. As might be expected, results show sensitivity with respect to elasticity parameters and assumptions as to how supply prices vary across countries, but the main themes of results remain.

References

Brown, DK (1987). Tariffs, the terms of trade, and national product differentiation. *Journal of Policy Modelling*, **9**, 503–526.

Cline, WR (1987). *The Future of World Trade in Textiles and Apparel.* Washington: Institute for International Economics.

Europa (1987). *The Europa Yearbook* 1987: *A World Survey*, Vols. I and II. Europa Publications Ltd.

European Commission (1987). Microfiche Eurostat sce 1520.

Food and Agricultural Organisation of the United Nations (FAO) (1985). *World Apparel Fibre Consumption Survey.* FAO.

General Agreement on Tariffs and Trade (GATT) (1984). *Textiles and Clothing in the World Economy.* Background study prepared by the GATT Secretariat to assist work undertaken by the contracting Parties in pursuance of the decision on textiles and clothing taken at the November 1982 ministerial meeting. Geneva: GATT.

Hamilton, C (1986). An assessment of voluntary restraints on Hong Kong exports to Europe and USA. *Economica*, 53.

——(1988). Restrictiveness and international transmission of the "new" protectionism. In *Issues in US-EC Trade Relations*, R Baldwin, C Hamilton and A Sapir (eds.). National Bureau of Economic Research and University of Chicago Press.

Hufbauer, GC, DT Berliner and KA Elliont (1986). *Trade Protection in the United States*: 31 *Case Studies.* Washington: Institute for International Economics.

Jenkins, GP (1980). *Costs and Consequences of the New Protectionism: The Case of Canada's Clothing Sector.* Ottawa: North–South Institute.

Mansur, A and J Whalley (1984). Numerical specification of applied general equilibrium models: Estimation, calibration and data. In *Applied General Equilibrium Analysis*, H Scarf and J Shoven (eds.). Cambridge: Cambridge University Press.

Shoven, J and J Whalley (1984). Applied general equilibrium models of taxation and international trade. *Journal of Economic Literature*, 1007–1051.

Tarr, DG (1989). *A General Equilibrium Analysis of the Welfare and Employment Effects of U.S. Quotas in Textiles, Autos and Steel.* Bureau of Economics Staff Report to the Federal Trade Commission.

Trela, I and J Whalley (1988). Do developing countries lose from the MFA? National Bureau of Economic Research Working Paper No. 2618, Cambridge, Massachusetts.

——(1990). Unraveling the threads of the MFA. In *Textiles Trade and the Developing Countries*: *Eliminating the Multi-Fibre Arrangement in the* 1990*s*, CB Hamilton (ed.). Washington, D.C.: World Bank.

United Nations (1986). *Industrial Statistics Yearbook* 1984. Vol. I: *General Industrial Statistics.* New York.

United Nations Industrial Development Organisation (UNIDO) (1985). *Handbook of Industrial Statistics* 1984. New York.

U.S. Department of Commerce. Office of Textiles and Apparel (June 1987a). *U.S. General Imports of Cotton Manufacturers* (TQ 2730).

——(June 1987b). U.S. *General Imports of Wool Manufacturers* (TQ 2740).

——(June 1987c). U.S. *General Imports of Man-Made Fibre Manufacturers* (TQ 2760).

——Bureau of Industrial Economics (1987d). *U.S. Industrial Outlook.* Washington.

——(1985). *U.S. Production, Imports and Import/Production Ratios for Cotton, Wool and Man-Made Fiber Textiles and Apparel.*

U.S. International Trade Commission (USITC) (1987). *U.S. Imports of Textiles and Apparel Under the Multifiber Arrangement: Statistical Report Through* 1986. USITC Publication, 1986.

Whalley, J (1985). *Trade Liberalization Among Major World Trading Areas*, Cambridge: MIT Press.

World Bank (1986). *World Development Report* 1986. New York: Oxford University Press.

Chapter 10

Immiserizing Growth and Endogenous Protection*

Ramon L. Clarete
School of Economics, University of the Philippines, Diliman, Quezon City, The Philippines

John Whalley†
Department of Economics, University of Western Ontario, London, Canada N6A 5C2
National Bureau of Economic Research (NBER)

This chapter focuses on immiserizing growth in the two senses of Bhagwati (1958) and Johnson (1967), and how both the likelihood that either may occur and their extent can be affected by the presence of endogenous protection; i.e., quota and other forms of protection for which the *ad valorem* equivalent level of protection is endogenously determined. We use a general equilibrium model of the Philippines due to Clarete (1984) to compute counterfactual equilibria involving changes in domestic policies, terms of trade, and resource endowments. Immiserizing growth, in the sense of Bhagwati, is less likely because the terms-of-trade fall required to offset the growth of resources has to be significantly larger if no distortions are in the model. Immiserizing growth in the sense of Johnson tends to be more likely if endogenous protection is present. As unbalanced growth occurs focused on the factor intensive in the protected sector, resources are drawn out of the export sector and export earnings decline and, if the level of protection is endogenously determined, the welfare costs of protection increase.

1. Introduction

This chapter discusses how either physical or value-based quotas (rationed foreign exchange) used in developing countries as part of the trade regime affect both the likelihood and extent of immiserizing growth in the two senses of Bhagwati (1958) and Johnson (1967). The former is where

*This chapter was first published in (1994). *Journal of Development Economics*, **45**(1), 121–133.
†We are grateful to two referees for helpful comments on an earlier draft of our paper.

resource growth induces a deterioration in the terms of trade leaving the country worse off. The latter is where domestic distortions are present and unbalanced growth involving augmentation of the factor used intensively in the protected sector is welfare-worsening (even at fixed terms of trade).

We argue that the presence of such distortions tends to reduce the likelihood of immiserizing growth occurring in the sense of Bhagwati (1958). This is because the *ad valorem* protective equivalents (quota premia) are endogenously determined for these forms of protection. A deterioration in the terms of trade induced by resource growth reduces premium values, which improves efficiency and offsets some of the loss from the terms-of-trade deterioration. Where rent seeking accompanies such quotas, these effects are larger.

In contrast, protection of this form tends to increase the likelihood that immiserization in the sense of Johnson (1967) will occur. This is because augmenting the factor used intensively in the protected sector draws resources away from the export sector, reduces export earnings, and increases *ad valorem* equivalents for endogenously determined protection. Endogenous protection thus has opposite effects on the likelihood that immiserizing growth in the two senses of Bhagwati and Johnson will occur.

In this chapter, we both present diagrammatic arguments to support these contentions, and explore the extent of these effects using a numerical general equilibrium model of the Philippines due to Clarete and Roumasset (1987) which we have extended here to capture endogenous protection of the type we analyze diagrammatically. Numerical results from the model confirm the intuition given above for the role that endogenous protection plays in affecting both types of immiserization. They also suggest that influences from other domestic policies can be significant. Analysis of immiserizing growth which does not take into account the presence of quota trade-based and other domestic distortions can, therefore, be misleading.

2. Endogenous Protection and the Likelihood of Immiserizing Growth

Ever since Bhagwati's classic 1958 paper, the literature on immiserizing growth has continued to expand. It is now widely accepted that there are two different senses of immiserizing growth; the first as originally discussed by Bhagwati (1958); the second as set out in Johnson (1967).[a]

[a]Bhagwati (1968) subsequently pointed out that these can, in principle, be combined into a single generalized concept.

Bhagwati's original analysis showed that balanced growth in the economy can lead to a sufficiently large deterioration in the terms of trade that the economy is left worse off. In Johnson's analysis, no terms-of-trade effects come into play but unbalanced growth occurs. If this growth is concentrated on the factor used intensively in a tariff-protected sector, the efficiency cost of the tariff distortion is increased by the unbalanced growth, and this can more than offset the direct benefits of factor growth. Here we investigate how the likelihood that each of these two forms of immiserization will occur is affected by the presence of trade policies which are part of a class we call "endogenous protection".

Endogenous protection refers to situations in which the *ad valorem* equivalent protection implied by a trade policy measure changes as endowments, technology or other policies change. One example is the practice of rationing foreign exchange in developing countries. What happens in this case is that exporters are required to surrender foreign exchange to the central bank at a fixed exchange rate, at which there is also excess demand for foreign exchange from importers. An implicit premium value associated with the scarce foreign exchange is established, effectively resulting in a two-tier exchange rate system for importers and exporters. When changes in endowments occur in the economy involving either balanced or unbalanced growth, the *ad valorem* equivalent protection operating against imports changes because the excess demand for foreign exchange is affected. If the premium associated with rationed foreign exchange changes as growth occurs, then the possibility that immiserizing growth will occur will be correspondingly affected.[b]

In the case of immiserizing growth in the sense of Bhagwati, the intuition is that as growth occurs and the terms of trade deteriorates, the demand for imports will fall, reducing excess demand for foreign exchange. This weakens the severity of foreign exchange rationing which also lowers the *ad valorem* equivalent protection implied by it. The likelihood of immiserization occurring in the presence of endogenous protection would, therefore, seem to be lowered.

Bhagwati immiserizing growth in the with and without endogenous protection cases is illustrated by the two panels in Fig. 1. In the case where no endogenous protection is present (Panel A), pre-growth equilibrium is characterized by production at point P and consumption at point C. The welfare level is U and the terms of trade are reflected in the world

---

[b]See the analyses of foreign exchange rationing in Clarete and Whalley (1991) and Dervis *et al.* (1981).

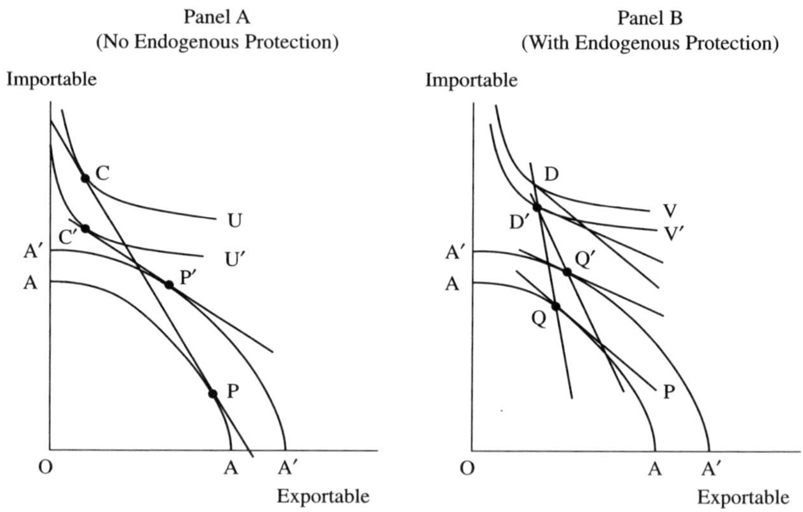

Fig. 1. Immiserizing growth in the sense of Bhagwati (terms of trade change).

price line PC. Balanced growth implies a parallel shift of the production possibility curve from AA to $A'A'$, production moves from P to P', and consumption to C'. If the terms of trade also deteriorates along with the growth, as indicated by the new world price line $P'C'$, post-growth welfare is U' which is less than U. The terms-of-trade decline more than offsets the direct benefits of growth and immiserization occurs.

Panel B indicates that if growth occurs when endogenous protection is present, the chance of immiserizing growth occurring is lower. In Panel B, initial equilibrium output, given that a trade-protective instrument is in place is at Q and consumption is at D. The world price line is QD, while the domestic price line is the line tangent to the production possibility frontier at Q. The presence of protection is reflected in the difference between the slopes of these two price lines.

With balanced growth reflected in a parallel shift in the production possibilities frontier, production changes to Q', and consumption to D'. Reduced imports lower *ad valorem* equivalent protection as indicated by the smaller wedge between domestic prices (i.e., the price line tangent to D') and the world prices (e.g., the line through $D'Q'$). The welfare level is V' which is lower than V, again indicating immiserization. But the reduction of real income from V to V' is less than that from U to U' in Panel A, suggesting that immiserizing growth in the sense of Bhagwati may be less likely to occur in the presence of endogenous protection.

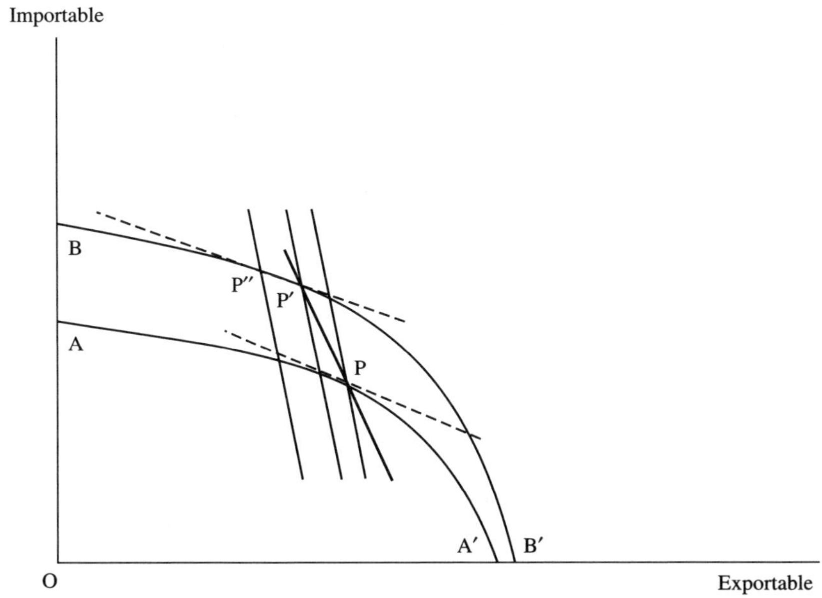

Fig. 2. Immiserizing growth in the sense of Johnson (fixed terms of trade).

Figure 2 illustrates how endogenous protection can affect the likelihood of immiserization occurring in the sense of Johnson. Johnson immiserization occurs where a tariff is used to protect a sector, and unbalanced growth is concentrated on the factor in which the protected sector is intensive. The effect of growth is to pull more resources into the protected sector and immiserization occurs if the induced additional costs of protection negate the benefits from augmentation of the factor. A necessary and sufficient condition that this type of immiserizing growth occur in the fixed tariff rate case is that the slope of the Rybszynski line associated with the growth of the factor used intensively in the protected sector is less than that of the international price line (Bhagwati and Srinivasan, 1983).[c]

Endogenous protection changes this analysis in so far as unbalanced growth of this form tends to reduce export earnings, which, in turn, tend

[c]This is equivalent to the condition that the productivity of the factor not used intensively in the protected sector is higher in the protected sector than in the unprotected sector, evaluated at world prices (Bertrand and Flatters, 1971), or the condition that the trade bias (i.e., the ratio of internal to external prices) is less than the ratio of the labor share in the exportable sector to the labor share in the protected import substituting sector (Martin, 1977).

to worsen the severity of foreign exchange rationing. In Fig. 2, the pre-growth output level is given by P and real income is defined by the (solid) world price line drawn through P. Unbalanced growth is concentrated on importables, and is indicated in the shift of the production possibility frontier from AA' to BB'. In this case, output changes to P' and real income falls, as indicated by the world price line drawn through P'; i.e., in this case immiserization occurs. The Rybszynski line in this case is also given by $P'P$.

If the level of protection is instead endogenously determined, production shifts to P'', since due to factor augmentation concentrated on the factor-intensive in the protected sector the level of endogenously determined protection will rise. Real income is now indicated by the world price line through P'', and thus the extent of immiserization is worse compared to the case of tariff protection. The likelihood of immiserization in the sense of Johnson occurring would seemingly have been increased by the presence of endogenous protection.

Endogeneity of the level of protection and the likelihood of immiserization occurring, thus seem interrelated. Immiserization seems to be made less probable in the Bhagwati sense by the presence of endogeneity in the level of protection, and made more probable in the Johnson sense.

3. Results on the Likelihood and Extent of Immiserization from a Numerical General Equilibrium Model of the Philippines

Whether immiserizing growth has occurred, or could potentially occur in various economies around the world has not been extensively discussed in the literature. Here we investigate the effects of various trade and domestic distortions, including the endogenous protection variety we stress above, on both the likelihood and extent of immiserization occurring in any particular case. We use the applied general equilibrium model of the Philippines presented in Clarete and Whalley (1988, 1991) which captures small open economy with production facing fixed terms of trade.[d] Into this model both domestic distortions and trade policies are incorporated. In analyzing how

[d]There is by now a substantial literature on numerical general equilibrium modelling applied to developing countries, of which our particular model is but one. The early volume by Dervis *et al.* (1982) sets out early applications, and more recent surveys by Robinson (1989a,b), and de Melo (1988) substantially update these. The majority of

both the likelihood and extent of Bhagwati or Johnson immiserization may be affected by endogenous protection, various changes in factor endowments and the terms of trade are considered and corresponding counterfactual experiments conducted with the model.

3.1. *Model structure*

Seven sectors, each producing a traded product, are specified in the model. Foreign and local goods are assumed to be identical, with excess demands of traded goods absorbed by the rest of the world. Each industry uses two variable factors (capital and labor), and an industry-specific fixed factor.[e] Production in each industry is described by a Leontief function defined over its value-added and a Leontief composite of intermediate inputs. The arguments of each industry value-added function are the two variable factors and a sector-specific factor.[f] Intermediate goods are used in fixed proportion to output. Since there are also nontraded goods in the model, their price relative to that of traded goods (the real exchange rate) has to be computed to obtain a general equilibrium in the model.

Domestic absorption of products in the model is reflected in the final demands of consumers. Each consumer has a Cobb–Douglas utility function and owns the domestic factors identified in the model. Incomes of consumers are derived from factor payments to resource owners and lump-sum income transfers from the government. Government income is derived from tax revenues and rents from quantitative and value-based import restrictions (i.e., licenses are assumed to be auctioned, and receipts are used to finance both transfers and real expenditures by government).

The model incorporates a number of domestic and trade-related policy distortions; quantitative import restrictions, foreign exchange rationing, trade taxes, rent seeking, and a fixed urban wage and associated urban–rural migration as in Harris and Todaro (1971). The presence of some of these features reflects earlier applications of the model. Trade taxes

---

these models use a so-called Armington country qualitatively different good assumption unlike our model; although see de Melo (1978) for a further homogeneous good treatment.

[e]The fixed factor in each industry production function precludes specialization effects occurring as can happen in homogeneous good trade models; see the discussion of this in Shoven and Whalley (1984).

[f]A reason for using Cobb–Douglas functions is that the share parameter on the sector-specific factor can be directly related to industry supply elasticities; see Clarete and Whalley (1988, 1991) for more details.

including import tariffs and export taxes are modeled in *ad valorem* form and are applied to the international value of imports and exports. Revenues collected from these are transferred back to consumers.

The model treatment of quantitative import restrictions implies that the domestic price of importables is endogenously determined, as is also the case with nontraded goods. Domestic prices for quota-restricted importables adjust until domestic output plus quota-restricted imports equal domestic demands. The government sells import licenses to importers, with a license required to import a unit of any good subject to quantitative restrictions. The price of the import license represents the scarcity premium associated with the import quota (Clarete and Whalley, 1988). The scarcity premium associated with the quantitative import restriction constitutes an element of the endogenously determined protection in the model.

The model also incorporates foreign exchange rationing, reflecting the pursuit of a fixed exchange rate but with nonaccommodative domestic monetary policy. A monetized extension of the model is used with a fixed domestic money supply and a simple Cambridge equation of exchange; i.e., money is held solely for final demand transactions (Clarete and Whalley, 1991).[g]

Under this treatment, the government announces a fixed exchange rate at which exporters must surrender all foreign exchange earnings to the central bank. The government then auctions off foreign exchange licenses to importers since there is an excess demand for foreign exchange at the official exchange rate. The scarcity premium associated with the shortage of foreign exchange operates akin to a trade-restricting measure and is another element of endogenous protection for local producers in the model. Unlike import licensing, this applies equally to all sectors. The income from auctioning foreign exchange licenses is assumed to be transferred back to consumers in lump-sum manner as with commodity-specific quotas.

We also consider rent-seeking along with licensing in an extended version of the model. The treatment assumed is that import licenses and foreign exchange are provided to importers at cost (i.e., without the premium). This induces agents to allocate resources to seek out access to import licenses and foreign exchange from the government (Bhagwati, 1982; Krueger, 1972). Under competitive rent seeking, the rents which would

[g]The difference from the earlier formulation due to Dervis *et al.* (1981) is the explicit incorporation of a monetary specification, and the associated nonneutrality of monetary policy given the fixed nominal exchange rate.

otherwise accrue to recipients of licenses are thus completely dissipated in resource costs devoted to rent seeking. The proportion of each factor used in rent seeking is assumed to reflect the relative economy-wide endowments of each factor input (Hamilton *et al.*, 1984).

Economic and policy data for the Philippines in 1988 are used to implement the model; a fuller description of this data set is available in Clarete and Whalley (1991). Following standard practice with numerical general equilibrium modeling, the model is first calibrated to a benchmark equilibrium data set (see Mansur and Whalley, 1984), with counterfactual equilibrium analysis performed around this. Here we highlight the main features of the calibrated model.

The seven traded goods sectors of the model are crops, livestock and natural resources, milling, other processed agricultural products, manufacturing, other industries, and services. The first three are exportables while the remaining four are importables. There are 11 consumers in the model grouped according to their respective incomes. Information about the distribution of resources among the 11 consumers is obtained from Habito (1984).

Premium values associated with quantitative import restrictions are obtained from Clarete (1984) who derives estimates from price comparisons. The premium value associated with foreign exchange rationing is assumed to be 20%. The model features three indirect taxes; the import tariff, excise tax, and the value-added tax; and two direct taxes, personal, and corporate income taxes.

Different versions of the model are used in analyzing the likelihood and extent of immiserization. The simplest model variant incorporates only tax distortions. A further variant includes both tax distortions and quantitative import restrictions. Yet a further variant includes tax distortions and foreign exchange rationing. And a final model variant includes all distortions for these model variant which include quotas and foreign exchange rationing. There are also model subvariants where quotas and/or rationed foreign exchange is present which include competitive rent-seeking activity.

3.2. *Model results*

We have made a number of calculations with the models described above using Philippine data for 1988 which allow us to analyze how endogenous protection and other distortions affect both the likelihood and extent of immiserization occurring in the senses of Bhagwati and Johnson.

Table 1. Welfare Costs of a 20% Terms-of-Trade Deterioration in the Presence of Different Combinations of Trade and Domestic Distortions (1978 Philippine Hicksian Equivalent Variations as a Percent of Base-Period Income).

Combinations of trade and domestic distortions present in the model	Welfare cost as a % of 1978 base-period income
All distortions present	2.37
No distortions present	5.77
All distortions present except export taxes	1.48
All distortions present except tariffs present	2.34
All distortions present except tariffs and export taxes	2.14
All distortions present except import quotas	2.37
All distortions present except import quotas and trade taxes	2.37
All distortions present except foreign exchange rationing	1.96
All distortions present except rent seeking	3.60
All distortions present except urban-rural migration	2.24

In Table 1, we analyze immiserization in the Bhagwati sense, reporting results from an assumed 20% deterioration in the Philippines terms of trade for a variety of model variants. Across the variants, we make different assumptions as to which policies are present in the model as the terms of trade declines. In all cases, the sum of Hicksian equivalent income variations across households in the model is reported as both the welfare criterion of any economy-wide real income gain or loss and the measure. This is calculated as a percent of base-period income in each of the model variants considered.

Results in Table 1 support the arguments made earlier in this chapter; namely, that in the presence of endogenous protection, a secondary benefit is induced by a terms-of-trade deterioration which partially offsets the welfare cost of the deterioration and hence makes immiserization less likely to occur. As we stress above, the way this arises is that as the terms of trade declines, the demand for imports falls and hence the endogenous protection associated with both foreign exchange and import rationing falls. The effect is to reallocate resources to export sectors and improve efficiency.

Hence, in Table 1 welfare goes down by 2.37% relative to the base-period equilibrium due to the lowered terms of trade when all distortions are present in the model. In contrast, when all distortions are removed before the terms-of-trade decline is considered, the same terms-of-trade deterioration imposes a welfare cost of 5.77% of base-period income. The role played by adverse terms-of-trade effects in generating immiserizing growth in the sense of Bhagwati for any given increase in endowments is thus reduced, and for any given resource endowment increase, the presence of endogenous protection reduces the likelihood of immiserization in the sense of Bhagwati. These analyses also directly indicate the extent of immiserization for a given (assumed) terms-of-trade deterioration.

When tariffs are excluded in Table 1, the terms-of-trade decline reduces welfare by 2.34%, but when both tariffs and export taxes are absent, the percent fall in welfare is only 2.14%. A regime without export taxes has the smallest welfare loss from a lowered terms of trade (1.48%), and removing foreign exchange rationing generates a welfare cost of only 1.96%. There is no incremental benefit if tariffs are removed, because protection through tariffs is redundant due to the presence of foreign exchange rationing. Other results (not reported in Table 1 due to space constraints) also show that when the Philippine terms of trade is 20% lower the welfare gains of removing distortions tend to be smaller; a result consistent with our argument above. Removing all distortions, for instance, implies efficiency gains equal to 8.05% compared to 11.96% of income under the benchmark terms-of-trade case.

We have also used the model to analyze how endogenous protection affects the likelihood of immiserization occurring in the sense of Johnson. We determine the terms-of-trade deterioration required to offset the beneficial effects of resource growth, and assess whether this is greater or smaller than the case where distortions are absent. Table 2 shows the welfare effects of a 3% growth of resources for four different cases: (i) Case A involves growth in all resources (capital, labor, and sector-specific factors); (ii) Case B considers growth of only capital and labor; (iii) Case C considers growth only of labor; and (iv) Case D growth of capital. Along with factor growth in these cases, equal percent increases are allowed for in the money supply, and the import quotas. We consider five variations on the policy mix assumed to be present. These are: all distortions present; no distortions present; tariffs present; foreign exchange rationing present; and a fixed urban wage.

In each of these calculations, we make the economy just as well off as before the growth occurred by calculating a post-growth equilibrium at fixed terms of trade, and then iteratively adjusting the terms-of-trade fall required to offset the effects of growth. We thus change the terms of trade and recompute equilibria in each case until a zero welfare effect is obtained. The upper level numbers reported in Table 2 are Hicksian equivalent variations as a percent of benchmark income; the lower level

Table 2. Welfare Effects of 3% Resource Growth and Terms-of-Trade Changes Needed to Offset the Benefits from Growth (1978 Philippine Hicksian Equivalent Variations as a Percentage of Base-Period Income; Lower Case Numbers in Parentheses give Terms-of-Trade Deterioration Needed to Offset the Effects of Growth).

	Factor growth assumptions[a]			
Distortions present	A	B	C	D
All distortions present[b]	3.00	0.13	−0.283	−0.76[c]
	(−23.08)	(−1.19)	(2.56)	(7.35)
No distortions present	3.00	1.05	0.72	0.33
	(−9.99)	(−3.57)	(−2.44)	(−1.12)
Tariffs	3.00	1.05	0.73	0.32
	(−10.47)	(−3.71)	(−2.53)	(−1.16)
Foreign exchange rationing	3.00	0.53	0.17	−0.31
	(−13.42)	(−2.51)	(−0.76)	(1.47)
Fixed urban-rural wage differential	3.00	1.06	0.73	0.33
	(−10.01)	(−3.57)	(−2.48)	(−1.12)

Notes:
[a]Cases of resource growth are: A — 3% growth of capital, labor, and all sector specific factors; B — 3% growth of capital and labor; C — 3% growth of labor; and D — 3% growth of capital. Upper level numbers are Hicksian equivalent income variation in percent of base case income associated with growth; lower level numbers in parentheses are percent change in the terms of trade which fully offset resource growth.
[b]Distortions include: export taxes, tariffs, import quotas, fixed exchange rate, rent seeking, and a fixed urban–rural wage differential.
[c]A reversal in the pattern of trade occurs with growth in this case.

numbers in parentheses give the percentage changes in the terms of trade needed to offset the effects of growth.

Three percent growth in all factors results in a 3% improvement in welfare, as shown in the results for Case A in Table 2. However, a larger deterioration in the terms of trade is required to offset this growth in resources when the economy has, rather than does not have, distortions (−23.08% versus −9.99%). A similar pattern is obtained for policy regimes with tariffs and rationed foreign exchange (−10.47% and −13.42%). These results clearly indicate that the decline in the terms of trade needed to offset growth has to be larger when endogenous protection exists, because of the induced secondary benefit from a lower terms of trade.

The welfare gains reported in Table 2 also generally follow a general declining pattern moving from Cases A through D, because growth is concentrated on progressively smaller factor bases. However, the occurrence of immiserizing growth becomes more frequent as growth becomes unbalanced in favor of the protected sectors. Thus, under Case D where capital grows by 3% and foreign exchange rationing occurs, we obtain a result showing immiserizing growth (−0.31%). Immiserizing growth is also obtained when all distortions are present and either labor or capital is increased by 3% (−0.28% and −0.76%, respectively for Case C and Case D). The explanation for this is that as growth occurs and real income increases, the demand for imports also expands, tightening the rationing process in foreign exchange. This, in turn, heightens the level of protection, increasing inefficiency in the economy. Thus, as we argue above, immiserizing growth in the sense of Johnson is more likely if levels of protection are endogenously determined due to physical or foreign exchange quotas.

4. Summary and Concluding Remarks

This chapter focuses on immiserizing growth in the two senses of Bhagwati (1958) and Johnson (1967), and how both the likelihood that either may occur and its extent can be affected by the presence of endogenous protection; i.e., quota and other forms of protection for which the *ad valorem* equivalent level of protection is endogenously determined.

We use a general equilibrium model of the Philippines due to Clarete (1984) to compute counterfactual equilibria involving changes in domestic policies, terms of trade, and resource endowments. When distortions include endogenous protection in the form of import or foreign exchange rationing, results indicate that a terms-of-trade decline is accompanied by a reduction in the level of protection through quota or foreign exchange premia. This secondary benefit (or induced trade liberalization) tends to make immiserizing growth in the sense of Bhagwati less likely because the terms-of-trade fall required to offset the growth of resources has to be significantly larger than if no distortions were in the model. However, the induced changes in protection work in the opposite way when immiserization in the sense of Johnson is considered. As unbalanced growth occurs focused on the factor-intensive in the protected sector, resources are drawn out of the export sector and export earnings decline and, if the level of protection is endogenously determined, the welfare costs of protection increase. Thus, immiserizing growth in the sense of Johnson tends to be more likely if endogenous protection of the type we discuss is present.

References

Bertrand, T and F Flatters (1971). Tariffs, capital accumulation, and immiserizing growth. *Journal of International Economics*, **1**, 453–460.

Bhagwati, J (1958). Immiserizing growth: A geometrical note. *Review of Economic Studies*, **25**(3), 201–205.

Bhagwati, J (1968). Distortions and immiserizing growth: A generalization. *Review of Economic Studies*, **35**(104), 481–485.

Bhagwati, J (1982). Lobbying, DUP activities and welfare: A response to Tullock. *Journal of Public Economics*, **19**(3), 395.

Bhagwati, I and TN Srinivasan (1983). *Lectures on International Trade*. Cambridge, MA: The MIT Press.

Clarete, RL (1984). The cost and consequences of trade distortions in a small-open economy: An illustration with Philippine tariffs. PhD dissertation, Economics Department, The University of Hawaii, Honolulu.

Clarete, RL and I Roumasset (1987). A Shoven–Whalley model of a small open economy: An illustration with Philippine tariffs. *Journal of Public Economics*, **32**, 247–261.

Clarete, RL and J Whalley (1988). Interactions between trade policies and domestic distortions in a small open developing country. *Journal of International Economics*, **24**, 281–598.

Clarete, RL and J Whalley (1991). Foreign exchange premia and non-neutrality of monetary policy in general equilibrium models. *Journal of International Economics*, **30**(1–2), 153–166.

de Dios, N (ed.) (1984). *An Analysis of the Philippine Economic Crisis*. Philippines: University of the Philippines Press.

de Melo, J (1978). Estimating the costs of protection: A general equilibrium approach. *The Quarterly Journal of Economics* XCII, **2**, 209–226.

de Melo, J (1988). Computable general equilibrium models for trade policy analysis in developing countries: A survey. *Journal of Policy Modeling*, **10**(4), 469–503.

Dervis, K, JD Melo and S Robinson (1981). A general equilibrium analysis of foreign exchange shortages and adjustment mechanisms in a developing economy. *Economic Journal*, **91**, 891–906.

Dervis, K, JD Melo and S Robinson (1982). *General Equilibrium Models for Development Policy*. Cambridge: Cambridge University Press.

Habito, CF (1984). Equity and efficiency trade-offs in Philippine tax policy analysis: A general equilibrium approach. Unpublished PhD dissertation (Harvard University, Cambridge, MA).

Hamilton, B, S Mohammed and J Whalley (1984). Rent seeking and the North–South terms of trade. *Journal of Policy Modeling*, **6**, 485–511.

Harris, T and M Todaro (1970). Migration unemployment and development: A two-sector analysis. *The American Economic Review*, **60**, 126–142.

Johnson, HG (1967). The possibility of income losses from increased efficiency or factor accumulation in the presence of tariffs. *Economic Journal*, **77**, 151–154.

Krueger, AO (1974). The political economy of the rent-seeking society. *American Economic Review*, **64**(3), 291–303.

Mansur, A and J Whalley (1984). Numerical specification of applied general equilibrium models: Estimation, calibration, and data, In Applied General Equilibrium Analysis, HE Scarf and JB Shaven (eds.). New York: Cambridge University Press.

Martin, R (1977). Immiserizing growth for a tariff distorted economy. *Journal of International Economics*, **3**(4), 323–326.

Robinson, S (1989a). Computable general equilibrium models of developing countries: Stretching the neoclassical paradigm. Working Paper No. 513, Department of Agricultural and Resource Economics, University of California, Los Angeles, CA.

Robinson, S (1989b). Multisectoral models. Handbook of development economics, HB Chenery and TN Srinivasan (eds.). Amsterdam: North-Holland.

Shoven, J and J Whalley (1972). A general equilibrium calculation of the effects of differential taxation of income from capital in the U.S. *Journal of Public Economics*, **1**.

Shoven, J and J Whalley (1984). Applied general equilibrium models of taxation and international trade. *Journal of Economic Literature*, **22**(3), 1007–1051.

Part III

Regional Trade Agreements

Chapter 11

Geographically Discriminatory Trade Arrangements*

Bob Hamilton and John Whalley[†,‡]
University of Ontario, Canada
[†]*National Bureau of Economic Research (NBER)*

An eight-region numerical general equilibrium model of global trade is used to investigate the impacts of various geographically discriminatory trade policy arrangements (GDAs) on regional trade and welfare. Results suggest that the important factors determining gains and losses in any GDA are such issues as whether initial levels of protection are asymmetric, the relative sizes of participating regions, and the pattern of trade between participating and nonparticipating countries. Results also appear to confirm the implication of Wonnacott and Wonnacott (1981) that the gain from reducing a partner's tariff is typically a more important consideration in evaluating potential benefits from a customs union, than the traditional concerns of trade creation and trade diversion.

1. Introduction

Current concerns among trade policymakers over GDAs reflect a number of different factors. One is that many commentators on trade policy matters are now taking an increasingly pessimistic view on the future of multilateralism under the GAFF. Another is the increasing discussion of geographically discriminatory arrangements as instruments of trade policy.

These raise a number of important issues. Is it true that trading regions can improve on current multilateral GATT arrangements through bilateral or other GDAs? If so, what form are regional groupings likely to take if there is further fragmentation in the GATT, and how do the competing interests of the major industrialized countries come into play in determining

*This chapter was first published in (1985). *Review of Economics and Statistics*, **67**(3), 446–455.
‡We are grateful to seminar groups at the National Bureau of Economic Research and Western Ontario for helpful comments. We wish to acknowledge financial support from SSHRC, Ottawa.

what could happen? Should the GATT continue to operate on its present multilateral basis involving (effectively) only developed countries, and how can developing countries be brought into this trade liberalization process?

In this chapter, a numerical eight-region general equilibrium model of world trade is used[a] to evaluate the impacts on both global and regional trade and welfare of alternative GDAs. The results presented bear on these questions, but are also relevant to theoretical debates on the customs union issue. A recent paper by Wonnacott and Wonnacott (1981) implicitly argues that much of the previous customs union literature[b] may have neglected a significant factor in both explaining customs union formation and analyzing gains and losses to individual countries. They suggest that the major reason any country participates in a customs union is to penetrate the partner's market, and the main source of increased penetration (and the main benefit from participation) comes from the reduction of the partner tariff. Wonnacott and Wonnacott emphasize that in most cases where customs unions are involved, negotiators concentrate almost exclusively on the reduction of the partner tariff.

Our results suggest that in any particular GDA it is usually relatively easy to identify the main considerations in determining both the total size of the joint gain and its division between regions. Whether any individual country gains or loses, for instance, is most heavily influenced by the initial level of protection in the partner country. Traditional trade creation/trade diversion effects come surprisingly low on the list.

2. A General Equilibrium Model of World Trade

The eight-region numerical general equilibrium model of world trade used to analyze impacts of GDAs is based on earlier four- and seven-region global trade modeling efforts in which the second author has been involved. The description here is kept brief since the main focus is on results and the model is described elsewhere; see Whalley (1985).

The model is most easily thought of as a numerical analog of a Heckscher–Ohlin trade model, with the two departures from pure Heckscher–Ohlin form that demand and production function parameters differ across regions, and that products are heterogeneous across regions rather than homogeneous. The model incorporates eight trading regions: the U.S., the EEC, Japan, Canada, Other Developed, New Industrialized

[a]This is an extension of earlier four- and seven-region models due to Brown and Whalley (1980) and Whalley (1985).
[b]See, for example, Berglas (1979), Johnson (1965), Lipsey (1957), and Viner (1950).

(NICs), and Less Developed Countries (LDCs). The size of these regions in the model reflects their relative U.S. dollar GNP for 1977 in the World Bank Atlas.[c]

The model incorporates six products produced in each region: (1) Agriculture and Food; (2) Mineral Products and Extractive Ores; (3) Energy Products (including oil); (4) Nonmechanical Manufacturing; (5) Machinery and Transport Equipment (including vehicles); and (6) Construction, Services, and Other Nontraded Goods. Each of the first five goods are internationally traded, with an assumed heterogeneity by region prevailing across production sources. The sixth commodity is nontraded for all regions.

The same commodity classification is used for trade, domestic production, and final demands, with an approximate concordance adopted between the different classification systems appearing in the basic data used to parametrize the model. Problems of data availability for all regions, plus the dimensions involved in obtaining a general equilibrium solution for an eight-region model, limit the model to six products and eight regions; 48 products in total.

The assumption of product heterogeneity by region (the so-called "Armington" assumption) implies that products are differentiated on the basis of geographical point of production as well as by physical characteristics. Similar products are imperfect substitutes in both demand and production, i.e., Japanese manufactures are treated as qualitatively different products from U.S. or EEC manufactures. This treatment is used both to accommodate the statistical phenomenon of cross-hauling in international trade data, and to exclude specialization in production occurring as a behavioral response in the model.[d] This structure also enables empirically based import demand elasticities to be incorporated into the model specification.

Explicit demand functions for each region are derived from hierarchical CES/LES preference functions, and CES production functions are used.[e]

---

[c]See the discussion in Whalley (1985).

[d]In some of the earlier numerical general equilibrium models where homogeneous products were assumed, large production responses were encountered even for cases where the change in trade policies was quite small. This reflected the limited curvature of production surfaces in these models. The use of the "Armington" assumption on the demand side removes extremes of specialization from the model.

[e]It is important to note that constant rather than increasing returns to scale production functions are used. This issue as it relates to numerical general equilibrium modeling is discussed in Harris (1984) and Whalley (1984).

Producers maximize profits and competitive forces operate such that in equilibrium all supernormal profits are competed away. Trade in newly produced investment goods (investment flows), interest and dividends, and foreign aid also enter the model, with the latter two being treated as income transfers between regions.

The model examines international trade equilibria, where demands equal supplies for all products, and in each region a zero-profit condition is satisfied for each industry, representing the absence of supernormal profits. In equilibrium, a zero external sector balance condition (including investment flows, dividends, interest, and transfers) holds for each region.

Production and demand patterns in each of the regions revolve around the domestic and world price systems. For each product the market price is taken to be the price at point of production. Sellers receive these prices, purchasers (of both intermediate and final products) pay these prices gross of tariffs, NTB tariff equivalents, and domestic taxes. No transportation costs are considered.

An important feature of the model is the structure of substitution possibilities on both the demand and production sides, as represented by the CES and CES/LES functions. The elasticities of substitution in these functions determine price elasticities of goods and factor demands. Because of the product heterogeneity assumption, these elasticities also control import and export demand elasticities for each region.

In production, each industry has a CES value-added production function which specifies substitution possibilities between the primary factor inputs, capital and labor services. No technical change is incorporated, and both factor inputs are assumed immobile between regions. In addition, each industry uses the outputs of other industries (both domestic and imported) as inputs in its own production process. Substitution between intermediate products is incorporated, while fixed coefficients in terms of composite goods are assumed.

Each fixed coefficient requirement is specified in terms of a composite good, which itself is represented by a nested CES function, with elements of the composite (i.e., products identified by geographical point of production) entering as arguments. Substitution occurs between comparable domestic and composite imported commodities at the top level of nesting, with further substitution taking place between import types differentiated by location of production.

On the demand side, final demand functions are used for each region, derived from nested CES/LES utility functions. A hierarchy of substitution possibilities is used, involving similar products imported from the various regions and composites of imports across sources and comparable domestic products. Use of these nested functions enables empirical estimates of price and income elasticities in world trade to be incorporated into the model. These values guide parameter choice for elasticity values in the nested CES functions (i.e., between similar products subscripted by location of production). The LES features allow income elasticities in import demand functions to differ from unity.

Since each region generates demands from utility maximization, the market demand functions in the model satisfy Walras' Law, i.e., that at any set of prices the total value of demands equals the total value of incomes. The incomes of regions are derived from the sale of primary factor endowments, plus transfers received (including foreign aid).

The model incorporates tariffs and nontariff barriers (NTBs) in *ad valorem* equivalent form, along with domestic tax policies. Other domestic distortions, such as those in labor and capital markets, are ignored. Impacts of various GDAs can be considered by computing equilibria associated with alternative policy regimes.

The procedures used in applying the model are summarized in Whalley (1985). A worldwide general equilibrium constructed from 1977 data is assumed in the presence of existing trade policies in all regions. The model is calibrated to this data set through a procedure which determines parameter values for the model functions consistent with this equilibrium observation. Counterfactual analysis then proceeds for any specified policy change. A counterfactual equilibrium for a policy or other change is found using a Newton method involving an estimate of the Jacobian matrix of excess factor demands and government budget imbalances.

This calibration procedure first involves constructing a data set for a given year in a form which is consistent with the equilibrium solution concept of the model; a "benchmark equilibrium data set." Once assembled, parameter values for equations can be directly calculated from the equilibrium conditions using the calibration procedure described in Mansur and Whalley (1984). Since the model specification must be capable of reproducing the benchmark data as equilibrium solution, this calibration procedure requires more information than contained in the benchmark equilibrium data set when CES/LES functional forms are used. This is met by specifying elasticities of substitution and minimum requirements in the functional forms. Once these are chosen, demand functions are solved for share parameters consistent with both equilibrium prices and quantities.

On the supply side, cost functions are similarly solved for share and unit parameters consistent with equilibrium prices and input use by industry.

As might be expected, the values chosen for substitution elasticities have a substantial impact on the results produced by the model, and so a central case model specification is adopted around which sensitivity analysis can be performed. Given the present focus on effects of changes in trade policies, an especially important set of parameters are the substitution elasticities which determine trade elasticities. Import price elasticities for developed countries in the model reflect the Stern *et al.* (1976) compendium of trade elasticities, and estimates for developing countries are due to Khan (1974). Estimates for the U.S., EEC, and Japan by Stone (1979) provide detailed estimates by product, and are approximately consistent with the values used in the model. The low values (in absolute terms) of import price elasticities produced by these and other studies have been extensively commented on in the literature. In the present model, these produce significant terms of trade effects under alternative GDAs, and their role should thus be highlighted.

3. Results

We consider a number of bilateral trade arrangements each involving various combinations of the regions identified in the model. Counterfactual equilibria under these alternative policy regimes are computed and compared to the 1977 benchmark equilibrium. We focus on the annual welfare effects by region as measured by Hicksian equivalent variations in 1977 billions of dollars, and on regional terms of trade effects. We initially concentrate on free trade areas to abstract from the terms of trade effects which may accompany the adoption of common external protection.

In Table 1, results are reported for a series of two-region free trade areas, each involving the U.S. This series of free trade areas is somewhat arbitrarily chosen from the many combinations of regions which can be considered with the model. Although all protection is bilaterally removed in these cases, we have also considered comparable cases in which we eliminate only tariffs. These are not reported due to space constraints.

In the U.S.–EEC case, the U.S. receives a welfare gain, the EEC a somewhat smaller gain, while most other regions lose. The terms of trade effects are positive for the U.S., and small negative for the EEC. The single most important factor determining the outcome in this particular case is

Table 1. Results for a Series of Bilateral Free Trade Areas (FTAs) Involving the U.S. (All Protection Bilaterally Removed).

	U.S.–EEC FTA	U.S.–Japan FTA	U.S.–Canada FTA	U.S.–Other Dev. FTA	U.S.–NIC FTA	U.S.–LDC FTA
(A) Annual Welfare Impacts (EVs in $billions, 1977)						
U.S.	5.1	2.8	0.6	2.0	8.1	8.0
EEC	0.7	0.0	−0.2	−0.9	−0.4	−1.0
Japan	0.2	1.2	−0.1	−0.1	−0.4	−0.3
Canada	−0.4	−0.3	1.3	0.0	0.2	0.0
Other Dev.	−2.6	−1.5	0.0	0.5	0.0	0.5
OPEC	0.1	0.0	0.0	0.0	−0.1	−0.5
NIC	−0.9	−0.5	−0.2	0.0	−2.9	0.6
LDC	−1.8	−1.2	−0.1	−0.2	0.0	−0.2
(B) Terms of Trade Impacts (% change, positive indicates improvement)						
U.S.	2.5	1.4	0.0	0.7	3.4	3.6
EEC	−0.3	0.0	−0.1	−0.4	−0.1	−0.5
Japan	0.2	0.1	−0.1	0.0	−0.4	−0.2
Canada	−0.8	−0.6	0.7	−0.1	0.2	−0.2
Other Dev.	−1.2	−0.7	0.0	−0.2	0.0	0.2
OPEC	0.2	0.1	0.1	0.1	−0.1	0.2
NIC	−0.6	−0.4	−0.1	0.0	−6.4	0.3
LDC	−1.0	−0.7	0.0	−0.1	−0.1	−4.6

differences in the initial levels of protection in the U.S. and the EEC, particularly the higher NTB's on agricultural products in the EEC. The terms of trade effects are explained primarily by the U.S. penetration of EEC markets as the EEC removes its agricultural NTBs against the U.S.[f] A comparable pattern occurs in the U.S.–Japanese case, where significant gains also occur for the U.S., with smaller gains for Japan and small terms of trade improvement. Again, the asymmetries in initial levels of protection, particularly in the NTBs, are a dominant factor in determining the outcome.

In the U.S.–Canadian case, most of the gains go to Canada since Canada is a small region relative to the U.S. This accord with the intuition that the relative size of regions can also be a dominant factor in determining the division of gains from a free trade arrangement. The U.S. gains in this case because of the removal of NTB's in Canada; where tariffs alone are eliminated bilaterally, the U.S. loses.

[f] In other results for a U.S.–EEC free trade area (not reported here) where only tariffs are removed and agricultural NTBs remain unchanged, the terms of trade effect for the EEC becomes positive.

In the U.S.–Other Developed case, once again, asymmetries in the initial levels of protection are the dominant consideration in determining who gains and who loses. The Other Developed region includes the smaller GATT members (e.g., Australia, New Zealand, Austria) who have higher levels of protection than larger countries such as the U.S. In the two final cases in Table 1, involving free trade between the U.S. and NICs and the U.S. and LDCs, the importance of these asymmetries in the initial levels of protection become even clearer. In these cases both the NICs and LDCs, which are sharply more protectionist than the U.S., have a significant terms of trade loss, and the U.S. a marked terms of trade gain.

In each of these cases the U.S. experiences gains of varying sizes. However, rather than trade creation/trade diversion effects being the important consideration, the initial levels of protection in the regions participating in the free trade arrangement, and differences in relative sizes of regions, principally determine gains and losses.

In Table 2, further free trade areas are evaluated. In the EEC–Japanese case, where the initial levels of protection are more symmetric than in the U.S. cases, both the EEC and Japan gain, with a slightly larger terms of trade improvement for Japan.

Table 2. Welfare Results from Further Free Trade Areas (All Protection Removed Within FTA).

	EEC–Japan FTA	"Northern" FTA (U.S., EEC, Japan, Canada, Other Dev.)	"Southern" FTA (NIC, LDC)
(A) Annual Welfare Impacts (EVs in $billions 1977)			
U.S.	−0.3	5.0	0.0
EEC	0.8	9.5	−0.2
Japan	1.0	2.0	−0.2
Canada	−0.0	2.4	0.1
Other Dev.	−0.7	0.3	−0.1
OPEC	0.0	−0.8	−0.0
NIC	−0.4	−4.8	−0.1
LDC	−0.6	−9.6	3.7
(B) Terms of Trade Impacts (% change, positive indicates improvement)			
U.S.	−0.2	1.4	−0.0
EEC	0.3	2.8	−0.1
Japan	0.8	0.1	−0.2
Canada	−0.1	2.5	0.1
Other Dev.	−0.3	−1.6	−0.1
OPEC	−0.1	−0.6	−0.1
NIC	−0.2	−3.2	−1.4
LDC	−0.3	−5.1	1.4

Results for a "Northern" free trade area (Table 2, column 2) provide some insight on the issue of whether or not countries gain more from multilateral rather than bilateral arrangements. In this case, all five participants in the free trade arrangement improve their welfare by the free trade arrangement. Only the Other Developed suffers a terms of trade deterioration, although they still receive a welfare gain due to the consumption effects associated with the free trade area. The gains to all other participating regions are large. For the U.S., the $5 billion gain is dominated only by a free trade arrangement with the EEC. The $9.5 billion gain to the EEC compares to a $0.7 billion gain from a free trade arrangement with the U.S. The Japanese gain of $2 billion compares to a $1.2 billion gain from a free trade area with the U.S., and Canada also gains more than it would from a free trade arrangement with the U.S.

These results suggest that a major effect of the GATT is an improvement in the terms of trade of developed countries with NICs and LDCs. GATT trade liberalization stimulates trade in manufactured products among developed countries, and developed countries improve their terms of trade with exporters of agricultural products and raw materials (LDCs).

The final column of Table 2 examines a Southern free trade area between NICs and LDCs. In this case, NICs participating in the free trade area suffer a welfare loss. NICs are a significant importer of raw materials and agricultural products from LDCs, while LDC imports from NICs are much smaller. LDCs increase their penetration of NIC markets more than NICs increase their access to LDC markets. This result emphasizes that a third consideration, the initial pattern of trade between the participating regions, can also be crucial in determining results, as well as asymmetries in initial levels of protection or size of regions.

In Table 3, we examine the U.S.–Canadian case in more detail, emphasizing the importance of factors beyond trade creation and trade diversion in determining regional gains or losses from GDAs. The first column reports the same U.S.–Canadian free trade arrangements as considered in Table 1, the abolition of all protection. The second column reports results of abolition of only tariffs. As already mentioned, the U.S. suffers both a terms of trade and welfare loss in this case. Subsequent columns investigate the impacts of using alternative common levels of external protection in the GDA, on regional gains or losses.

In the U.S.–Canada customs union case, where only tariffs are eliminated and the common tariff is set at U.S. rates, welfare effects are

Table 3. Further Investigation of U.S.–Canadian Trade Arrangements.

	U.S.–Canada FTA[a] all protection	U.S.–Canada FTA tariffs only	U.S.–Canada CU[b]-tariffs-common tariff U.S. rates	U.S.–Canada CU-all protection-common protection U.S. rates	U.S.–Canada CU-tariffs common-tariff Canadian rates	U.S.–Canada CU-all protection-common protection Canadian rates	U.S.–Canada CU-all protection-10% common external protection	U.S.–Canada CU-all protection 20% common external protection	U.S.–Canada CU-all protection-30% common external protection
(A) Annual Welfare Impacts (EVs in $billions, 1977)									
U.S.	0.6	−0.6	−0.7	0.4	1.6	2.8	0.0	8.2	14.9
EEC	−0.2	−0.1	0.0	0.1	−1.2	−1.3	1.0	−1.9	−4.5
Japan	−0.1	−0.1	−0.0	−0.1	−0.8	−0.9	−0.2	−1.9	−3.3
Canada	1.3	1.1	1.0	1.1	1.1	1.3	1.1	1.9	2.4
Other Dev.	0.0	0.0	0.1	0.0	−0.4	−0.4	0.4	−0.2	−0.7
OPEC	0.0	0.0	0.0	0.0	0.0	−0.1	−2.0	−4.7	−7.1
NIC	−0.2	−0.0	0.0	0.0	−0.4	−0.5	3.1	0.8	−1.2
LDC	−0.1	0.0	−0.0	−0.2	−0.0	−0.2	2.3	1.5	1.3
(B) Terms of Trade Impacts (% change, positive indicates improvement)									
U.S.	0.0	−0.4	−0.5	−0.1	1.0	1.5	−0.9	4.5	9.6
EEC	−0.1	−0.1	0.0	0.1	−0.5	−0.5	0.4	−0.8	−1.9
Japan	−0.1	−0.1	−0.1	−0.1	−0.9	−0.9	−0.3	−1.9	−3.3
Canada	0.7	1.8	1.4	−0.1	1.8	0.7	−0.1	1.6	3.1
Other Dev.	0.0	0.0	0.0	−0.0	−0.1	−0.2	0.1	−0.1	−0.3
OPEC	0.1	0.0	0.0	0.0	0.1	0.1	−1.4	−2.8	−4.3
NIC	−0.1	−0.0	0.0	0.0	−0.2	−0.3	2.0	0.5	−0.9
LDC	0.0	0.0	0.0	−0.0	−0.1	−0.1	1.4	0.9	0.3

[a]FTA = Free Trade Area.
[b]CU = Customs Union.

comparable to the free trade arrangement with tariffs only. However, where the common protection is set at Canadian levels, a sharp gain accrues to the U.S. with a larger gain to Canada. These results occur because when U.S. protection is raised to Canadian levels, Canada (being the relatively smaller country) gains from the higher protection in the U.S., and further penetrates the U.S. market. In the all protection case, setting common external protection at either U.S. or Canadian levels also makes a major difference to the size of gains or losses. A terms of trade deterioration occurs for the U.S. with common protection set at Canadian rates.

The final three columns emphasize how the level of common external protection in a customs union can sharply affect the size of regional gains or losses. Varying common external protection between 10% and 30% increases the welfare gain to the U.S. from a customs union with Canada in the all protection case from \$0 to \$14 billion, with the latter case resulting in a terms of trade improvement of nearly 10%. The impact of the level of common external protection on the terms of trade for Canada also shows through in these cases.

We conclude from this table that the usual focus in the customs union literature on trade creation and trade diversion effects not only neglects the important issue of the initial level of partner protection, but also neglects the potential for joint terms of trade improvement through common external protection. This in turn suggests that while the threat to multilateralism in the GATT from bilateral free trade arrangements may be small, the threat from groups of countries breaking away and forming customs unions who then exploit common external protection for a terms of trade gain may be more pronounced.

Table 4 reports impacts on trade flows for the U.S.–EEC bilateral free trade arrangement considered earlier, and reveals some of the difficulties in separately identifying trade creation and trade diversion effects from GDAs. This table emphasizes the differences between general equilibrium calculations of the effects of GDAs in which all effects, including terms of trade changes, are captured, and the partial equilibrium analyses in theoretical literature which abstract from terms of trade effects. In the U.S.–EEC free trade area case, for example, there is an increase in imports by the U.S. from the EEC of approximately \$6 billion. However, because of the trade balance condition, the import change column for the EEC is completed by a series of negatives, and the column for the U.S. by a series of positives. Because of the change in relative prices it becomes difficult to

Table 4. Impacts of Geographically Discriminatory Arrangements on Trade Flows (Changes in Trade Flows in 1977 $billions).

U.S.-EEC free trade (all protection)								
Exporting Region	Importing region							
	U.S.	EEC	Japan	Canada	Other Dev.	OPEC	NIC	LDC
U.S.	0.0	9.7	−0.4	−0.4	−0.7	−0.4	−0.5	−0.6
EEC	5.8	0.0	0.1	0.1	−0.6	0.3	0.1	0.0
Japan	0.6	−0.2	0.0	0.0	−0.2	0.0	0.0	−0.2
Canada	0.7	−0.5	0.0	0.0	0.0	0.0	0.0	0.0
Other Dev.	0.8	−2.1	0.3	0.1	0.0	0.2	0.1	0.1
OPEC	0.8	−0.4	0.0	0.0	−0.2	0.0	−0.1	−0.2
NIC	0.7	−0.9	0.0	0.0	−0.1	0.0	0.0	0.0
LDC	0.7	−1.2	0.2	0.0	0.0	0.2	0.0	0.0

separately identify the trade creation and trade diversion effects from these numbers alone.

An understandable concern with the approach used here is that the particular numerical specification in the model may be crucial for results. This issue is investigated in Table 5. In these sensitivity analyses, we focus on the U.S.–EEC free trade area case from Table 1 and vary elasticities from the values used in the central case specification of the model. Central case welfare and terms of trade results from Table 1 are given in the final column on the right-hand side of the table.

Varying elasticities of substitution for import types from the central case values (in the neighborhood of 1) between 1.5 and 5 for all products in all regions sharply increases the welfare gains and terms of trade improvements which accrue to the EEC and the U.S. This occurs because the key margin of substitution in a free trade area is between the geographically subscripted products. The larger is this elasticity, the larger the substitution effect in favor of partners in the free trade arrangement.

On the other hand, varying the elasticity of substitution between composite imports and domestic products can change results the other way. If the elasticity of substitution between domestic and imported products is set at 0.75, the terms of trade improvement for the EEC in the central case changes to a terms of trade deterioration. The terms of trade improvement for the U.S. is larger in this case because in the central case the import price elasticity in the U.S. is larger than in the EEC. The use of a common 0.75 value thus removes the effect of the difference across regions.

Table 5. Sensitivity Analysis for U.S.–EEC Free Trade Area (All Protection).[a]

	Elasticity of substitution between import types set at 3.0 all regions	Elasticity of substitution between import types set at 5.0 all regions	Elasticity of substitution between domestic products and imports set at 0.75 all regions	Elasticity of substitution between domestic products and imports set at 1.5 all regions	Elasticity of substitution between domestic products and imports set at 3.0 all regions	Import income elasticity = 0.9 for regions 1–6, 1.1 for regions 7,8	Import income elasticity = 0.75 for regions 1–6, 1.25 for regions 7,8	Import income elasticity 1.5 for all regions	Central case
(A) Annual Welfare Impacts (EV's in $billions, 1977)									
U.S.	9.2	12.5	9.6	5.8	3.3	5.2	5.1	4.8	5.1
EEC	2.6	3.3	−0.2	−0.8	−0.5	0.9	1.3	0.4	0.7
Japan	0.1	0.2	−0.4	0.0	0.6	0.2	0.2	0.1	0.2
Canada	−1.4	−2.1	−1.7	−0.4	0.4	−0.4	−0.4	−0.4	−0.4
Other Dev.	−5.2	−6.9	−3.5	−1.4	−0.1	−2.7	−2.8	−2.3	−2.6
OPEC	−0.4	−0.8	0.1	−0.1	0.0	0.1	0.1	0.1	0.1
NIC	−2.7	−4.2	−2.3	−0.7	1.0	−0.8	−0.7	−0.7	−0.9
LDC	−3.9	−5.3	−2.8	−1.3	0.6	−1.7	−1.6	−2.8	−1.8
TOTAL	−1.7	−3.2	−1.3	1.2	5.3	0.7	1.4	−1.0	1.0

(*Continued*)

Table 5. (*Continued*)

	Elasticity of substitution between import types set at 3.0 all regions	Elasticity of substitution between import types set at 5.0 all regions	Elasticity of substitution between domestic products and imports set at 0.75 all regions	Elasticity of substitution between domestic products and imports set at 1.5 all regions	Elasticity of substitution between domestic products and imports set at 3.0 all regions	Import income elasticity = 0.9 for regions 1–6, 1.1 for regions 7,8	Import income elasticity = 0.75 for regions 1–6, 1.25 for regions 7,8	Import income elasticity 1.5 for all regions	Central case
(B) Terms of Trade Effects (% change, positive indicates improvement)									
U.S.	4.5	5.9	5.5	3.0	1.2	2.5	2.3	2.6	2.5
EEC	0.8	1.4	−0.5	−1.1	−1.5	−0.3	−0.3	−0.1	−0.3
Japan	0.1	0.2	−0.4	0.1	0.6	0.3	0.3	0.1	0.2
Canada	−3.0	−4.3	−3.5	−0.8	0.5	−0.8	−0.7	−1.0	−0.8
Other Dev.	−2.3	−2.9	−1.6	−0.6	0.0	−1.1	−1.1	−1.3	−1.2
OPEC	−0.2	−0.6	0.4	0.3	0.3	0.2	0.2	0.2	0.2
NIC	−1.7	−2.5	−1.7	−0.4	0.5	−0.6	−0.6	−0.7	−0.6
LDC	−2.2	−3.0	−1.8	−0.7	0.2	−1.0	−1.0	−1.0	−1.0

[a]The elasticity configuration used in the central case is as follows:
Substitution elasticity between import types is 1.5 for all countries.
Substitution elasticity between domestic and imported products for regions 1–8 are 1.66, 0.9, 0.78, 1.02, 1.02, 0.89, 1.38, 1.28.
Unit income elasticities in demands in all regions.

When the elasticity of substitution between domestic products and import composites is raised, terms of trade effects become more negative for the EEC and smaller for the U.S. because of the change in the relative elasticities between composites of imports and domestic products, and import types. Under changes in import income elasticities, results are relatively unaffected, confirming that the key parameters affecting results in GDAs are those producing the substitution effects between products subscripted by region, rather than income effects.

4. Conclusion

In this chapter, an eight-region numerical general equilibrium model of global trade is used to investigate the impacts of various GDAs on regional trade and welfare. Our analysis is motivated both by the policy concern that pressures for regional fragmentation of existing multilateral trade arrangements are growing, and recent debates in the customs union literature as to the significance of various factors in determining the outcome in any particular union.

Results suggest that the important factors determining gains and losses in any GDA are such issues as whether initial levels of protection are asymmetric, the relative sizes of participating regions, and the pattern of trade between participating and nonparticipating countries, rather than the trade creation/trade diversion issues usually emphasized in theoretical literature. Results also suggest that while the incentives to engage in bilateral free trade areas rather than to participate in multilateral negotiations (such as the GATT) may be small, use of common external protection by participants in a customs union may make participants better off compared to wider multilateral arrangements. Finally, results appear to confirm the implication of the recent paper by Wonnacott (1981) that the gain from reducing a partner's tariff is typically a much more important consideration in evaluating potential benefits from a customs union, than the traditional concerns of trade creation and trade diversion.

References

Berglas, E (1979). Preferential trading theory: The n commodity case. *Journal of Political Economy*, **87**, 913–931.

Brown, F and J Whalley (1980). General equilibrium evaluations of tariff-cutting proposals in the Tokyo round and comparisons with more extensive liberalisation of world trade. *Economic Journal*, **90**, 838–866.

Harris, RG and D Cox (1984). *Trade, Industrial Policy, and Canadian Manufacturing.* Toronto: Ontario Economic Council.

Johnson, HG (1965). An economic theory of protectionism, tariff bargaining and the formation of customs unions. *Journal of Political Economy*, **73**, 256–283.

Khan, MS (1974). Import and export demand in developing countries. *IMF Staff Papers*, **21**(3), 678–693.

Lipsey, RG (1957). Trade diversion and welfare. *Economica*, **24**, 40–46.

Mansur, A and J Whalley (1984). Numerical specification of applied general equilibrium models: Estimation, calibration and data. In *Applied General Equilibrium Analysis*, H Scarf and J Shoven (eds.). New York: Cambridge University Press.

Stern, RM, J Francis and B Schumacher. *Price Elasticities in International Trade: An Annotated Bibliography.* New York: Macmillan Publishing Co. for the Trade Policy Research Centre.

Stone, JA (1979). Price elasticities of demand for imports and exports: Industry estimates for the U.S., the EEC, and Japan. *Review of Economics and Statistics*, **61**, 306–312.

Viner, J (1950). *The Customs Union Issue*, New York: Carnegie Endowment for International Peace.

Whalley, J (1984). Trade, industrial policy, and Canadian manufacturing. *Canadian Journal of Economics*, **18**, 386–398.

Whalley, J (1985). *Trade Liberalization Among Major World Trading Areas.* Cambridge, MA: MIT Press.

Wonnacott, P and R Wonnacott (1981). Is unilateral tariff reduction preferable to a customs union? The curious case of the missing foreign tariffs. *American Economic Review*, **71**, 704–714.

Chapter 12

The New Regionalism: Trade Liberalization or Insurance?[*,†]

Carlo Perroni
University of Warwick, Coventry, U.K.

John Whalley
University of Western Ontario
National Bureau of Economic Research (NBER)

Several of the recently negotiated regional trade agreements contain significantly fewer concessions by the large countries to smaller countries than vice versa. In this chapter, we compute post-retaliation Nash tariffs by region under various regional trade arrangements using a calibrated numerical general equilibrium model of world trade. Regional agreements constrain strategic behavior within each trading area, and in the Customs Union (CU) case, enhance it outside the bloc. Results confirm the intuition that without side payments large–small country regional agreements (such as the Canada–U.S. agreement) would not have occurred.

1. Introduction

The new regionalism that has entered global trade arrangements in the last few years (Canada–U.S., NAFTA, EU accession agreements with Eastern European countries), has received considerable attention in both academic and popular literature.[a] A striking feature of these new regional agreements,

*Earlier versions of this chapter have been presented at seminars at Western Ontario, Warwick, and Exeter, as well as to an NBER Universities International Trade Conference. We are grateful to seminar and conference participants for helpful comments. Financial support from the ESRC during the final stages of this project is gratefully acknowledged. Email: jwhalley@uwo.ca

†This chapter was first published by National Bureau of Economic Research in its series NBER Working Papers 4626.

[a]See the two edited research volumes on the new regionalism from the World Bank (De Melo and Panagariya, 1993) and GATT (Anderson and Blackhurst, 1993). There is also substantial discussion of it in issues of the trade policy journal, *World Economy*; see

which has been noted by a number of authors,[b] is that they appear to have been "one-sided". In both the Canada–U.S. and the NAFTA agreements, the majority of the concessions have been made by the smaller acceding country. These include restraints on their domestic policies affecting patent and royalty arrangements (in pharmaceuticals), energy pricing, security of energy supply arrangements, as well as explicit trade concessions. Domestic policy changes sought by the larger country in smaller countries have also occurred simultaneously with the negotiations and, while not being part of an explicit treaty arrangement, became implicit.[c]

In this chapter, we interpret these characteristics of new regional trade agreements as reflecting smaller countries with little negotiating power seeking safe-haven trade arrangements with larger countries primarily to make their access to large markets more secure. In the resulting agreements, larger countries have been able both to extract a price for their participation in the form of nontrade concessions, as well as to enhance their power in bloc-wide negotiation. As such, we argue that these agreements should be seen as insurance arrangements (with premia paid by smaller countries to large countries) as much as conventional trade liberalization.

This view of the new regionalism contrasts with the more conventional reciprocity-based approach to Free Trade Area (FTA) or CU agreements widely analyzed in theoretical literature. In reality, and as noted in Whalley (1996), various country objectives in negotiating these agreements co-mingle, including the desire to use international commitments to make more secure domestic policy reform, as was the case with Mexico's participation in NAFTA. Where the dominant motive for the small country is to achieve a safe-haven or insurance arrangement, we suggest that without side payments by the small to the large country, such an agreement would likely not have been negotiated.

To develop these arguments, we use a general equilibrium trade model of tariff retaliation and use numerical simulation methods to evaluate recent regional agreements in this light. Our model incorporates seven regions (U.S., Canada, Mexico, Japan, the European Community, Other

---

Bhagwati (1992), Jackson (1993), Sapir (1993), Winters (1992), and the January 1992 symposium on model-based evaluations of NAFTA.

[b]See the discussion of the Canada–U.S. agreements and NAFTA in Whalley (1993), comments in similar vein about the NAFTA outcome in Wonnacott (1993), and discussion of E.C. accession agreements for the Eastern European countries in Winters (1993).

[c]These have included changes in patent protection for foreign pharmaceuticals in Canada and commitments of funds to environmental programs in Mexico.

Western Europe, and a residual Rest-of-the-World), allowing us to capture some of the key regional features of the current global economy, and is calibrated to 1986 intercountry trade flow data and to literature-based trade elasticities. Because of the large dimension involved in computing Nash equilibria in the presence of multiple goods and countries,[d] we limit ourselves to formulations with two goods (importables, exportables) for each country, with the importables being treated as qualitatively different across sources of supply (by exporting country). We compute post-retaliation Nash outcomes in global tariff games under the various restraints on retaliation that regional agreements imply. In the presence of FTAs, we model members as maintaining zero barriers to each other even in a global trade war, although each retaliates separately against non-members. In the presence of a CU, retaliation against third countries takes place via a common external tariff used jointly by all members of the Union.

We illustrate the application of our model to regional agreements by assessing the country gains and losses of the Canada–U.S. Free Trade Agreement of 1988 and by comparing model country welfare effects under Nash tariff retaliation with those from a more conventional trade creation/trade diversion approach. The different country incentives to participate under these two approaches reflect the difference in comparing constrained and unconstrained Nash outcomes on the one hand, and incremental effects of barrier changes relative to the status quo on the other.

Results suggest that for the U.S. it did not pay to conclude a regional agreement with Canada if no side payments were allowed. Even in the case of the formation of a CU, under which there would be more leverage for the U.S. in a tariff war with the European Community and Rest-of-the-World (ROW), losing the opportunity to play strategically against Canada more than offsets this source of gain. On the other hand, since Canada benefits substantially from preferential dutyfree access to U.S. markets in a bloc-wide rather than country-wide trade war, the side payment that the U.S. can demand of Canada more than compensates for such losses. Thus, in a trade war between blocs with side payments within blocs, the U.S. is better off participating in the regional agreement than not. Under this scenario, both large and small countries see it as in their interests to form insurance-based regional blocs, even if the barrier changes relative to the pre-trade war status quo are small.

[d]Also see the discussion of this issue in Hamilton and Whalley (1983).

The plan of the chapter is as follows. In Section 2, we describe the numerical general equilibrium model of tariff retaliation and bargaining that we use to analyze their effects and the data and parameters used to calibrate the model. In Section 3, we present results of numerical simulations. In Section 4, we present our conclusions.

2. A Global Trade Model for the Analysis of Trade Retaliation

To analyze the incentives for countries of different size to enter a regional trade agreement, we use an enlarged version of the retaliatory Nash tariff and trade structure first set out in Johnson (1954) and Gorman (1957) and subsequently expanded on in Hamilton and Whalley (1983), Kennan and Riezman (1990), and Markusen and Wigle (1989). Our contribution here is to compute Nash equilibrium tariff rates in higher-dimensional space than used in previous literature, with a more complex analytical structure and without the restriction to constant-elasticity excess demand forms used in much of the earlier work and with the constraints on retaliation implied by regional trade agreements.

Relative to an unconstrained trade war, the introduction of such constraints produces gains or losses for the countries involved. If losses occur for particular countries, then compensation in the form of side payments or other nontrade concessions may be required for an agreement to proceed. For each of the agreements we analyze, we can trace out the bargaining set, to which we can then apply a bargaining solution concept (Nash). This allows us to analyze the size of side-payments in such cases using a two-stage structure that determines constrained Nash tariff outcomes after side-payments have been made.[e]

The model incorporates seven regions: U.S., Canada, Mexico, Japan, the European Community, Other Western Europe (OWE), and a residual ROW. A number of data sources are used in model calibration, and elasticities adopted are based on literature estimates. Data and elasticity values and sources are set out in more detail in Appendix A.

[e]This is related to the procedures for a two-stage game used by Riezman (1985) and Kennan and Riezman (1990), with the difference here that the formation of regional trade groupings is not endogenous to the game-theoretic structure.

2.1. *Technology and preferences*

The trade model we use is a simplified version of the older competitive numerical models which incorporate internationally differentiated products[f] (referred to as "Armington" trade models), but here, owing to the dimensionality restrictions imposed by optimal tariff calculations, only one good is produced in each region.[g] This implies that, if primary factors are assumed to be internationally immobile, we can represent production as being in fixed supply.

In effect, this specification amounts to a pure exchange economy, where trade offer curves are fully determined by endowments and preferences. A fixed supply of $\bar{S}^j$ a single good is produced in each region $j = 1, \ldots, R$, but consumers in region j demand both domestic output and an aggregate of imports from all other regions. Thus, the supply of exportables by each region is perfectly inelastic, although by an appropriate setting of elasticities in demand functions, trade responses similar to those from models with less-than-perfectly inelastic supply responses can be generated.

We use an LES representation of preferences. For region j's representative consumer, the utility function is

$$U^j(D^j, A^j) = [(b_D^j)^{1/\sigma^j}(D^j - \bar{D}^j)^{(\sigma^j-1)/\sigma^j} + (b_A^j)^{1/\sigma^j}(A^j - \bar{A}^j)^{(\sigma^j-1)/\sigma^j}]^{\sigma^j/(\sigma^j-1)}, \quad \forall j, \qquad (1)$$

where D^j and A^j represent final demands for domestic output and for an import aggregate, respectively. The b^j's are share parameters and σ^j is the elasticity of substitution between domestic production and the import aggregate. $\bar{D}^j$ and $\bar{A}^j$ are LES shift parameters that can be interpreted as subsistence consumption levels.

Consumption of the import composite A^j is a CES aggregate of imports, M_i^j, from all regions $i = 1, \ldots, R$ (other than region j).

$$A^j(M_1^j, \ldots, M_{j-1}^j, M_{j+1}^j, \ldots, M_R^j) = \left[\sum_{i \neq j}(a_i^j)^{1/\mu^j}(M_i^j)^{(\mu^j-1)/\mu^j}\right]^{\mu^j/(\mu^j-1)}, \quad \forall j, \qquad (2)$$

[f] As in Whalley (1985) or, more recently, in Nguyen *et al.* (1993a).
[g] Our choice of a single-good model structure is also dictated by the sparsity of available empirical estimates of income and price trade elasticities disaggregated by product type.

where the a_i^j are share parameters and μ^j is the elasticity of substitution in region j among imports from different regions.

This use of LES preferences allows us to set both income and price elasticities of demand for imports at values other than unity. These utility functions are not restricted to yield constant-elasticity excess demand functions, for which computation of Nash tariffs is simplified and optimal strategies by countries are independent of responses; as noted by Johnson (1954) and Gorman (1957).

2.2. *Market equilibrium (for given tariffs)*

We describe first a competitive equilibrium for this structure given tariff rates in each region and subsequently the computation of Nash equilibria. In this model, global equilibrium involves full market clearing in each country-specific commodity and government budget balance. A property of such an equilibrium is that trade will be balanced for each country. More concretely, if p_D^j denotes the net-of-tariff price of region j's goods (i.e., the domestic price in region j), t_i^j the *ad valorem* tariff rate on imports by region j from region i, and Y^j is disposable income in region j; the latter is equal to the sum of the value of output and tariff revenues.

$$Y^j = p_D^j \bar{S}^j + \sum_{i \neq j} t_i^j p_D^i M_i^j, \quad \forall j. \tag{3}$$

Domestic demand for domestic production is given by

$$D^j = b_D^j \frac{Y^j - p_D^j \bar{D}^j - p_A^j \bar{A}^j}{[b_D^j (p_D^j)^{1-\sigma^j} + b_A^j (p_A^j)^{1-\sigma^j}](p_D^j)^{\sigma^j}} + \bar{D}^j, \quad \forall j, \tag{4}$$

where p_A^j is the gross-of-tariff price of region j's import aggregate:

$$p_A^j = \left\{ \sum_{i \neq j} a_i^j [(1 + t_i^j) p_D^i]^{1-\mu^j} \right\}^{1/(1-\mu^j)}, \quad \forall j. \tag{5}$$

Export supply for region j is then

$$X^j = \bar{S}^j - D^j, \quad \forall j. \tag{6}$$

Given domestic demand for the import aggregate in region j,

$$A^j = b_A^j \frac{Y^j - p_D^j \bar{D}^j - p_A^j \bar{A}^j}{[b_D^j (p_D^j)^{1-\sigma^j} + b_A^j)(p_A^j)^{1-\sigma^j}](p_A^j)^{\sigma^j}} + \bar{A}^j, \quad \forall j, \tag{7}$$

import demands for good i (from region i) by region j are

$$M_i^j = A^j a_i^j \left[\frac{p_A^j}{(1+t_i^j)p_D^i} \right]^{\mu^j}, \quad i \neq j. \tag{8}$$

Total demand for region i's exports is then given by

$$I_i = \sum_{j \neq i} M_i^j, \quad \forall i. \tag{9}$$

International market clearing requires equality between export supplies from each region and total import demands for the product in all other regions:

$$X^i = I_i, \quad \forall i. \tag{10}$$

A global equilibrium in this structure is thus given by values p_D^j, p_A^j, Y^j, $D^j, A^j, X^j, \forall j, M_i^j, i \neq j$, and $I_i, \forall i$, which satisfy Eqs. (3)–(10). Computation is straightforward, and for any given change in tariff rates by region, such as that occurring as a result of regional trade agreements, new equilibria can be computed.

2.3. *Computation of noncooperative tariff equilibria*

To evaluate the effects of a regional trade agreement relative to an unconstrained noncooperative global outcome, we also compute Nash tariff equilibria; both unconstrained and constrained through the application of various trade agreements. A bilateral Canada–U.S. Free Trade Agreement, for instance, is modeled as a bilateral restriction that allows both countries to play noncooperatively with other countries, while they maintain tariffs against each other at zero.

Computation of Nash tariff equilibria was first discussed by Johnson (1954), who noted that in the case where net trade functions are of constant elasticity form, optimal tariff rates for one country are independent of any retaliation by the other country, making computation of Nash equilibria trivial. Subsequent authors, such as Hamilton and Whalley (1983), have noted the constraints that dimensionality impose, once the analysis departs from the simple Johnson formulation. Here, we extend the computation of Nash tariff games in several directions relative to previous literature. With multiple countries and imperfect substitution among sources of imports, the simplifying features of the Johnson formulation no longer hold; and with more than two regions, retaliation can take place against different regions at different levels. Also, using nested LES functional forms implies that excess demand functions are not restricted to the constant-elasticity form.

Computation of Nash tariff equilibria proceeds by sequential computation of optimal tariff rates for each region, holding the other regions' tariff rates constant in each calculation.[h] All of the regions in the model are assumed to play strategically in their tariff setting with the exception of the ROW, who, we assume, offers no strategic response. This assumption is made because the trade policies in the large number of countries belonging to the ROW bloc are not, in reality, coordinated in any meaningful way, implying that the strategic power of each individual country in the ROW bloc is negligible.[i]

In the central-case version of the model, the objective assumed for the tariffsetting authority in each region is welfare maximization for its representative consumer. Individual region welfare maximization is maintained for the analysis of FTAs. For CUs involving groupings of regions in the model, the tariff setting authority is assumed to maximize a linear combination of the welfare of the representative consumers in member countries, with weights proportional to benchmark GNP levels.[j]

We iterate through a sequence of calculations of optimal policy responses by region, moving across regions until we achieve convergence to Nash equilibrium where assumed and actual optimal policy responses are mutually consistent. Successful application of this approach relies heavily on the stability of such equilibria (which, in turn, depends on the monotonicity and slope of reaction functions). As Hamilton and Whalley (1983) found earlier in lower-dimensional space, for the class of functional forms we use here (CES, LES), our experience is that this procedure works well in practice. We also note that this computational procedure does not check for the presence of multiple Nash equilibria.[k]

---

[h]We use the GAMS (Generalized Algebraic Modeling System) numerical optimization software, see Brooke *et al.* (1988).

[i]This assumption is perhaps a little strong, as the ROW includes a number of larger economies such as China, India, and Brazil, although their individual shares in total world trade are small.

[j]Although this appears to be a heuristically appealing rule, it has been shown that under certain conditions it may be optimal for smaller countries to fully delegate tariff setting to larger countries when forming a CU, that is, to have a zero weight in the objective of the tariff-setting authority. See Gatsios and Karp (1991).

[k]For the model parametrizations we use here the reaction functions generated by our model are monotonic, but as Johnson (1954) noted over 40 years ago, multiple equilibria in tariff games can occur even with monotonic reaction functions. We have repeated our

In cases where two or more regions form a regional trade agreement, our computation of Nash equilibria reflects the presence of additional constraints on regions' optimization problems. Regions within FTA have tariffs on trade within the Area frozen at zero. For CUs, external barriers are identical for all members of the Union, in addition to freezing tariffs on trade within the region.[l] We also require that import levies set by all other regions be uniform across exports originating from all members of the Union.[m]

In our model specification, post-retaliation Nash tariffs increase sharply as import demand elasticities approach unity (in absolute value), since they are inversely related to import demand elasticities (and hence also to export supply elasticities). With the Armington treatment in preferences adopted here, two levels of substitution are involved; one between imports as a composite and domestically produced goods (determined by σ^j), and the other between imports from different origins (determined by μ^j). These two separate substitution elasticities jointly determine import demand elasticities for imports from the various regions and, at the same time, export supply elasticities in all regions.

2.4. *Bargaining and side-payments*

To explore the role of side-payments between members of a trade arrangement as a supporting mechanism for the agreement, we embed the noncooperative Nash equilibrium structure described above within a model of cooperative bargaining under uncertainty. Since no markets in state-contingent claims exist and regions cannot provide each other with full insurance, trade agreements accompanied by side payments provide a way of making inter-country trades across states of the world possible. Thus, to assess both the viability and the impact of a given prospective trade agreement, we seek state-independent, interregional lump-sum transfers, which in combination with the agreement itself, produce an expected utility gain for all participating regions (i.e., a Pareto improvement).

---

computational procedure for a number of model solutions using different starting points, however, without detecting such an occurrence.

[l]A looser arrangement would be one where the CU plays strategically as a single bloc by coordinating its individual members' policies, but no constraints are placed on its external tariffs or on other countries' external tariffs.

[m]The ROW, which does not set its tariffs strategically, is also assumed to conform to this rule. The common tariff rate levied by the ROW on its imports from the CU is set equal to the lowest tariff rate on imports from any member of the CU in the initial equilibrium.

For simplicity, we consider two possible states of the world in the bargaining model: N, in which regions do not engage in strategic tariff setting ("No Trade Wars"); and W, where a full noncooperative Nash outcome prevails ("TradeWars"). We assume that the representative consumer in each region, j, attaches subjective probabilities, π_N^j and π_W^j to each of these states.[n] For simplicity in our analysis, these probabilities are taken as given and hence are independent of trade arrangements. This specification can be interpreted as a very stylized representation of a situation where status quo tariff levels reflect a tacit collusion long-run equilibrium, which could be disrupted by shocks to the system (Riezman 1991).[o] In this interpretation, although a country's participation in a trade war is a matter of active choice, the probability of an outside event's triggering retaliation can be regarded by all countries as being exogenous.

We represent preferences over these two states by means of a linear homogeneous Constant-Coefficient-of-Relative-Risk-Aversion (CCRRA) expected utility function. This takes the form

$$EU^j\big(U_N^j, U_W^j\big) = \left[\pi_N^j (U_N^j)^{1-\rho^j} + \pi_W^j (U_W^j)^{1-\rho^j}\right]^{1/(1-\rho^j)}, \quad \forall j, \tag{11}$$

where U_N^j and U_W^j are utility levels of region j in states N and W, and ρ^j is region j's coefficient of relative risk aversion. Thus, when two or more regions form FTA or CU, expected payoffs are computed by comparing expected utility levels with and without the agreement.

If a particular trade agreement implies losses for some regions, we assume side payments from gaining to losing regions will be needed for the agreement to come into force. C_i^j denotes (positive or negative) transfers from region i to region j.[p] Disposable income in region j, Y^j is then equal to the sum of the value of output, tariff revenues and transfers to and from other regions.

$$Y^j = p_D^j \bar{S}^j + \sum_{i \neq j} t_i^j p_D^i M_i^j + \sum_i C_i^j, \quad \forall j. \tag{12}$$

If a Pareto improvement for all regions in the model is possible through a transfer scheme, such an outcome will typically not be unique: There will

[n] Alternatively, these can be interpreted as weights, reflecting a "partial" reversion to a noncooperative tariff equilibrium (i.e., a weakening of the system rather than a full implosion).

[o] An explicit representation of this idea would require us to depart from our static, one-shot specification and model strategic interaction as a repeated game (which would be computationally forbidding).

[p] It follows trivially that $\sum_i \sum_j C_i^j = 0$.

exist many configurations of transfers that support a Pareto improvement for the participating regions in an agreement, each corresponding to a different distribution of the surplus from the agreement among regions. In order to select one of these configurations, we adopt Nash's (1953) axiomatic bargaining solution concept. Since these transfers have an effect both on trade flows and on other characteristics of noncooperative tariff equilibria, they must be computed in conjunction with all the other variables in the model. A bargaining equilibrium is obtained by computing noncooperative and status quo tariff outcomes for different values of C_i^j and then selecting the values that maximize the Nash product,

$$\prod_{r \in R} (EU^r - \overline{EU}^r), \tag{13}$$

where R is the subset of countries joining the regional agreement, $\overline{EU}^r$ is expected utility for region r in the absence of the agreement, and EU^r is expected utility in the presence of the agreement and side-payments.[q,r]

2.5. *Model data and calibration*

To calibrate the model described above, we use a 1986 data set drawn from a larger data set used by Nguyen *et al.* (1993b). The main features of the data are displayed in the tables in Appendix A. GNP levels for each region (Table A1) are taken from the Penn World Tables. Aggregate bilateral merchandise trade flows for the year 1986 are from UNCTAD bilateral trade data, adjusted for consistency and discrepancies, and summarized in Table A2. Benchmark average *ad valorem* combined tariff and nontariff rates of protection by region as used in the model base case (and also based on Nguyen *et al.*, 1993b) are summarized in Table A3.[s]

We base our model specification of import demand elasticities on the results of several empirical studies, which are summarized in Table A4 and, in turn, based on Marquez (1990). As we note above, trade elasticities,

[q]This first-stage bargaining game thus abstracts from other potentially important aspects of bargaining in trade negotiations, such as the choice of the weights to be used in the tariff setting rule for CUs.
[r]Notice that the Nash bargaining solution is not invariant with respect to transformations of the players' utility functions. In the absence of any economic criterion to guide the selection of a cardinal representation of preferences, our choice of a linearly homogeneous specification appears to be a natural one.
[s]*Ad valorem* equivalent levels of protection by region are difficult to determine with precision. The estimates we use include protective effects of domestic agricultural programs, textile quotas and other VERs, and trade-restrictive practices in services.

and specifically import demand elasticities, are crucial parameters in the determination of Nash tariffs. It is also the case that conclusive evidence as to appropriate values for use in a model such as ours remains elusive, with significant variation across studies. Beginning with Houthakker and Magee (1969), most studies find import income elasticity values above one for all developed countries, with the notable exception of Japan. The estimates obtained by Marquez are also less than unity for LDCs. Own-price elasticity estimates for imports vary widely across studies. Overall, these studies seem to suggest high-elasticity values for the U.S., Japan, and EU countries and lower values for Canada and LDCs. We adopt a central-case configuration of price and income elasticities for the model based on our survey of elasticity studies, supplemented by information on relative country size (Table A5). We subsequently perform sensitivity analysis around this specification by varying elasticities values; this is inevitably limited by the number of potential elasticity configurations.

On the basis of the data and elasticity parameters set out in Appendix A, remaining model parameters are then determined using the calibration procedures described in Mansur and Whalley (1984). The application of calibration methods to our model is straightforward. Given bilateral trade flow and protection data and given import price and income elasticities, we infer parameter values for the elasticity of substitution between imports and domestic production, σ^j, subsistence levels and $\bar{D}^j$ and $\bar{A}^j$, and all share parameters. In the absence of firm empirical estimates for the second-tier "Armington" elasticities (the elasticities of substitution among imports of different origin), we use a value that is 50% higher than the upper-tier elasticities; that is, $\mu^j = 1.5\sigma^j, \forall j$. This reflects the intuition that importables from different regions are likely to be more substitutable for one another than is the case between imports and domestic goods.[t]

3. Model Results

The model described in the previous section has been used to compute competitive equilibria with different tariff rate configurations (reflecting negotiation of regional trade agreements); Nash (post-retaliation) equilibria where trade wars are unconstrained; cases where Nash equilibria and hence trade wars are constrained by prior regional agreements (member countries of a FTA or CU do not retaliate against each other); and, for

[t]This intuition has received some limited support in empirical studies. See Reinert and Shiells (1993).

the sake of comparison, cases where trade wars occur between differing regional groupings. These computed equilibria allow recent regional trade agreements to be evaluated, either by comparison with the base case (status quo) to which the model is benchmarked, or by comparison with noncooperative equilibria to which the world could revert with varying probability links. As noted earlier, in all noncooperative equilibrium computations, we make the assumption that the ROW (in reality an aggregation of a large number of smaller countries) uses no retaliatory tariffs, implying that retaliation is limited to only six regions in the model rather than the seven included.

3.1. *Unconstrained global trade war*

In Table 1, we report model results for a full Nash tariff war involving all six (non-ROW) regions setting their external tariffs strategically, with no prior regional or other trade agreement constraining retaliation. We use the central case elasticity specification of the model and compute tariffs, trade, and other characteristics of the post-retaliation Nash equilibrium.

As can be seen from the results, post-retaliation Nash tariffs are extremely high in this scenario, the more so the larger the country. These high post-retaliation tariffs are a direct reflection of the elasticity values used in the central-case specification of the model,[u] which might nonetheless seem to many to be on the low side. This finding, however, supports the widespread intuition that an all-out global war would be extremely destructive of trade and yield large shocks to individual economies. Thus, in the case of the European Union, tariffs in the range of 900% to 1,000% are generated by the model, with rates around 500% in the case of the U.S.,[v] the difference between these two reflecting the relative importance of trade to GDP in these countries. Much smaller estimates are obtained for Mexico and Canada, which have less retaliatory power than the European Union, the U.S., and Japan.

In the upper panel of Table 2, we report recomputations of post-retaliation Nash tariffs for cases where all trade elasticities are increased by 33%. In this case, post-retaliation optimal tariffs fall substantially: from

[u]The U.S.–Canada Nash tariffs computed by Markusen and Wigle (1989) are much smaller than the ones reported here. Their model, however, is calibrated to demand and supply elasticities, not directly to literature estimates of trade elasticities, as is the case here.

[v]In some cases, such high tariff rates effectively amount to prohibitive import barriers, resulting in reductions in trade flows of almost 100%, although with internationally differentiated products in the model, trade flows can never become zero.

Table 1. Post-Retaliation Nash Equilibrium for the Central Case Elasticity Model Specification.[a]

	Destination							
Origin	U.S.	Canada	Mexico	Japan	EU	OWE	ROW	
(A) *Tariff rates* (%)								
U.S.		123	132	228	931	167	38	
Canada	514		131	226	935	167	44	
Mexico	480	118		223	923	168	48	
Japan	430	118	131		897	168	42	
EU	426	118	131	220		179	49	
OWE	435	118	131	220	890		57	
ROW	481	117	131	235	1013	170		
(B) *Changes in trade flows* (%)								
U.S.		−81	−82	−87	−95	−77	−75	
Canada	−37		+1	+1	−27	−2	+33	
Mexico	−48	−21		−25	−46	−15	+9	
Japan	−79	−54	−56		−77	−52	−39	
EU	−98	−87	−89	−93		−87	−85	
OWE	−24	−12	−13	−21	−43		+18	
ROW	+48	+33	+40	+35	+8	+29		
	Region							
	U.S.	Canada	Mexico	Japan	EU	OWE	ROW	World
(C) *Welfare effects*								
EV(U.S. \$B)	+52.5	−100.2	−32.1	−73.9	+128.4	−131.7	−1051.0	−1208.1
EV (% of income)	+1.2	−25.5	8.5	−5.2	+3.7	−32.2	−10.6	−6.0

[a]The first six regions above are assumed to play strategically against all regions (including the ROW). The ROW is treated as passive and its tariffs remain at benchmark levels (see text for details). Because imports from different regions are treated as imperfect substitutes in the model, each region has differential optimal tariffs across imports from other regions.

nearly 1,000% to around 150% for the European Union. In the lower panel of the same table, we report equilibrium tariffs for a parametrization involving the same higher import price elasticities, but where the second-tier "Armington" substitution elasticities equal the elasticity of substitution between domestically produced goods and the import aggregate. These rates are higher than those in the upper panel (around 400% for the European Union) but still considerably lower than those used in our central-case calculation. These findings emphasize that, given current literature uncertainties as to model elasticity values, all estimates of characteristics

Table 2. Sensitivity Analysis of Post-Retaliation Equilibrium Tariff Rates (%), Higher Uncompensated Import Price Elasticities (+33%).

	Destination						
Origin	U.S.	Canada	Mexico	Japan	EU	OWE	ROW
(A) $\mu^j = 1.5\sigma^j$							
U.S.		66	69	94	144	83	38
Canada	140		68	93	147	84	48
Mexico	135	65		92	147	84	48
Japan	123	64	68		144	84	42
EU	120	64	68	91		86	49
OWE	122	64	68	91	153		57
ROW	129	64	68	96	161	86	
(B) $\mu^j = \sigma^j$							
U.S.		126	146	222	409	138	38
Canada	363		147	227	414	139	44
Mexico	360	128		227	414	140	48
Japan	338	128	147		412	139	42
EU	350	128	147	226		138	49
OWE	356	128	147	228	407		57
ROW	367	128	147	229	428	140	

Notes: μ^j refers to the elasticity of substitution between import types (by region of origin). σ^j refers to the elasticity of substitution between the domestic good and the import composite. In the central case, we assume $\mu^j = 1.5\sigma^j$.

of Nash equilibria reported here have to be taken as indicative of ranges rather than as providing precise estimates.

In Table 1, we report associated impact on trade flows in the Nash tariff equilibrium, showing large reductions in particular bilateral trade linkages, such as those between Canada and the U.S., where high retaliatory tariffs occur in the larger country. In Table 1, we also report the long-run equilibrium welfare effects implied by an unconstrained trade war. Welfare changes are computed with reference to the status quo scenario. In our calculations, the large blocs (the European Union and the U.S.) benefit from unconstrained retaliation, while small countries (Canada and Mexico) experience large losses.

Although the size and even the sign of these impacts are highly dependent on the parameter specification and on our assumptions about retaliation,[w] these results do underscore the notion that a small country

[w]In particular, the finding that large countries gain from a trade war can be attributed in part to the assumption that the ROW does not retaliate.

would be more adversely affected than a large country by a trade war, and that, consequently, large and small countries face differential risk of a reversion to a global retaliatory regime. These results also underscore the point that it is the threat of global trade wars during which small countries would face reductions in access to large-country markets, as much if not more than the hope of achieving reductions in prevailing levels of protection in the larger countries that propels smaller countries into trade negotiations with larger countries.

3.2. *Regional trade agreements*

In Table 3, we report results showing the welfare effects of alternative regional arrangements in the absence of any strategic tariff setting — the conventional approach based on competitive equilibria with different tariff configurations. The effects are generally small. In most cases, all participants in regional arrangements benefit, the more so with CUs than with FTAs. In the few cases where regional participants lose — such as the U.S. in FTA with Canada and the U.S. and European Union with the simultaneous formation of North American and European FTAs — this is a reflection of elasticity parameters and asymmetrical initial protection levels.

The small size of the welfare effects from regional agreements in this table stands in contrast to the large effects using unconstrained Nash outcomes as the reference point. These are shown in Table 4, which reports Nash equilibrium welfare impacts (relative to the 1986 base case) for a number of regional trade agreements, modeled as constrained retaliation in a noncooperative tariff game. The second column, for instance, reports welfare effects under a trade war in the presence of a Canada–U.S. Free Trade Agreement in which Canadian and U.S. tariffs are bilaterally constrained to remain at zero in the war. Large benefits accrue to Canada from this arrangement because of both continued and ever more valuable preferential access to U.S. markets as U.S. tariffs against third parties increase.

Instead of gains to the U.S. (as in Table 3), losses now occur, and the previous large loss to Canada is now converted to a small gain. This small gain reflects not only continued access to the U.S. market, but the added feature that this access is preferential. As barriers rise progressively against suppliers from Japan, the European Union and elsewhere, in the U.S. market trade preferences to Canada becomes progressively more important. It is interesting that the European Union gains from a Canada–U.S. FTA relative to an unconstrained trade war, because the Free Trade Agreement constrains retaliation by the U.S., since there is a significantly lowered tariff

Table 3. Welfare Effects of Alternative Regional Arrangements, No Retaliation Equilibria (Impact of Liberalization Relative to 1986 Benchmark).

	1	2	3	4	5	6	7	8	9
Region	Global Free Trade[a]	Canada–U.S. FTA[b]	Canada–U.S. CU[c]	Mexico–U.S. FTA[b]	Mexico–U.S. CU[c]	North American FTA[b]	North American CU[c]	Simultaneous[d] North American and European FTA[b]	Simultaneous[d] North American and European CU[c]
(A) Hicksian EVs (U.S. $B)									
U.S.	+9.2	−1.6	−1.3	+0.4	+3.6	−1.2	+1.7	−1.8	+3.2
Canada	+4.0	+4.0	+4.3	−0.2	−0.2	+3.9	+4.3	+3.8	+4.6
Mexico	+0.9	−0.1	−0.1	+0.9	+0.9	+0.8	+0.8	+0.7	+0.9
Japan	+9.4	−0.5	−0.6	−0.2	−1.5	−0.7	−2.2	−1.0	−0.8
EU	+22.7	−0.8	−1.2	−0.3	−0.7	−1.2	−1.7	−5.3	−15.9
OWE	+13.2	−0.1	−0.1	−0.04	−0.1	−0.1	−0.2	+8.2	+8.0
ROW	−8.7	−1.1	−0.8	−0.5	−0.9	−1.6	−1.6	−6.0	+6.3
World	+50.8	−0.3	+0.1	−0.06	+1.1	−0.2	+1.1	−1.5	+6.2
(B) Hicksian EVs in per cent of National Income									
U.S.	+0.2	−0.04	−0.03	+0.01	+0.8	−0.03	+0.04	−0.004	+0.1
Canada	+1.0	+1.0	+1.1	−0.04	−0.1	+1.0	+1.1	+1.0	+1.2
Mexico	+0.2	−0.03	−0.02	+0.7	+0.2	+0.2	+0.2	+0.2	+0.2
Japan	+0.7	−0.04	−0.04	−0.01	−0.1	−0.05	−0.2	−0.07	−0.05
EU	+0.7	−0.02	−0.04	−0.01	−0.02	−0.03	−0.04	−0.2	−0.5
OWE	+3.2	−0.02	−0.03	−0.01	−0.02	−0.02	−0.05	+2.0	+1.9
ROW	−0.1	−0.01	−0.01	−0.01	−0.1	−0.02	−0.05	−0.06	+0.06
World	+0.3	−0.001	+0.0005	−0.0003	+0.005	−0.0008	+0.006	−0.007	+0.03

[a] All trade barriers are removed.
[b] In an FTA, tariffs are bilaterally zero among member countries.
[c] In a CU, tariffs are bilaterally zero among member countries, remaining so throughout any retaliatory trade war, and a common external tariff applies to imports from third countries. See text for more details.
[d] North America is U.S., Canada, and Mexico; European implies EU plus Other Western Europe.

Table 4. Welfare Effects in Nash Post-Retaliation Trade War Equilibria in the Presence of Alternative Retaliation Constraining Regional Trade Agreements (Comparison: 1986 Benchmark).

	1	2	3	4	5	6	7	8	9
Region	Unconstrained Trade War[a]	Canada–U.S. FTA[b]	Canada–U.S. CU[c]	Mexico–U.S. FTA[b]	Mexico–U.S. CU[c]	North American FTA[b]	North American CU[c]	Simultaneous[d] North American and European FTA[b]	Simultaneous[d] North American and European CU[c]
(A) Hicksian EVs (U.S. $B)									
U.S.	+52.5	−9.5	+22.1	+22.2	+46.5	−15.3	+18.6	−4.5	+19.6
Canada	−100.2	+5.1	+3.4	−77.4	−101.5	+1.2	+1.5	+13.6	−2.9
Mexico	−32.1	−19.9	−32.2	+7.2	+2.9	−0.3	+0.5	+4.6	−1.2
Japan	−73.9	−33.8	−73.7	−49.2	−74.2	−28.7	−73.6	−17.4	−76.7
EU	+128.4	+142.0	+119.4	+135.0	+125.2	+145.3	+116.6	+38.7	+87.3
OWE	−131.7	−119.7	−135.5	−123.4	−134.7	−118.1	−137.0	+42.3	+41.5
ROW	−1051.0	−879.1	−1082.5	−933.8	−1082.6	−857.9	−1101.9	−461.7	−1330.0
World	−1208.1	−914.8	−1179.0	−1019.8	−1218.2	−873.9	−1175.2	−384.4	−1262.3
(B) Hicksian EVs in per cent of National Income									
U.S.	+1.2	−0.2	+0.5	+0.5	+1.1	−0.4	−0.1	+0.5	+0.1
Canada	−25.5	+1.3	+0.9	−19.7	−25.8	+0.3	+3.5	−0.7	+1.2
Mexico	−8.5	−5.2	−8.5	+1.9	+0.8	−0.07	+1.2	−0.3	+0.2
Japan	−5.2	−2.4	−5.2	−3.9	−5.2	−2.0	−1.2	−5.4	−0.05
EU	+3.7	+4.1	+3.4	+3.9	+3.6	+4.2	+1.1	+2.5	−0.5
OWE	−3.2	−29.2	−33.1	−30.1	−32.9	−28.9	+10.3	+10.1	+1.9
ROW	−10.6	−8.8	−10.9	−9.4	−10.9	−8.6	−4.6	−13.4	+0.06
World	6.0	−4.5	−5.8	−5.0	−6.0	−4.3	−1.9	−6.2	+0.03

[a]Unconstrained trade war involves all regions except ROW adopting optimal bilateral tariffs against each and all trading partners.
[b]In an FTA, tariffs are bilaterally zero among member countries, and remain so throughout any retaliatory trade war.
[c]In a CU, tariffs are bilaterally zero among member countries, remaining so throughout any retaliatory trade war, and a common external tariff is set strategically by the union against third countries. See text for more details.
[d]North America is U.S., Canada, and Mexico; European implies EU plus Other Western Europe.

that Canada applies to third-country markets even in the event of a global trade war between Canada and the U.S. The size of duty-free trade between Canada and the U.S. reflects this.

The last result is reversed, however, if the U.S. and Canada form a CU rather than a FTA, since their retaliatory power against the European Union is now enhanced (third column of Table 4). In the CU case, bilateral tariffs are zero, as in FTA, but a common external tariff now applies against third countries. A surprisingly large difference in the results for the U.S. occurs with this change, with significant benefits to the U.S. and reduced benefits to Canada. The positive benefits for the U.S. reflect the feature that, with a common external tariff, the U.S. can now induce Canada to follow the higher U.S. tariff against third countries. As a result, gains to the European Union in a trade war are reduced. These findings also suggest that the bilateral trade agreement between Canada and the U.S. would not have occurred were it not also accompanied by side-payments, since it would represent a losing proposition for the U.S. compared with a full Nash equilibrium, while it would be a dramatically gaining proposition for Canada.

Table 4 also reports welfare effects under a trade war in the presence of a Mexico–U.S. FTA or Customs Union, as well as a North American FTA or CU. Mexico benefits substantially from these arrangements; and, as in the Canada–U.S. case, the U.S. is better off under a Customs Union than under a FTA. In the absence of side payments, the U.S. is better off entering FTA with Mexico than it is under a U.S.–Canada FTA, because U.S.–Mexico trade flows are smaller than U.S.–Canada flows in our 1986 data set. This implies that the retaliatory power of the U.S. is less affected by a FTA with Mexico than by one with Canada.

North American trilateral arrangements have effects similar to those of the bilateral Canadian and Mexican agreements, except that the benefits of access are now shared by Canada and Mexico, and benefits to the U.S. are lowered. Under a trade war in the presence of a North American FTA, the U.S. loses rather than gains as it would with a CU. Also, the U.S. gains less with a three-way CU than it would in a two-way union with either Canada or Mexico.

Welfare effects of simultaneous bloc enlargements in Europe and in North America[x] are reported in the final two columns of Table 4. The gains

[x]The European trade arrangements considered are more comprehensive than the current EC–EFTA agreement, since the OWE bloc includes countries that do not belong to EFTA.

to the European Union and the U.S. are significantly lower than in a full unconstrained trade war. Also, a trade war with the simultaneous formation of both a North American and a European Customs Union produces a larger negative aggregate welfare effect than an unconstrained trade war.[y]

3.3. *Side-payments and transfers*

We have elaborated on the analyses in Tables 3 and 4 for the Canada–U.S. FTA and CU cases by calculating side payments that would support a Pareto improvement for U.S. and Canada relative to an unconstrained scenario, showing how they further affect the analysis of regional trade agreements. We assume a value for each region for the subjective probability of a trade war's occurring and for the coefficient of relative risk aversion, as discussed in the previous section. We then make a series of calculations to trace out the bargaining sets (i.e., the sets of points that are Pareto superior to the disagreement point) for Free Trade and CU agreements by varying transfers between members, choosing the bilateral agreement between Canada and the U.S. for purposes of illustration.

These bargaining sets are shown in Fig. 1. Point D, the disagreement point, represents the expected payoffs to the U.S. and Canada in the absence of a bilateral agreement, while the expected payoffs from an agreement with no side payments are represented by point A. The solid sections of the curve represent the bargaining sets, while the dashed sections represent constrained efficient points that are not Pareto superior to D. For both FTA and CU, in the absence of side payments the expected payoff to the U.S. is below its reservation expected utility. The Nash bargaining outcome is shown as point Q in Fig. 1. As we note above, in the absence of side payments (point A), the U.S. is better off in CU than in FTA, whereas Canada is almost indifferent between the two. For Canada, this implies lower equilibrium side payments and a higher expected payoff (point Q) in the CU case than in the FTA case.

We also compute side payments associated with a Nash bargaining outcome for different values of the coefficient of relative risk aversion and various values of subjective probabilities of trade wars' occurring (assuming these parameters to be identical across countries). These are reported in

[y]As Kennan and Riezman (1990) have shown, the formation of a CU in a strategic tariff setting has ambiguous welfare effects, whereas the formation of a FTA unambiguously improves world welfare. More recently, Krugman (1991) and Haveman (1992) have described examples where the formation of CUs reduces world welfare.

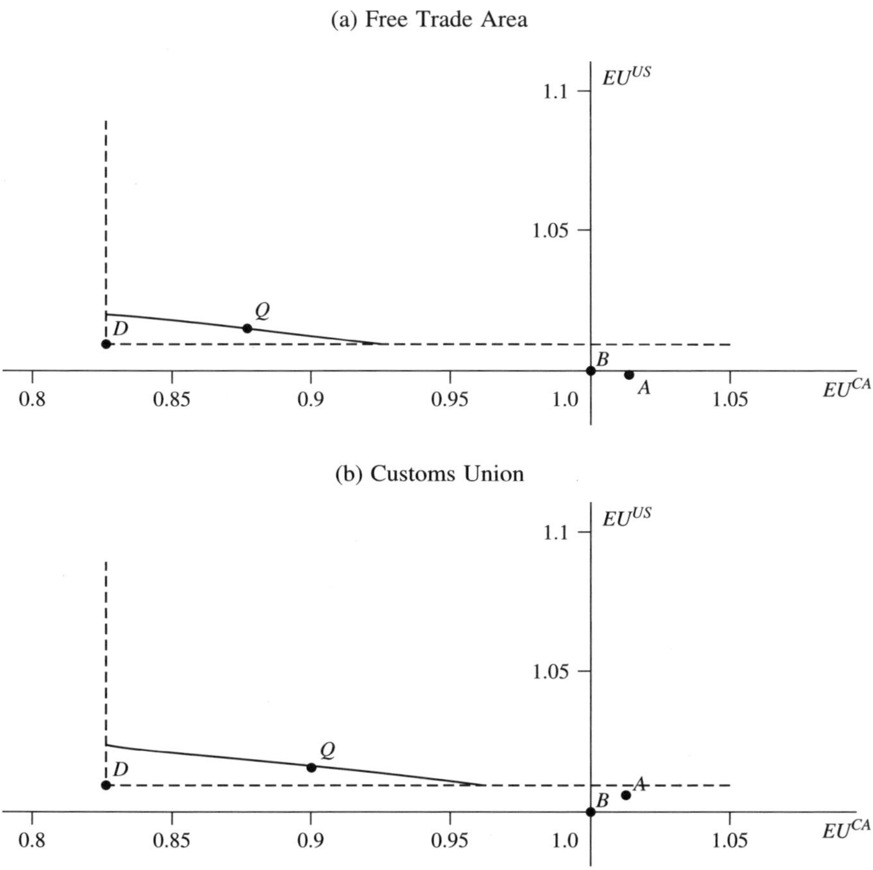

B: 1986 benchmark (no retaliation)
D: unconstrained trade war
A: trade agreement with no side payments
Q: Nash bargaining solution
$\pi_W^{CA} = \pi_W^{US} = 0.5$ (π_W : subjective probability of a trade war occurring)
$\rho^{CA} = \rho^{US} = 1.0$ (ρ: coefficient of relative risk aversion)

Fig. 1. Bargaining sets for alternative Canada–U.S. trade arrangements.

Table 5. The side payment needed to support a CU agreement is smaller than in the FTA case, as would be expected from the results in Table 4, and this difference increases with higher probabilities of a trade war.[z]

[z]Estimating the actual side payments implied by the 1988 Canada–U.S. FTA (and its accompanying process) is difficult, of course, but with stronger patent protection, pricing restraints implied by the energy provisions, and other features in the agreement, implicit

Table 5. Side-Payments from Canada to the U.S. Supporting a Nash Bargaining Model Outcome (per cent of Canada GDP) Central Case Elasticity Model Specification.

ρ	0.25	1.0	5.0	10.0
(A) Free Trade Area				
π_w				
1%	0.6	0.7	0.8	1.4
25%	4.0	4.3	5.8	7.5
50%	7.3	7.6	8.9	10.0
75%	10.4	10.6	11.4	11.8
99%	13.2	13.3	13.3	13.3
(B) Customs Union				
π_w				
1%	0.6	0.6	0.8	1.3
25%	3.3	3.6	5.0	6.5
50%	6.0	6.3	7.6	8.4
75%	8.5	8.7	9.4	9.8
99%	10.8	10.8	10.8	10.8

Notes: ρ: coefficient of relative risk aversion. π_w: subjective probability of the occurrence of a trade war.

These results show that substantial side payments may be required to induce a large trade bloc to accept a new smaller member. Furthermore, since the entry of a small country into a FTA undermines the retaliatory power of its larger partners, the required side payments in the FTA case is larger than under a CU.

4. Concluding Remarks

In this chapter, we use a calibrated model of global trade to examine the incentives for countries of different size to enter into regional trade agreements, computing constrained and unconstrained global Nash equilibria. We also characterize the side payments needed to support agreements. The model covers seven major trading regions and allows us

side payments by Canada to the U.S. in the range of 15 billion dollar per year, representing around 4 per cent of Canada's GDP, may not be an unreasonable estimate. This is based on conjectures circulating at the time of the agreement that firmer intellectual property protection for U.S. firms in Canada might be worth around 5 billion dollar a year. We add to this the value of the guarantee of no differential domestic and export pricing for sales of energy from U.S. company owned leases. Lenjosek and Whalley (1986) report estimates of the rent losses to Canada from eliminating differential energy pricing that range from \$2.5 to \$10 billion U.S. (using 1980 data). Further smaller concessions were made by Canada in the investment screening and security of energy supply areas.

to explore the consequences of various regional trade arrangements, given the risk of trade war. We calibrate our model to literature-based elasticities and share parameters on the basis of 1986 bilateral trade flow data, and compute both competitive and post-retaliation Nash tariff equilibria under various constraints implied by alternative trade agreements. These include Canada–U.S. FTAs and CUs, related Mexico–U.S. and North American arrangements as well as enlargement of the European Union.

More specifically, our model analysis of the 1988 Canada–U.S. FTA suggests that the insurance value to Canada is large, but that it did not pay for the U.S. to negotiate a regional agreement without side payments. This is because, while they may have more leverage with the regional agreement in place in a tariff war with the European Community or the ROW (at least in the CU case), losing the opportunity to play strategically against Canada more than offsets the source of gain. Since Canada benefits substantially from preferential duty-free access to U.S. markets in a bloc-wide rather than country-wide trade war, the side payment that the U.S. can demand of Canada is substantial. The U.S. thus will only participate in a regional bloc if side payments occur, and under the Canada–U.S. agreement both countries saw it as in their interest to sign a trade agreement because of the insurance and side-payment elements involved. We use Nash bargaining to compute side payments and conjecture that the ranges involved in the Canada–U.S. case may not fall too far short of the implicit side-payments accruing with the 1988 Canada–U.S. Agreement.

Similar themes emerge for other regional arrangements, although with nuances. The U.S. is better off in a regional arrangement with Mexico with side-payments than not, and similarly the European Union with Other Western European countries. CUs seem preferred by all members over a FTA, since their joint retaliatory power is increased; but the side payments that can be extracted are typically lower.

The central theme is thus that recent regional trade agreements, which are simultaneously complex and seemingly of little trade-liberalizing substance, are more readily understandable as insurance arrangements with premia than as conventional reciprocity-based trade liberalization, especially since it is the smaller countries who have sought them. We also note that their value to large countries rises as the risk of global trade conflicts rises, because they can extract increasingly larger premia. The threat they present to the stability of the multilateral trading system thus becomes more apparent when viewed in this light than a more conventional assessment might reveal.

Appendix A. Data and Parameter Values Used in the Model

Table A1. 1986 Gross World Product, by Region (U.S. $B).

Region	GNP
U.S.	4,266.500
Canada	393.700
Mexico	378.990
Japan	1,415.380
European Union	3,462.120
OWE[a]	409.370
ROW[b]	9,947.854

[a]OWE denotes "Other Western Europe".
[b]ROW denotes "Rest of the World".
Source: Nguyen *et al.* (1993b).

Table A2. 1986 Bilateral Merchandise Trade Flows between Regions (U.S. $B).

	Destination						
	U.S.	Canada	Mexico	Japan	EU	OWE	ROW
U.S.	—	48.844	11.917	23.864	69.578	8.013	87.453
Canada	50.611	—	0.396	4.244	9.354	0.964	12.482
Mexico	13.441	0.997	—	1.616	5.672	0.487	5.971
Japan	70.748	5.544	1.328	—	38.810	6.427	89.113
European Union	88.477	13.989	4.879	25.856	—	67.774	236.090
OWE	13.492	2.198	0.901	4.621	74.885	—	41.997
ROW	110.882	11.395	2.918	61.925	188.682	19.895	—

Source: Nguyen *et al.* (1993b).

Table A3. Average Rates of Protection by Region, Against Imports from Other Regions (%).

	Destination						
Origin	U.S.	Canada	Mexico	Japan	EU	OWE	ROW
U.S.	—	9.4	19.5	22.7	19.8	13.1	38.5
Canada	8.2	—	23.7	23.5	19.1	14.3	43.9
Mexico	10.2	10.0	—	17.5	18.7	17.2	48.2
Japan	9.3	10.5	18.2	—	18.3	10.3	42.4
European Union	12.3	12.7	22.0	15.3	—	6.9	48.9
OWE	11.4	12.7	20.8	13.1	10.1	—	56.8
ROW and Developing Countries	14.7	14.4	25.3	20.7	22.8	17.3	—

Source: Nguyen *et al.* (1993b).

Table A4. Import Elasticity Estimates: Comparison of Results from Selected Studies.

	A	B	C	D	E	F	G
Uncompensated own price elasticities							
U.S.	−0.54	−1.46	−1.66	−4.8/−8.8	−0.20	−1.2/−3.2	−0.63/−0.92
Canada	−1.46	−0.61	−1.30	−1.2/−2.8	−0.46	0.1/−1.0	−0.33/−1.02
Japan	−0.72	−0.93	−0.78	−1.3/−7.7	−0.33	−0.7/−0.9	−0.28/−0.93
Germany	−0.24	−1.00	−0.88	0.1/−1.9	−0.30	0.5/−1.3	−0.58/−0.60
U.K.	0.22	n/a	−0.65	0/−3.2	0.14	−1.4/−2.4	−0.47/−0.49
Other OECD	n/a	n/a	n/a	n/a	n/a	n/a	−0.26/−0.49
LDCs	n/a	n/a	n/a	n/a	n/a	n/a	−0.34/−0.81
Income elasticities							
U.S.	1.51	n/a	n/a	4.03	1.72	2.01	1.89/1.94
Canada	1.20	n/a	n/a	1.87	1.35	1.82	1.06/1.84
Japan	1.23	n/a	n/a	1.69	1.17	0.41	0.35/0.48
Germany	1.80	n/a	n/a	1.46	1.59	1.49	1.88/2.09
U.K.	1.66	n/a	n/a	2.58	1.12	−1.10	2.09/2.51
Other OECD	n/a	n/a	n/a	n/a	n/a	n/a	2.02/2.03
LDCs	n/a	n/a	n/a	n/a	n/a	n/a	0.38/0.40

A: Houthakker and Magee (1969).
B: Adams and Junz (1971).
C: Stern *et al.* (1976).
D: Wilson and Takacs (1979).
E: Thursby and Thursby (1984).
F: Warner and Kreinin (1983).
G: Marquez (1990).

Table A5. Central Case Specification of Import Elasticities.

Region	Uncompensated own price elasticity	Income elasticity
U.S.	−1.50	1.50
Canada	−0.85	1.25
Mexico	−0.85	1.00
Japan	−1.01	1.00
European Union	−1.25	1.25
OWE	−0.85	1.25
ROW	−0.85	1.00

References

Adams, FG and HB Junz (1971). The effect of the business cycle on trade flows of industrial countries. *Journal of Finance*, **26**, 251–68.

Anderson, K and Blackhurst (eds.) (1993). *Regional Integration and the Global Trading System.* New York: St Martin's Press.

Bhagwati, J (1992). Regionalism versus multilateralism. *World Economy*, **15**, 535–555.

Brooke, A, D Kendrick and A Meeraus (1988). *GAMS: A User's Guide* San Francisco: Scientific Press.

De Melo, J and A Panagariya (eds.) (1993). *The New Regionalism in Trade Policy.* Washington, DC: World Bank.

Gatsios, K and L Karp (1991). Delegation games in customs unions. *Review of Economic Studies*, **58**, 391–397.

Gorman, WM (1957). Tariffs, retaliation, and the elasticity of demand for imports. *Review of Economic Studies*, **25**, 133–162.

Hamilton, B and J Whalley (1983). Optimal tariff calculations in alternative trade models and some possible implications for current world trading arrangements. *Journal of International Economics*, **15**, 323–348.

Haveman, JD (1992). Some welfare effects of dynamic customs unions formation. mimeo, Purdue University.

Houthakker, H and S Magee (1969). Income and price elasticities in world trade. *Review of Economics and Statistics*, **52**, 111–125.

Jackson, J (1993). Regional trade blocs and GATT. *World Economy*, **16**, 121–131.

Johnson, HG (1954). Optimal tariffs and retaliation. *Review of Economic Studies*, **21**, 142–143.

Kennan, J and R Riezman (1990). Optimal tariff equilibria with customs unions. *Canadian Journal of Economics*, **23**, 70–83.

Krugman, PR (1991). Is bilateralism bad? In *International Trade and Trade Policy*, (eds.) E Helpman and A Razin. Cambridge, MA: MIT Press.

Lenjosek, G and J Whalley (1986). A small open economy model applied to an evaluation of Canadian energy policies using 1980 data. *Journal of Policy Modelling*, **8**, 89–110.

Mansur, AH and J Whalley (1984). Numerical specification of applied general equilibrium models: Estimation, calibration and data. In *Applied General Equilibrium Analysis*, (eds.) HE Scarf and JB Shoven. Cambridge: Cambridge University Press.

Markusen, JR and RM Wigle (1989). Nash equilibrium tariffs for the United States and Canada: The roles of country size, scale economies, and capital mobility. *Journal of Political Economy*, **97**, 368–386.

Marquez, J (1990). Bilateral trade elasticities. *Review of Economics and Statistics*, **72**, 70–77.

Nash, J (1953). Two-person cooperative games. *Econometrica*, **21**, 128–140.

Nguyen, TT, C Perroni and RM Wigle (1993a). An evaluation of the Draft Final Act of the Uruguay Round. *Economic Journal*, **103**, 1540–1549.

—— (1993b). Micro-consistent data for the analysis of world trade. Mimeo, University of Waterloo, Canada.

Reinert, KA and CR Shiells (1993). Armington models and terms-of-trade effects: Some econometric evidence from North America. *Canadian Journal of Economics*, **26**, 299–316.

Riezman, R (1985). Customs Unions and the core. *Journal of International Economics*, **19**, 355–366.

—— (1991). Dynamic tariffs with asymmetric information. *Journal of International Economics*, **30**, 267–283.

Sapir, A (1993). Regionalism and the new theory of international trade. *World Economy*, **16**, 423–438.

Stern, RM, J Francis, and B Schumacher (1976). *Price Elasticities in International Trade: An Annotated Bibliography.* London: Macmillan for the Trade Policy Research Centre.

Thursby, J and M Thursby (1984). How reliable are simple, single equation specifications of import demand?. *Review of Economics and Statistics*, **66**, 690–695.

Warner, D and M Kreinin (1983). Determinants of international trade flows. *Review of Economics and Statistics*, **65**, 96–104.

Whalley, J (1985). *Trade Liberalization among Major World Trading Areas.* Cambridge, MA: Cambridge University Press.

—— (1993). Regional trade arrangements in North America: CUSTA and NAFTA. *New Dimensions in Regional Integration* (eds.) J de Melo and A Panagariya. Cambridge: Cambridge University Press.

—— (1996). Why do countries seek regional trade agreements?. NBER Working Paper No. 5552.

Wilson, J and W Takacs (1979). Differential responses to prices and exchange rate influences in the foreign trade of selected industrial countries. *Review of Economics and Statistics*, **51**, 267–279.

Winters, A (1992). Goals and own goals in European trade policy. *The World Economy*, **15**, 557–574.

—— (1993a). The European community: A case of successful integration? In *New Dimensions in Regional Integration.* (eds.) J de Melo and A Panagariya. Washington, DC: The World Bank.

—— (1993b). Expanding E.C. Membership and association accords: Recent experience and future prospects. In *Regional Integration in the Global Trading System.* (eds.) K Anderson and R Blackhurst. Harvester Wheatsheaf for the GATT.

Wonnacott, P (1993). Letter. *Wall Street Journal*, October 1993.

Chapter 13

How Often are Propositions on the Effects of Regional Trade Agreements Theoretical Curiosa?*,†

Lisandro Abrego
IMF

Raymond Riezman
University of Iowa, Iowa

John Whalley
University of Western Ontario
National Bureau of Economic Research (NBER)

This chapter uses computational techniques to assess whether or not various propositions that have been advanced as plausible in the literature on regional trade agreements may actually hold. The idea is to make probabilistic statements as to whether propositions of interest might hold, rather than to restrict assumptions so they unambiguously hold. Our aim is to blend theory and numerical simulation and go beyond the ambiguous analytically derived propositions that dominate the theoretical literature so as to assess the likelihood of propositions holding for particular model specifications.

1. Introduction

In this chapter, we generate repeated model solutions for alternative numerical specifications of a simple (few countries and commodities) general

*We are grateful to the Center for the Study of Globalization and Regionalization at the University of Warwick and the ESRC for financial support and we acknowledge comments at Center seminars. The chapter was mostly written while the first author was a research fellow at the University of Warwick. Jon Eaton, Scott Page, Carlo Perroni, Danny Tsiddon, Chuck Whiteman, Ben Zissimos and a referee have also provided helpful comment and input. An earlier version was presented to a conference on the WTO and World Trade held in Seattle, December 4, 1999, the Ecole de Printemps held in Aix-en-Provence, May 2000 and the CESifo conference on Globalization, Inequality and Well-Being, November 2002. We thank participants in these conferences for useful comments.
†This chapter was first published in (2006). *Journal of International Economics*, **68**(1), 59–78.

equilibrium trade model so as to map out the extent of the parameter space for which each of a series of propositions regarding CUs is true.[a] The idea is to blend theory and numerical simulation, in contrast to theoretical work in this area which sets out assumptions under which propositions unambiguously hold, and demonstrates their validity using analytical techniques. Here we take a different approach of trying to determine the frequency with which various results hold so as to obtain an indication of which statements are more likely to hold and which not.

We apply the techniques we develop to the analysis of various propositions in the customs union (CU) literature because despite nearly 50 years of research on regional trade agreements, which originates with Viner's (1950) work on CUs, no set of generally accepted propositions regarding the effects of regional trade agreements has yet emerged to guide policy makers and public officials. Whether individual countries necessarily gain by entering a CU is unproven, and the use of alternative reference points, such as free trade or noncooperative Nash, only further clouds the picture. Whether world welfare is higher under a CU is also unknown, as is whether CUs generate higher external tariffs compared to a noncooperative Nash equilibrium in tariffs. Other propositions are widely thought to be true, but without explicit confirmation; such as that CUs generally improve the terms of trade of member countries; and that non-member countries prefer that no CU be formed against them.

Specifically, we consider a three-country, three-good, pure exchange model with CES preferences, and use both random draws and a grid search over the space defining preference parameters and endowments. We compare both free trade and three-country noncooperative (Nash) equilibria to partial cooperation regional agreement equilibria where two countries form a regional agreement and play noncooperatively against the third country (CU). If we assume uniform prior over the parameter space (admittedly a strong assumption) and then calculate the percentage of cases for which certain results hold, our sample frequencies can be interpreted as

[a]This differs from previous work on systematic sensitivity analysis for general equilibrium models due to Pagan and Shannon (1986) and Harrison and Wigle (1993) which focuses on the sensitivity of counterfactual equilibrium results to key parameters, such as elasticities, in calibrated models for which parameter estimates are scarce. Sample frequencies for propositions are our objective more so than sensitivity analysis of central case results. In the process, we compute noncooperative game theoretic solutions as well as cooperative solutions for draws from the entire parameter space and we also go beyond existing literature in this dimension.

the probability of particular propositions holding conditional on both the model and the assumed prior.

Taken as a set, our results show that numerical simulation can be an important and useful adjunct to theory in economics. None of the propositions we consider holds unambiguously; some hold over 80% of the time, others considerably less frequently. We also investigate the reasons why particular propositions seem to hold more frequently than others using additional model analyses. Thus, where theory does not yield clear and unambiguous results, numerical simulation can be used to generate insights as to the likelihood of and reasons for particular propositions holding and, we believe, yield significant benefits in many other areas.

2. CU Literature and Theory-Simulation Interactions

Because of our focus on ambiguous propositions in the CU literature, prior to presenting our analyses it is helpful to provide some background. Ambiguity in theoretical outcomes has been a constant in this literature since its inception. In 1950 Jacob Viner, the initiator of subsequent CU literature, pointed out that regional trade agreements do not necessarily result in gains to members, even though some tariffs are eliminated by the agreement. He developed what later became known as the trade creation–trade diversion approach to regional trade agreements to help understand this ambiguity. Following Viner's work, for many years trade creating regional agreements were seen as good and trade diverting regional agreements were seen as bad.[b]

Viner's work was also the driving force behind later literature that subsequently sought to set out the conditions under which regional trade agreements would either improve or worsen welfare. This work was still based on trade creation–trade diversion considerations; but Meade (1955), Lipsey (1957) and others discovered that preference considerations also

[b]These two forces can be explained with a simple example. Suppose countries 1 and 2 initially have no tariffs, but form a CU while country 3 remains outside the agreement. If we suppose that before the agreement country 1 imports clothing from country 3, a low cost producer of clothing, and that as a result of the agreement, then 1 imports clothing instead from 2 because 2 had the advantage of tariff-free access to 1's market, trade into 1 is diverted from low cost producer 3 to high cost producer 2 and welfare may be lowered. However, if 1 formed a union with 3, then 1 would import more from low cost producer 3 and less from high cost producer 2; trade would be created and welfare increased.

enter in trying to make such determinations; this was to lead to Lipsey and Lancaster's (1958) characterization of the general theory of the second best; confirmation that no general CU results were possible. Dissatisfaction with the trade creation–trade diversion dichotomy resulted in Kemp (1969), Lipsey (1970), Riezman (1979) and others trying to develop other approaches that would yield clear propositions.[c] A new approach known as the terms of trade–volume of trade approach became popular, under which the impact of a regional trade agreement can be summarized by its effects on both terms of trade (prices) and trade volumes.[d] This terms of trade–volume of trade approach uses general equilibrium instead of Vinerian partial equilibrium analysis, and emphasizes the impacts of the union on individual countries as integration occurs, instead of on world welfare.

However, even with the adoption of a new approach the same lack of general results has continued to characterize the literature. Indeed, few if any propositions are true for all parameter values even in highly simplified models. Consider the conjecture: "In a three-country pure exchange economy, any pair of countries can benefit by forming a regional trade agreement." In a world where countries are of the same size this conjecture is true, but as Riezman (1999) shows, this conjecture fails to hold more generally. In a world with one large and two smaller countries, a regional trade agreement between the large country and either smaller country can result in the large country doing worse than in the initial equilibrium. In the initial equilibrium, the large country benefits from its use of tariffs against both countries, while small countries lose. When the large country forms a CU it shares some of its tariff advantages with the other union partner, but foregoes the opportunity to play strategically against the small partner. Thus, even in a very simple model there are still no general results even for a more restricted set of questions.[e]

In other literature, such as Kennan and Riezman (1990), strategic considerations underlying the formation of regional trade agreements have served to further cloud the picture. Thus, one objective behind the

[c]See Kemp and Wan (1976), Lloyd (1982), Riezman (1985), Wooton (1986).

[d]Kowalczyk (2000) provides a comprehensive critique of the trade diversion and trade creation methodology, and argues that the terms of trade and volume of trade approach constititues an attractive alternative.

[e]There has nonetheless been intense recent policy debate over whether or not regional trade agreements are desirable in which strong positions are advanced (Bhagwati and Panagariya, 1996; Summers, 1991; Riezman, 1999).

formation of the EU in the late-50s was to enhance joint country bargaining in the GATT with the U.S.; and Mercosur was, in part, an attempt by four countries (Brazil, Argentina, Uruguay, Paraguay) to strengthen their bargaining position for an eventual accession negotiation with NAFTA. Such considerations naturally suggest treating countries as strategic players in a multi-country mixed cooperative–noncooperative trade policy game, but such considerations have made the search for clear propositions as to the effects CUs even more difficult.

This chapter begins then from the ambiguity of most, if not all, theoretical propositions as to what happens when regional trade agreements form. Whether individual countries benefit, whether trade volumes expand, whether tariffs rise globally are all uncertain. Such propositions are further complicated by whether a regional agreement is to be compared to free trade or a multi-country Nash outcome. Our approach is to build on the applied general equilibrium modeling literature and use numerical simulation methods to investigate the frequency with which various propositions hold. Since Miller and Spencer (1971), Shoven and Whalley (1974) and Whalley (1985), researchers have used numerical equilibrium models to simulate the effects of regional trade agreements as well as to address a range of policy questions. They were used extensively in the WTO Uruguay Round process (see Harrison *et al.*, 1996; Francois *et al.*, 1996) as well as in the earlier Tokyo Round. They have also been used to explicitly model the effects of regional trade agreements (Hamilton and Whalley, 1985; Perroni and Whalley, 2000). These models are richer (more countries, production, more commodities) than the trade models that theorists frequently use. However, propositions of the form we investigate here are not explored.

Our blend of theory and numerical simulation seeks to assess whether propositions hold most of the time, and thus stand as reasonable working hypotheses; or whether they hold seldom, and are thus largely theoretical curiosa. We do this by using numerical simulation techniques to compute equilibria for a large number of model parametrizations and then to assess the likelihood of a given proposition holding generally by computing sample frequencies.

3. Implementing Propositional Analysis

The literature on CUs has focused on the effects of the formation of CUs on the welfare of individual countries, as well as on the world as a whole. In addition, there has been work on the effects of CU formation on the terms of trade and volume of trade of both member and non-member countries. Understanding how CU formation affects country terms of trade and their volume of trade helps in understanding the welfare effects of CUs. Older literature concentrates on comparing CUs to an exogenously given initial equilibrium. More recent literature endogenizes the initial equilibrium and also compares CU equilibria to free trade.[f] We follow more recent literature and focus on comparisons of CU equilibria with three-country Nash equilibria and free trade. For each of these three equilibria, we compare welfare, terms of trade, and volume of trade. We assume countries 1 and 2 in a three-country world are the union members. We do not consider the added complication of endogenous membership of the union (see footnote j).

We consider eight propositions as to the effects of regional trade agreements that we feel reflect central themes that the theoretical literature in the area has explored. They are widely discussed in the previously cited literature, are of theoretical interest, and have important policy implications. These are that:

(1) Both members benefit from a CU relative to free trade.
(2) Both members benefit from a CU relative to a Nash equilibrium.
(3) A CU increases world welfare relative to a three-country Nash equilibrium.
(4) CUs are a "stepping stone" to free trade (i.e., members are better off in CU relative to Nash, and members gain from free trade).
(5) A CU results in higher external tariffs for member countries relative to a Nash equilibrium.
(6) A CU improves member countries' terms of trade relative to a Nash equilibrium.
(7) A CU increases member countries' volume of trade relative to free trade.
(8) A CU increases member countries' volume of trade relative to a Nash equilibrium.

We assess the likelihood that each of these propositions hold in a particular case; a three-country pure exchange model based on Kennan and Riezman (1990) and specify functional forms and admissible ranges of parameter values. We consider both random parametrizations of the model drawn from the admissible parameter space and parametrizations represented by a lattice of grid points in the parameter space. For each

[f]See Kennan and Riezman (1990) and Krugman (1991), for example.

parametrization, we compute equilibria in the presence of regional trade agreements, as well as three-country noncooperative Nash equilibria and free trade equilibria.[g] From these computed equilibria we calculate the impacts on world welfare, individual country welfare, prices, tariff levels, and trade volumes as regional agreements form, and hence assess whether each of the propositions holds for that parametrization.[h]

3.1. *Model structure*

Each country has a single representative consumer with endowments of three goods, and a utility function of the form

$$U^i = U^i(X_1^i, X_2^i, X_3^i), \quad (i = 1, \ldots, 3), \tag{1}$$

where X_1^i, X_2^i, X_3^i represent consumption of goods 1, 2, and 3 in country i and U^i is country i's utility. Endowments are given by $\overline{E}_1^i, \overline{E}_2^i, \overline{E}_3^i$, where i denotes the country, and 1, 2, and 3 denote the goods.

Because each country can impose nonnegative tariffs at rate t_j^i on good j imported by country i, we define the sellers prices (i.e., net of tariff prices) as P_j for any good j. This implies that internal (gross of tariff) prices π_j^i in any country are

$$\pi_j^i = (1 + t_j^i)P_j. \tag{2}$$

Tariffs are set to zero on any good exported by country i. Countries (or regions) set tariffs on all imported goods, typically in some optimal fashion although we also consider free trade cases with zero tariffs. Tariff revenues collected by country i are

$$T^i = \sum_{j=1}^{3} t_j^i P_j \max\{(X_j^i - \overline{E}_j^i), 0\}. \tag{3}$$

[g]We assume uniqueness of these equilibria, and have done various *ad hoc* tests (changing the speed of approach and the initial starting point) to search for multiple equilibria. None have been found, although Kehoe's (1980) discussion suggests that, for competitive equilibria, even in small dimensional examples multiple equilibria can occur.

[h]We use Hicksian equivalent money metric measures by country which we aggregate as necessary across countries for this purpose.

The income of country i is thus given by

$$I^i = \sum_{j=1}^{3} \pi_j^i \overline{E}_j^i + T^i. \tag{4}$$

It is easily shown that (2)–(4) imply that the balance of trade for each country is zero.

We use constant elasticity of substitution (CES) (and in special cases Cobb–Douglas) preferences to represent the utility functions (1), for which (in the CES case) utility maximizing demands are given by

$$X_j^i = \frac{\alpha_j^i I^i}{(\pi_j^i)^{\sigma^i} \sum_{j=1}^{3} \alpha_j^i \pi_j^{i(1-\sigma^i)}}, \tag{5}$$

where the α_j^i are CES preference shares on good j in country i, and the σ^i are country i CES substitution elasticities in preferences. Equation (2) presumes knowledge of the direction of trade for any country in any commodity. In the theoretical literature this is assumed to be given and unchanging as we move between alternative equilibria (free trade; three-country Nash; with regional trade agreements).

In the model we use, the direction of trade is endogenously determined as part of the equilibrium solution. This endogeneity of trade patterns is an important feature of this model and differentiates it from previous work in this area. We achieve endogeneity by performing sequential equilibrium calculations in which the direction of trade is given by the previous iteration and then checked for consistency with the resulting model solution.[i] Only when full consistency is achieved we accept this as a bonafide equilibrium solution. We find that changes in the direction of trade across equilibria occur surprisingly frequently (see Abrego *et al.*, 2001), calling into question the use of this assumption in theoretical work.

3.1.1. *Equilibrium solution concepts*

We examine a range of solution concepts for our model, each relevant to the propositions listed above whose frequency we analyze.

Competitive Free Trade Equilibria In free trade, tariff rates are all zero on all products in all countries, and equilibrium prices clear markets globally, i.e., equilibrium prices (P_1^*, P_2^*, P_3^*) are determined such that for

[i]Initially, we use the base case trade pattern.

each good j

$$\sum_{i=1}^{3} X_j^i - \sum_{i=1}^{3} \overline{E}_j^i = 0, \tag{6}$$

and global excess demands are all zero for all three commodities. Given that only relative prices matter in such a structure; we can normalize prices to sum to unity i.e.,

$$\sum_{j=1}^{3} P_j = 1; \quad P_j \geq 0. \tag{7}$$

Three-Country Noncooperative Nash Equilibria We also compute three-country noncooperative Nash equilibria. In these, each country takes other countries' tariffs as given and computes its own optimal tariffs by commodity. In equilibrium country computations of optimal tariffs are mutually consistent. The t_j^i are thus endogenously determined for country i.

Specifically, each country determines its own optimal tariff vector $(t_j^i)^*$ by maximizing U^i subject to the constraint that their balance of trade equals zero. Equilibrium occurs where global markets clear and each country charges optimal tariffs given the tariffs of other countries. Tariff revenues, T^i, enter this version of the model, and affect demands since they are redistributed to the country's representative consumer in lump sum fashion.

Equilibrium requires consistent optimizing behavior with tariffs by country, market clearing and government budget balance in each country. Thus each country i solves an optimization problem

$$\max U^i$$

subject to

$$\sum_{j=1}^{3} P_j (X_j^i - \overline{E}_j^i) = 0. \tag{8}$$

In the problem (8), t_j^i for $j \neq i$ are taken as given and denoted by $\hat{t}_j^i$. In a Nash equilibrium, optimal tariff rates $t_j^{i*} = \hat{t}_j^i$ for all i, j and markets clear, i.e.,

$$\sum_{j=1}^{3} X_j^i - \sum_{j=1}^{3} \overline{E}_j^i = 0 \quad \forall i. \tag{9}$$

CU Equilibria We also compute CU equilibria for this model. In these, we assume that countries 1 and 2 form a CU with zero tariffs between them, and set a common external tariff against country 3.[j] Thus, countries 1 and 2 jointly set an optimal tariff against country 3, and country 3 sets an optimal tariff against the other two countries. Members of the Union receive the tariff revenues collected on their own imports.

In this mixed cooperative, noncooperative case, countries 1 and 2 set zero tariffs against each other, i.e., $t_j^1 = t_j^2 = 0$ if the supplying country is 1 or 2, but jointly set optimal tariffs against country 3. Since countries 1 and 2 typically have a conflict of interest over how their joint external tariff is set, we assume that this tariff is set to maximize the sum of country 1 and 2's utilities. We then use different weights on country utilities in this joint sum in subsequent sensitivity analyses.

The CU optimization problem is given by

$$\max U^1 + U^2$$

subject to

$$\sum_{i=1}^{2}\sum_{j=1}^{3} P_j(X_j^i - \overline{E}_j^i) = 0. \tag{10}$$

3.2. *Implementing the approach*

To compute sample frequencies for the propositions we list above, we use two different procedures for generating alternative model parametrizations. One is a randomization which, in our central case analysis, we implement across both preference parameters (both shares and elasticities) and endowments. In this, we consider CES preferences and generate share and substitution parameters in preferences for all three countries as well as endowments normalized to lie in a unit interval for each good for each country. The other uses a search over a grid defined only on endowment configurations since the dimensionality of the grid becomes unworkably large if we also include preference parameters.

The reason for using these two methods is both to check that they yield comparable results, and to provide a better understanding of the

[j]We have not considered cases where CUs are themselves endogenously determined, but this is clearly an important issue. We assume that countries 1 and 2 are exogenously chosen as the countries which form a union.

factors underlying computed sample frequencies. Since our central case involves randomizing over both preference parameters and endowments, for comparability to our grid search in which we only consider endowment configurations, we later analyze randomizations restricted to endowment configurations only. In our grid search, we focus on the case where share parameters are identically symmetric across countries (all one third), and substitution elasticity values are common to all countries. We search across equilibria associated with parametric specifications of the model given by a lattice grid of points in the parameter space. In these cases we first restrict ourselves to Cobb–Douglas preference functions, and later do CES sensitivity analysis with different preference share parameters across goods and use varying elasticities of substitution.

Table 1 sets out the key features of the procedures we use in computing equilibria on which our sample frequencies are based. Table 2 sets out in more detail an example of the parametric variations, we make over the endowment parameter space in the grid search cases, we have constructed. We assume that the global endowment of each good is 1 by choice of units, and consider own country endowments of goods that range between 0.1 and 0.9. We consider off diagonal elements of the endowment array to be symmetric. Table 2 indicates how a case of (0.1, 0.3, 0.4) translates into the endowment array by good by country given in Table 2.

Table 1. Key Features of the Procedures Used in Propositional Analysis in the Central Case.

Dimensionality:	3 countries, 3 goods.
Preferences:	Randomization: CES.
	Grid search: Cobb–Douglas — symmetric identical preferences across countries, with shares equal to 1/3 for each good.
Endowments:	Randomization: Randomly drawn from the interval 0.05–1.0 for each good for each country.
	Grid search: Lattice grid of model specifications, with country endowment intervals for each good of 0.1. Off-diagonal elements are treated as symmetric. Thus, each model specification is given by a three-dimensional vector (see below) from a range of endowments is generated.
Number of cases:	Randomization: We consider 2,000 draws from the range of potential parametric specifications.
	Grid search: We consider 769 different model specifications reflecting a single integer grid in own endowments.
Equilibria computed for each case for each method	Competitive equilibria, three-country Nash equilibria, CU equilibria (the sum of member utilities is maximized).

Table 2. An Example of a Model Parametric Specification Generated by the Grid Search Procedure.

	Country		
Endowment of goods	1	2	3
1	0.10	0.45	0.45
2	0.35	0.30	0.35
3	0.30	0.30	0.40

The grid search procedure we consider involves all possible own endowment configurations across the three countries with single digit decimals; a total of 769 cases. Cases which by construction are symmetric are excluded [e.g., (0.2, 0.4, 0.6) gives the same equilibrium solution as (0.4, 0.2, 0.6)].

In randomization cases, we limit our parametric specification to the relevant range for each parameter, e.g., 0.1 for share parameters. We consider 2,000 draws in our central case analysis. For all the specifications generated by both methods we compute free trade, three-country Nash, and CU equilibria and compare across these to assess sample frequencies as to how often the propositions we list above hold in the cases we consider. Assuming a uniform prior, we can interpret the computed sample frequencies in probabilistic form as the likelihood of whether or not any particular proposition holds. As noted above, an important difference between the randomization and grid search procedures is that the grid search is limited to endowments, while the randomization is over all model parameters.

In three-country Nash cases, we encounter difficulties in computing equilibria reflecting a lack of monotonicity in the individual country utilities when they are maximized with respect to their own tariff vector. Such problems are confined to the three-country Nash cases (and occur in between 17% and 20% of cases in our central case). They do not arise with CU or free trade equilibrium computations. These problems manifest themselves in the GAMS optimization code we use in the form of cycling between local equilibria. They are more common in cases where trade patterns change.[k]

[k]In the cases in which we cannot compute Nash equilibrium, we drop all results for that endowment and preference specification.

4. Results

4.1. *Central case results*

Table 3 presents results for the central case where all model parameters (preferences and endowments) are randomized. In these, we randomly draw preference (share and elasticity) parameters and endowment configurations for 2,000 cases, and for each compute free trade, CU, and Nash equilibria. We compile sample frequencies for the eight propositions holding that we listed earlier in Section 3.

Results in Table 3 indicate that some propositions hold in a clear majority of computed cases (proposition 6, whether a CU improves the members' terms of trade relative to Nash) while others hold less frequently. For instance, both members benefit by forming a CU relative to the three-country Nash outcome in only 48% of the cases. A CU improves world welfare relative to a Nash equilibrium in 76% of computed cases. CUs result in higher external tariffs for member countries compared to Nash in 72% of

Table 3. Central Case Analyzes of CUs Propositions Under Randomization Over Both Preference Parameters and Endowments.

Proposition	Sample frequencies of computed model parametrizations for which the proposition is true
(1) Both members benefit from a CU relative to free trade	22.9
(2) Both members benefit from a CU relative to a Nash equilibrium	47.6
(3) CU increases world welfare relative to a three-country Nash equilibrium	76.0
(4) CUs are a "stepping stone" to free trade (i.e., members are better off in CU relative to Nash, and members gain from free trade)	3.6
(5) CU results in higher external tariffs for member countries relative to a Nash equilibrium	72.2
(6) CU improves member countries' terms of trade relative to a Nash equilibrium	88.6
(7) CU increases member countries' volume of trade relative to free trade	27.1
(8) CU increases member countries' volume of trade relative to Nash equilibrium	86.9

cases. CUs lead to more international trade for member countries (relative to Nash) 87% of the time. At the other end of the spectrum only in 4% of the cases are CUs a "stepping stone" to free trade. We next discuss each of the results in more detail.

Propositions 1 and 2 look at welfare changes between equilibria. Proposition 1 suggests that *both* members of a CU do better than at free trade in about 20% of the cases while that number jumps to almost 50% (Proposition 2) when the comparison is made to Nash equilibrium rather than free trade. Moving from a Nash equilibrium (or free trade) to a CU improves the union member's bargaining power and the members should gain *vis-à-vis* the non-member. From Johnson (1953) and Kennan and Riezman (1988) we know that only where there are significant asymmetries of size in a two-country case will a country gain in Nash equilibrium relative to free trade. The same logic applies to the union-nonunion distinction and in our computations both members gain (i.e., the CU is big enough) about 20% of the time.

To see the intuition for these results it helps to decompose the change into terms of trade effect and volume of trade effect. Moving to a CU from either free trade or Nash equilibrium will usually improve the terms of trade of union members with respect to the rest of the world (see Proposition 6.) However, within the CU one country will see its terms of trade improve at the expense of the other member.[1] So, for one member the terms of trade improve with respect to all trading partners while for the other the change in overall terms of trade is ambiguous and will depend on what percentage of its trade is within the CU. The volume of trade will usually fall moving from free trade to CU (Proposition 7) and increase moving from Nash equilibrium to CU (Proposition 8). Putting these effects together it follows that welfare gain for both members of a CU is more likely when the comparison is to a Nash equilibrium rather than to free trade.

The fundamental significance of Proposition 1 lies in the fact that it gives a measure of the stability of free trade. If free trade existed, then more than 20% of the time there would be a CU that would benefit both member countries. In those cases, free trade would not be very stable in the sense that there would be a tendency to defect and form a CU. Proposition 2 implies that about half the time in a tariff ridden world there will be at

---

[1]Riezman (1979) stresses the importance of this effect.

least one pair of countries that can benefit from forming a CU. Hence, in this situation there would be a strong tendency to move towards regionalism.

The world welfare, results for Proposition 3, suggest a bias in favor of CUs over three-country Nash equilibria when one looks at world welfare. Theoretically, here we are comparing two distorted equilibria and moving from a Nash equilibrium to a CU gives some tariff reduction. However, members of the CU coordinate their external tariffs which leads to higher protection. The results, therefore, indicate that from a global point of view the benefits of tariff reduction outweigh the costs of tariff coordination, with a sample frequency of considerably more than half.

One traditional view of regional trade agreements is that starting from an initial tariff equilibrium, one could view CUs as an intermediate step or "stepping stone" on the path to free trade. In the context of our model, this means that starting at Nash equilibrium two countries could benefit from forming a CU (and would presumably do so) and starting from the CU equilibrium all countries would do better at free trade (and would presumably move to free trade). In this context, CUs facilitate the attainment of free trade by providing a path along which countries gain each step of the way until free trade is obtained.[m] In our numerical analysis, we start with the result that in 48% of the cases both members benefit by moving from a three-country Nash equilibrium to a CU. Result 4 tells us that starting from the CUs equilibrium in less than 10% of these cases will all countries benefit from a further move to free trade. The view that CUs are likely to be an intermediate step on the way to free trade is not supported by our results.

Results for Proposition 5 suggest that in more than 70% of the cases, CUs raise common external tariff rates relative to three-country Nash levels. Krugman (1991) shows that CUs always increase tariffs, a proposition that is not generally true once asymmetric cases are considered. The intuition for why CUs lower tariffs some of the time can be found in a paper by Syropoulos (1999). Here he argues that when two countries form a CU there are two effects working against each other in determining the optimal external tariff for the union. First, there is a tariff reduction effect. As CUs

[m]Starting at Nash equilibrium the country excluded from the CU would probably be worse off, but they would be unable to stop the CU from forming. GATT/WTO rules under Article 24 require a regional agreement both to broadly cover all trade and not to raise barriers against third parties. These rules, in practice, could restrain the formation of a CU.

members eliminate tariffs between them the optimal external tariff falls. Second, there is a tariff increasing effect as the CU internalizes the tariff externality that occurs when members import the same good. Thus, there are two forces working in opposite directions. This intuition suggests that CU external tariffs fall when the tariff externality is small accounting for the results here, generally cases where the CU members do not import much of the same good.

Results for Proposition 6 suggest that CUs improve their external terms of trade relative to Nash in a large majority of cases. Subsequent sensitivity analysis suggests that this result depends on country size, since a CU's external terms of trade deteriorates when the CU is small relative to the third country. This result is not surprising if one views the problem from non-member country's point of view. In Nash equilibrium, they compete against two other countries that are setting their tariffs independently. When those two countries form a CU the third country now faces what is essentially one country from the point of view of trade policy. Hence it is not surprising that the non-member's terms of trade deteriorate vis a vis the member countries.

Propositions 7 and 8 indicate the extent to which CUs are protrade, in the sense that they lead to more trade among member countries. Proposition 7 shows that a quarter of time CU countries trade more than they would at free trade. Proposition 8 results suggest that if we compare CU to Nash equilibria nearly 87% of the time members trade increases moving to the CU. Theory suggests that with a CU the volume of internal trade increases while external trade falls, but provides no guidance as to which effect will dominate. These results indicate that at least compared to Nash equilibrium the increase in internal trade will usually dominate.[n]

4.2. *Discriminant analysis*

We have also undertaken further analyses of our results in which we impose various conditions in an attempt to ascertain whether these conditions make it more or less likely that particular propositions will hold. We term this discriminant analysis. Results in Table 4 show the deviation in sub-sample frequencies where propositions hold from full sample frequencies.

[n]It is possible that a CU, due income effects, can lead to increased trade with non-members; see Kowalczyk and Wonnacott (1992).

Table 4. Discriminant Analysis of CU Proposition Frequencies.*

Full sample percentage relative frequency	Proposition 1 18.8	Proposition 2 44.6	Proposition 3 75.3	Proposition 4 3.0	Proposition 5 71.3	Proposition 6 90.1	Proposition 7 23.8	Proposition 8 89.1
(A) Member Country Relative Size								
(1) Income of country 1 exceeds that of country 2	−0.6	10.0	2.0	−3.0	1.4	−1.5	−10.1	−5.0
(2) Income of country 1 exceeds 1.5 times that of country 2	−2.1	−2.9	12.3	−3.0	3.7	−2.6	−15.4	−9.9
(3) Income of country 1 exceeds twice that of country 2	−5.5	−17.9	18.1	−3.0	−4.6	−3.4	−10.4	−9.1
(B) Union–Nonunion Relative Size								
(4) Income of CU countries combined exceeds twice income of country 3	4.1	7.5	12.3	−3.0	−10.9	−6.8	5.4	4.6
(5) Income of CU countries combined exceeds 4 times income of country 3	−18.8	−6.1	17.1	−3.0	−17.4	−13.2	14.7	10.9
(6) Income of CU countries combined exceeds 6 times income of country 3	−18.8	−4.6	4.8	−3.0	8.7	9.9	36.2	10.9

Note: Results show percentage deviation of sub-sample frequencies for propositions from full sample frequencies.
*We consider 2,000 randomization cases in generating these results.
***These are

P1: CU welfare compared to FT
P2: CU welfare compared to Nash
P3: World welfare compared to Nash
P4: Stepping stone
P5: External tariff
P6: TT improvement for CU as a whole
P7: CU trade volume increase relative to FT
P8: CU trade volume increases relative to Nash.

In the intracustoms union country size cases, for example, we calculate the number of cases for which the income of country 1 exceeds that of country 2 and then determine the sample frequency for each proposition in that sub-sample. We then deduct the full sample frequency from this sample frequency, giving the deviations (in percentages) of sub-sample from full sample frequencies. Numbers which are small (closer to zero) indicate that the discriminant has little impact on sample frequencies. We consider two types of discriminants in Table 4; some relating to the relative incomes of member countries in a union to capture the importance of country size within the union, and others relating to relative incomes across the union and nonunion countries. We impose conditions of increasing stringency in applying these tests, and as we do so the number of cases in the larger sample meeting those restrictions falls.

Consider for example, Proposition 7 which implies that in 23.8% of cases CU increases member countries' volume of trade relative to free trade. If we then take our 2,000 randomizations and select all those in which the income of country 1 exceeds the income of country 2 then that percentage of cases for which Proposition 7 holds falls by 10.1% so that for that particular sub-sample, trade volume increases in 13.7% of cases. For the case in which income of country 1 exceeds 1.5 times the income of country 2 the percentage of cases for which Proposition 7 holds falls by 15.4% meaning that it holds 12.4% of the time. Using this discriminant analysis in this way we try and get some insight into the role that relative incomes play, both internal and external to the CU, in driving the results we have. The discriminant analysis for Propositions 7 and 8 provide some interesting results. Taken together these results suggest that size inequality within the CU make it less likely that CUs increase trade volume, while size inequality between union and nonunion members make it more likely. This is an intriguing finding that suggests interesting directions for future theoretical research.

4.3. *Sensitivity analysis*

The results we report above for the various CU cases will also produce different frequencies for different parametrization procedures. In Table 5, we report results in which the number of randomizations used to generate frequency results is varied. Our central case results in Table 2 use 2,000 randomizations. Here, we report additional cases for 500, 1,000, and 3,000 randomizations. Results indicate minor variations in results across these

Table 5. Sensitivity Analysis to Full Randomization Sample Frequencies.

Proposition	Central case	3,000 randomizations	1,000 randomizations	500 randomizations
(1) Both members benefit from a CU relative to free trade	22.9	22.2	23.3	25.0
(2) Both members benefit from a CU relative to a Nash equilibrium	47.6	47.2	47.4	48.1
(3) CU increases world welfare relative to a three-country Nash equilibrium	76.0	76.3	74.8	77.9
(4) CUs are a "stepping stone" to free trade (i.e., members are better off in CU relative to Nash, and members gain on free trade)	3.6	3.6	2.9	3.3
(5) CU results in higher external tariffs for member countries relative to a Nash equilibrium	72.2	72.0	73.2	72.2
(6) CU improves member countries' terms of trade relative to a Nash equilibrium	88.6	89.8	88.9	88.4
(7) CU increases member countries' volume of trade relative to free trade	27.1	27.4	27.7	24.9
(8) CU increases member countries' volume of trade relative to a Nash equilibrium	86.9	87.7	88.2	88.4

Note: Percentage sample frequencies for which the proposition holds.

different procedures. This suggests that the frequencies obtained using 2,000 randomizations have small standard errors.

4.4. *Grid search versus randomization*

In Table 6, we report results which compare grid search and randomization procedures. Because the grid search is restricted only to endowments, for the reasons of tractability noted above, we undertake a randomization analysis

Table 6. Proposition Sample Frequencies Computed Using Both Grid Search and Randomization Techniques.

Proposition	Using grid search procedure	Randomization over endowments only	Using full randomization procedure (central case)	Randomization over preference parameters only
(1) Both members benefit from a CU relative to free trade	30.3	29.9	22.9	23.2
(2) Both members benefit from a CU relative to a Nash equilibrium	81.6	75.7	47.6	57.4
(3) CU increases world welfare relative to a three-country Nash equilibrium	95.4	87.0	76.0	78.9
(4) CUs are a "stepping stone" to free trade	21.9	22.4	3.6	4.6
(5) CU results in higher external tariffs for member countries relative to a Nash equilibrium	79.5	83.6	72.2	72.4
(6) CU improves member countries' terms of trade relative to a Nash equilibrium	98.5	98.2	27.1	96.2
(7) CU increases member countries' volume of trade relative to free trade	8.1	3.1	27.1	19.4
(8) CU increases member countries' volume of trade relative to a Nash equilibrium	91.6	89.1	86.9	88.9

Note: Percentage sample frequencies for which the proposition holds.

only over endowments using 2,000 randomizations as in the central case. We also report the full randomization results from Table 3, *and a case in which randomization is restricted to preference parameters only rather than endowments.*

These results show a high degree of similarity between grid search and *endowment restricted* randomization. There are, however, large differences between these cases and the complete randomization case. Taken together,

Table 7. Quantitative Orders of Magnitude of Gains and Losses from Cases Considered in Table 3 (Welfare Effects (EV) as % of Income).

	Across gaining cases			Across losing cases		
Comparisons	Mean gain	Max gain	Smallest gain	Mean loss	Max loss	Smallest loss
(1) CU versus free trade	0.53	8.52	2.00e–05	0.74	9.17	1.00e–05
(2) CU versus a Nash equilibrium	2.58	10.21	5.00e–07	1.34	11.72	7.00e–09
(3) Nash equilibrium versus Free Trade	0.21	9.63	1.00e–10	2.07	14.17	2.00e–06

Note: Percentage sample frequencies for which the proposition holds.

these results suggest that the method used to generate sample frequencies may be less important than the restrictions placed on the search made, independent of the method used. In other words, it may not make much difference whether grid search or randomization is used, but inclusion of different variables appears to have an important effect on the outcome.

4.5. *The size of gains and losses*

While our analysis has concentrated on purely qualitative propositions of gain and loss and their likelihood of occurring, we are also able to make statements about the size of gains and losses across the cases we consider. In Table 7, we consider the same cases as for our central case analyzes in Table 3 but now report the mean welfare gain and loss across gaining and losing cases comparing free trade, CU, and Nash equilibrium. We calculate a money metric measure of the welfare change (the Hicksian equivalent variation) which we report as a percentage of base case income, and also give ranges of effects. These results are dependent on the parametric specification used for the model, but provide quantitative instead of qualitative information. The results indicate that, on average, the welfare effects of the changes we consider are significant. In addition, in some instances the welfare effects are quite large.

5. Conclusion

In this chapter, we use computational methods to calculate sample frequencies for parametrizations for which various propositions in the CU literature hold for a given model. Our motivation is that despite

50 years of research, most if not all propositions in CU literature remain ambiguous. These include whether CUs raise world welfare, the welfare of particular countries, tariff levels, and other variables, and for each relative proposition alternative base cases as the reference point are investigated. The usual argument made against numerical analysis is that only statements conditional on a particular numerical specification be made. Here we examine equilibria associated with different parametrizations drawn from the admissible parameter space using both randomization and grid search techniques. We use a three-country, three-good Cobb–Douglas/CES pure exchange economy. Our results show, for example, that for the model we consider, world welfare increases under a CU relative to Nash equilibrium more than 70% of the time.

Taken as a set, we interpret our results as suggesting that few (or none) of the propositions we investigate are extrema; they are neither theoretical curiosa nor largely true. Whether they hold depends on model characteristics that are amenable to investigation. Results seem robust to alternative procedures for analysis and constraints are applied in propositional analysis to demonstrate this. Blending theory and numerical simulation thus provides useful insights as to when propositions may hold in these cases and we suggest that this may also be so in other cases where theory does not yield unambiguous conclusions.

References

Abrego, L and J Whalley (2001). How reasonable are the assumptions used in theoretical models?: Computational evidence of the likelihood of trade pattern changes (mimeo). *NBER* WP #W8169.

Bhagwati, J and A Panagariya (1996). Preferential trading areas and multilateralism: Strangers, friends or foes? In *Free Trade Areas or Free Trade? The Economics of Preferential Trading Agreements*, J Bhagwati and A Panagariya (eds.). Washington, D.C.: AEI Press.

Francois, JF, B MacDonald and H Nordstrom (1996). The Uruguay round: A numerically based qualitative assessment. In *The Uruguay Round and the Developing Countries*, W Martin and A Winters (eds.). Cambridge, New York and Melbourne: Cambridge University Press.

Hamilton, R and J Whalley (1985). Geographically discriminatroy trade arrangements. *Review of Economics and Statistics*, **67**, 446–55.

Harrison, G, R Jones, L Kimbell and R Wigle (1993). How robust is general equilibrium analysis. *Journal of Policy Modelling*, **15**(1), 99–115.

Harrison, GW, TF Rutherford and DG Tarr (1996). Quantifying the Uruguay round. In *The Uruguay Round and the Developing Economies*, W Martin and LA Winters (eds.). Cambridge: Cambridge University Press; *Economic Journal*, 1997, **107**(44), 1405–1430; World Bank Discussion Paper No. 307, 1995.

Johnson, HG (1953). Optimum tariffs and retaliation. In *Elgar Reference Collection. International Library of Critical Writings in Economics*, 115. *Economic integration and international trade*, C Kowalczyk (ed.). Cheltenham, U.K. and Northampton, Mass.: Elgar; distributed by American International Distribution Corporation, Williston, Vt., 1999; 140–51. Previously published: 1953.

Kehoe, T (1980). An index theorem for general equilibrium models with production. *Econometrica*, **48**, 1211–32.

Kemp, M (1969). *The Pure Theory of International Trade and Investment.* London: Prentice-Hall.

Kemp, M and H Wan (1976). An elementary proposition concerning the formation of customs unions. *Journal of International Economics*, **6**, 95–97.

Kennan, J and R Riezman (1988). Do Big Countries Win Tariff Wars? *International Economic Review*, **29**(1), 81–85.

Kennan, J and R Riezman (1990). Optimal tariff equilibria with customs unions. *Canadian Journal of Economics*, **90**, 70–83.

Kowalczyk, C and R Wonnacott (1992). Hubs and spokes, and free trade in the Americas. *NBER* WP#4198.

Kowalczyk, C (2000). Welfare and integration. *International Economic Review*, **41**(2), 483–94.

Krugman, P (1991). Is bilateralism bad? In *International Trade and Trade Policy*, E Helpman and A Razin (eds.). Cambridge: MIT Press.

Lipsey, RG (1957). The theory of customs unions: Trade diversion and welfare. *Economica*, **24**, 40–46.

Lipsey, RG (1960). The theory of customs unions: A general survey. *Economic Journal*, **70**, 498–513.

Lipsey, RG (1970). *The theory of Customs Unions: A General Equilibrium Analysis.* London: Weidenfeld and Nicholson.

Lipsey, RG and K Lancaster (1956). The general theory of second best. *Review of Economic Studies*, **24**, 11–32.

Lloyd, PJ (1982), A 3×3 theory of customs unions. *Journal of International Economics*, **12**, 41–63.

Meade, JE (1955). *The Theory of Customs Unions.* Amsterdam: North-Holland.

Miller, MH and JE Spencer (1971). The static economic effects of the UK joining the EEC: A general equilibrium approach. *Review of Economic Studies*, **44**, 71–93.

Pagan, A and JH Shannon (1986). Sensitivity analysis for linearized computable general equilibrium models. In *New Developments in Applied General Equilibrium Analysis*, J Piggott and J Whalley (eds.). Cambridge: Cambridge University Press, 104–18.

Perroni, C and J Whalley (2000). The new regionalism: Trade liberalization or insurance? *Canadian Journal of Economics*, **33**, 1–24.

Perroni, C and J Whalley (1996). How severe is global retaliation risk under increasing regionalism? *American Economic Review*, **86**, 57–61.
Riezman, R (1979). A 3×3 model of customs unions. *Journal of International Economics*, **9**, 341–354.
Riezman, R (1985). Customs unions and the core. *Journal of International Economics*, **19**, 355–365.
Riezman, R (1999). Can bilateral agreements help induce free trade? *Canadian Journal of Economics*, **32**, 751–766.
Shoven, JB and J Whalley (1974). On the computation of competitive equilibrium on international markets with tariffs. *Journal of International Economics*, **4**, 341–354.
Summers, L (1991). Regionalism and the world trading system. In *Federal Reserve Bank of Kansas City* (Policy Implications of Trade and Currency Zones), pp. 295–301.
Syropoulos, C (1999). Customs unions and comparative advantage. *Oxford Economic Papers*, **51**, 239–266.
Viner, J (1950). *The Customs Union Issue.* New York: Carnegie Endowment for International Peace.
Whalley, J (1985). *Trade Liberalization Among Major World Trading Areas.* Cambridge, Mass. London: MIT Press.
Wigle, R (1991). The Pagan–Shannon approximation: Unconditional systematic sensitivity in minutes. In *Studies in Empirical Economics Applied general equilibrium*, J Piggott and J Whalley (eds.). New York: Springer; Heidelberg: Physica, 35–49.
Wooton, I (1986). Preferential trading agreements: An investigation. *Journal of International Economics*, **21**, 81–97.

Chapter 14

Developing Country Benefits from MFN Relative to Regional/Bilateral Trade Arrangements*,†

Madanmohan Ghosh
University of Western Ontario, Canada

Carlo Perroni
University of Warwick, Coventry, U.K.

John Whalley
Universities of Western Ontario
National Bureau of Economic Research (NBER)

This chapter discusses the ways in which most favored nation (MFN) treatment in multilateral trade agreements benefits developing countries relative to bilateral or regional trade agreements. We analyze rights to MFN treatment in foreign markets, and the obligation to grant MFN treatment in home markets; the key features of nondiscrimination in the post-war GATT/WTO multilateral trading system. We first argue that MFN gives benefits to small countries in being able to free ride on bilateral tariff concessions exchanged between larger countries in MFN based GATT/WTO negotiating rounds. We evaluate these benefits numerically using a traditional competitive framework. We then argue that MFN also restrains retaliatory actions by other countries to be nondiscriminatory and analyze them using a cooperative Nash equilibrium framework. Finally we use a cooperative bargaining framework in which trade policies are jointly set and argue that MFN changes threat points

*An earlier version of this chapter was presented at the Summer Meetings of the Econometric Society, June 25–29th, Pasadena, California, 1997. The second and third authors acknowledge support from the U.K. ESRC under an award for "General Equilibrium Modeling of U.K. Policy Issues". We are grateful to the Associate Editor, Mario Crucini, and a referee for helpful comments. We also thank Hari Govindran, Anne Kreuger, and Uzi Segal for discussions of the issues addressed in the chapter, and to Ayhan Kose for helpful detailed comments.
†This chapter was first published in (2003). *Review of International Economics*, **11**(4), 712–728.

and hence affects the bargaining solution of multilateral MFN-based trade negotiation compared to a bilateral/regional arrangement. We use a calibrated numerical model of global trade in which developing countries appear to analyze these three sources of potential benefit for developing countries. We compute solutions for all three equilibrium concepts and compare MFN and nonMFN equilibria in each case. We use the GTAP (1992) data base in these analyzes, concluding from model results that quantitatively the most significant effect of MFN for developing countries seems to be in its impact on bargaining outcomes rather than on competitive and Nash equilibrium solutions.

1. Introduction

The principle of nondiscrimination states that countries should grant other countries their MFN treatment when using trade restrictions at their border. It simultaneously stands as the major GATT/WTO right that contracting parties/members can demand of others in markets abroad and their major obligation to other member countries. While in practice MFN operates as a diluted principle through GATT/WTO sanctioned trade discrimination covering regional trade agreements (Article 24), the Generalized System of Preferences (GSP), trade restrictions covering products such as textiles and apparel [Multi-Fiber Arrangement (MFA)], and the use of trade instruments such as anti-dumping/countervailing actions (Article 6), it is the central element of system participation that is aggressively sought by potential new entrants to the WTO (such as China). It lies at the heart of the post-war GATT/WTO trading system and stands in GATT 1994 Article 1 as the central GATT obligation that WTO members grant to all other WTO members in their own market. It is also the principle whose application developing countries tried to strengthen in the Uruguay Round, and a principle to which larger powers in the trading system are supposedly still committed.

Despite its central role in modern trade policy there is little literature that attempts to evaluate the benefits and costs of MFN for various types of countries,[a] and specifically for developing countries. Here we suggest that countries receive various benefits from and incur costs because of their MFN rights and obligations relative to regional or bilateral agreements, and we use numerical simulation techniques to investigate their implications

[a]Here we have in mind literature that values MFN from different country perspectives (small, large for example).

by focusing on three different model solution concepts; comparative static competitive equilibria, tariff game Nash equilibria, and bargaining solutions (with side-payments), each of which is affected in different ways by the MFN commitment relative to a nonMFN world. We model MFN as a constraint on the relevant model solution concept, and use a seven region global trade model calibrated to the 1992 GTAP Version 3 data base to compute equilibria, and value MFN benefits by comparing across MFN and nonMFN equilibrium outcomes. In doing so, we draw on code and model structure used earlier by Perroni and Whalley (1994).

The first source of MFN benefit for developing countries that we analyze is their ability to free ride through MFN on trade concessions agreed to bilaterally by large countries in their own trade negotiations with each other. This has been extensively discussed in the literature, beginning with Baldwin and Murray (1977),[b] and we investigate this here by computing comparative static competitive equilibria under MFN and nonMFN (bilateral) tariff elimination between the larger regions in the model (North America and the EU).[c] We compare the outcomes under changes to MFN arrangements relative the 1992 base case to which the model is calibrated.

The second source of MFN benefit to developing countries we analyze are the constraints that MFN imposes on retaliation, should it occur in the system, as MFN restrictions imply that small countries cannot be singled out for retaliatory trade actions. We compute MFN constrained and MFN unconstrained retaliatory Nash equilibria which models an outbreak of retaliatory trade wars between countries, even though a global round of trade retaliation would very likely result in violations of GATT/WTO tariff bindings.[d] We again compare outcomes for each region under MFN restraints to nonMFN retaliation.

Finally, we evaluate the effects on developing countries of the constraints that MFN imposes on multilateral trade bargaining both in the GATT/WTO and outside. The benefit of MFN here for developing countries is that they cannot be forced into making adverse concessions

[b]For further discussion of the merits and demerits of MFN as free riding. See Baldwin (1987), Jackson (1987), Caplin and Krishna (1988), Ludema (1991) and Staiger (1995).
[c]The extent by which small countries have actually been able to free ride in the sense discussed here is a separate issue and has been discussed elsewhere. See Finger (1979).
[d]In the model MFN requires that uniform tariff rates to be applied to all similar products supplied by all members of the GATT/WTO.

through bilateral bargaining with larger countries, since under MFN all bargaining effectively becomes multilateral. For larger countries, this feature of MFN treatment potentially involves a significant cost since countries forgo the opportunity to separately bilaterally bargain with a number of smaller countries. We compute both Nash (1950) and Kalai–Smorodinsky (1975) trade policy bargaining outcomes supported by appropriate side-payments; the effect of MFN being to change the threat point, and hence affect the bargaining outcome. We interpret side-payments in trade policy bargaining as domestic policy restraints (such as intellectual property protection) which are advantageous to partner (large in the developing country case) countries.

In the 1992 base data set we use, OECD tariffs are already low and hence our numerical simulations suggest that for smaller countries the value of MFN treatment in the first sense of free riding on further large country tariff cuts is small. Our model results also show only small gains for developing countries from MFN treatment in the second sense (MFN restraints on retaliation). This is because when global retaliation occurs, the influence that countries have over their terms of trade with all other countries reflects their being able to restrict their trade in aggregate rather than that with individual countries. Results suggest the benefits to developing countries of not being selectively targeted for retaliation are relatively small.

In contrast, the benefits to developing countries from MFN treatment in the third sense emerge from our model calculations as large. Developing countries benefit substantially from not being forced to bargain bilaterally with large countries (or to make side-payments to maintain MFN treatment). Our simulations thus suggest that for larger countries MFN obligations impose a substantial cost on them insofar as they forgo the opportunity to bargain bilaterally on trade policy with small countries, since if they do so it must be within the framework of a set of multilateral nondiscriminatory disciplines. Multilateral nondiscriminatory rules prevent the use of bilateral threats to extract maximal concessions.

Our results thus shed light on why it is that developing countries remain so concerned over nondiscrimination in the trading system. The impacts on them of adverse bilateral negotiation are potentially large. The same results also account for the concerns of developing countries expressed during the Uruguay Round of a weakening of multilateral GATT/WTO disciplines from the surge of regional trade agreements which occurred contemporaneously with the Round. The same results also raise the issue of why it is that large countries or regions, such as the U.S. and the EU, should remain committed to the maintenance of MFN as the central element in the WTO.

Model results also shed light on the trade policy implications of the end of the Cold War. In the early post-war years, when the strategic interests of the large powers overrode their immediate trade interests, MFN treatment was often granted to smaller countries as a way of securing strategic alliances. Accession to GATT by smaller post-colonial countries in the 1960's occurred with little or no conditionality attached. Commitment by the large powers to a system, even if based on MFN, reflected an overriding strategic interest and markets of those countries were small. In the post-Cold War period, however, where trade interests dominate and markets in developing countries have grown, larger countries seek ways of proceeding bilaterally despite earlier MFN obligations. The system erodes, with even more bilateral pressure exerted by larger powers. In such a world, developing countries may now need to offer asymmetric trade concessions (effectively side-payments) to maintain an MFN-based system, as indeed many of them have done. In this way, their MFN benefits become diluted.

We conclude by noting that despite our analysis and model results, recent game theoretic literature questions the significance of any negotiated trade (or other) commitments, including MFN. This is because the Folk theorem stresses that any outcome that Pareto dominates threat point utilities can be supported as a sub-game perfect equilibrium of a repeated game.[e] This theorem emphasizes the multiplicity of equilibria potentially emerging from trade policy games, and suggests that supporting mechanisms, not negotiated commitments, are the key to understanding trade policy. But despite these considerations, multilateral trade negotiations have grown in the post-war years with ever widening negotiated trade commitments being linked with other international treaty networks to support their enforcement. Eight post-war GATT/WTO negotiating rounds have occurred, and their central role in modern trade policy to us justifies better understanding the implications of MFN for the

[e] Also see the discussion of this point in Perroni and Whalley (1996), p. 59. This same argument could also be made for domestic as well as international law, namely that legal commitments are less the issue than enforceable cooperation via supporting strategies.

developing countries who seek to use this system to speed their growth and development.

2. Assessing the Benefits to Developing Countries from Most Favored Nation

2.1. *The rationale for MFN*

As we note in our introduction, MFN treatment implies that countries extend to other countries the same trade treatment as that granted to their most favored trading partners, effectively a rule that no country will discriminate against other countries in its use of trade measures at the border. MFN has long been the source of discussion in policy based literature as to who gains and who loses from it, and in which ways. MFN became the cornerstone of the modern GATT/WTO system in 1947 when it was enshrined as the central principle of the General Agreement in Article 1. MFN first entered the trade policy world through the bilateral European trade treaties of the 19th century (such as the U.K.–France Cobden–Chevalier treaty of the 1860's). In this case, bilateral signatories to the treaty committed that should they negotiate with third parties any benefits of improved access that may result had to also accrue to other treaty signatories as a result of third party negotiations. Under the U.K.–France treaty, the U.K. was thus also to share in improved access to, say, Spain if France was to negotiate with Spain.

After long being opposed to unconditional MFN the U.S. embraced the idea in the 20th century in its bilateral trade agreements of the 1930's. These followed the 1933 U.S. Reciprocal Trade Agreements Act which gave the president authority to negotiate bilateral trade deals if foreign countries reciprocated U.S. tariff cuts. MFN at this time was believed to be a vehicle for more quickly spreading the benefits of trade liberalization to other countries, and speeding the recovery of the global economy from the recession of the early 1930's, and hence in interest of both the U.S.

MFN next became the centerpiece of the GATT as it was negotiated in 1947 as effectively the multilateralization of U.S. pre-war bilateral agreements (the GATT was modeled on the 1942 U.S.–Mexico agreement). As in pre-war days, MFN was seen as a vehicle for speeding whatever trade liberalization the GATT negotiating process generated to more countries than would have been true in a nonMFN world.

In policy-based literature, there is a widely held presumption that small countries benefit from MFN in not being discriminated against, and large countries lose since they forgo the opportunity to extract more beneficial trade terms from smaller trading partners through bilateral pressure.[f] This raises the issue of why it is that large countries or regions such as the U.S. and the EU remain committed today to MFN, and why it was agreed in the first place.

A variety of explanations exist in the policy literature. One is that cooperation is difficult to establish, and once in place costly to remove and replace with noncooperative outcomes. Under this view, large countries might no longer agree to MFN in a *de novo* negotiation today, but it is accepted as part of functioning cooperation that dominates noncooperation. Another explanation is that the trading system is effectively a 2 or $2^1/_2$ large power system (the U.S., the EU and Japan), and MFN means that, in principle at least, the EU and the U.S. each share in whatever agreements are negotiated with third parties. Yet another explanation is that in its early years, the interest of larger countries in the GATT were as much strategic as economic; OECD countries saw an MFN-based GATT as one way of pulling newly independent developing countries away from a Communist embrace. Finally, policy-based literature notes the many ways the MFN rule in GATT/WTO is breached in practice, allowing large countries some latitude in how it is applied.

Despite these various explanations of large country acceptance, the fact remains that MFN is a central part of GATT/WTO system and has been so for over 50 years. They also leave in place the question for developing countries as to whether this rule is in their interest, and if so how. Here, we evaluate three sources of benefit from MFN for developing countries. One is that MFN allows them to free ride on bilateral agreements to lower trade barriers among large countries. A second is that any trade retaliation a large country engages in must be nondiscriminatory. A third is that MFN changes the threat points entering any trade bargaining by effectively eliminating bilateral bargaining. It is these that we investigate in this chapter.

---

[f] A number of recent pieces, however, touch on related issues. Bond and Syropolous (1996) discuss the size of trading blocs and the world welfare implications, Ludema (1996) discusses the value of preferential arrangements in multilateral trade negotiations, and Siedman and Winter (1997) discuss the endogenous expansion of preferential trading arrangements.

2.2. *A model for evaluating MFN benefits*

To assess how MFN treatment affects developing countries, both through rights to MFN in markets of trading partners and own country MFN obligations towards other countries, we use a seven-region numerical global trade model, calibrated to 1992 trade, consumption, and production data by region. The regions we consider are Australia–New Zealand–Japan (ANJ), Rich Asia (RIA), Poor Asia (POA), North America (NAM), South America (SAM), Europe (EUR) and the Rest-of-the-World (ROW). Developing countries dominate POA, SAM and the ROW. The production, consumption, and trade structure of the model is similar to that used earlier by Perroni and Whalley (1994) to evaluate the insurance component of new regional trade agreements such as NAFTA, where they compute both Nash bargaining and Nash retaliatory equilibria.

2.2.1. *Production*

The model assumes regionally differentiated products (the "Armington" assumption), with each region, j, producing only one good, which it both consumes and exports. Consumers in region j demand both the region j good, and a composite of goods from other regions (imports) which enter preferences as a composite imported good. We take the single good in each region j to be in fixed supply, S^j, $(j = 1, \ldots, K)$; where K denotes the total regions. This treatment implies that regional offer curves in the model are determined solely by endowments and preferences; effectively a pure exchange formulation. Importantly, we do not consider production distortions in our analysis, and were they to be incorporated results would differ.

The one good per region treatment reflects dimensionality restrictions when computing Nash retaliatory (optimal tariff) equilibria. These are discussed both in Perroni and Whalley (1994), and in Hamilton and Whalley (1983). Earlier literature (Johnson, 1954; Gorman, 1957; Kuga, 1973) typically used simple functional forms (constant elasticity excess demand functions) in which optimal tariff setting elicits no further response, and computation of Nash equilibria is trivial. Subsequent literature has used more conventional demand functions, for which Nash equilibrium computation requires repeated iteration. The difficulty of calculation increases rapidly both with regions and goods. Most other literature uses 2×2 or 3×3 formulations; and so in using seven regions here we numerically generalize earlier analyses.

2.2.2. *Preferences*

Demands in region j are determined by utility maximization subject to a regional budget constraint. We assume a representative consumer for each region and use CES preferences, where

$$U^j = \left(\alpha_D^j D_j^{\frac{\sigma_j-1}{\sigma_j}} + \alpha_c^j C_j^{\frac{\sigma_j-1}{\sigma_j}}\right)^{\frac{\sigma_j}{\sigma_j-1}} \quad (j = 1, \ldots, K) \tag{1}$$

and U^j defines utility, D_j and C_j are quantities of the domestic (own region) good and the composite import good consumed by region j. α_{D}^j and α_{c}^j are share parameters in region j's preferences applying to the domestic and composite import goo, and σ_{j} is the CES substitution elasticity in region j's preferences.

The import composite for region j, C_j, is, in turn, a CES aggregate over the imports M_i^j purchased by region j from region i, i.e.,

$$c_j = \left[\sum_{i \neq j} \beta_i^j M_i^{j\,\frac{\lambda_j-1}{\lambda_j}}\right]^{\frac{\lambda_j}{\lambda_j-1}} \quad (j = 1, \ldots, K) \tag{2}$$

where β_i^j are CES share parameters on imports by region j from region i, and λ_j is the bottom level CES substitution elasticity parameter in region j among imports.

Tariffs affect demands by raising the price of imported goods, and generate a substitution effect away from imports towards domestic products. Tariffs also raise revenues, which are treated as recycled to consumers as lump sum transfers, and hence affect incomes. σ_j determines the import demand elasticity in region j, λ_j the ease of substitution among import types.

2.2.3. *Trade barriers*

We consider each region to have available to them the use of (potentially regionally discriminatory) tariffs, t_i^j, i.e., tariff rates on imports by region j from region i. In the various model solutions where we consider the effect of MFN treatment on individual regions, we impose the condition on tariff setting that

$$t_i^j = t_k^j; \quad \forall i, k; \quad i \neq j, \quad k \neq j. \tag{3}$$

In nonMFN cases tariff rates in all regions remain unrestrained by condition (3). Revenues raised by these tariffs are given by

$$R_j = \sum_i t_i^j P_i M_i^j \tag{4}$$

where R_j refers to aggregate tariff revenues raised in region j, and P_i is the sellers price (the world price) of good i (sold by region i to region j).

2.3. *Model solution concepts*

We numerically explore three alternative solution concepts using the model, each one relevant to the three senses of MFN benefits for developing countries we set out above. We compute counterfactual competitive equilibria (without retaliation) for both MFN and nonMFN trade policy changes by the large regions in the model (North America and the EU); comparing each counterfactual solution to the base case (1992) model solution. Results of these comparisons are used to value the first source of developing country benefit from MFN treatment we list above, namely access benefits generated by free riding under MFN on trade liberalization agreed among larger countries. From a small country perspective, the MFN benefit here is the ability to gain improved market access from bilaterally agreed tariff reductions extended multilaterally to all parties through Article 1 of GATT/WTO.

We also compute post-retaliation noncooperative Nash equilibria for global (seven region) tariff games in the model with and without an MFN restraint applying to retaliation by individual regions against other regions. With an MFN restraint in place, countries who use retaliatory trade actions must use the same measure against all countries, without any country differentiation in retaliatory tariff rates. These computations allow us to assess the benefits of MFN to developing countries (and costs to larger countries) in not being selectively discriminated against in a noncooperative retaliatory trade war.[g] These involve the admittedly strong assumption that in a trade war, even if countries violate their own GATT/WTO bound tariff levels, they still abide by the terms of GATT Article 1.

We also compute cooperative bargaining solutions to the model to enable us to assess the impact of MFN treatment on the outcome of trade negotiations. We model cooperative agreements on trade as needing supporting mechanisms in the form of side payments to achieve mutual

[g]These model analyses are also relevant to the issue of how bloc size affects Nash tariff levels, and hence world welfare. See also Haveman (1996) for a recent discussion.

agreement to lower trade barriers. We make calculations of what side-payments might be needed by small regions to support free trade under nonMFN and MFN trade bargaining by comparing across model solutions for alternative bargains; and hence the value (or cost) of MFN as a restraint on bargaining. We trace out inter-regional utility possibility frontiers using alternative side payments, adopting alternative axiomatic bargaining solution concepts (Kalai and Smorodinsky, 1975; Nash, 1950). We interpret side payments in trade policy negotiations as the value of concessions made on domestic policies (intellectual property, services regulation, GSP graduation, energy and resource royalties, domestic tax treatment and other measures) that countries can make as an accompaniment to trade bargaining rather than as payments of cash (which do not occur in current trade policy bargaining).

2.3.1. *Competitive equilibria*

We compute global competitive equilibria for the model for given tariff rates in all regions (treated as exogenous). We use these to assess developing country benefits from free riding on exogenous large country tariff cuts. These equilibria involve market clearing in each country specific product, government budget balance in each region, $(K-1)$ relative goods prices, and K revenue levels in each country; with all of these endogenously determined in equilibrium. We make equilibrium computations using the GAMS (Generalized Algebraic Modeling System) Software due to Brooke *et al.* (1988).

More concretely, income in region j, I^j, is given by

$$I^U = P_j \bar{s}^j + R^j \tag{5}$$

where tariff revenues in region jR^j are given by

$$R^j = \sum_{i \neq j} t_i^j P_i M_i^j \tag{6}$$

and domestic demands in each region are

$$D_j = \frac{(\alpha_D^j)^{\sigma_j} I^j}{[(\alpha_D^j)^{\sigma_j} P_j^{1-\sigma_j} + (\alpha_c^j)^{\sigma_j} (P_j^M)^{(1-\sigma_j)}] P_j^{\sigma_j}} \tag{7}$$

where P_j^M is the composite import price in region j given by

$$P_j^M = \left[\sum_{i \neq j} (\beta_i^j)^{\lambda_j} [(1+t_i^j) P_i]^{(1-\lambda_j)} \right]^{\frac{1}{(1-\lambda_j)}} \tag{8}$$

It follows that exports by region j, X_j, are given by

$$X_j = \bar{S}^j - D_j \tag{9}$$

The demand in region j for the regional import composite, C_j, is given by

$$C_j = \frac{\left(\alpha_c^j\right)^{\sigma_j} I^j}{\left(P_j^M\right)^{\sigma_j}\left[\left(\alpha_D^j\right)^{\sigma_j}(P_j)^{(1-\sigma_j)} + \left(\alpha_c^j\right)^{\sigma_j}\left(P_j^M\right)^{(1-\sigma_j)}\right]} \tag{10}$$

and demands in region j for imports from region i are given as

$$M_i^j = \frac{(\beta_i^j)^{\lambda_j}(P_j^M C_j)}{((1+t_i^j)P_i)^{\lambda_j}\left[\sum_{i\neq j}(\beta_i^j)^{\lambda_j}[(1+t_i^j)P_i]^{(1-\lambda_j)}\right]} \tag{11}$$

The total demand for the exports of any region, l, is given by

$$T_l = \sum_{j\neq l} M_l^j; \quad \forall l \tag{12}$$

and, in equilibrium, prices of the K regional products P_i and the K tariff revenues R^j, are such that

$$T_l = X_l; \quad j\forall l \tag{13}$$

As only relative product prices matter in this equilibrium formulation, a numeraire can be chosen, say, (the price of one of the regional products), or a price normalization (such as $\sum_i P_i = 1$) can be used.

2.3.2. *Noncooperative Nash equilibria*

We compute noncooperative Nash equilibria in this model to evaluate developing country benefits from MFN restraints on retaliation using a tariff game structure similar to that set out in Johnson (1954). Unlike for competitive equilibria above, under this solution concept tariff rates are endogenously determined rather than set exogenously, and reflect country utility maximization across global competitive equilibria for alternative own country tariff rates which change country or region in terms of trade. In this case, tariff rates for each region are obtained by maximizing own country welfare subject to global market clearing; in effect, solving a series of optimization problems across regions in which other region tariffs are successively taken as given. These optimization problems are repeatedly solved until mutual consistency is obtained i.e., tariff rate values for regions taken as exogenous in other regions optimization problems are the solutions for the corresponding own region's optimization problem.

More formally, given tariff rates, t_j^k, in all other countries $k \neq j$, and the competitive equilibrium conditions (13) for each region j, when computing noncooperative Nash equilibria, we repeatedly maximize (1) to generate a set of endogenously determined optimal tariffs, t_j^l, as a best response to the other region tariff rates t_j^k, $k \neq j$. We represent these in the form of reactions functions as

$$\hat{t}_j^l = r(t_j^k); \quad k \neq j \tag{14}$$

In a noncooperative Nash equilibrium, best response tariff rates generated by regional optimizing behavior need to be mutually consistent across all regions i.e.,

$$\hat{t}_j^l = t(\hat{t}_j^k); \quad k \neq l, \ \forall l \tag{15}$$

We compute Nash equilibria for cases where both the MFN restraints (3) apply to retaliation (best responses) by region (i.e., t_j^l are the same for all j), and also for cases where MFN restraints are absent.

2.3.3. *Bargaining and side-payments*

We also compute both Nash (1950) and Kalai–Smorodinsky (1975) bargaining solutions for the model to evaluate the impact of MFN treatment on trade policy bargaining. MFN treatment excludes pairwise bargaining between regions because of its nondiscrimination provisions, and is advantageous to developing countries since they cannot be selectively pressured in negotiation by larger countries using threats of bilateral actions against them. The effect of MFN in this case is to limit the admissible threat points that can be used in bargaining. This element of MFN treatment is disadvantageous to large countries since they forgo their opportunity to bilaterally pressure small countries into disadvantageous trade concessions. We compute solutions from the model under different bargaining solution concepts so as to give a range of measures of bargaining outcomes.

Thompson (1994) surveys axiomatic bargaining solution concepts and describes nine different axiomatic solution concepts, suggesting that Nash and Kalai–Smorodinsky are the most widely used. We implement these two bargaining solution concepts by tracing out utilities possibility frontier for the parties to the bargain, which we generate by parametrically varying side-payments between them and computing Pareto optimal (zero tariff competitive equilibria) allocations. We take the Nash noncooperative equilibrium to be the threat point, and compute bargaining outcomes under both Nash and Kalai–Smorodinsky axioms. MFN treatment constrains the threat point and hence changes the bargaining solution. We consider single period one-shot games. No repeated game structure enters this analysis, and issues of sub-game perfection do not arise.

As with noncooperative Nash equilibrium computation, there are difficulties with dimensionality in computing such model solutions. Generating the utilities possibility frontier in high-dimensional space is tedious, because it does not reflect an analytical solution. We therefore limit ourselves to various pairwise bilateral bargaining between large and small countries for this solution concept, arguing that such bargaining would be ruled out by MFN treatment. We approximate the frontier for each pairwise bargain by the utilities generated in a sequence of computed equilibria under pairwise bilateral transfers. The value of MFN for smaller developing countries in the third sense above lies in avoiding such bilateral bargaining, and the cost for large countries lies in forgoing such opportunities.

As a result, we compute mixed cooperative/noncooperative equilibria in which two regions bargain and can potentially engage in trade retaliation one against another, while the parties not involved in bargaining play passively and maintain their base year tariff levels. This equilibrium yields the threat points for the participants in bilateral bargaining. Using permutations of side payments between the two regions involved in bargaining, we then trace out the utility frontier for the parties to the bargaining by computing cooperative equilibria in which these regions eliminate their tariffs. Each point on the frontier is supported by a configuration of side-payments between the parties; the threat point being given by utility levels in the noncooperative (retaliation) equilibrium.

Thus, if T_i^j represents the side-payment received (or made, if negative) by j from i in such an equilibrium, the income Eq. (5) is modified to

$$I^j = P_j \bar{S}^j + T_i^j \tag{16}$$

where, by construction

$$\sum_i \sum_j T_i^j = 0 \tag{17}$$

We use a Nash criterion for a bargaining solution to the model, appealing to Nash's (1951) axioms. This is the best known of the various axiomatic bargaining solution concepts and maximizes

$$\cup = \prod_l (U_l - U_l^R) \tag{18}$$

with U_l representing region l's utility on the utility possibility frontier we generate (l referring to the regions involved in the bargaining), and U_l^R referring to region l's utility at the threat point, R. This and other axiomatic bargaining solution concepts are discussed in more detail in Thompson (1994), who points out, among other things, that such bargaining solutions are not invariant to a monotonic transformation of individual region utilities.

We also make computations using the Kalai–Smorodinsky (1975) bargaining solution concept. The difference between this and the Nash concept is shown in Fig. 1. While Nash maximizes a criterion function

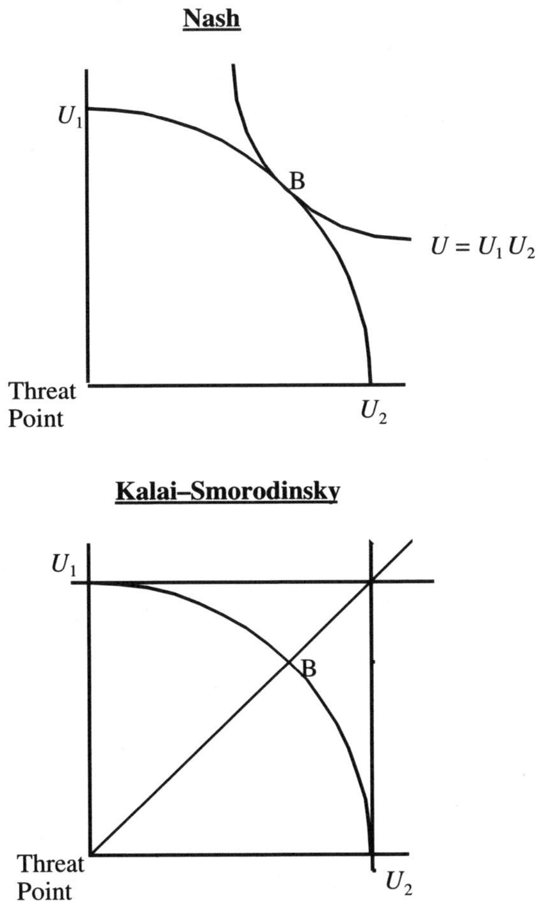

Fig. 1. Nash and Kalai–Smorodinsky bargaining solutions used in model solution (B denotes bargaining outcome).

subject to the utilities possibility frontier, Kalai–Smorodinsky takes maximal utilities for regions and constructs a ray through the utilities possibilities set from the origin to the point B on the frontier. Thompson also discusses the properties of this solution concept.

We also compute power indices for regions on the basis of marginal contribution to broader coalitions in the spirit of Shapley (1953) values.[h] Here we show that the marginal contribution of larger regions in a coalition is higher indicating that such a region could extract a larger share of the surplus from trade bargaining with the rest of the world.

3. Parametrizing and Implementing the Model

We have numerically implemented the model set out above by calibrating it to a benchmark global equilibrium data set for 1992 covering consumption, production, trade, and tariffs for the seven regions we study.[i] Calibration is the procedure described in Mansur and Whalley (1984) and Shoven and Whalley (1992), under which the first use of the model is to solve for model parameter values given an initial (or base case) equilibrium represented by data, rather than the more usual computation of equilibrium given model parameters. The effects of this procedure is to impose equilibrium as an identifying restriction on the model parametrization used. If simple functional forms (Cobb–Douglas) are used, calibration is sufficient to exactly identify all model parameter values. With the CES forms used here, substitution elasticity parameters are required prior to implementing calibration procedures. We draw here on literature values of import demand elasticities by region to guide the key trade related substitution elasticities in the model.

In producing a data set to which we calibrate the model, we first aggregate unadjusted GTAP country data into the regional classification we use here. The links between country classification under which data is reported in the GTAP data base and the regions used in the model is shown in Table 1. We have chosen the seven regions in the model to reflect both large trade entities and significant geographical groupings. We make adjustments to the raw GTAP data so as to satisfy both trade

[h] Shapley values are preferable to bilateral bargaining solutions in that they are consistent with multilateral bargaining (see Hart and Mas-Colell, 1996).

[i] As noted above, the regions are Australia, New Zealand, Japan (ANJ), RIA, POA, NAFTA (NAM), SAM, Europe (EUR), and ROW. We use data from the GTAP (Version 3) data base (see Hertel *et al.*, 1996) for 1992.

Table 1. Regional Aggregation of GTAP Country Data Used in Constructing Model Base Case Data.

Regions in the model		Countries in GTAP data base included in the region
1. ANJ	Australia, New Zealand and Japan	Australia, New Zealand and Japan
2. RIA	Rich Asia	Korea, Indonesia, Malaysia, Philippines, Singapore, Thailand, Hong Kong and Taiwan
3. POA	Poor Asia	China, India, Rest of South Asia
4. NAM	NAFTA	Canada, U.S.A. and Mexico
5. SAM	South America	Central American and Caribbean, Argentina, Brazil, Chile, Rest of South America
6. EUR	Europe	European Union of the 12, Austria, Finland, Sweden, European Free Trade Area and Central European Countries with EU Association Agreements
7. ROW	Rest of the world	Former Soviet Union, Middle East and North Africa, Sub Saharan Africa and Rest of the World

balance conditions and other equilibrium conditions required by the model, including market clearing by product.

Table 2 reports the resulting base case data for 1992 on production and bilateral trade for the seven regions in the model. The value of production in these regions implies a gross world product of $20.6 trillion in 1992. The large regions are NAM and EUR; the small regions are RIA, POA, and SAM. Our base period tariff data come from the same GTAP source, and are shown in Table 3. These include both tariffs and *ad valorem* equivalents of quotas and other trade policy interventions. In reality, MFN trade rules already apply to the base case data, but in the data in Table 3 some element of discrimination in tariff rates across regional imports already appears. This reflects the differing product composition of bilateral trade between regions, and elements of nondiscrimination formally allowed within the system (such as the Generalized System of Preferences, and arrangements under the Lomé Convention).

The key behavioral parameters in the model are the elasticities of substitution in preferences for the two levels we specify. These determine the ease of substitution, first, between types of imports (by region of origin), and, second, between imports as a composite and domestic production. These are important parameters in the model since they determine the strength of terms of trade effects across competitive equilibria, and through these terms of trade effects, both the level of optimal tariffs in

Table 2. Base Case (1992) Regional Data Used in Global General Equilibrium Model.

	Region	Production in ($B)
(A) Production Data[1]		
1.	ANJ	3,451.7
2.	RIA	900.7
3.	POA	641.8
4.	NAM	6,099.0
5.	SAM	792.0
6.	EUR	7,158.7
7.	ROW	1,491.1
	TOTAL	20,595.0

1992 Benchmark Trade Flows (U.S. Billions)

	Importing region						
Exporting region	ANJ	RIA	POA	NAM	SAM	EUR	ROW
ANJ		112.5	27.1	115.8	12.2	92.5	27.6
RIA	91.3		35.3	91.8	7.6	82.3	22.0
POA	25.7	28.9		26.7	2.5	37.2	12.9
NAM	114.9	74.9	19.0		41.1	202.8	42.8
SAM	12.5	6.9	2.7	37.0		41.8	6.4
EUR	85.1	80.3	35.3	187.3	37.6		181.6
ROW	58.2	26.6	14.5	37.0	6.3	150.6	

[1]Based on data from GTAP (Version 3) 1992 data base, with adjustments made to satisfy model consistency conditions.

Table 3. Data on 1992 Tariff and Tariff Equivalents by Region Used in Base Case Model Solution.

	Ad valorem equivalent import tariffs[1] on imports from each region						
Region	ANJ	RIA	POA	NAM	SAM	EUR	ROW
ANJ	—	14.0	34.0	19.0	22.0	13.0	21.0
RIA	12.0	—	38.0	10.0	21.0	8.0	24.0
POA	16.0	15.0	—	10.0	18.0	9.0	22.0
NAM	21.0	17.0	20.0	—	14.0	6.0	13.0
SAM	12.0	10.0	14.0	10.0	—	16.0	13.0
EUR	9.0	10.0	26.0	6.0	15.0	—	16.0
ROW	4.0	7.0	17.0	3.0	7.0	6.0	—

[1]Based on data drawn from 1992 GTAP data base (Version 3).

Table 4. Import Price Elasticity Estimates by Region Used in Model Calibration.

Region	Uncompensated import demand elasticity[1]
ANJ	−1.15
RIA	−1.12
POA	−0.95
NAM	−1.50
SAM	−0.85
EUR	−1.25
ROW	−0.85

[1]The sources used for these values include Marques (1990), and Stern *et al.* (1976).

noncooperative Nash equilibria and the size of side-payments in bargaining solutions (through their impacts on threat points).

The substitution elasticity values used in the model are obtained by calibrating implied point estimates of import price elasticities by region evaluated at the base case equilibrium to literature values of trade elasticities. The model parameters generated in this way are, thus, a reflection of literature-based estimates of trade elasticities; the values we use by region are reported in Table 4. Values such as these, in the neighborhood of one, are widely used in other trade modeling literature (see the discussion in Whalley, 1985), and reflect the range of estimated import price elasticity values that have been generated for over 40 years, going back to Orcutt's (1950) classic work on trade elasticities. Despite their widespread use, such values continue to strike many trade economists as low, and in this present model are the source of strong inter-regional effects from trade policy changes in the model. As a result, we conduct limited sensitivity analyses exploring the impacts of alternative import elasticity parameter values on model results.

4. Model Results

We have used the model and its associated 1992 calibration-based parametrization to compute the three forms of model solutions we set out above; competitive equilibria, noncooperative Nash equilibria in tariffs, and bargaining solutions with side-payments. We use these solution concepts in turn to assess the value of MFN treatment to developing countries in the model in the three senses discussed above; free riding on large country liberalization, constraints on retaliation, and impacts on bargaining.

Table 5. Model Results for Competitive Equilibria Under MFN and NonMFN Bilateral Trade Barrier Elimination.

	Hicksian equivalent variations by region in 1992 when MFN and nonMFN bilateral trade liberalization occurs			
	(1) EU and NAFTA engage in MFN tariff elimination		(2) EU and NAFTA engage in nonMFN tariff elimination	
Region	$Billion, 1992	% of GDP	$Billion, 1992	% of GDP
ANJ	32.1	0.93	−2.1	−0.061
RIA	8.3	0.92	−1.7	−0.189
POA	3.6	0.56	−0.6	−0.093
NAM	−27.6	−0.45	2.5	0.041
SAM	9.7	1.22	−1.0	−0.126
EUR	−26.8	−0.37	5.5	0.077
ROW	9.2	0.62	−2.8	−0.188
WORLD	8.5	0.04	−0.09	−0.000

Table 5 presents results from the first of these model solutions showing benefits from free riding, competitive equilibria under alternative tariff regimes. In both of two cases we consider the EU and North America engage in bilateral tariff elimination. In one this is done on an MFN basis, so that the benefits of bilateral EU–North America tariff elimination are automatically extended to all the other five regions in the model. In the other, bilateral tariff elimination is restricted to bilateral trade between North America and the EU. Computing these equilibria allow us to compare the two different counterfactual equilibria to the benchmark equilibrium and gauge the incremental effects of MFN compared to an exclusionary regional trade agreement.

Results in Table 5 show that under nonMFN bilateral tariff elimination North America and the EU both gain, while all other regions lose due to trade diversion and adverse terms of trade effects. But when MFN-based bilateral tariff elimination occurs between North America and the EU, the other five regions all gain due to improved market access to the EU and North America, while the EU and North America lose from a worsened terms of trade as their tariffs against the other five regions fall further below their optimal tariffs. There are thus differences in the sign of the welfare effects for individual regions (measured in terms of Hicksian equivalent variations between the counterfactual and benchmark equilibria). The benefit of MFN over nonMFN liberalization to poor Asia is 4 billion dollar, for rich Asia is around 10 billion dollar, and for South

Table 6. Effect of MFN Restraints on Nash Noncooperative (Tariff) Equilibria Under Global Retaliatory Trade War Scenarios.

	Hicksian equivalent variations relative to 1992 base case under global retaliatory trade war outcomes relative model base			
	(1) With no MFN restraint on tariff retaliation by region		(2) With MFN restraints on tariff retaliation by region	
Region	$Billion, 1992	% of GDP	$Billion, 1992	% of GDP
ANJ	−112.2	−3.3	−108.1	−3.1
RIA	−132.0	−14.7	−132.9	−14.8
POA	−68.3	−10.6	−68.0	−10.6
NAM	−90.0	−1.5	−100.8	−1.7
SAM	−78.5	−9.9	−75.9	−9.6
EUR	−31.4	−0.4	−26.7	−0.4
ROW	−281.4	−18.9	−299.1	−20.1
WORLD	−793.8	−3.9	−811.4	−4.0

America is around 11 billion dollar. As a fraction of GDP, however, these effects are small primarily because initial tariff levels in the 1992 base case data are low reflecting the global tariff liberalization that occupied under the GATT between 1947 and 1992.

Table 6 reports computations of Nash noncooperative equilibria using the model, reporting the outcome of global trade wars under retaliatory tariff setting by all regions in the model. We consider cases where this retaliatory process either is and is not constrained by MFN. MFN restrained retaliation here means that tariff rates imposed by a region on imports from any region are the same while under nonMFN retaliation they could differ depending upon the origin of the imports. As we note above, these scenarios both assume that MFN treatment (GATT Article 1) will survive increases in tariffs beyond current GATT tariff bindings, and that retaliation continues to a full Nash equilibrium, rather than stopping through arbitration in some trigger supported cooperative equilibrium.[j] We consider two different cases. In one, MFN restraints apply to retaliation, implying nondiscriminatory treatment across import sources in any region importing from the other regions in the model. In the other case, no MFN restraints apply to such retaliation.

Strikingly, the differences between results with and without MFN constrained retaliation in Table 6 are small in part because unconstrained

[j] Also see the discussion in Perroni and Whalley (1996).

retaliatory tariff rates are not that different across country sources into any importing country. In each case, Hicksian equivalent variations relative to the benchmark equilibrium are reported; and in each case all regions lose. As a proportion of national income, losses are smallest in the large regions (North America and the EU). However, the differences between the two cases remain small.

The reason why MFN restraints on retaliation seem to have such small effects on the outcome in a Nash noncooperative equilibrium is that MFN only limits country specific retaliation rather than retaliation in general. The gains to importing countries from retaliation occur from driving down the price of all other products against that of their own product i.e., restricting trade in their own good relative to all imports. The benefit to any region in the model from retaliation occurs from restricting trade in general (as also occurs in the MFN case), more than from restricting trade along particular bilateral channels. MFN restraints, in this case, have little direct effect on the outcome, and both the value of MFN treatment to small regions and the benefits of MFN to smaller regions in the second sense set out above appear small.

Table 7 reports post retaliation tariff rates for the same case considered in Table 6. Rates are reported on a pairwise regional basis. For any importing region, tariff rates across export sources do not vary that much; consistent with the welfare results on MFN constraints on retaliation set out in Table 6.

In Table 8, we report model results which show the impacts of MFN on bargaining outcomes. We analyze these in an indirect way because of the

Table 7. NonMFN Tariff Rates Under Global Retaliatory Trade War Scenarios.

	ANJ	RIA	POA	NAM	SAM	EUR	ROW
ANJ	—	152.8	125.3	187.7	107.8	250.9	21.0
RIA	138.9	—	129.3	189.2	107.4	249.7	24.0
POA	140.6	147.9	—	191.5	107.3	253.6	22.0
NAM	135.5	136.7	121.5	—	109.6	250.7	13.0
SAM	136.2	137.2	122.3	201.8	—	278.3	13.0
EUR	133.9	138.8	124.4	174.1	109.4	—	16.0
ROW	149.9	143.1	124.3	181.4	107.0	272.1	—

Note: ROW is treated as a passive region in the model and hence do not participate in retaliation. The tariff rates imposed by regions under MFN restrained retaliation are 142.0, 147.0, 127.2, 188.3, 108.0, and 278.9% respectively by ANJ, RIA, POA, NAM, SAM, and EUR.

Table 8. Bilateral Side-Payments Needed to Support Bargained Free Trade Between Small and Large Countries.[1]

	Nash bargaining		Kalai–Smorodinsky bargaining	
Payment by	$Billion, 1992	% of GDP	$Billion, 1992	% of GDP
POA to NAM	13.3	2.1	17.2	2.7
POA to EU	29.3	4.6	54.2	8.4
RIA to NAM	55.5	6.2	55.5	6.2
RIA to EU	109.5	12.2	109.5	12.2
SAM to NAM	9.5	1.2	21.6	2.7
SAM to EU	46.9	5.9	62.9	7.9

[1]The model solutions reported on in this table use aggregations of the full seven region model to more manageable four region sub-models as discussed in the text.

dimensionality problems involved in generating utility possibility frontiers for the model (see above). These frontiers are not analytic, and are instead generated by computing a sequence of distortion free (Pareto Optimal) competitive equilibria, where transfers (side-payments) occur between the parties to the bargain. Because of the implications of MFN treatment for small and large regions bargaining on trade policy, we consider various combinations of two region bargaining using the model and compute a number of model solutions.

In these, we treat POA, RIA and SAM as the small regions in the model, and consider the implications of bilateral bargaining occurring for each alternatively with the large regions, Europe and NAFTA. In each case, side-payments need to be made by the small to the large countries to support bilateral free trade as a bargained outcome. The benefit to smaller developing countries of MFN treatment (and the cost to larger countries) is that such bilateral negotiations are effectively excluded, and hence that these side-payments will not be made. As we comment above, we interpret side-payments in this case as the value of concessions made in nontrade areas in linked trade and nontrade bargaining, such as in intellectual property protection, domestic energy policies, and foreign investment policy. As noted by Perroni and Whalley (1994) these are additional areas that have entered recent bilateral trade negotiations, and represent in kind payment by smaller to larger countries for conventional trade benefits.

In each case we use aggregations of the seven-region model into a sequence more manageable four region sub-model (i.e., POA/EU/NAFTA/ROW; RIA/EU/NAFTA/ROW; SAM/EU/NAFTA/ROW), and consider bilateral bargaining between the small (POA, RIA, SAM) and large regions (EU, NAFTA). We compute both the Nash and Kalai–Smorodinsky bargaining solutions discussed earlier. From these solutions we are also able to determine the side-payments made by each region to the other party to the bilateral bargain to support bilateral free trade with the larger region.

Results are reported in Table 8 and their striking feature is the size of the side-payments involved. These are sometimes 8–10 times larger than the benefits of MFN treatment in the first two senses computed earlier and described above. The implication would seem to be that the main advantage (cost) to smaller (larger) countries from MFN treatment may well lie in avoiding bilateral trade bargaining (regional arrangements), rather than in the conventionally discussed benefits of free riding on other countries tariff cuts. There are differences in these results across bargaining solution concepts, and these are more pronounced in some cases (such as POA to EUR and SAM to NAM) than others, but the main theme of the results is common to the results from the two solution concepts.

We have performed a number sensitivity analyses with the model to test out the robustness of the model results reported in Table 7. In Table 9, we

Table 9. Sensitivity Analysis of Side-Payment Calculations Reported in Table 7.

Bilateral side-payments made by POA to NAM ($billion, 1992)				
	Nash bargaining		Kalai–Smorodinsky bargaining	
	$Billion, 1992	% of GDP	$Billion, 1992	% of GDP
A. Central case model specification	13.3	2.1	17.2	2.7
B. Increase top level preference substitution elasticities (Domestic/Composite imports) by 50% in all regions	20.5	3.2	18.2	2.8
C. Cut top and bottom level preference substitution elasticities (Domestic/Composite Imports) by 25% in all regions	22.7	3.5	22.7	3.5
D. Increase bottom level preference substitution elasticities (Among Imports) by 50% in all regions	14.7	2.3	14.7	2.3

report a sample of these results for the case of bilateral bargaining between POA and North America. We vary model elasticities increasing some by 50%, and cutting others by 25%. These elasticity variations have a large effect on noncooperative Nash equilibrium tariff levels (not reported here), but they have more limited effects on the side-payments needed to support multilaterally negotiated free trade.

A weakness of the calculations reported in Tables 8 and 9 is that they do not represent comprehensive measures of the value of MFN treatment, merely illustrating the importance of MFN in the sense of restraints on bargaining for particular pairwise bargains. Another way to proceed is by appealing to notions of marginal contributions of regions to broader coalitions implicit in Shapely's (1953) measure of power; the Shapely value. We have thus also used the model to construct power indices in the spirit of Shapely values, on which we report in Table 10. These measure the marginal contribution individual regions can make to the joint gain a larger coalition can receive from trade bargaining with the ROW. These are still not comprehensive measures of the value of MFN, but nonetheless show how an alternative measure to that used in Tables 8 and 9 points to the same conclusion that the source of major benefit from MFN for smaller countries lies in its impacts on bargaining.

We use the same four-region version of the model as above, but instead consider Nash noncooperative equilibrium outcomes rather than bargained outcomes. We compute Nash equilibria for a no coalition case, for the three pairwise coalitions between POA, Europe, and NAFTA, and also for the grand coalition of the three. ROW is treated as passive in the Nash retaliatory process, and does not enter into any coalitional activity.

Comparing the Nash outcomes for the three-region coalition and the three two-region coalitions, we can calculate the marginal contribution of

Table 10. Marginal Contributions to Three-Region Joint Coalitional Gains from Strategic Trade Policy Setting Against ROW by Individual Regions.

Marginal contribution to the joint gain of a three-region (POA, EU NAFTA) coalition from trade retaliation against ROW (1992 U.S.$billion)

	Gain in $billion, 1992	Gain As % of combined three-region GDP
POA	238.6	1.72
EU	636.4	4.58
NAFTA	611	4.4

each region to the joint three-region gain from forming the coalition. These measures are in the spirit of Shapely values and can be thought of as a measure of region power in wider trade negotiations. Table 10 indicates a small measure for POA, with much larger measures for Europe and NAFTA. These, in turn, suggest more limited bilateral bargaining power for POA relative to the larger Europe and NAFTA regions, a situation which MFN redresses for Poor Asia by effectively ruling out bilateral bargaining.

Thus, the conclusion that we draw from our model results taken as a set is that MFN treatment in the trading system seems to have its largest impacts on the trade bargaining process; and this occurs by effectively ruling out explicit bilateral bargaining between large and small (developing) countries. These effects seem to dominate benefits from free riding for developing countries on MFN tariff cuts by large countries, and any nondiscrimination restraints on global retaliation. These results also seem to explain why developing countries have been concerned about new regional trade arrangements in the trading system such as NAFTA, even though the computed comparative static trade effects against these countries are small in most studies. Their concern is the weakening implied of MFN, and the potential adverse effect on them in terms of trade bargaining, rather than the direct trade effects.

5. Conclusions

This chapter reports on numerical simulation results through which we try to shed light on the value of MFN treatment under global trade rules for developing countries (or regions). We use a seven-region global trade model, calibrated to a 1992 base case data set, in which we are able to compute not only traditional comparative static competitive equilibria under different tariff regimes (and assess free rider benefits), but also noncooperative Nash equilibria with and without MFN restraints on retaliation; and both Nash and Kalai–Smorodinsky bargaining solutions, supported by side-payments. Previous literature has stressed the free rider benefits to small or developing countries, who benefit through MFN from large country tariff cuts. Here we also analyze other developing country benefits from MFN in the form of restraints on retaliation and impacts on bargaining by effectively excluding bilateral bargaining. These three forms of benefits are captured by these solution concepts, and each is evaluated through numerical solution both in the presence and absence of MFN. The incremental effect of MFN is evaluated for each benefit source.

Model results indicate large effects from MFN in influencing bargaining outcomes (and associated side-payments), and only small direct effects from free riding and retaliation constraining considerations. The main benefit (cost) to smaller (larger) countries from MFN treatment seems to be the effective restraint it imposes on regional or bilateral trade policy bargaining to be equivalent to multilateral bargaining. We suggest this also explains why developing countries (such as India) have been concerned about recent regional trade agreements, such as NAFTA, even though repeated studies show that the direct trade effects from diversion are negligible. The concern is the erosion they see of MFN through these arrangements, and the implied impacts on bargaining within the trading system, more so than the direct trade effects.

References

Baldwin, RE (1987). Multilateral liberalization. In *The Uruguay Round: A Handbook on the Multilateral Trade Negotiations*, JM Finger (ed.). Washington D.C: World Bank.

Baldwin, RE and T Murray (1977). MFN tariff reductions and developing country trade benefits under the GSP. *Economic Journal*, **87**, 30–46.

Bond, E and C Syropolos (1996). The size of trading blocs: Market power and world welfare effects. *Journal of International Economics*, **40**, 411–437.

Brooke, A, D Kendrick and A Meeraus (1988). *GAMS: A User's Guide*. California: Scientific Press.

Caplin, A and K Krishna (1988). Tariffs and the most-favored-nation clause: A game theoretic approach. *Seoul Journal of Economics*, **1**, 267–289.

Finger, JM (1979). Trade liberalization: A public choice perspective. In *Challenges to a Liberal International Economic Order*, RC Amacher, G Haberler and TD Willett (eds.). Washington D.C.: American Enterprise Institute.

Gorman, WM (1957). Tariffs, retaliation, and the elasticity of demand for imports. *Review of Economic Studies*, **25**, 133–162.

Hamilton, RW and J Whalley (1983). Optimal tariff calculations in alternative trade models, and some possible implications for current world trading arrangements. *Journal of International Economics*, **15**, 323–348.

Hart, S and A Mas-Colell (1996). Bargaining and value. *Econometrica*, **64**(2), 357–380.

Haveman, J (1996). Some welfare effects of sequential customs union formation. *Canadian Journal of Economics*, **29**(4), 941–958.

Hertel, TW (ed.) (1997). *Global Trade Analysis: Modelling and Applications*. Cambridge: Global University Press.

Johnson, HG (1954). Optimal tariffs and retaliation. *Review of Economic Studies*, **21**, 142–153.

Kalai, E and M Smorodinsky (1975). Other solutions to Nash's bargaining problem. *Econometrica*, **43**, 513–518.

Kuga, K (1973). Tariff retaliation and policy equilibrium. *Journal of International Economics*, **3**, 351–366.

Ludema, R (1991). International trade bargaining and the most-favored-nation clause. *Economics and Politics*, **3**(1), 1–20.

Ludema, R (1996). On the value of preferential trading agreements in multilateral negotiations. Mimeo, University of Western Ontario, Canada.

Mansur, AH and J Whalley (1984). Numerical specification of applied general equilibrium models: Estimation, calibration and data. In *Applied General Equilibrium Analysis*, HE Scarf and JB Shoven (eds.). Cambridge: Cambridge University Press.

Marques, J (1990). Bilateral trade elasticities. *Review of Economics and Statistics*, **72**, 70–77.

Nash, JF (1950). The bargaining problem. *Econometrica*, **28**, 155–162.

Orcutt, GH (1950). Measurement of price elasticities in international trade. *Review of Economics and Statistics*, **32**, 117–132.

Perroni, C and J Whalley (1994). The new regionalism: Trade liberalization or insurance? NBER Working Paper #4626, National Bureau of Economic research, Inc.

Perroni, C and J Whalley (1996). How severe is global retaliation risk under increasing regionalism? *American Economic Review*, **86**, 57–61.

Shapley, LS (1953). A value for n-person games. In *Contributions to the Theory of Games*, HW Kuhn and AW Tuckerz (eds.), Vol. 2, pp. 307–317. Princeton, NJ: Princeton University Press.

Shoven, JB and J Whalley (1992). *Applying General Equilibrium.* Cambridge: Cambridge University Press.

Siedman, DJ and E Winter (1997). The endogenous expansion of preferential trading arrangements: Theory and applications. Mimeo, European University, Department of Economics.

Staiger, RW (1995). International rules and institutions for cooperative trade policy. In *Handbook of International Economics*, GM Grossman and K Rogoff (eds.), Vol. 3, Chapter 29, pp. 1495–1551. Elsevier.

Stern, RM, JF Francis and BF Schumacher (1976). *Price Elasticities in International Trade: An Annotated Bibliography.* London: MacMillan Press.

Thompson, W (1994). Cooperative models of bargaining. In *Handbook of Game Theory*, RJ Aumann and S Hart (eds.), Vol. 2. Elsevier Science B.V.

Whalley, J (1985). *Trade Liberalization Among Major World Trading Areas.* Cambridge, M.A.: MIT Press.

Part IV

Money and Taxes in General Equilibrium Trade Models

Chapter 15

Tax Structure and Revenue Instability Under External Shocks: Some General Equilibrium Calculations for Côte D'Ivoire*

Cristina Dawkins and John Whalley[†,‡]
Centre for the Study of International Economic Relations,
University of Western Ontario, London, Canada N6A 5C2
University of Warwick, Coventry CV4 7AL, U.K.
[†]*National Bureau of Economic Research (NBER)*

This chapter presents some general equilibrium calculations for Côte D'Ivoire which explore the significance of tax structure for the relationship between external shocks and revenue instability, an issue until recently little explored in the literature, either for Côte D'Ivoire or other developing countries. Results suggest that a low-rate broadly based value-added tax, as advocated by the World Bank in its structural adjustment lending, may be a poor revenue stabilizer compared with existing trade-based tax regimes in many lower-income commodity exporting countries. With high trade taxes, the external sector is smaller, and external sector shocks general less revenue instability under existing arrangements compared with a broadly based yield-neutral alternative, such as a VAT.

1. Introduction

This chapter presents some general equilibrium calculations for Côte d'Ivoire which explore the significance of tax structure for the relationship between external shocks and revenue instability, an issue until recently little explored in the literature, either for Côte d'Ivoire or other developing countries. Available literature (e.g., Bleaney *et al.*, 1992) uses econometrics techniques to analyze the relative contribution of external and other shocks as sources of aggregate revenue instability, rather than explicitly using

*This chapter was first published in (1997). *Review of Development Economics*, **1**(1), 23–33.
[‡]We acknowledge support from the program on Institutional Reform and the Informal Sector (IRIS) at the University of Maryland at College Park, under their IRIS Scholars Program.

the economy-wide modeling techniques that we apply here. Tax structure, *per se*, does not explicitly enter such analyses. We use the numerical general equilibrium model of Côte d'Ivoire developed by Chia *et al.* (1992) and calibrated to a 1986 benchmark data set, and shock the model by changing externally set world prices for key commodity exports (coffee and cocoa).

Model results suggest that aggregate revenue impacts from global commodity price declines can differ substantially under alternative tax regimes. Tax structure affects the sectoral composition of the economy and thus matters for the propagation of external shocks onto revenues. In particular, the existing tax structure with high trade taxes outperforms a broadly based VAT. With high trade taxes, the external sector is smaller, and external sector shocks generate less revenue instability under existing arrangements compared with a broadly based yield-neutral alternative, such as a VAT. These results suggest that a low-rate broadly based VAT, as advocated by the World Bank in its structural adjustment lending, may be a poor revenue stabilizer compared with existing trade-based tax regimes in many lower-income commodity exporting countries. Other factors also come into play, such as whether household groups that bear the burden of particular taxes spend large or small fractions of their income on lightly taxed (usually traditional agricultural) products. Thus, under some tax structures, falls in world commodity prices can depress incomes of particular groups and have smaller revenue impacts that would be true under a broadly based VAT which would tax all of their expenditures.

These considerations raise a number of questions. Which tax systems best insulate revenues from external shocks? What changes in revenues are implied by differing size changes in commodity prices? Is the relationship approximately linear across both large and small changes, or is it significantly nonlinear? Our results also shed light on these for the Ivorian case.

2. Assessing Revenue Instability Using a General Equilibrium Model of Côte D'Ivoire

After string growth in Côte d'Ivoire in the first two decades following independence in 1961, world prices for key exports (coffee and cocoa), which have historically accounted for well over 50% of export earnings, began to fall sharply in the early 1980's. A decade of negative growth followed and, with it, major internal dislocation. Some estimates suggest that real per-capita income may have fallen by as much as 25% between 1985 and 1990. Many of the ensuing adjustment problems fell into the fiscal domain, with sharp falls in revenues leading to pressures on the expenditure side. By 1990, the public-sector deficit, which was inconsequential in the early 1980's, was approaching 10% of GDP.

Here, we use a numerical general equilibrium model for Côte d'Ivoire to analyze how tax structure affects the extent to which external shocks over this period may have translated into revenue instability. The model, due to Chia *et al.* (1992), is a numerical open economy general equilibrium model in the tradition of the computable equilibrium models deriving from Shoven and Whalley (1972, 1984). It captures the main features of the Ivorian economy: Production sectors, household sectors, the government sector (which includes public enterprises) and the rest of the world, along with the key elements of the tax system (trade taxes, corporate and personal income taxes, production and excise taxes). Other elements of fiscal structure such as the Stabilization Fund, a tax transfer scheme aiming to stabilize domestic producer prices (and represented here in *ad valorem* equivalent form), enter the model along with interhousehold and government-household transfers. The model is calibrated to a 1986 Benchmark Data Set for Côte d'Ivoire, and uses Cobb–Douglas and CES functions and literature-based elasticity estimates.

2.1. *Production*

The production side of the model includes seven tradable and eight nontradable sectors. Tradable sectors include: A food crop sector, a traditional export sector, a nontraditional export sector, a food processing sector, and manufacturing sectors. Nontradable sectors include: Gas and electricity, construction, transport, financial services, government services, and other services. Given the importance of agriculture in Côte d'Ivoire (46% of GDP, and 91% of exports in 1986), more detail appears in the model for the agricultural sector, through a separate specification of the food crop sector, the traditional export sector (coffee, cocoa, cotton), and the nontraditional sector (sugar, palm oil, rubber). Although not central to the model analysis undertaken here, the model also includes separate representations of formal and informal sectors in the Ivorian economy; the informal sector reflecting activities under-represented in the annual financial survey of enterprises. These typically neither pay taxes nor receive subsidies.

Production in each sector is represented by nested functions; the top level nest being Leontief in intermediate demands and value-added.

Intermediate demands are a CEF function of domestically produced and imported goods; with value-added a nested CES function of capital and labor (the latter being further disaggregated into labor types). The tradable goods sector produces exports and domestically consumed goods according to a CET function. Firms determine factor demands and output supplies by maximizing profits. All sectors are assumed to be competitive. Capital and labor are assumed to be internationally immobile. Factor mobility between sectors is constrained by the presence of sector-specific factors.

2.2. *Factor markets*

The model structure includes a more detailed treatment of the labor market than in many other numerical general equilibrium models. Labor is disaggregated into three types: Agricultural, skilled, and unskilled. Skilled and unskilled labor move freely across sectors, while agricultural labor is sector-specific. In the agricultural sector, unskilled labor, skilled and agricultural labor enters a CES aggregate function. In the nonagricultural formal sectors, labor is a nested CES function of skilled and unskilled labor. The informal sector uses only unskilled labor.[a] With unskilled and skilled labor mobile across sectors, this treatment of the labor markets captures movements between formal and informal sectors, as well as migration between agricultural and nonagricultural sectors (i.e., rural-urban migration).

Four types of capital appear in the model: Food crop capital, traditional export-sector capital, capital used in the nontraditional export sector, and nonspecific sector capital. Each of the first three of these are sector-specific capital, the only capital employed in that sector, and the shocks of each type of capital are fixed. More than half of the capital in the economy is treated as fixed and is split between the three agricultural sectors. This has implications both for the incidence of taxes and the measurement of revenue instability.

2.3. *Households*

Households maximize nested utility functions subject to budget constraints. The top nest is a Cobb–Douglas function defined over goods; the lower

[a]For a more detailed discussion of the structure of these value-added functions, see Chia *et al.* (1992).

nest is a CES function defined over domestic and imported goods. Each household consumes the ten consumer goods identified in the model, is endowed with an exogenous and fixed amount of both mobile (labor and capital) and sector-specific factors, and preferences (which differ by household group). Given the static nature of the model, household shares of consumption and savings in post-tax income are assumed constant, with all household savings treated as paid into a savings pool from which domestic investment is financed.

Besides income from endowments, households also receive transfers from the government, from abroad, and from other households. Households engage in independent trades and the inactive households receive net subsidies from the government. Unlike in developed countries, interhousehold transfers play a major role in the economy and reflect a strong rural–urban linkage in income transfers. These are also captured in the model.

Households in the model are represented by seven socioeconomic groups: Export households, food crop households in the Savannah region, households who are administrative government employees, households in the formal sector, households engaged in independent trades or in the informal sector, and inactive households. Classifying households in this manner allows us to identify the impacts of external price shocks on different segments of the economy.

2.4. *External sector*

The treatment of the external sector in the model reflects the widely used "Armington" (1969) assumption which models domestic and foreign products as imperfect substitutes. With imperfect substitution on the import side we avoid problems with complete specialization and cross hauling which have traditionally kept numerical modelers away from a homogeneous goods treatment for tradables. Tariffs apply to imported products, and domestic import composites enter both intermediate demands and household final demands. On the export side, the extent to which world commodity shocks are fully and instantaneously transmitted to the domestic economy depends on the substitution elasticities assumed between comparable domestic and foreign goals.

The model treatment thus departs from the "price taker" on imports and "price maker" on exports assumption used by Dervis *et al.* (1982), and others, and discussed at some length in Whalley and Yeung (1984).

We assume small open price-taking behavior for both imports and exports; but with imperfect substitutability between domestic and foreign products on both import and export sides. These elements of model structure have implications for the questions we address, since with insulation from the world economy, world prices will no longer directly determine domestic factor prices and production which in turn affects the tax base. Here both exported and imported products are imperfect substitutes across domestic and foreign sources, with the degree of substitutability determining the extent of transmission of price disturbance.

2.5. *Government sector and tax structure*

The tax structure in the base-case specification of the model encompasses production taxes in all the formal sectors of the economy as well as export taxes levied on the traditional export and processed food sectors. Imports of manufactured goods, rice, processed foods, and food crops are subject to import duties. The activities of the Caisse de Perequation (Marketing Board for rice) and the Caisse de Stabilization (Marketing Board for cocoa, coffee) are modeled as *ad valorem* taxes or subsidies on output, depending on whether or not revenues are raised by the fund on a net basis. Finally, the government collects income taxes from each household and corporate taxes from firms.

In the model, the government also provides various services such as public administration, economic and social planning, and defence and security services to the public either free or with a small user fee. Goods and services used by government to provide public services enter government demands and public-sector transfers to households for education and other objectives also enter the model. All of these activities are financed by a number of *ad valorem* taxes, with the level of provision of government services decided through government utility maximization defined over inputs (mainly labor) used to provide these services. No mechanism exists in the model whereby households directly articulate demands for public goods.

The relative importance of these various government revenue sources in the 1986 base-case data used in the model is shown in Table 1. Trade taxes, and particularly taxes on the traditional export sector, dominate taxes on other exports. Taxes on goods for domestic consumption (including excises) are the major category source, with income taxes more minor.

Table 1. Percentage Contribution of Component Taxes to Government Tax Revenues in the 1986 Base-Case Data Used in the Côte d'Ivoire Model.

Traditional sector exports (coffee, cocoa, cotton)[a]	22
All other exports[a]	7
Imports	29
Domestic production (all informal sectors)	37
Income taxes from households	5

[a]Taxes on the export sectors include export duties as well as *ad valorem* production taxes on exported goods.

2.6. *Calibration and model solution*

The model is calibrated to a 1986 base-period micro-consistent data set for Côte d'Ivoire. These data are drawn from a Social Accounting Matrix (SAM) constructed for Côte d'Ivoire for 1986. The basic input data are from the National Accounts (Republique de Côte d'Ivoire, 1991) and related sources, such as the Balance of Payments from the Banque de Donnees Financieres, Household Survey data, and Tax data.

The SAM provides a consistent accounting of the circular flow of incomes and expenditures in the Ivorian economy for 1986, and serves as a base-period model-admissible equilibrium data set for calibration. Constructed so as to be micro-consistent, it satisfies all the equilibrium conditions of the model: Markets clear for all goods and factors; all 15 sectors earn zero profit; budget balance holds for all seven households groups and the government; and the aggregate supply of each good equals aggregate demand. Aggregate supply includes both domestic production and imports, while aggregate demand includes intermediate and final demands. Private consumption expenditures, government expenditures, capital formation, and exports are components of final demand. Zero-profit conditions imply that industries earn normal economic profits, and hence total receipts from sales in each sector equals total expenditures. Total sales include payments for intermediate demands, final demands, and net trades, while total costs of production include costs of intermediate inputs, payments to primary factors, net payments to the Caisse de Stabilization, Caisse de Perequation, and taxes. Taxes paid by production sectors in the model include production taxes, import duties, and export taxes.

Calibration of the model to the 1986 SAM produces parameter value for the various behavioral functions in the model such that the model reproduces the benchmark data as an equilibrium solution, if no changes in policies or other model characteristics occur.[b] Calibration of Cobb–Douglas functions is relatively straightforward since share parameters in Cobb–Douglas functions can be determined simply from the input shares of factors or expenditure shares. Procedures used to determine share and other parameters in the CES/CET functions we use here through calibration are slightly more complex, insofar as elasticities of substitution must first be set.

In implementing our calibration procedures, we follow Harberger (1962) in adopting a unit's convention to separate benchmark equilibrium value data into separate price and quantity observations. Thus, assuming the net-of-tax price of mobile labor to be one, the quantity of labor used in sector i in the benchmark equilibrium is determined from the value-added data showing the returns paid to labor in sector i. With this separation complete, model calibration is implemented in the ways described in Mansur and Whalley (1984), using elasticity parameters from related literature for the CES components of calibration.[c] The key elasticity parameters used in the model on the production side for capital-labor and qualified–nonqualified labor substitution are set out in Chia *et al.* (1992). MPS/GE, a software package developed by Rutherford (1989), is used to solve the model for counterfactual equilibria; these typically reflect commodity price shocks of varying severity.

3. Model Results on the Role of Tax Structure in Revenue Instability

We have used the model described in earlier sections to analyze the effects of external shocks on revenue instability in Côte d'Ivoire in the presence of alternative tax structures. We use a number of model specifications and analyze a variety of shocks. The model revenue instability results jointly project several key themes that stand in contrast to received wisdom on what constitutes an appropriate tax structure in a developing country.

In Table 2, we present results from the base-case model variant and a case where the pre-existing tax system is replaced by a broadly based

[b]See also the discussion of calibration in Michel and Noel (1984), and especially the modele de prevision macro-economique used by the planning department in Côte d'Ivoire. See also Benjamin and Devarajan (1985).
[c]Scale parameters in the Cobb–Douglas function are determined from the input shares of factors.

VAT before the exogenously specified shock affects the economy. In the first of these cases we calculate the percentage changes in real revenues under the existing tax system, given different percentage falls in world prices of traditional exports (coffee and cocoa). We use 1986 benchmark equilibrium data as our reference point. In further computations we first replace the existing tax structure with a yield-neutral equivalent VAT on all consumption, including imports, and then compute the percentage change in real revenues generated by the model for the same shocks as those we impose on the existing tax structure.

The striking feature of Table 2 is the sharply elevated revenue instability under the VAT compared with the existing tax system. This feature primarily reflects the importance of high trade taxes in the existing system in insulating the economy from external shocks. The existing tax system is concentrated on a narrow revenue base from which adjustments have already taken place, so that as price changes increase, little further adjustment is possible, and revenues are relatively stable. With a prior move to a VAT, the traded-goods sector is enlarged, and the propagation

Table 2. Base-Case Model Evaluation of Revenue Instability (Under Alternative Tax Structures).

Fall in prices of traditional exports (coffee, cocoa) (%)	Change in real revenues under the existing tax system[a] (%)	Change in real revenues under a VAT-based system[b] (%)
0	0.00	0.00
5	−0.13	−0.19
10	−0.26	−0.38
15	−0.40	−0.58
20	−0.54	−0.79
25	−0.70	−1.00
30	−0.86	−1.23
35	−1.02	−1.46
40	−1.20	−1.69
45	−1.39	−1.94
50	−1.58	−2.20
55	−1.79	−2.47
60	−2.01	−2.75
65	−2.25	−3.04
70	−2.51	−3.35

[a]Using 1986 benchmark equilibrium data as a base or reference.
[b]Using equilibria generated by the replacement of the existing tax system by a VAT as a reference point.

of external shocks through the rest of the economy, and therefore onto revenues, is also larger than under the existing tax structure. We thus conclude from this that in being concentrated on narrow bases, and in particular being linked through high trade taxes to smaller trade volumes in the economy, the existing tax system generates lower degrees of revenue instability than a VAT-based system. The implications of this are that a VAT-based tax system provides less revenue stability than the current tax system for the types of price shocks to which the Ivorian economy is typically subjected over an average cycle. In contrast to traditional efficiency arguments that argue for the implementation of VAT, the revenue instability properties of a VAT compared with existing tax systems maybe a drawback to its implementation.

Table 3 displays the effects of the same shocks on revenues under a number of model variants. We once again compute the percentage changes

Table 3. Revenue Instability Under Model and Parameter Sensitivity.

Fall in prices of traditional exports (coffee, cocoa) (%)	Change (%) in revenues under the existing system[a]			Change (%) in revenues under a VAT-based system[b]		
	Model 1	Model 2	Model 3	Model 1	Model 2	Model 3
0	0.00	0.00	0.00	0.00	0.00	0.00
5	−0.35	−0.17	−0.04	−0.38	−0.23	−0.15
10	−0.72	−0.35	−0.09	−0.78	−0.46	−0.31
15	−1.08	−0.54	−0.14	−1.18	−0.70	−0.47
20	−1.28	−0.73	−0.20	−1.57	−0.95	−0.64
25	−1.29	−0.93	−0.26	−1.95	−1.21	−0.83
30	−1.29	−1.14	−0.34	−2.25	−1.47	−1.02
35	−1.28	−1.36	−0.42	−2.31	−1.75	−1.22
40	−1.28	−1.58	−0.51	−1.88	−2.03	−1.42
45	−1.27	−1.81	−0.61	−1.83	−2.33	−1.65
50	−1.27	−2.06	−0.72	−1.81	−2.64	−1.88
55	−1.27	−2.31	−0.84	−1.80	−2.96	−2.12
60	−1.26	−2.58	−0.97	−1.80	−3.30	−2.38
65	−1.26	−2.86	−1.12	−1.79	−3.65	−2.66
70	−1.26	−3.17	−1.29	−1.79	−4.02	−2.95

Model 1: Mobile capital between all sectors.
Model 2: Decreased productivity in the food crop sector.
Model 3: Unitary import CES substitution elasticity between domestic and foreign goods.
[a]Using 1986 benchmark equilibrium data as a base or reference.
[b]Using equilibria generated by the replacement of the existing tax system by a VAT as a reference point.

in real tax revenues under the existing tax structure and under a VAT-based system, but in this case for three model variants. In the first of these, we assume mobile capital between sectors. In the second, productivity shocks affect the food crop sector and change relative prices of domestic products. In this case, the shocks on the external sector affect an economy where production functions in the food crop sectors have lower efficiency parameters. Finally, we use different substitution elasticities in the import demand functions for Côte d'Ivoire; these affect the numerical specifications of the CES functions defined over domestic and foreign products.

With a change in the model treatment towards more capital mobility, the behavior of the revenue change in columns 1 and 4 becomes highly nonlinear. Initial adjustments take place as mobile capital leaves the tax sectors, with large adjustments taking place for relatively modest shocks. Once most of the capital has left the sector, subsequent shocks result in relatively little further adjustment, and the revenue impacts become progressively smaller. Hence, with more factor mobility the extent of revenue instability as reported in Table 3 tends to be accentuated for smaller price shocks because of the heightened mobility of factors out of sectors subject to shocks.

The second set of sensitivity results show that, with different productivity parameters, the food crop sector results (compared with Table 2) remain largely the same, insofar as the existing tax structure still provides more stability than a VAT, in this case because the food crop sector is lightly taxed. While the evaluation of the relative stability properties of alternative taxes is a function of both the type and size of shock involved, in this case the stability superiority of the existing tax structure over a VAT is preserved under a different parametric specification.

Changing import substitution elasticities in columns 3 and 6 also has relatively little impact on reported revenue instability results, because import prices remain unchanged as a result of the external shock, and the effects operating through the trade sector on the import side are largely income rather than price effects. These income effects have significant revenue instability implications because of the impact on trade taxes, but changes in the elasticity of substitution between domestic and foreign products have little impact on revenue instability.

In Table 4, we further analyze the earlier revenue instability results under alternative model parametrizations, concentrating on elasticities between domestic and export production which affect the supply elasticities of sectors subject to shocks. With a zero substitution elasticity in

Table 4. Model Sensitivity to Changes in the Elasticity Between Domestic and Export Production.

Decrease in world price of traditional exports (%)	Elasticity of transformation					
	0.0	0.5	1.0	1.5	2.0	5.0
	Change in revenue under existing system (%)					
0	0.00	0.00	0.00	0.00	0.00	0.00
10	−0.31	−0.27	−0.26	−0.26	−0.25	−0.27
20	−0.65	−0.56	−0.54	−0.53	−0.53	−0.55
30	−1.03	−0.88	−0.85	−0.83	−0.83	−0.85
40	−1.44	−1.24	−1.19	−1.16	−1.15	−1.16
50	−1.90	−1.64	−1.56	−1.52	−1.50	−1.50
60	−2.42	−2.09	−1.97	−1.91	−1.88	−1.87
70	−2.99	−2.61	−2.45	−2.36	−2.31	−2.27
	Change in revenue under VAT-based system (%)					
0	0.00	0.00	0.00	0.00	0.00	0.00
10	−0.55	−0.41	−0.38	−0.36	−0.34	−0.29
20	−1.13	−0.85	−0.79	−0.74	−1.71	−0.59
30	−1.75	−1.33	−1.23	−1.15	−1.09	−0.91
40	−2.39	−1.85	−1.69	−1.58	−1.50	−1.25
50	−3.08	−2.41	−2.20	−2.05	−1.94	−1.61
60	−3.84	−3.04	−2.75	−2.55	−2.41	−2.00
70	−4.67	−3.73	−3.35	−3.10	−2.91	−2.41

production between domestic and export products in the constant elasticity-of-transformation function assumed in the model, results for the existing tax system and a VAT are sharply different; the differences narrowing as the elasticity increases. The substitution elasticity in technology thus emerges as a key parameter affecting model behavior. This is because the price shock affects domestic products, and the elasticity value assumed between domestic and foreign products, particularly in agricultural food crop sectors, controls the substitution effects out of the products whose prices have been sharply lowered. With a zero rather than unity elasticity as in the base-case, the revenue instability functions once again change.

The conclusion from these results, therefore, is that changes in model structure will affect both the pattern and form of revenue instability, particularly where assumptions on factor mobility or variations in key substitution elasticities related to the portion of the economy on which the external shock is most directly felt are concerned. The superiority of the existing tax system to the VAT on revenue stability grounds, however, persists through all the cases.

4. Conclusions

In this chapter, we have analyzed the effects of tax structure on revenue instability in Côte d'Ivoire. We used a general equilibrium model constructed for the analysis of Ivorian social programs, adapted here to analyze revenue instability issues. The motivation of our analysis was that literature there is on revenue instability, and the role it plays in wider economic and macro-dislocation in developing countries, tends to focus on econometric analyses which run regressions to isolate the role of country and other characteristics on different revenue instability patterns. Relatively little micro-based analysis exists of revenue instability in developing countries.

For the external shocks which we consider as the revenue instability source for Côte d'Ivoire, our results suggest that the existing tax structure tends to outperform a broadly based VAT on revenue stability grounds. The key reason is that the high reliance on trade taxes under the existing regime implies that a move to a VAT will expand the traded-goods sector. Hence, the extent to which any external sector shock in the form of reduced external sector prices maps through into reduced revenues depends on the tax structure. Because the existing tax system is concentrated on fairly narrow tax bases, large tax changes also result in progressively smaller adjustments, and so for changes of a given size the existing tax system outperforms the VAT-based system less dramatically.

We suggest that improved performance of the existing structure relative to a VAT in terms of its relative revenue stability properties provides a rationale against its introduction in lower-income commodity-exporting developing countries and contrasts with those traditionally offered on efficiency grounds. We also analyzed the size and nature of the shocks involved to see if they affect stability properties, performing a number of sensitivity analyses with the model. All indicate the importance of model structure and parameter specification for the precise revenue stability performance, while leaving unchanged the central result of revenue stability superiority of the existing tax regime over the VAT.

References

Armington, P (1969). A theory of demand for products distinguished by place of production. *IMF Staff Papers*, **16**, 159–178.

Benjamin, N and S Devarajan (1985). Oil revenue and economic policy in Cameroon. World Bank Staff Working Paper 745, Washington, DC.

Bleaney, M, N Gemell and D Greenaway (1992). Tax revenue and instability in sub-Saharan Africa: Causes and consequences. CREDIT Research Paper 92/2.

Chia, N, S Wahba and J Whalley (1992a). A general equilibrium-based social policy model for Côte d'Ivoire, Poverty and Social Policy Series, Paper No. 2, Washington, DC: World Bank.

Dervis, K, JD Melo and S Robinson (1982). *General Equilibrium Models for Development Policy.* Cambridge: Cambridge University Press.

Harberger, A (1962). The incidence of the corporate income tax. *Journal of Political Economy*, **70**, 215–240.

Mansur, A and J Whalley (1984). Numerical specification of applied general equilibrium models: Estimation, calibration and data. In *Applied General Equilibrium Analysis*, H Scarf and J Shoven (eds.). New York: Cambridge University Press.

Michel, G and M Noel (1984). Short term responses to trade and incentive policies in the Ivory coast: Comparative static simulations in a computable general equilibrium model. World Bank Staff Working Paper 647, Washington, DC.

Republique de Côte d'Ivoire (1991). Les comptes de la nation 1986. Direction de la statistique et de la comptabilite nationale. Mimeo, Côte d'Ivoire.

Rutherford, T (1989). General equilibrium modeling with MPS/GE. University of Western Ontario, Canada.

Shoven, J and J Whalley (1972). A general equilibrium calculation of the effects of differential taxation of capital in the U.S. *Journal of Public Economics*, **1**, 281–322.

Shoven, J and J Whalley (1984). Applied general equilibrium models of taxation and international trade. *Journal of Economic Literature*, **22**, 1007–1051.

Whalley, J and B Yeung (1984). External sector closing rules in applied general equilibrium models. *Journal of International Economics*, **16**(2), 123–138.

Chapter 16

Discriminatory Features of Domestic Factor Tax Systems in a Goods Mobile-Factors Immobile Trade Model: An Empirical General Equilibrium Approach*

John Whalley†
University of Western Ontario
National Bureau of Economic Research (NBER)

A recently constructed numerical general equilibrium model of domestic and foreign trade activity for the U.S., the (nine-member) EEC, and Japan is used to analyze the effects of removing distortions in domestic factor taxes, taking into account international trade flows. As is conventional in the general equilibrium tax literature, corporate and property taxes are treated as *ad valorem* taxes on capital use by industry and social security taxes as *ad valorem* taxes on labor use by industry. National accounts sources are used both to obtain model equivalent tax rates by trading area and to construct a benchmark data set with which to estimate the model. Results suggest that under some assumptions current factor tax structures can produce significant terms-of-trade gains, and in the U.S. case results show welfare losses occurring from the removal of existing distortions. This result contrasts with conventional closed economy analysis of distorting factor taxes and is explained by national terms-of-trade losses which more than outweigh the gains from removal of domestic distortions. The policy significance of this and other findings is discussed.

1. Introduction

This chapter reports some numerical results on the strength of relative price effects in international trade caused by the different domestic factor

*This chapter was first published in (1980). *Journal of Political Economy*, **88**(6), 1177–1202.
†An earlier version of this chapter was presented at the Econometric Society Meeting, August 31, 1978, Chicago. I am especially grateful to Wayne Thirsk for bringing an important error in an earlier draft to my attention which, in turn, resulted in substantial recomputation. I also wish to acknowledge comments from Roger Gordon, Jim Melvin, Greg Ballantine, and two referees and credit Fred Brown, Bob Hamilton, and Jon Fuller with invaluable research assistance. This work has been supported by the Ford Foundation under their competition in International Economic Order.

taxes which operate in the major trading areas of the U.S., the (nine-member) EEC, and Japan.[a] These have been obtained from a recently constructed empirically based static general equilibrium model of domestic economic activity and international trade involving these major trading areas.[b] The model follows the tradition of theoretical Heckscher–Ohlin trade models and incorporates numerical specifications of demand and production functions in each trading bloc along with estimates of factor tax rates by industry. The model has fixed factor endowments by trading area. It departs from traditional Heckscher–Ohlin in that the "Armington" assumption of product and factor heterogeneity across trading areas is used and technology therefore differs across areas. Trade occurs in commodities but, unlike traditional Heckscher–Ohlin, arises from more than differences in factor endowments. A feature of the model is its multipurpose character, having been constructed to aid evaluation of several forms of price-distorting interferences in world trade. Tariffs, other taxes, and selected nontariff barriers are also present in the model but are not changed in the experiments discussed.

A striking finding is the strength of the terms-of-trade effects which domestic factor taxes can induce.[c] These effects are sufficiently strong that under some assumptions the U.S. is better off with existing distorting factor tax systems compared with revenue-preserving broadly based sales taxes which are usually considered nondistorting in the public finance literature. This result occurs because existing policies are closer to a set of optimal export taxes than are uniform taxes, and the terms-of-trade gains through the indirect exercise of national monopoly power implicit in factor tax systems can more than offset the domestic distortionary losses. Results

---

[a]See the discussion in Melvin (1975) of some of the issues investigated here empirically and the thesis work by Schmundt (1975).

[b]The details of this model are more fully described in Whalley (1978). A mathematical appendix was provided with earlier versions of this paper; this appendix has had to be deleted due to space constraints but is available upon request.

[c]Boadway and Treddenick (1978), in their analysis of the Canadian tariff structure, report findings yielding conclusions not dissimilar from some of those arrived at here in cases where they allow terms-of-trade effects to operate. Many economists would argue that Canada should be modeled as close to a small open price-taking economy with limited potential for terms-of-trade manipulation, and Boadway and Treddenick also consider such cases. The importance of the specification of the external sector in general equilibrium tax analysis is a conclusion also arrived at by Piggott and Whalley (1977) in their study of the U.K. tax system.

also portray factor tax systems as being more significant for some of the trading areas in distorting international trade than their tariff policies, with the obvious suggestion that their role in world trade has been insufficiently investigated. This finding is important for current and future negotiations on world trade liberalization under the GATT. Recent GATT negotiations have tended to concentrate on multilateral tariff reductions with only limited discussion of other components of commercial and domestic policies which affect world trade.

An important qualification of the results is that the strength of tax-induced terms-of-trade effects depends on the values assigned for price elasticities of import demand functions for the trade areas in the model. The majority of empirical estimates of price elasticities in world trade strike many people as surprisingly small and since Orcutt's (1950) paper there has been considerable discussion of downward bias in estimated values. The model used here incorporates demand functions with import price elasticities approximately consistent with the central tendency values suggested in the recent compilation of estimates by Stern *et al.* (1976). Additionally, there are grounds for arguing that the "Armington" assumption may unduly strengthen terms-of-trade effects compared with an alternative specification incorporating incomplete specialization and homogeneous products across trading areas.

2. Characteristics of Tax Structures in Major Trading Blocs and Their Role in World Trade

In this section, the factor tax structures in each of the three major trading blocs considered in the model are briefly reviewed and their likely impact on international trade activity outlined.[d]

In the model, the domestic tax systems for each of the trading blocs are represented in model-equivalent form and components of each tax system are aggregated into model subsystems for this purpose. The factor taxes

[d]Tax rates in the rest of the world in the model are taken simply as the arithmetic averages of the corresponding taxes in the U.S., the EEC, and Japan. This is not particularly realistic, as the rest of the world includes all developing and less developed economies, many of whom collect a major fraction of tax revenues from selective taxes (frequently export taxes) on only a few items. The assumption adopted is one of convenience rather than accuracy.

examined here comprise the taxes on capital and labor use by industry. The corporate tax and the property tax are treated as taxes on capital use by industry. Social security taxes are treated as taxes on labor use by industry. For the other taxes, the broadly based value-added taxes, commodity taxes, and retail sales taxes are treated as consumer taxes on products purchased as are the selective excise taxes on drink, tobacco, hydrocarbon oil, and other specific products. Income taxes are treated as taxes on incomes accruing to the household sector.

As with other general equilibrium exercises which investigate factor tax policies, the model specification, of necessity, assumes a particular treatment of certain taxes, and this is inevitably contentious. There has been discussion of the corporate tax as a lump sum tax (Stiglitz, 1973) rather than as a distorting tax on capital use by industry as modeled by Harberger (1962). There has been extensive discussion of the appropriateness of treating property taxes as factor taxes or excise taxes. With social security contributions there is the issue of whether they constitute a true tax or are partly a purchase of future security. Although the model treatment adopted here for all these taxes can be argued for as "conventional" in the general equilibrium tax literature, readers should be clear that these debates are not resolved merely by adopting a particular treatment, and the results which follow hinge crucially on this aspect of the modeling.

A further issue is the interlinkage between factor taxes and the income tax. Income taxes can compound or offset factor tax distortions. This is true of the dividend tax credits which operate within the integrated personal and corporate taxes common in several EEC countries and also present in Japan. A further feature of the income tax is tax treatment of owner-occupied housing. The focus here is on factor tax systems narrowly defined to include corporate, property, and social security taxes; but the role of additional distortionary features in the income tax should be taken into account in interpreting the results reported later.[e]

[e]These features of the income tax should also ideally be taken into account in the generation of the "benchmark" equilibrium data set described later, as has been done by Whalley (1975, 1977) and Fullerton *et al.* (1978) in single economy, general equilibrium tax models. The scope of the present model makes such corrections infeasible because of the data requirements imposed on all individual country statistics, and none has been attempted. This does not, however, prevent the linkage features referred to above from being incorporated as part of the income tax in each trading bloc and also from affecting resource allocation when income taxes are modified.

Differences in factor tax structures between the trading blocs originate from a number of different sources. Generally, EEC countries have only limited property taxes, which results in a lower total tax applying to capital income. This feature is reinforced by substantial acceleration in the provisions for depreciation under the corporate tax. In certain EEC countries full depreciation of capital expenditures can be deducted when incurred, and in one EEC country it is possible to deduct capital expenditures in anticipation of future outlay. This relatively light tax treatment of capital income contrasts with, on average, a somewhat more progressive rate structure under the personal income tax than in the U.S.[f]

In Japan capital income is also relatively lightly taxed. As in the EEC there is a relatively limited property tax, while under the corporate tax there are more extensive deductibility provisions than in the other trading areas. There is also an integrated corporate and personal income tax,[g] and under the personal income tax there is limited progression in taxes on capital income. The characteristic that, on average, capital income is differentially taxed between the major trading blocs is important for the determination of world trading patterns and shows through in the results presented later.

Taxes on labor are significant in their effects but are closer to uniform taxes than capital taxes are, and their distorting effects are milder. The use of national accounting data implies that manufacturing industries (export industries) are more labor intensive than other areas of the economy. This same feature is present in the data used by Harberger (1962) in his analysis of the U.S. corporate income tax and appears in other data used in the general equilibrium tax literature.

The model-equivalent *ad valorem* tax rates which are used are given in Table 1. The pattern of tax rates by factor, industry, and product is clearly differentiated by trading bloc although a number of points need to be kept in mind in interpreting the numbers. In the model products are treated as heterogeneous across the trading blocs in line with the "Armington" (1969) type of Heckscher–Ohlin model, where products are differentiated by their

[f]France and Italy are exceptions due to the special structure of their income tax systems. Both of these countries raise relatively small amounts of revenue through the income tax. A further offsetting feature is the absence of capital gains taxes in Europe (outside of the U.K.).

[g]A "split rate" corporate tax currently operates with a 30% tax on distributed profits and a 40% tax on undistributed profits.

Table 1. Model-Equivalent *Ad Valorem* Tax Rates Used in the Model.

(a) *Factor tax system**

	EEC		U.S.		Japan	
Industries	Tax on Capital Use† (%)	Tax on Labor Use‡ (%)	Tax on Capital Use (%)	Tax on Labor Use (%)	Tax on Capital Use (%)	Tax on Labor Use (%)
Agriculture and food	3.4	33.0	18.4	9.0	20.2	4.9
Raw materials and extractive	4.6	22.0	33.7	9.6	9.0	4.9
Nondurable manufacturing	16.0	20.8	62.3	10.9	36.6	4.9
Durable manufacturing	18.9	20.6	84.8	10.3	30.4	4.9
Services	5.6	21.1	56.5	10.4	15.5	4.9

(b) *Commodity tax system*

	EEC		U.S.	Japan
Commodities	Consumer Output Taxes§ (%)	VAT Rate (%)	Consumer Output Taxes (%)	Consumer Output Taxes (%)
Agriculture and food	7.5	9.1	12.8	13.7
Raw materials and extractive	0.0	12.2	8.8	4.8
Nondurable manufacturing	10.2	14.9	8.5	6.8
Durable manufacturing	2.4	14.1	4.7	13.6
Services	0.0	10.1	6.7	0.9

(*Continued*)

Table 1. (*Continued*)

(c) *Personal tax system*

	EEC	U.S.	Japan
Marginal income tax rate assumed¶	32.5#	27.0	15.8**

Source: Author's own calculations using data for 1973; sources given in Appendix B of Whalley (1978) and interpretations given in the text. Data for the U.S. draw on data compiled by Fullerton *et al.* (1978).

*These rates are all calculated as rates of tax on net of tax factors incomes: A 100% tax rate on a net basis corresponds to a 50% tax on a gross basis.

†Taxes on capital use are corporate and property taxes.

‡Taxes on labor use are social security taxes.

§Consumer output taxes (all treated as destination-based taxes) are: in the EEC, specific commodity excise taxes; in the U.S. specific commodity excise taxes and statewide retail sales taxes; in Japan, specific commodity excise taxes and commodity tax. Tariffs are not included in the reported tax rates under the commodity tax system.

¶These rates are calculated at an estimated mean taxable income per tax unit for each area. Imputed income from housing is tax free under all systems.

#The model also incorporates a dividend tax credit common under EEC integrated corporate and personal tax structures.

**A lower tax rate on capital income is assumed.

point of production as well as by their physical characteristics.[h] This means that the tax rates reported in Table 1 apply to industries which, by trading bloc, produce qualitatively different products. Also, certain high tax rates (e.g., on drink and tobacco) are averaged out in the aggregation used in Table 1.

The tax rates in Table 1 are inevitably obtained after some approximate use of data, particularly in the case of the EEC, where several aggregations over countries are involved with different elements of the data set. The sources used along with an outline of data adjustments and modifications are given in Whalley (1978). Broadly speaking, national accounts data for a single year are followed in constructing the estimates of these effective tax rates; some volatility may therefore be present in the one year's data (1973) used. These tax rate calculations (outside of the income tax) all assume that average and marginal rates of tax are the same and are calculated using methods similar to those adopted in the Harberger corporate tax model (1962)[i] and subsequent extensions to include all elements of tax systems due to Whalley (1975), Piggott and Whalley (1977), and Fullerton, Shoven, and Whalley (1978). The estimates of U.S. factor tax rates draw heavily on the data used in the last of these studies. On the factor side

[h]This type of model is used because of the presence of cross hauling in international trade statistics, in which a country can appear to be importing, producing, and exporting the same product. This observation is inconsistent with perfectly competitive assumptions if homogeneous products are assumed and is frequently accommodated in empirical international trade models by treating similar products produced in different locations as heterogeneous while remaining close substitutes in demand.

[i]Units for factors are defined under this approach as those amounts which generate factor rewards of $1.00 net of taxes in an assumed equilibrium state before any tax changes are considered. In the present model national accounts data in national currencies for 1973 are transformed into a consistent international equilibrium data set for the purpose of estimating both tax rates and other parameters in the model. Exchange rate conversions take place at published yearly average exchange rates; for the EEC countries conversions are first made into European Units of Account and then into U.S. dollars. The constructed equilibrium data sets are internationally consistent in domestic and foreign currencies for any country. Within the model the classical dichotomy between real and monetary phenomena in general equilibrium models holds so that the specification of an exchange rate regime is inconsequential for real behavior in long-run equilibrium.

Taxes on factors are on factor services measured in terms of (National Accounts adjusted) profit type return and labor bill by industry. Units for outputs are those amounts of products selling for $1.00 net of taxes in the assumed equilibrium. Household gross incomes are factor incomes plus transfers; income taxes apply to taxable incomes (gross incomes less deductions and allowances). The imputed income to home ownership appears as part of the profit type return in services, and a portion of income thus accrues tax-free to households.

tax rates apply to the net of tax factor price (the market price). Factors are assumed completely mobile between domestic industries but immobile between countries.

The broad picture conveyed in Table 1 is that significantly heavier taxation of labor exists in the EEC than in the U.S. or Japan, with heavier taxation of capital in the U.S. Limited selectivity is present in labor tax rates, but significantly differentiated capital tax rates are present with higher rates for manufacturing industries. Higher marginal income tax rates occur in the EEC than the U.S., but both EEC and Japanese systems have features favoring capital income. In the commodity tax structure some differentiation exists with the high selective excise tax rates missed by the aggregation used in Table 1.

Important characteristics of the factor tax rates in the model are (a) the heavier capital use taxes on manufacturing, especially in the U.S. and (to a lesser extent) in the EEC, which, given that both economies export manufactured products, act partially as origin-based export taxes; (b) heavier capital taxation (on average) in the U.S. than in either the EEC or Japan along with heavier labor taxes in the EEC; and (c) substantial differences in the average tax treatment of labor by trading area, although these are approximately uniform by industry.

3. The Structure of the Model

The empirical general equilibrium international trade model used incorporates both the domestic and foreign trade activity of four major blocs chosen to reflect the major participants in world trade.[j] These are the (nine-member) EEC, the U.S., Japan, and the rest of the world. The relative sizes of these blocs in the model reflect their relative GNP in U.S. dollars for these areas for 1973.[k] The EEC, the U.S., and Japan between them account for some 60% of the gross world product and jointly participate in a large, although somewhat smaller, fraction of world trade.

[j]This model has also been used to evaluate the effects of alternative tariff-cutting formulae in negotiations in the recent Tokyo Round in the GATT; see Brown and Whalley (1980) where a similar model description appears.

[k]Conversion between figures in national currencies for the EEC and Japan is made at average exchange rates used in the EEC and Japanese balance-of-payments accounts. The GNP for the rest of the world is taken to equal GNP for non-U.S., EEC, and Japanese countries from the World Bank Atlas (1975).

The model considers a number of products, each of which is treated as being produced solely in the trading bloc concerned. Under this "Armington" variant of a Heckscher–Ohlin model products are differentiated on the basis of geographical point of production as well as their physical characteristics, with "similar" products being treated as close substitutes in demand. This approach is followed both to accommodate the empirical observation of "cross hauling" and to remove cases of complete specialization in response to a tax change. As noted in the introduction, in an "Armington" variant of Heckscher–Ohlin, trade originates from more than differences in factor endowments; a further feature is that with products differentiated by trading area, a specification consistent with observed trade flows will typically not have any meaningful autarky solution if continuously substitutable preference functions are used.

An aggregated version of the model described in Whalley (1978) is used which allows functional forms to be incorporated which capture substitution between domestic production and imports in intermediate as well as final demands. The computational costs involved in repeated solution of the detailed variant considered by Whalley (1978) increase if this feature is used. The smaller size enables richer functional forms to be considered compared with those used in the earlier, more detailed, model. The products considered in these variants are listed in Table 2; each variant of the model uses a product and industrial classification which is identical. The detailed variant used in Whalley (1978) considers 33 product categories, and the aggregate variant used here five. While some of the effects of tax discrimination are lost in aggregation, the main discriminatory effects between manufacturing and nonmanufacturing remain.

An outline of the model is given in Fig. 1. The model incorporates production and demand patterns in each of the trading blocs. Producers are assumed to maximize profits and the competitive forces to operate in such a manner that in equilibrium all supernormal profits are competed away. Fixed factor endowments in each trading bloc are assumed; factors by trading area are treated as heterogeneous, and international factor markets are not incorporated. Products can be sold in any trading area but can only be produced in one location (following the "Armington" formulation in the model). A single household consumer group is considered in each trading bloc with explicit demand functions covering both consumption and investment derived from utility maximization. Demand patterns also enter the model for government expenditures.

Table 2. Product and Industrial Classifications Considered in the World General Equilibrium Models.

Detailed variant used in Whalley (1978)	Aggregated variant used in this paper
Agriculture:	Agriculture and food: 1–4 + 8–11
1. Meats and dairy products	
2. Cereals	
3. Other agricultural products	
4. Forestry and fisheries	
Mining:	Raw materials and extractive products: 5–7
5. Coal	
6. Oil, natural gas	
7. Metallic, nonmetallic, and other	
Manufacturing (nondurable goods prepared food and kindred products):	Nondurable manufacturing: 12–17
8. Tea, sugar, coffee, spices, cocoa	
9. Alcoholic drinks	
10. Other foods	
11. Tobacco	
12. Apparel and textile products	
13. Paper, printing, publishing	
14. Pharmaceuticals and toiletries	
15. Other chemical and allied products	
16. Petroleum and coal products	
17. Rubber and plastics	
Manufacturing (durable goods):	Durable manufacturing: 18–24
18. Lumber, wood, and furniture	
19. Primary and fabricated metals, stone, glass	
20. Machinery except electrical	
21. Electrical machinery	
22. Transport vehicles	
23. Scientific and precision instruments	
24. Miscellaneous manufacturing	
Services:	Services: 25–33
25. Construction*	
26. Water transportation	
27. Other transportation and communications	
28. Housing services*	
29. Electricity and gas services	
30. Wholesale and retail trade*	
31. Finance, insurance, and real estate	
32. Other services	
33. Government*	

Source: Whalley (1978) and this article.
*Denotes a nontraded good.

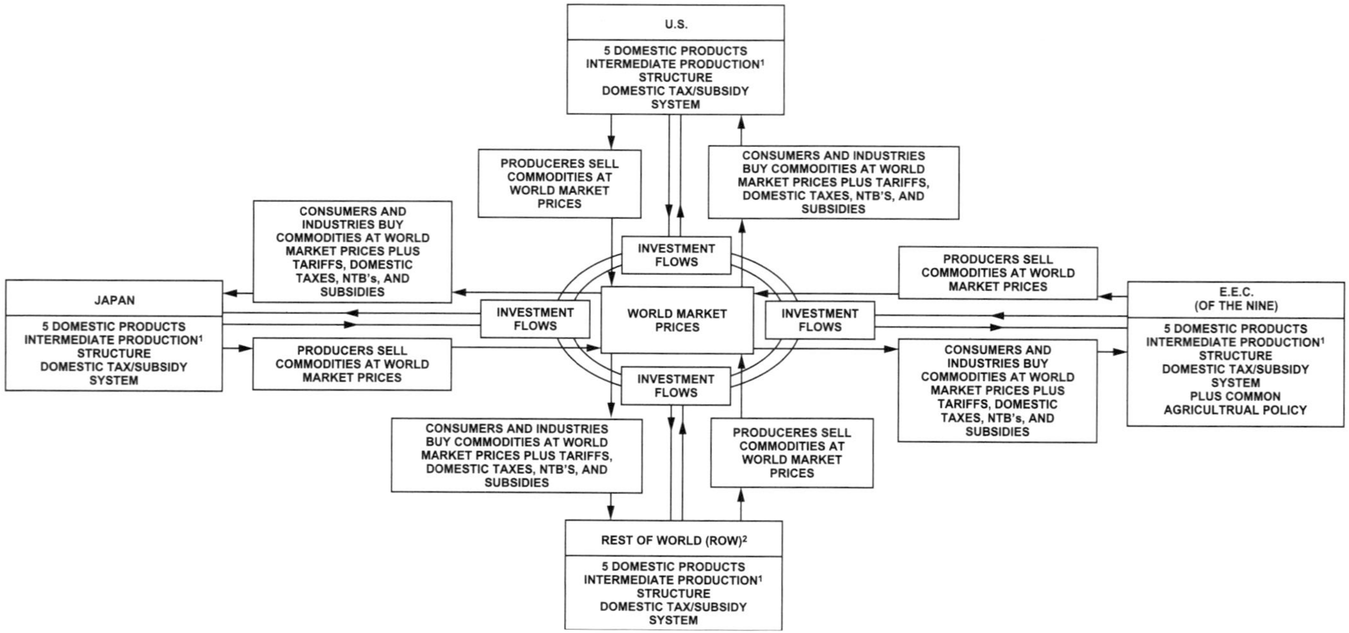

Fig. 1. The general equilibrium model of U.S.–EEC–Japanese trade — a structural outline. World general equilibrium: a set of world market prices such that (1) demand equals supply for all goods and factors; (2) no industry makes positive profits, with those in operation breaking even; and (3) each trading bloc is in zero trade balance (including investment flows, dividends and interest, and transfers). 1 = This incorporates intermediate substitution between similar inputs differentiated by country of origin, e.g., a fixed steel requirement per car produced in the U.S. might be specified, but this can be met by a substitutable mix of domestically produced steel and steel and steel imported from the various trading blocs. 2 = The rest of the world is specified schematically, and no strong claims to realism are made. An arithmetic average of comparable parameters in the three major trading areas is used. The factor endowments in the rest of the world are, however, selected to reflect the relative capital abundance of the three major trading areas. The capital-to-labor ratio in the rest of the world is considered to be in aggregate one-fifth of that in the combination of the three major trading areas with a ratio of 1:10 for manufacturing.

For each product the market price of a good is the price at point of production. Producers take these prices as selling prices; consumers take these prices gross of tariffs and any domestic taxes which operate as their consumption prices. Traded commodities flow through a world trade network and in world markets uniform world prices prevail. Investment flows also enter the trade network and are represented as purchases of newly produced capital goods by agents located in the country of source of the capital funds. The difference between investment flows and merchandise trade is that the capital goods acquired are not repatriated to the country of location of the purchaser but remain in the source country to generate income in future time periods. It should be noted that since investment decisions involve a choice between heterogeneous capital goods (by trading area) and fixed factor supplies are assumed, no mechanism exists in the model by which rates of return across trading areas are equalized. The role played by an international capital market in which rates of return are equalized across trading areas is not captured in the model, and an alternative specification of the world economy in terms of a single homogeneous capital market would produce findings different from those reported here.

Nested CES functions are used for utility functions, from which demand functions in each trading bloc are derived. For these functions all compensated own-price elasticities of demand functions are negative. Values of the substitution elasticities appearing in demand functions are discussed below, but in broad terms their values are chosen for the various nests to calibrate implied (uncompensated) own-price elasticities to literature estimates.[1] Unitary income elasticity in demand for all products is assumed. A CES/LES type of demand system which would relax this assumption is more complex to work with. Nested CES functions capture the "Armington" assumption of a higher degree of substitution between comparable domestic and imported products than between product groups in general. With these nested forms a different elasticity of substitution can be assumed between imported products from the various trading areas

[1]A particularly important characteristic of demand functions derived from directly additive preferences (of which the CES function is an example) is what Deaton (1974) terms "Pigou's Law". This is the property that ratios of own-price and income elasticities for all products are approximately constant. This clearly gives less freedom in the selection of parameter values to calibrate in this way and partly explains the reason for nesting, since additional parameters are created for use in the calibration.

and domestic products of a similar type from the elasticity of substitution between the composite products.

The demand functions for each trading bloc and for the world in total satisfy Walras's Law. This specifies that at any set of prices the value of demands equals the value of incomes. The incomes of consumer groups are derived from the ownership of primary factors located in each trading bloc plus transfers received from the government. The government in each trading bloc collects taxes from households and also disperses transfer incomes. Government expenditures enter as a separate demand category and are financed by tax collections.

Each industry in each trading bloc uses two different types of inputs. The first set of inputs is primary factors: substitutable capital and labor service inputs located in that country. Each industry is given a value-added production function of CES form which specifies the substitution possibilities for that industry between capital and labor. In addition to these value-added functions, each industry uses the outputs of other industries (both domestic and imported). In the version of the model used here substitution between intermediate products enters. Fixed coefficient requirements are specified, but only in terms of composite goods. Each fixed coefficient in composite goods is a CES function with each type of the composite good (products designated by point of production) entering as arguments. Thus substitution is possible between, for example, foreign and domestic steel in car production while a fixed per unit steel requirement applies. No technical change is incorporated, and the possibility of country relocation by industries in response to tax changes is excluded.

A number of different components of commercial policy are considered in the model beyond domestic tax policies.[m] Tariffs, nontariff barriers, and domestic tax policies are all incorporated in *ad valorem* form, and distorting features of domestic factor taxation policies are evaluated in the model in the presence of other distortions which may either partially or fully offset (or compound) their trade effects. An example of this would be the substantial nontariff barriers to agricultural products in the EEC and Japan which, to some degree, reinforce the manufacturing industry capital tax features referred to earlier; in the U.S., agricultural nontariff barriers, while present, are milder.

[m]See Whalley (1978) for more details.

An equilibrium in the model is a situation where, at the prevailing market prices, demands equal supplies for all products, and in each industry a zero-profit condition is satisfied, representing the absence of supernormal profits. Each country is also in zero balance in its foreign trade transactions, and each government has a balanced budget. At equilibrium there is full employment of all factors. The model is solved for equilibria achieved under different policy regimes and the equilibria compared.

4. Estimation and Computer Solution of the Model

The model described in Section 3 contains a large number of parameter values which must be determined before the model can be used to evaluate the effects of alternative tax policies in the various trading blocs. Such a large-scale model cannot be easily estimated in its entirety using conventional econometric methods, and resort is therefore made to a sequence of procedures which have been developed in recent years for estimation of large-scale general equilibrium models.

The method is to assemble a set of data for a given period of time in a form which is consistent with the equilibrium conditions of the model. This data set (termed as "benchmark equilibrium data set") satisfies the properties required of a worldwide competitive equilibrium in that demands and supplies for products balance, no profits occur in any of the domestic industries, and each country is in zero balance in its trade with all other countries. This data set is then used to estimate parameter values of equations from the equilibrium conditions. In broad terms, the model is solved "backward" from equilibrium to parameters rather than "forward" from parameters to equilibrium as is done in the subsequent counterfactual policy change situations.

The adoption of this overall approach implies the need to construct a benchmark equilibrium data set involving both the domestic and trading activity of each of the trading blocs. Many of the interpretations of the role of domestic factor tax structures in foreign trade which this chapter offers can be seen, *ex post*, as implications of the underlying data set, and an important spin-off from the assembly of the model is the construction of such a data set which can be used in other studies.[n]

[n]This data set, though, needs several divergent sets of source materials which must be assembled and converted into consistent classifications and definitions. Even when this has been completed, further adjustments are necessary to mutually adjust the

The nonstochastic estimation procedure used is to solve the equilibrium conditions of the model for parameter values of the assumed functional forms. Depending upon the complexity of functional forms used for demand and production functions, additional information beyond the single equilibrium observation may be necessary in this procedure. If Cobb–Douglas functional forms are assumed for demand functions, the exponents in the Cobb–Douglas functions are given directly by the expenditure shares from the benchmark equilibrium data set. With the nested CES functions used, more information is needed than that contained in the equilibrium data set because of the additional parameters compared with the Cobb–Douglas case.

This need for additional information is met by specifying elasticities of substitution in the CES functional forms. On the production side these are obtained from a literature search.[o] On the demand side no empirical evidence on substitution elasticities in preference functions is directly available, and a procedure is used of relating substitution elasticities in preference functions to econometric estimates of own-price elasticities of market demand functions. At the benchmark equilibrium given by the consistent data set it is possible to calculate the implied point estimates of the price elasticities of demand for imports and composite goods in each of the trading blocs. These values can be compared with estimates obtained from a literature search and, on that basis, modifications made to the estimates of the substitution elasticities. Sensitivity analysis is then performed around the values selected.

The most important area of parameter sensitivity arises with the import price elasticities by product and by trading bloc. Heavy reliance has been placed on the recent compendium of elasticity values in world

data so that the equilibrium conditions of the model are satisfied. This is a substantial undertaking and must be done with care and attention to detail before full confidence can be attached to results. The data set which has been assembled thus far should only be considered as a first approximation to an ideal data set for the model. There are problems of inconsistent classifications and definitions, gaps in data availability, and differences in the dates of data sources. The steady improvement of this data set is a task which could easily preoccupy many years, and the results with this first assembled data set may be modified by such improvements if and when they are made. Sources for this data set are given in Appendix B of Whalley (1978).

[o]The recent survey by Caddy (1976) provides the main source for these estimates. An average over the estimates reported by Caddy is used for each industry in the model. The values adopted are the same for each trading area and are: Agriculture and food, 0.64; raw materials, 0.50; nondurable manufacturing, 0.93; durable manufacturing, 0.79; services, 0.97.

trade produced by Stern *et al.* (1977). Although these authors emphasize that the literature on price elasticities in world trade is not wholly reliable and conclude that limited faith can be placed in elasticity values available for detailed product classifications, they produce "best-guess" estimates for price elasticities for imports by country for a single-digit SITC classification. The majority of these elasticities are in the neighborhood of −1.0. This is somewhat larger in absolute value than the region suggested by Houthakker and Magee (1969) in their earlier survey of trade elasticities, although some researchers, such as Balassa and Kreinin (1967), have argued for and used substantially higher values on the grounds of a downward bias associated with time series estimation of import functions. Literature discussion of downward bias in estimates of import demand functions begins with the paper by Orcutt (1950) and remains unresolved, although a number of recent contributions suggest the bias may not be as serious as once imagined.

Two sets of elasticity values are used in the model. One uses a different substitution elasticity between products for each trading area with the same value for substitution between product types within the area. Values close to the aggregate Stern *et al.* import price elasticities are used as the substitution elasticities in preference functions, and this gives import price elasticities with limited variation across products. In the other set, different values are used by product. These are chosen to calibrate approximately to the best-guess Stern *et al.* import price estimates on a single-digit SITC product classification for each trading area.[p]

The model also incorporates substitution between domestic and imported products in intermediate use, and a value of 1.15 has been used for this substitution elasticity for all areas in the calculations reported. This is slightly lower than intermediate substitution elasticity values recently estimated using Australian data in connection with the Impact project,[q] but provides closer consistency with empirical trade elasticities by area.

Once specified and estimated, the model is solved for a general equilibrium using a Newton method. The programs used have been developed from routines originally designed to refine the approximation

[p]For the EEC this involves some degree of averaging over individual country estimates.
[q]This is an extensive study of Australian tariff and trade policies using a detailed general equilibrium model supported by the Australian Industries Assistance Commission and described in Powell (1977) and Dixon *et al.* (1977). Work on estimation of the elasticity of substitution between imported and domestically produced goods classified at an input–output level of aggregation has been done by Alaouze *et al.* (1977).

obtained from the application of Scarf's algorithm (Shoven and Whalley, 1972, 1974; and Whalley, 1977). These Newton methods work swiftly, and, although there is no *ex ante* argument of convergency built into the procedures, they have been successful in implementation. Because of the complexity of the model no analytic argument for uniqueness of equilibrium is available, although, with other general equilibrium models which are similar in structure, experimentation has been done in displacing equilibria once found and then checking that these are returned to, and also approaching equilibria from different points and at different speeds. None of these tests has yet to reveal a situation of nonuniqueness of equilibria in these complex environments, although nonuniqueness is certainly not excluded.

5. Results from the Model

A number of changes in factor taxes in the trading blocs have been considered in the model. In this section, the findings from some of these experiments have been synthesized and the implications drawn for current perceptions of the role of factor taxes on foreign trade.

After each change in the factor taxes in any (or all) of the trading blocs a new competitive equilibrium is calculated and compared with the benchmark equilibrium. The major statistics used as summary measures of the changes between the new and old equilibria are the compensating and equivalent variations for each of the trading blocs. Since there is only one household agent considered in each of the trading blocs along with the demand patterns of government, the procedure used is to sum the monetary measures of the changes in utility implied by the utility functions underlying the demand functions for each of these sectors in the economy. Since utility yields no easily interpretable results, changes in utility levels between equilibria have been converted into dollar measures by using Hicksian compensating and equivalent variations. A sign convention is adopted such that a welfare-improving change gives both compensating and equivalent variations which are positive.[r]

These measures of the change between equilibria for the trading blocs capture a number of different components. Removing domestic distortions

[r]The compensating variation is the amount needed to compensate a consumer for a price change which has occurred. Strictly speaking, this should be negative for a welfare-improving price change.

of production decisions will typically yield a positive compensating or equivalent variation, since there is a gain in productive efficiency. A positive compensating or equivalent variation can also occur due to the removal of the implicit distortions of consumer choice which differential factor taxes can cause through effects on output prices. Lastly, in the international trade setting considered in the model, terms-of-trade effects associated with tax changes will also have effects on compensating and equivalent variations. One trading bloc may improve its terms of trade with another, giving an increase in welfare for one bloc and a reduction in welfare for the other. The focus in results is on movements in the aggregate of these effects.

Table 3 reports on four experiments performed with the model. Under these experiments the existing capital and labor tax systems have been

Table 3. Welfare Effects of Equal Yield, Broadly Based Sales-Tax Replacement of Existing Capital and Labor Taxes INI Trading Blocs ($ Million, 1973).

Trading bloc	Compensating variation	Equivalent variation
Experiment 1. *Replacement of U.S. Factor Taxes Alone*		
EEC	2220.9	1950.2
U.S.	−4259.5	−3635.0
Japan	276.1	241.1
ROW	2869.6	2515.7
Experiment 2. *Replacement of EEC Factor Taxes Alone*		
EEC	254.1	235.1
U.S.	−123.8	−114.3
Japan	−26.9	−24.9
ROW	568.6	525.4
Experiment 3. *Replacement of Japanese Factor Taxes Alone*		
EEC	69.5	67.8
U.S.	462.3	451.6
Japan	−739.0	−713.9
ROW	963.4	940.2
Experiment 4. *Simultaneous Replacement of EEC, U.S. Japanese, and ROW Factor Taxes*		
EEC	2916.6	2343.5
U.S.	−3799.1	−2961.0
Japan	−394.2	−311.3
ROW	3999.0	3203.1

Note: ROW = Rest of the world.

abolished and replaced by a yield-preserving broadly based neutral tax. These are in no way represented as politically feasible alternatives for the trading blocs but enable some overall appraisal to be made of the role of factor taxes in world trade. The replacement tax is a destination-based tax on all final expenditures within the trading bloc. This experiment is performed separately in the EEC, the U.S., and Japan and, lastly, in all trading areas. For each of these four experiments, calculations have been made of the compensating and equivalent variations implied for each of the trading blocs.

A striking result is that with the abolition of factor taxes in the U.S., the U.S. loses around 4 billion dollar per year. This suggests that, contrary to current opinion, the existing distortionary factor tax system is not a source of loss to the U.S. and may not be distortionary enough. The 1973 GNP in the U.S. is approximately U.S. 1,200 billion dollar; this loss from removing these taxes is thus around 0.33% of the GNP but is important when compared with estimates of productive efficiency losses from distorting factor taxes in closed economies, since it goes in the opposite direction. This negative effect occurs in spite of both a domestic productive efficiency gain and the removal of distortions of consumer choice through the heavier taxation of manufacturing products. The reason for the negative effect is a terms-of-trade loss which the U.S. suffers as a result of the abolition of its factor taxes, which outweighs the efficiency gain.

At first sight this is a surprising result but is explained by the characteristics of the U.S. factor taxation system as reflected in the model. Taxes on factor use by industry operate in the form of origin-based taxes, since in a competitive model they contribute to factor cost and are not rebated on exports. Competing imports are not liable for these taxes. Since the U.S. exports manufactured products and these industries are more heavily taxed under the factor tax system, the U.S. is able to obtain a terms-of-trade gain by operating what is in effect a tax on exports. While not explicitly an export tax in affecting the price of exported products alone, it taxes more heavily the products which are exported and, therefore, changes the terms of trade in their favor. Under the U.S. capital taxation system heavier taxes exist for manufacturing industries than for nonmanufacturing industries.

The terms-of-trade loss associated with the removal of the factor taxes in the U.S. is larger than any effects calculated thus far with this model for changes in or abolitions of existing U.S. tariffs. This suggests that the effects on world trade from variations in domestic factor taxation policies may well be more powerful than those which occur through tariffs.[s]

In experiment 2, the EEC receives a small gain from the removal of distortions in their domestic factor taxes; as in the U.S. case, the world in total gains. In the EEC factor tax rates on capital income are lower than in the U.S., with lower rates on manufacturing industry. The terms-of-trade loss which the EEC suffers as a result of the abolition of its factor tax system is less pronounced than in the case of the U.S. and does not offset the domestic welfare gains. Japan, like the U.S., loses through the abolition of its factor taxes while other trading blocs in the model gain.

Experiment 4 in Table 3 considers the simultaneous abolition of all factor taxes in the model by the U.S., the EEC, Japan, and the ROW (the ROW tax rates are averages of the tax rates in the EEC, U.S., and Japan by industry).[t] In this case the rest of the world obtains a gain in the region of 4 billion dollar per year. The EEC gains 2 billion dollar per year, and the U.S. loses 3 billion dollar–3.5 billion dollar. Japan is a loser by slightly less than 0.5 billion dollar per year. The simultaneous abolition case produces larger gains for the EEC and smaller losses for the U.S. and Japan because the terms-of-trade losses associated with tax abolitions on a unilateral basis are partially offset by terms-of-trade gains to trading partners when the tax abolitions occur on a multilateral basis.

In Table 4, the abolition of the capital tax system alone is considered instead of the combined abolition of capital and labor taxes. With the abolition of U.S. capital taxes alone, the U.S. loses around 6 billion dollar a year, more than in the case of all factor taxes. The EEC gains as does the rest of the world. In the case of the abolition of capital taxes in the EEC smaller negative effects are obtained, but the gain from abolition of all factor taxes is converted into a loss. In the Japanese case with labor taxes being exactly uniform by industry the losses in Tables 3 and 4 differ hardly

[s]This finding can be rationalized in that the rates of tax involved in domestic factor taxation structures are on average more substantial than the rates which are involved products among major trading blocs are in the region of 10% with perhaps slightly higher rates in Japan than in the EEC or the U.S. The rates involved are sufficiently small that variations in these rates produce relatively mild effects on international trade. In addition, the differentiation in tariff rates is not as pronounced as that which is produced indirectly through the operation of domestic factor taxation structures.

[t]The rest of the world, however, has different factor intensities than occur in the three major trading areas. In aggregate it is assumed the rest of the world has a capital–labor ratio equal to one-fifth of the average capital–labor ratio in the three trading blocs.

Table 4. Welfare Effects of Equal Yield, Broadly Based Sales Tax Replacement of Capital Taxes Alone ($ Million, 1973).

Trading bloc	Compensating variation	Equivalent variation
Experiment 1. *Replacement of U.S. Capital Taxes Alone*		
EEC	2927.4	2800.5
U.S.	−6092.1	−5609.4
Japan	513.4	488.1
ROW	3701.2	3532.6
Experiment 2. *Replacement of EEC Capital Taxes Alone*		
EEC	−953.2	−1004.3
U.S.	442.4	467.2
Japan	−30.4	−32.0
ROW	973.6	1027.4
Experiment 3. *Replacement of Japanese Capital Taxes Alone*		
EEC	73.6	74.0
U.S.	517.4	520.7
Japan	−854.3	−849.2
ROW	1017.1	1022.6

Note: ROW = Rest of the world.

at all; the source of the difference lies in a small revenue effect between government and the household sector due to the way in which the equal tax yield experiment is specified.

The investigation of the changes in capital taxes alone in Table 4 suggests that, for the U.S. with sharply differentiated and high capital tax rates by industry, the strong terms-of-trade effects from factor taxes derive exclusively from the capital tax system. For the EEC and Japan this is also the case, but the terms-of-trade effects are weaker than in the U.S. case.

The role of the labor taxes is confirmed by results reported in Table 5, where an abolition in labor taxes with equal yield tax replacement is considered in the EEC, the U.S., and Japan. In the cases of the EEC and the U.S., an abolition in labor taxes leads to gains of 1.25 billion dollar and 1.75 billion dollar per year, respectively. These gains are accounted for by the removal of mild distortions in a tax which affects a large fraction of value added; the terms-of-trade movements in these cases are not pronounced. In the case of Japan, an abolition in labor taxes alone produces a small gain accounted for by small income effects between government

Table 5. Welfare Effects of Equal Yield, Broadly Based Sales Tax Replacement of Labor Taxes Alone ($ Million, 1973).

Trading bloc	Compensating variation	Equivalent variation
Experiment 1. *Replacement of U.S. Labor Taxes Alone*		
EEC	−551.6	−553.5
U.S.	1713.9	1735.0
Japan	−210.0	−210.7
ROW	−936.5	−938.9
Experiment 2. *Replacement of EEC Labor Taxes Alone*		
EEC	1331.6	1277.3
U.S.	−473.4	−452.3
Japan	10.9	10.4
ROW	−587.8	−561.4
Experiment 3. *Replacement of Japanese Labor Taxes Alone*		
EEC	93.5	99.1
U.S.	44.0	46.6
Japan	128.7	136.4
ROW	−237.5	−251.3

Note: ROW = Rest of the world.

and the household sector accompanying the removal of the uniform labor tax.

Table 6 explores the sensitivity of some of the results reported in Table 3 to changes in parameter values used in the model.[u] The case of the equal yield abolition of all factor taxes simultaneously in the EEC, the U.S., Japan, and the rest of the world is considered. In the first variation, different substitution elasticities by product are used in the utility functions for substitution between domestic and imported products. The Stern *et al.* (1976) import elasticity estimates by single-digit SITC classification are

[u]In other runs not reported here variations in the policy changes considered also affect results. An interesting finding is that the income tax tends to magnify the terms-of-trade gains achieved through distorting taxes through the light tax treatment of housing (a nontraded good); the expectation is that this feature, for the same reason, would be more pronounced were the tax distortion of the labor/leisure choice also incorporated into the model.

Table 6. Equal Yield Replacement of all Factor Taxes in EEC, U.S., Japan, and ROW Simultaneously (Experiment 4, Table 3) (U.S.$ Million, 1973).

	Experiment 4, Table 3		Substitution elasticities differ by product		"High" substitution elasticities (3.0) between domestic and foreign goods in final demands in all trading blocs and in intermediate production	
Trading bloc	Compensating variation	Equivalent variation	Compensating variation	Equivalent variation	Compensating variation	Equivalent variation
EEC	2916.6	2343.5	1057.7	869.8	1020.7	1243.9
U.S.	−3799.1	−2961.0	−7537.6	−6201.7	−5466.1	−6603.3
Japan	−394.2	−311.3	167.7	132.2	241.7	307.3
ROW	3999.0	3203.1	11083.6	8111.2	5347.6	7258.9

Note: This table is a sensitivity analysis on the results presented in Table 3, Experiment 4. ROW = Rest of the world.

adopted.[v] In the second, a uniform "high" value of 3.0 is used for these substitution elasticities and for the substitution elasticity in intermediate production.

These sensitivity variations, perhaps not surprisingly, have a significant impact on results. Under both variations the U.S. loss is magnified, and the EEC gain falls, while the gain of the rest of the world rises sharply. Use of elasticity values by product doubles the estimated losses of the U.S. Use of high substitution values increases the loss for the U.S. by around one-half.

Despite the sensitivity findings the suggestion remains that contemporary factor taxation systems in the major developed economies may well exert a significant effect on the pattern and structure of world trade, with the possibility that existing "distorting" systems need not be nationally inferior to the "nondistorting" alternatives usually considered in calculations of domestic welfare cost.

6. Conclusion

This chapter has presented some numerical results on the effects of changes in domestic factor taxes on world trade. A recently constructed general equilibrium model which incorporates the tariff, nontariff, and domestic taxation policies of major trading blocs (the EEC, the U.S., and Japan) in a price-endogenous Heckscher–Ohlin-type framework has been used to investigate the effects of changes in domestic taxation policies. Fixed factor supplies by trading area are assumed, and an international capital market in which rates of return across countries are equalized is not captured in the model. A prior data exercise is necessary with national accounts and related statistics to obtain estimates of tax rates by type, product, and industry for the trading blocs involved along with an equilibrium data set for use in the model.

[v]The values used are as follows:

	EEC	U.S.	Japan
Agriculture and food	0.78	0.80	0.66
Extractive products	1.17	0.96	0.57
Nondurable manufacturing	2.53	1.84	1.42
Durable manufacturing	2.53	1.84	1.42
Services	0.88	1.66	0.78

For the ROW an arithmetic average by-product is used.

For the U.S. existing factor taxes yield a significant terms-of-trade gain. Results indicate that the abolition of existing discriminatory features of distorting taxes in the U.S., while leading to a domestic gain in production efficiency, would lead to welfare losses because of the movement in the terms of trade against the U.S. A similar feature is also present for Japan, although it is not as pronounced. In the EEC, this terms-of-trade effect, while present, is milder; small gains occur from the removal of distortions in factor taxes with losses occurring when capital tax distortions are removed. The role of domestic factor taxation systems in affecting the pattern of world trade and the distribution of the gains from trade appears to be surprisingly important and, in all probability, more important than other trade-distorting commercial policies, such as tariffs.

The rationalization offered for these results is that existing systems of factor taxation in the major trading blocs (and in particular the EEC and the U.S.) act as origin-based taxes at substantially higher effective rates on those industries which are export industries. They yield terms-of-trade gains for the major world trading blocs. An implication of these findings is that in future (post-Tokyo Round) multilateral trade negotiations substantially more emphasis could be placed on the role of distorting domestic tax policies than on the removal of the relatively small tariff rates currently operating in the post-Kennedy (and eventually post-Tokyo) Round trade environment. The elimination of these tax features could yield more substantial gains for Third World countries than the elimination of tariffs in the industrialized trading areas.

The results also have implications for existing analysis of incidence and efficiency effects of taxation. Even for a country such as the U.S. which has a relatively small external sector (perhaps some 8% of domestic activity) these results suggest that the adverse terms-of-trade effects against the U.S. under some assumptions can be sufficiently strong that the removal of distorting domestic taxes could lead to reductions in national welfare. This can occur despite a gain in production efficiency. If taken seriously, the implication of this finding is that from a national point of view existing factor taxes are not distortionary enough.

References

Alaouze, CM, JS Marsden and J Zeitsch (1977). Estimates of the elasticity of substitution between imported and domestically-produced commodities at the four digit ASIC level. Impact Project, Working Paper No. 0-11, Mimeographed. Melbourne: Indus. Assistance Commission.

Armington, PS (1969). A theory of demand for products distinguished by place of production. I.M.F. Staff Papers 16, 159–178.

Balassa, B and ME Kreinin (1967). Trade liberalization under the "Kennedy Round": The static effects. *Review of Economics and Statistics*, **49**, 125–137.

Boadway, RW and JM Treddenick (1978). A general equilibrium computation of the effects of the Canadian tariff structure. *Canadian Journal of Economics*, **11**, 424–446.

Brown, F and J Whalley (1980). General equilibrium evaluations of tariff cutting proposals in the Tokyo round and comparisons to more extensive liberalization of world trade. *Economic Journal*, **90**(363), 838–866.

Caddy, V (1976). Empirical estimation of the elasticity of substitution: A review. Mimeographed. Melbourne: Indus. Assistance Commission.

Deaton, A (1974). A reconsideration of the empirical implications of additive preferences. *Economic Journal*, **84**, 338–348.

Dixon, PB, BR Parmenter, GJ Ryland and J Sutton (1977). ORANI: A general equilibrium model of the Australian economy. First Progress Report of the Impact Project, Vol. 2. Canberra: Australian Government Publishing Service.

Fullerton, D, JB Shoven and J Whalley (1978). General equilibrium analysis of U.S. taxation policy. In 1978 *Compendium of Tax Research*. Washington: Office of Tax Analysis, Department of Treasury.

Harberger, AC (1962). The incidence of the corporation income tax. *The Journal of Political Economy*, **70**(3), 215–240.

Houthakker, HS and SP Magee (1969). Income and price elasticities in world trade. *Review of Economics and Statistics*, **51**, 111–125.

Melvin, JR (1975). *The Tax Structure and Canadian Trade: A Theoretical Analysis*. Ottawa: Economic Council of Canada.

Orcutt, GH (1950). Measurement of price elasticities in international trade. Review of Economics and Statistics, **32**, 117–132.

Piggott, JR and J Whalley (1977). General equilibrium investigations of U.K. tax subsidy policy: A progress report. In *Studies in Modern Economic Analysis*, AR Nobay and MJ Artis (eds.). Oxford: Basil Blackwell.

Powell, AA (1977). *The Impact Project: An Overview. First Progress Report of the Impact Project*, Vol. 1. Canberra: Australian Government Publishing Service.

Schmundt, M (1975). National and international tax incidence in simple general equilibrium models. PhD dissertation, Yale University.

Shoven, JB and J Whalley (1972). A general equilibrium calculation of the effects of differential taxation of income from capital in the U.S. *Journal of Public Economics*, **1**, 281–321.

Shoven, JB and J Whalley (1974). On the computation of competitive equilibrium on international markets with tariffs. *Journal of International Economics*, **4**, 341–354.

Stern, RM, J Francis and B Schumacher (1976). *Price Elasticities in International Trade: An Annotated Bibliography*. Toronto: Macmillan (for Trade Policy Res. Centre).

Stiglitz, JE (1973). Taxation, corporate financial policy, and the cost of capital. *Journal of Public Economics*, **2**, 1–34.

Whalley, J (1975). A general equilibrium assessment of the 1973 United Kingdom tax reform. *Economica*, **42**, 139–161.
Whalley, J (1977). The United Kingdom tax system, 1968–1970: Some fixed point indications of its economic impact. *Econometrica*, **45**, 1837–1858.
Whalley, J (1978). General equilibrium analysis of U.S.–EEC–Japanese trade and trade distorting policies. University of Western Ontario working paper. To appear in a Symposium on International Trade Models in Economic Appliquee.
World Bank (1975). *World Atlas*. Washington: World Bank.

Chapter 17

Foreign Exchange Premia and Nonneutrality of Monetary Policy in General Equilibrium Models*

Ramon Clarete
University of the Philippines, Manila, The Philippines

John Whalley[†]
University of Western Ontario, London, Ontario, Canada N6A 5C2
National Bureau of Economic Research (NBER)

We present a simple monetized extension of a traditional small-country, real-side, general equilibrium trade model in which premia on foreign exchange occur, with the value of the quota and the quota premium endogenously determined. Monetary policy is nonneutral in the model, and has real effects, illustrated using a small open economy general equilibrium model of the Philippines, which includes foreign exchange premia. The results emphasize the importance of incorporating domestic monetary policy, fixed exchange rates and associated foreign exchange premia when analyzing the trade policy regime in such a country.

1. Introduction

In this chapter, we present a simple monetized extension of a traditional small-country, real-side, general equilibrium trade model in which premia on foreign exchange occur, with both the value of the quota and the quota premium being endogenously determined. Monetary policy is nonneutral in the model, and has real effects. We differ from earlier work on foreign exchange rationing in developing countries in making explicit the equilibrium mapping involved through which premia and the value of

*This chapter was first published in (1991). *Journal of International Economics*, **30**(1), 153–166.
[†]We are grateful to two referees for comments on an earlier draft. Earlier versions of this chapter have been presented to a Trade Theory Conference at Western Ontario, April 12–13, 1986, and a NBER Applied General Equilibrium Conference at Stanford, April 17–18, 1986.

foreign exchange earnings are jointly determined.[a] We also introduce a simple monetary specification into the analysis, which in our opinion is essential to the analysis of foreign exchange rationing.

A series of modifications to our basic analysis allow us also to analyze how foreign exchange premia interact with real-side trade policies, including commodity-specific tariffs and quotas. We show how a reduction in a general tariff (one at the same rate on all importables) has no real effects on trade flows when a foreign exchange premium occurs, since it will be exactly offset by an increase in the foreign exchange premium value. However, where quotas apply for all imports and a positive foreign exchange premium value occurs, reductions in the foreign exchange premium value will generate offsetting increases in quota premium values and will have no real effects on trade flows.

We illustrate our approach using a small, open-economy general equilibrium model of the Philippines due to Clarete (1984), which is modified here to include foreign exchange premia. The importance of incorporating domestic monetary policy, fixed exchange rates and associated foreign exchange premia when analyzing the trade policy regime in such a country emerges strongly from these results.

2. Foreign Exchange Premia Equilibrium in a Small, Open-economy Exchange Model

To investigate an equilibrium structure in the presence of foreign exchange rationing, we first consider the case of a small, open price-taking economy in which, for simplicity, there is no production and all goods are traded. The world prices for the N goods are given as $\bar{\pi}_i^w$, $i = 1, \ldots, N$.

The economy has market demand functions, $\xi_i(\pi^d)$, and nonnegative endowments, ω_i, for each of the N goods, where π^d denotes the N-dimensional vector of domestic commodity prices. These demand functions are nonnegative, continuous, homogeneous of degree zero in π^d, and satisfy Walras' Law, i.e., at all price vectors, π^d.

$$\sum_{i=1}^{N} \pi_i^d[\xi_i(\pi^d) - \omega_i] = 0. \tag{1}$$

[a]See Dervis *et al.* (1981, 1982, Chapter 9) who use an *ad hoc* rationing rule in a barter economy with exchange rates but with no monetary specification. See also the comments by Srinivasan (1983) on the treatment of exchange rates by Dervis *et al.*

Without a foreign exchange premium, $\pi_i^d = \bar{\pi}_i^w$ for all i, and thus trade balance holds. Equilibrium in the domestic economy follows trivially; net trades are given by $[\xi_i(\pi^d) - \omega_i]$, which, in turn, are fully accommodated by the larger rest of the world.

To analyze the equilibrium structure in the presence of foreign exchange rationing, we assume that the government fixes the exchange rate at $\bar{e}$, and implements the policy by requiring all foreign exchange earned from exports to be surrendered to the Central Bank at the rate $\bar{e}$. It then allocates rights to purchase available foreign exchange at the same rate $\bar{e}$ to importers. We assume that exporters comply with this policy and fully meet the surrender requirement, even though there are obvious incentives for exporters to conceal foreign exchange and attempt to sell it on parallel (black) markets rather than surrender it at the lower fixed rate.

The simplest modeling for the allocation process of foreign exchange among importers is to assume that the government auctions (or sells) it. In practice, allocation schemes actually followed are more complex than this involving priority allocation of various forms, but for now we abstract from these. Under the simple auction scheme, if desired imports require more foreign exchange than the government offers for sale, the price of foreign exchange paid by importers will be bid up. This price will thus include a foreign exchange premium above the fixed rate $\bar{e}$, which we designate as λ. This premium acts as a surcharge on foreign exchange bought by importers, and adjusts so as to clear the foreign exchange market.

The net effect is akin to a general tariff on all imports, since the exchange rate received by exporters differs from the gross of premium exchange rate paid by importers. As modeled above, the foreign exchange premium accrues to the government, but if rights to purchase foreign exchange at the rate $\bar{e}$ are allocated by the government without charge, the premium would instead go directly to importers.

We introduce money into our small, open-economy model by requiring that domestic transactions be conducted in local currency, the "peso", and international trade be transacted using foreign exchange, the "dollar". Local exporters thus sell their dollar earnings to the Central Bank to acquire pesos, while importers buy dollars with pesos to purchase imports. The auction scheme produces a dual price system, since exporters surrender foreign exchange at a net of premium exchange rate, but sales of foreign exchange to importers occur at a gross of premium rate.

This is clearly the case where the government sells foreign exchange to importers. If, however, rights to foreign exchange are freely distributed to qualifying imports at the rate $\bar{e}$, and legal foreign exchange resale markets exist, the effect is similar, except that importers rather than the government receive the proceeds of the premia. If legal sale is prohibited, the premium value can instead be realized by importing goods and reselling them at domestic prices which reflect the foreign exchange premium, or by selling foreign exchange on black (or parallel) markets.

Our treatment of money in this model is deliberately kept simple; we follow the widely used "cash-in-advance" constraint approach (see Feenstra, 1985; Helpman, 1981; Obstfeld and Stockman, 1984). We assume that real balances are used solely for transactions purposes and that the velocity of circulation is fixed, i.e., money demand is of the simple Cambridge form. All domestic commodity prices are denominated in terms of money. Thus, if we choose units such that velocity is unity, the total demand for pesos, M^d, is given by the value of domestic demands in domestic currency, i.e.,

$$M^d = \sum \pi_i^d \xi_i(\pi^d). \tag{2}$$

The domestic supply of money is assumed set by the monetary authorities and is given by $\bar{M}^s$.

Because of the foreign exchange premium, relative domestic prices of the Ntraded goods will now differ from world prices, depending upon whether they are imported or exported. Domestic prices, π_i^d, are given by

$$\begin{aligned} \pi_i^d &= \bar{e}\,\bar{\pi}_i^w, & &\text{if } (\xi_i - \omega_i) < 0, \\ \pi_i^d &= \bar{e}(1+\lambda)\,\bar{\pi}_i^w, & &\text{if } (\xi_i - \omega_i) \geqq 0, \end{aligned} \tag{3}$$

where $\xi_i - \omega_i$ denotes the net import of goods i, and λ is the premium value over the official exchange rate paid by purchasers of imports.

Total revenues accruing to sellers of rights to purchase foreign exchange at the rate $\bar{e}$ are

$$R = \lambda\bar{e}\sum_{i=1}^{N} \bar{\pi}_i^w \max[0, \xi_i - \omega_i]. \tag{4}$$

These rents accrue either directly to the household sector as additional revenues of importers who are given allocations of foreign exchange by the government which they resell on premium markets, or indirectly as recycled government revenues.

Because anticipated revenues, L, from rights of access to foreign exchange affect commodity demands and are a component of income for at least one of the agents in the model, market demand functions have to be rewritten to reflect this, a feature similar to the tax general equilibrium models presented by Shoven and Whalley (1973, 1992). L and R are each endogenously determined, and only in equilibrium will $L = R$. Commodity demands are therefore written as $\xi_i - (\pi^d, L)$ with these functions homogeneous of degree zero in π^d, L, and $\bar{M}^s$. These demand functions are assumed to be nonnegative and to satisfy Walras' Law discussed below.

The rationale for the homogeneity property assumed for demand functions can be seen from the budget constraint for the household sector, which includes initial holdings of money balances, and is given by

$$I = \sum_{i=1}^{N} \pi_i^d \omega_i + \bar{M}^s + L. \tag{5}$$

Doubling π^d, $\bar{M}^s$, and L doubles both money incomes and buying prices of commodities, leaving real commodity demands unchanged. The demand for money in nominal terms also doubles.

$\bar{M}^s$ appears as part of the budget constraint since initial period money balances used for transactions purposes are assumed held by the household sector. Similarly, M^d appears on the expenditure side since money balances are demanded for transactions purposes. L defines the anticipated revenues from rights to buy foreign exchange at $\bar{e}$ in contrast to the revenues, R, which actually accrue to holders of foreign exchange. This is similar to the Shoven–Whalley general equilibrium tax models where a comparable simultaneity occurs between tax revenues redistributed by the government and revenues actually collected.

For this model Walras' Law states that at any set of domestic prices, whether or not they are equilibrium prices, the total value of expenditures satisfies the household sector budget constraint, i.e.,

$$\sum_{i=1}^{N} \pi_i^d \xi_i + M^d = \sum_{i=1}^{N} \pi_i^d \omega_i + \bar{M}^s + L. \tag{6}$$

Equation (6) implies that

$$\bar{e} \sum_{i=1}^{N} \bar{\pi}_i^w (\xi_i - \omega_i) + (M^d - \bar{M}^s) + (R - L) = 0. \tag{7}$$

Equation (7), in turn, implies that money is nonneutral when the exchange rate is fixed and domestic monetary policy is nonaccommodative. This is because an increase in the money supply cannot result in an increase in export prices since these are fixed in domestic currency prices. As a result, a monetary nonneutrality is present. Contractionary monetary policy can restore equilibrium in such circumstances and remove the need for rationing foreign exchange by the central bank. Monetary policy can thus have real effects on trade flows in the model.

A general equilibrium for this model is given by values of $[\lambda^*, L^*]$ which satisfy the conditions.

$$\sum_{i=1}^{N} \bar{\pi}_i^w (\xi_i - \omega_i) = 0, \quad (R - L). \tag{8}$$

In equilibrium, Walras' Law implies that

$$(M^d - \bar{M^s}) = 0. \tag{9}$$

As emphasized in Section 1, in contrast to equilibrium models that examine physical quantity constraints, which Van der Laan (1980) and others have shown can be supported by a system of virtual taxes, here both the virtual taxes (λ) and the value of the quota (foreign exchange earnings) are endogenously determined.

In this simple case, equilibrium involves two unknowns, λ and L, and two imbalances (trade balance and government budget balance). It is straightforward to apply a fixed point algorithm to this model, such as Van der Laan and Talman (1979) or Broadie (1983) to numerically determine an equilibrium. It is also possible to prove existence, which follows directly from an application of the Gale Nikaido mapping to this system above.

The only complication relative to the standard general equilibrium model is that the direction of trade needs to be assumed before computation begins, and the equilibrium solution may not yield trade flows that match these assumptions. While there are ways to deal with this by introducing additional dimensions to the equilibrium problem, which allow for the endogenous determination of the direction of trade, a simpler scheme in practice is repeated recomputation under modified assumptions on the direction of trade until consistency between assumption and solution is obtained.

3. Extending the Simple Model

While the simple model described in the preceding section serves to illustrate how the basic equilibrium structure involving value quotas and virtual taxes works in the presence of foreign exchange premia, for the modeling approach to be useful for the analysis of policy options for economies using such policies, a number of extensions to the basic model are needed. These include such features as multiple (nonsmall) countries, production, the presence of nontraded goods, parallel (black) markets in foreign exchange, tariffs and quantitative restrictions (QRs).

3.1. *Multiple (nonsmall) countries*

The model outlined above can easily be extended to the case where there are multiple (nonsmall) countries, rather than the single, open, price-taking economy case discussed above. In this extension of the model there are K countries, who trade with one another but have fixed exchange rate regimes, nonaccommodative domestic monetary policy, and foreign exchange premia. We assume that at least one country maintains full convertibility to provide a medium of exchange for all other countries to use (the λ value for this country is zero).

Instead of there being fixed world prices as above, these are now endogenously determined and denoted by π_i^w, $i = 1, \ldots, N$. Global equilibrium involves the same equilibrium conditions (8) in each country as in the model above, but in addition there is global market clearing at the equilibrium world prices π^{w^*}, i.e.,

$$\sum_{k=1}^{K} [\xi_i^k(\pi^{w*}, \lambda^{k*}, L^{k*}) - \omega_i^k] = 0, \tag{10}$$

where ξ_i^k and ω_i^k are demands for and endowments of good i in country k, λ^{k*} is the equilibrium foreign exchange premium value in country k, and L^{k^*} is the value of rents accruing to recipients of foreign exchange in country k.

3.2. *Production and nontraded goods*

Extending the approach outlined above to incorporate production and other features such as nontraded goods is also relatively straightforward. We use our approach to modeling equilibrium with foreign exchange premia in a small (price-taking) economy numerical general equilibrium model of the Philippines due to Clarete (1984) which uses production functions with both industry-specific factors and industry-mobile factors. We therefore describe a similar treatment of production here.

In this model variant, there are T tradable goods, NT nontraded (home) goods, $(T + NT)$ sector-specific factors and K industry-mobile factors of production. π^d and $\bar{\pi}^w$ are T-dimensional vectors of domestic and world prices of the traded goods; π^h is a NT-dimensional vector of domestic prices of home goods; and w a K-dimensional vector of factor prices. On the demand side we again consider a single consumer.

From profit maximization, the economy's aggregate profit function is $p(\pi^d, \pi^h w, \bar{z})$, where $\bar{z}$ is a $(T+NT)$-dimensional vector of industry-specific factors. We also assume this profit function to be linearly homogeneous in π^d, π^h, and w. The derivatives of the profit function with respect to its price arguments, p_{π^d}, p_{π^h}, and p_w give the net outputs of the $(N + NT)$ commodities and the K factor demands by firms. It follows from the homogeneity property of the profit function that $p(\pi^d, \pi^h, w, \bar{z}) = \pi^d p_{\pi^d} + \pi^h p_{\pi^h} + w' p_w \geqq 0$. The inequality allows for rents that accrue to the sector-specific factors.

From utility maximization, the consumer's expenditure function is $e(\pi^d, \pi^h)$, which we assume to be linearly homogeneous in π^d, π^h, and $\bar{M}^s$. The vectors of derivatives of the expenditure function with respect to its price arguments give the compensated consumer demand functions for $(T+NT)$ goods and real balances. The homogeneity property of the expenditure function implies that $e(\pi^h, \pi^d) = \pi^d e_{\pi^d} + \pi^h e_{\pi^h}$. We assume that consumer factor demands (e.g., demand for leisure) are zero. Since all factor endowments in the model are exogenous, the vectors of sectorally-mobile and industry-specific factor supplies, F and z, are respectively $\bar{F}$ and $\bar{z}$.

The income of the economy consists of the value of factors, the money endowment, and public income transfers (including the value of rights of access to foreign exchange). Household expenditures include both traded and nontraded goods, plus money demands.

Using the homogeneity property of $p(\pi^d, \pi^h, w, \bar{z})$ and $e(\pi^d, \pi^h)$, the general equilibrium conditions for this version of the model are

$$(-p_w - \bar{F}) = 0 \tag{11}$$

for the sectorally-mobile factors (we note that $p_w < 0$);

$$(e_{\pi^h} - p_{\pi^h}) = 0 \tag{12}$$

for home goods;

$$\bar{\pi}^{w'}(e_{\pi^d} - p_{\pi^d}) = 0 \tag{13}$$

as the trade balance condition; and

$$(R - L) = 0 \tag{14}$$

for the government budget balance condition.

Walras' Law implies that

$$(M^d - \bar{M}^s) = 0 \tag{15}$$

for domestic currency. The above system of equations can also be solved for w^*, π^{h^*}, λ^*, and L^*, using a fixed-point algorithm.

3.3. *Tariffs*

Tariffs are also relatively easy to incorporate into the approach. We represent tariffs by the *ad valorem* tariff rates t_i $(i = l, \ldots, N)$ on the N traded goods, noting that $t_i = 0$ where good i is exported. As already indicated, their inclusion leads to the proposition that a reduction in a general tariff on all imports will have no real effect on trade, since an adjustment in the foreign exchange premium value will occur so as to leave both real trade flows and household incomes unchanged.

The major changes in the model structure occur with the determination of domestic prices, which now include tariffs on imports, and in the determination of household incomes, which now include tariff revenues (assumed redistributed by the government to the household sector).

Domestic prices are given by

$$\begin{aligned} \pi_i^d &= \bar{e}\,\bar{\pi}_i^w, && \text{if } \xi_i - \omega_i < 0, \\ \pi_i^d &= \bar{e}(1+\lambda)(1+t_i)\,\bar{\pi}_i^w, && \text{if } \xi_i - \omega_i \geqq 0. \end{aligned} \tag{16}$$

The household sector budget constraint is given by (5) except that L now includes not only anticipated revenues from foreign exchange premia, but also anticipated tariff revenues.

In this case, actual revenues collected, R, also include both tariff revenues and those from foreign exchange premia, i.e.,

$$R = \bar{e}\sum_{i=1}^{N}(\lambda + t_i + \lambda t_i)\bar{\pi}_i^w \max[0, \xi_i - \omega_i]. \tag{17}$$

An equilibrium in the presence of both tariffs and a foreign exchange premium is again given by values of $[\lambda^*, L^*]$ such that the same conditions as in (8) hold.

The neutrality proposition that a general reduction in tariffs will have no real effects on trade flows and will be exactly offset by an increase in the premium value for foreign exchange follows from Eqs. (16) and (17). For instance, in the case where $t_i = t$ for all imports, an elimination of tariffs results in a new premium value $\hat{\lambda} = \lambda + t + \lambda t$. At this new premium value domestic prices are unchanged; combined revenues from tariffs and premia, R, are unchanged in Eq. (17); household sector incomes are unchanged; and the value of domestic transactions, and hence M^d, is unchanged. In short, all the real characteristics of the equilibrium will be preserved since there are no relative price changes, and in this one-household case there are no income effects between households from the reduction in tariffs and the increase in premium values.

In the case of sector-specific tariffs, the neutrality of tariff policy occurs where changes in tariff rates are equiproportional, i.e., $\Delta t_i/(1+t_i)$ is equal for all t_i. Otherwise, in removing sector-specific tariffs real effects will result. A change in tariffs can thus be decomposed into an average change which has no real effects, and a change in the dispersion of tariffs from which real effects result. For this reason, the liberalizing effect of lowering tariffs will typically be smaller under a trade regime in which foreign exchange premia occur than otherwise, and reductions in tariffs on a subset of goods which increase the dispersion of tariff rates can be trade restricting.

3.4. *Quantitative restrictions (quotas)*

QRs are slightly more complicated than tariffs to introduce into this, or any other, equilibrium structure, since each quota will have a separate premium value associated with it and all of these QRs will be endogenously determined in equilibrium. If we designate quota restrictions by $\bar{q}_i$, and the per unit value of the quota premium associated with each restriction as p_i^q, the adjustments to the model structure are similar to those needed for tariffs. Domestic prices are gross of the premium values associated with the quota restrictions, and household incomes include the value of quota premia. Where commodity i is exported, $\bar{q}_i = p_i^q = 0$. A major difference relative to the tariff case is that the quota premium values are endogenously determined in equilibrium.

Domestic prices are given by

$$\begin{aligned} \pi_i^d &= \bar{e}\,\bar{\pi}_i^w, && \text{if } \xi_i - \omega_i < 0, \\ \pi_i^d &= \bar{e}(1+\lambda)(1+p_i^q)\,\bar{\pi}_i^w, && \text{if } \xi_i - \omega_i \geqq 0. \end{aligned} \tag{18}$$

The household sector budget is given by Eq. (5), but revenues collected, R, include both revenues from foreign exchange premia and those accruing to holders of quota for imports, i.e.,

$$R = \bar{e} \sum_{i=1}^{N} (\lambda + p_i^q + \lambda p_i^q) \bar{\pi}_i^w \max[0, \xi_i - \omega_i]. \tag{19}$$

An equilibrium in the presence of QRs is given by values of $[p_i^{q*}, \lambda^*, L^*]$ such that the same conditions as in (8) hold, except that an additional set of market-clearing conditions are required for each quota, i.e.,

$$\xi_i - \omega_i - \bar{q}_i \leqq 0 \quad (= 0, \text{ if } p_i^q > 0). \tag{20}$$

In this version of the model, the foreign exchange premium only affects the domestic prices of imports for which there is either no quota or the quota is not binding. Where all imports are quota constrained, the foreign exchange premium, if positive, only has a redistributive role and has no real impact in the model. In such a case, a devaluation or a contractionary monetary policy will be neutral and have no real effects on trade flows. A reduction in quotas such that all quota premium values change proportionally, i.e., $\Delta p_i^q/(1 + p_i^q)$ is equal for all import quotas i, will also be neutral, provided all quotas continue to bind.

Where imports have no quotas or have redundant quotas, a devaluation or a contractionary monetary policy will again have real effects, although with smaller effects relative to a model without quotas. In these cases, quotas act to transfer rationing from the foreign exchange market to the goods markets.

3.5. *Priority allocation of foreign exchange and parallel markets*

Thus far we have assumed that foreign exchange received by the government from surrender by exporters is either sold by the government on a free market, or rights to purchase foreign exchange at the rate $\bar{e}$ are allocated to importers without charge. In practice, more complex allocation procedures are used, and we briefly mention how some of these can be incorporated into our equilibrium approach.

Certain imports can be classified as "essential" or "high priority", and others are classified as "nonessential". Importers then receive allocations of foreign exchange at the rate $\bar{e}$ for essential imports, which they use for one of two purposes. They either import essentials, which they sell at the going domestic price (and in the process implicitly receive a foreign exchange premium at rate λ), or they sell their foreign exchange on black (or parallel) foreign exchange markets. Buyers of foreign exchange on black markets use their dollars to finance nonessential imports, either through legal importation or through smuggling.

Black markets for foreign exchange can be incorporated into this model using a similar approach to that used by Nguyen and Whalley (1987) to examine the co-existence of equilibria on black and white markets. In this case the effective foreign exchange premia applying to imports of essential and nonessential imports are given by the two different values, λ_1, and λ_2, with the difference between the two reflecting the probability of sellers of foreign exchange on black markets being detected and fined.[b]

4. A Small Open-Economy Model of the Philippines

We have used a small open-economy numerical general equilibrium model of the Philippines due to Clarete (1984) into which we have introduced this formulation of foreign exchange premia, along with other trade distortions. The original model is presented in detail in Clarete (1984), and also described in Clarete and Roumasset (1987) and Clarete and Whalley (1988).

In the basic model, the government uses both tariffs and export taxes and redistributes the revenues in a lump-sum fashion to the single consumer. In the version used here, a fixed exchange rate, an exogenous domestic money supply, and a foreign exchange premium are introduced as modeled above. We also consider a case with import quotas, but we have not incorporated parallel markets for foreign exchange arising from the designation of priority and nonpriority imports.

This model is calibrated to a 1978 Philippine benchmark equilibrium data set using the procedure described in Mansur and Whalley (1984). Seven sectors are included: Three exportables, two importables, and two home goods. Exportables are commercial crops, agricultural food industries, and industrial exportables. Importables include industrial importables (consisting mainly of producer goods), and import substitutes. The home goods sectors are other agricultural products and services. Two variable

[b]We assume, for simplicity, that all penalties are incurred on the selling side of the black market for foreign exchange.

factors are specified, labor and capital, with the aggregate supply of each assumed to be fixed.

Tariff and export tax rates used in the model are trade-weighted averages of respective industry average rates using commodity-specific data listed in the Philippine Tariff Code for 1978. In the 1978 base year data, industrial importables have an ad valorem tariff rate equal to 23% and import substitutes face a rate of 62%. Export tax rates for commercial crops, agricultural food industries, and industrial exportables are set at 5.3% and 3%, respectively. We construct alternative micro-consistent economic data with import quotas as well as tariff rates. Quotas are set equal to the observed benchmark imports, and the respective quota premium values are assumed equal to 0% and 20% (i.e., one of the quotas is redundant).

We assume the benchmark value of the foreign exchange premium to be 20%, and set the money supply equal to nominal expenditures on all commodities in the benchmark data. These policy parameters are combined with other data from Clarete (1981) to yield the complete benchmark equilibrium data set used in the model. The calibration procedures used determine the parameters for the production and demand functions, which, in turn, are used in the counterfactual analyses reported below.

We have performed a series of experiments with this model. We first consider a version of the model in which quotas do not appear. The sector-specific tariffs in the 1978 data set are first reduced equiproportionately, and then are completely removed holding the exchange rate and money supply fixed at their benchmark values. We then reduce the money supply, by an amount sufficient to eliminate the foreign exchange premium, holding tariffs and exchange rates constant, demonstrating the nonneutral effects of monetary policy. We also allow the exchange rate to vary, keeping other policy parameters constant, demonstrating the real effects of devaluation in the model. In each case we calculate the welfare effect of the change implied by comparing counterfactual and original equilibria and calculating the Hicksian equivalent variation.

Results from these computations are reported in Table 1. They clearly show the neutrality of a general tariff reduction, and the real effects of either contractionary domestic monetary policy or a devaluation. Reducing tariff rates equiproportionately has no real effects, and the equivalent variation associated with this change is zero. The implication is that tariff reforms have smaller liberalizing effects where foreign exchange is rationed, evident in the small equivalent variation associated with removing all sector-specific tariffs of 0.91% of income. Removing the same set of tariffs without

Table 1. Welfare Impacts from Changes in Trade and Monetary Policies in a Philippine Trade Model[a] (Welfare Impacts Measured as Percent of National Income).

Policy change and model variant	
• No-quota model variant	
10% equiproportional reduction in tariff rates	0.00
Sector-specific tariffs removed	0.91
Money supply reduced so as to eliminate the foreign exchange premium	2.11
Devaluation of 10% in the peso	2.11
• With quota model variant	
Sector-specific tariffs and quotas removed	1.86

[a]See description in text.

including foreign exchange premia in this model yields a welfare gain of 3.3% of income (see Clarete and Whalley, 1988).

The equivalent variation implied by reducing the money supply so as to sufficiently eliminate the foreign exchange premium, holding the other policy parameters constant, is 2.11% of income. This confirms the proposition that monetary policy is nonneutral in this model and suggests that it has more effect on trade flows than tariff changes. Lastly, devaluation is equally effective.

Using a model variant that incorporates quotas, we then consider the removal of all sector-specific tariffs and quotas. There is no real impact from changes in tariffs in this case, because these policies have no marginal effects on imports. This is true independently of exchange rate and monetary policies. Changes in monetary policy and devaluation are also neutral in this case. Only when import quotas are changed (in the case reported, together with tariffs) do we observe any real effects, and in the case reported an improvement in economic welfare of 1.86% of national income occurs.

The implication we draw from these calculations is that it is important to incorporate foreign exchange premia as an integral part of the foreign trade regime in developing countries when assessing their trade policy options. In analyzing tariff reforms, for instance, the interaction of premia with tariffs can negate any real effects of tariff changes. In analyzing QRs the neutrality of exchange rate changes can be restored, but only where binding quotas apply to all imports. In general, changes in monetary policy or devaluations will have real effects in the type of model presented here.

5. Concluding Remarks

This chapter discusses general equilibrium models in which the government pursues a fixed exchange rate policy along with a nonaccommodative domestic monetary policy (typical of many developing countries). An associated foreign exchange premium results generating a dual price system under which exporters surrender foreign exchange at a net of premium exchange rate, but importers have to pay a gross of premium rate to acquire foreign exchange. We present an equilibrium formulation in which both the virtual tax rate and the value of the quota are endogenously determined, and contrast our equilibrium structure with that needed to analyze physical quotas. We indicate how trade taxes, quotas, parallel black markets for foreign exchange, production, and home goods all can be incorporated into the basic approach. Some general equilibrium calculations using a model for the Philippines incorporating rationed foreign exchange are presented.

References

Broadie, M (1983). OCTASOLV user's guide. Systems optimization laboratory technical report 83-9, Stanford University, Department of Operations Research.

Clarete, RL (1984). The cost and consequences of trade distortions in a small open economy: A general equilibrium model of the Philippines. PhD dissertation, University of Hawaii, Economics Department.

Clarete, RL and JA Roumasset (1987). A Shoven–Whalley model of a small open economy: An illustration with Philippine tariffs. *Journal of Public Economics*, **32**(2), 247–261.

Clarete, RL and J Whalley (1988). Interactions between trade policies and domestic distortions in a small open developing country. *Journal of International Economics*, **24**, 345–358.

Dervis, K, J de Melo and S Robinson (1981). A general equilibrium analysis of foreign exchange shortages in a developing country. *Economic Journal*, **91**(364), 891–906.

Dervis, K, J de Melo and S Robinson (1982). *General Equilibrium Models for Development Policy.* Cambridge: Cambridge University Press.

Feenstra. RC (1985). Anticipated devaluations, currency flight and direct trade controls in a monetary economy. *American Economic Review*, **75**(3), 386–401.

Helpman, E (1981). An exploration in the theory of exchange control regimes. *Journal of Political Economy*, **89**, 865–890.

Mansur, A and J Whalley (1984). Numerical specification of applied general equilibrium models: Estimation, calibration, and data. In *Applied General Equilibrium Analysis*, HE Scarf and JB Shoven (eds.), pp. 69–137. New York: Cambridge University Press.

Nguyen, TT and J Whalley (1987). General equilibrium analysis of black and white markets: A computational approach with an application to India. *Journal of Public Economics*, **40**(3), 331–347.

Obstfeld, M and AC Stockman (1984). Exchange rate dynamics. In *Handbook of International Economics*, Vol. 2, PB Kenen and RW Jones (eds.), pp. 917–978. Amsterdam: North-Holland.

Shoven, JB and J Whalley (1973). General equilibrium with taxes: A computational procedure and an existence proof. *Review of Economic Studies*, **40**, 475–490.

Shoven, JB and J Whalley (1992). *Applying General Equilibrium*. Cambridge: Cambridge University Press.

Srinivasan, TN (1983). Review of K Dervis, J de Melo and S Robinson. General equilibrium models for development policy. *Economic Journal*, **93**, 441–442.

Van der Laan, G (1980). Equilibrium under rigid prices with compensation for the consumers. *International Economic Review*, **21**(1), 63–74.

Van der Laan, G and A Talman (1979). A restart algorithm for computing fixed points without an extra dimension. *Mathematical Programming*, **17**, 34–43.

Chapter 18

Exploring Policy Options in Joint Intertemporal-Spatial Trade Models Using an Incomplete Markets Approach*,†

Hui Huang
Department of Economics, University of Waterloo, Waterloo, Ontario, Canada
School of Economics and Finance, Victoria University of Wellington, Wellington, New Zealand
hui.huang@vuw.ac.nz
h34huang@uwaterloo.ca

John Whalley
Department of Economics, The University of Western Ontario, London, Ontario, Canada
National Bureau of Economic Research (NBER)
jwhalley@uwo.ca

Shunming Zhang
Center for Macroeconomic Research and Department of Finance, School of Economics, Xiamen University Xiamen, Fujian, People's Republic of China School of Economics and Management, China Agricultural University, Beijing, People's Republic China

In this chapter, we discuss the desirability of service trade liberalization in the presence of incompleteness of markets where there is both inter-spatial and intertemporal trade between countries. We use numerical simulation methods for insights and relate our discussion to the General Agreement on Trade in Services (GATS) in the WTO. We interpret the absence of intertemporal trade as an absence of intermediation services provided by both domestic and foreign service providers. For simplicity, we consider extreme cases where intertemporal

*This paper draws in part on material of an earlier paper, "Financial Services Trade Liberalization in A Joint Spatial Intertemporal Multi-Country Model" by Huang *et al.* (2004). We acknowledge the financial support from the Center for International Governance Innovation (CIGI), Waterloo, Canada, and from National Social Science Foundation of China (SSFC Grant 07AJL002), National Natural Science Foundation of China (NSFC Grant 70825003) and "Humanities and Social Science" Major Project, Chinese Ministry of Education (Grant Number 07JJD790145).
†This chapter was first published in (2009). *Economic Theory*, **41**(1), 131–145.

intermediation services can only be provided by domestic providers, so that when intertemporal trade in services is not allowed, markets are not complete. To our knowledge, this type of models is not used in the trade literature as general comparative statics results are unavailable. We first consider the liberalization of trade in financial services in an inter-spatial and intertemporal model of two countries, and we show how services liberalization can be welfare worsening in the presence of a tariff on spatial trade in goods. We show that this can hold in an artificial world with no domestic financial services provider. We compare financial service trade autarky in which there is no intermediation to financial service trade liberalization which involves costless intertemporal intermediation provided by foreign service providers. We also consider a more complex (and realistic) world where costly intermediation services can be provided by both domestic and foreign providers.

1. Introduction

In this chapter, we discuss the policy implications of having incomplete markets in trade models where both intertemporal and inter-spatial trade between countries is possible and relate our discussion to the structure of the General Agreement on Trade in Services (GATS) in the WTO. We appeal directly to literature on multi-commodity intertemporal models of incomplete markets due to Duffie (1987), Duffie and Shafer (1985), Geanakoplos (1990), Geanakoplos and Tsomocos (2002), Hart (1975), Magill and Shafer (1991), Magill and Quinzii (1996), Radner (1972), and Werner (1985) in analyzing the effects of financial services liberalization. We use this literature on incomplete markets without the added complication of uncertainty; most of this literature is concerned with existence issues; our focus here is comparative statics. We interpret situations with no intertemporal trade as an absence of intertemporal intermediation services provided by both domestic and foreign service providers. For simplicity, we consider extreme cases where intertemporal intermediation services can only be provided by domestic providers so that when intertemporal trade in services is not allowed, markets are incomplete in that consumers only face period by period budget constraints.

We first consider a series of two country, two good, and two period numerical simulation analyses using a simple general equilibrium structure, and consider cases in which tariffs distort trade within periods both before and after financial service liberalization. Initially, there is intertemporal autarky (no intertemporal intermediation) in financial services, which, for simplicity, we characterize as no domestic provision of intermediation services. Using this framework, we are able to separately consider both tariff liberalization (removing or reducing tariffs) and financial services liberalization which allows for foreign providers to enter domestic markets and relax intertemporal budget constraints for borrowers and lenders. We are thus able to consider financial services liberalization in the presence of tariffs, tariff liberalization in the presence of financial service trade restrictions, and joint liberalization of both goods and financial services.

We explore whether financial services liberalization need be welfare improving using numerical examples. Initially, we consider a simple world in which there is no domestic provision of intermediation services but liberalization permits foreign entry of costless service providers who, in effect, relax period by period budget constraints. We then consider an extension to this model with costly intermediation and with both domestic and foreign financial service providers both before and after liberalization. These two service providers have differential costs. In this model, financial services trade liberalization typically increases the amount of intermediation; intertemporal intermediation services are used initially in both countries, but after liberalization are provided in both countries by the relatively more efficient domestic service provider. We report on examples where, with preexisting tariffs, financial services liberalization can be welfare worsening.

In the contemporary global economy, services trade is perhaps 1/3 of total goods and services trade,[a] and services are more heavily restricted than goods, albeit by regulatory devices more so than by tariffs. The severity of existing service trade restrictions seemingly suggests that it is more likely that services liberalization may be welfare improving, but this remains a judgmentally based evaluation rather than a clearly established result. General results are probably unattainable for the simulation structure we explore numerically here, but in the presence of goods trade restrictions the mere possibility that adding financial services liberalization to conventional goods liberalization could be welfare worsening is important for the ways in which GATS and services liberalization in the WTO are currently discussed. This implication is that, until such time that goods trade is free of restrictions, services trade liberalization in the GATS needs to be shown to be welfare improving in particular cases before it can be unequivocally advocated.

[a]See World Trade Organization (WTO) (2007).

2. A Two-Country Model of Joint Spatial and Intertemporal Trade used to Evaluate Financial Services Liberalization

To explore the impacts of financial services trade liberalization in the presence of goods market restrictions, we use a simple two period ($t = 0, 1$) two-country ($i = 1, 2$) two-good ($l = 1, 2$) pure exchange general equilibrium model. In this model,[b] each country has a single representative consumer, with endowments of the two goods in each period ($E^t_{il}; t = 0, 1, i = 1, 2, l = 1, 2$). For simplicity, a time-additive utility function is used of the form

$$U_i = \sum_{t=0}^{1} \frac{1}{(1+\rho_i)^t} u^t_i(X^t_{i1}, X^t_{i2}) = u^0_i(X^0_{i1}, X^0_{i2}) + \frac{1}{1+\rho_i} u^1_i(X^1_{i1}, X^1_{i2}), \quad i = 1, 2, \tag{1}$$

where $u^t_i(X^t_{i1}, X^t_{i2}) = [X^t_{i1}]^{\alpha^t_{i1}}[X^t_{i2}]^{\alpha^t_{i2}}$ for $t = 0, 1$ and $i = 1, 2$, ρ_i is the intertemporal discount factor for individual i, X^t_{il} denotes the consumption of good l for country i at date t, and α^t_{il} is the share parameter for good l for country i at date $t(\sum_{l=1}^{2} \alpha^t_{il} = 1)$.

For any good l, in any period t, we define the seller's (net of tariff) price as π^t_l and we allow each country i to impose tariffs at rate T^t_{il} on each imported good l (i.e., if $X^t_{il} \geq E^t_{il}$, then $T^t_{il} \geq 0$). Tariffs are set to zero for any export i (i.e., if $X^t_{il} \leq E^t_{il}$, then $T^t_{il} = 0$). Internal (gross of tariff) prices for good l in country i at date t are thus

$$P^t_{il} = (1 + T^t_{il})\pi^t_l, \quad t = 0, 1, \ i = 1, 2, \ l = 1, 2. \tag{2}$$

These are also sellers' prices of good l in country i.

Tariff revenues collected in country i in period t are

$$R^t_i = \sum_{l=1}^{2} T^t_{il}\pi^t_l(X^t_{il} - E^t_{il})^+, \quad t = 0, 1, \ i = 1, 2, \tag{3}$$

the total income of country i in period t is given by

$$I^t_i = \sum_{l=1}^{2} P^t_{il}E^t_{il} + R^t_i, \quad t = 0, 1, \ i = 1, 2. \tag{4}$$

[b]Also see the related structure, not used in trade analysis, in Geanakoplos (1990) and Geanakoplos and Tsomocos (2002).

To simplify matters, we initially assume that there is service autarky and that in this case (and as a strong assumption) there no intermediation provided by domestic service providers. This is clearly an artificial construct (which we relax later) whose main virtue is simplicity. This enables us to appeal directly to relevant literature on multi-commodity intertemporal models from Duffie (1987), Duffie and Shafer (1985), Geanakopolos (1990), Hart (1975), Magill and Shafer (1991), and Magill and Quinzii (1996), Radner (1972), Werner (1985), in analyzing the effects of service liberalization in a simple way. We do this without the added complication of uncertainty which is central to this literature. Most of this literature is concerned with existence issues; our focus here is comparative statics. We assume for now (and also for further simplicity) that under free trade in services, intermediation services are provided costlessly by foreign banks.[c]

In the initial autarky case, period by period budget constraints apply for each country i and in each period t, i.e.,

$$\sum_{l=1}^{2} P_{il}^{t} X_{il}^{t} = I_{i}^{t}, \quad t = 0, 1, \ \ i = 1, 2.$$

These imply that

$$\sum_{l=1}^{2}(1 + T_{il}^{t})\pi_{l}^{t} X_{il}^{t} = \sum_{l=1}^{2}(1 + T_{il}^{t})\pi_{l}^{t} E_{il}^{t} + R_{i}^{t}, \quad t = 0, 1, \ \ i = 1, 2. \tag{5}$$

The combined budget constraint for country i over the two periods is

$$\sum_{t=0}^{1}\sum_{l=1}^{2} P_{il}^{t} X_{il}^{t} = \sum_{t=0}^{1} I_{i}^{t}, \quad i = 1, 2$$

which implies

$$\sum_{t=0}^{1}\sum_{l=1}^{2}(1 + T_{il}^{t})\pi_{l}^{t} X_{il}^{t} = \sum_{t=0}^{1}\sum_{l=1}^{2}(1 + T_{il}^{t})\pi_{l}^{t} E_{il}^{t} + \sum_{t=0}^{1} R_{i}^{t}, \quad i = 1, 2. \tag{6}$$

Our treatment of financial services liberalization allows us to consider two different types of equilibria. In one, there are period by period budget constraints and in the other only across period budget constraints. Moving

[c]The discussion of barriers to trade in intermediation services in practice in Chen and Schembri (2002), Francois and Schuknecht (2000), Kalirajan *et al.* (2001), and Mattoo (1999), clearly indicates this is a strong simplification, which are adopt here to simplify the analysis.

from period by period budget constraints to an across period budget constraint can be thought of as allowing for intertemporal intermediation in consumption activities across periods where none previously occurred. The interpretation is that, initially, there is autarky in the trade of intermediation services since none can be provided domestically. We then open up each economy to international trade in intermediation services which are costlessly provided, a simple form of liberalization in intertemporal intermediation services. In this case, we can thus consider goods trade liberalization as a reduction in tariffs where no service liberalization occurs, or service liberalization where no tariff liberalization occurs. We can also consider services liberalization in a tariff-free world, and tariff liberalization in a world either with or without service restrictions. Finally, we can consider joint tariff and services liberalization. Comparisons of welfare outcomes across all these equilibria can be made and implications for policy drawn.

Vayanos and Vila (1999) and Kamiya and Shimizu (2007) study money and transaction costs in their general equilibrium models. Our joint spatial intertemporal economy can also be thought of as one in which there are a series of spot markets in goods and, in the presence of services liberalization, a system of asset markets which permit the transfer of income among spot markets in the sense first analyzed by Arrow (1964) and later by Hart (1975), Magill and Shafer (1991), and Werner (1985).[d] It contrasts with earlier intertemporal equilibrium formalizations of a set of Arrow–Debreu contingent commodity markets as in Debreu (1959).

The two types of equilibria we consider for this structure are:

General equilibrium with period by period budget constraints. A general equilibrium for this economy with period by period budget constraints is characterized by a price system and consumption of goods by countries $[(\pi_l^t : t = 0, 1; l = 1, 2), (X_{il}^t : t = 0, 1; i = 1, 2; l = 1, 2)]$ such that (1) given $(\pi_l^t; t = 0, 1, l = 1, 2)$, for $i = 1, 2, (X_{il}^t; t = 0, 1, l = 1, 2)$ solves the utility maximization problem subject to the period by period

[d]Hart (1975) showed, with uncertainty and hence incomplete markets, an equilibrium may not exist, or an inefficient equilibrium may result. Werner (1985) discusses the general issue of existence for such economies; Magill and Shafer (1991) show among others results how in the certainty case the multi-commodity intertemporal equilibrium is equivalent to one in which an interest rate is endogenously determined and equals the ratio of the shadow prices of period by period budget constraints for each of the individuals in the economy.

budget constraints (5), and (2) markets clear:

$$\sum_{i=1}^{2} X_{il}^{t} = \sum_{i=1}^{2} E_{il}^{t}, \quad t = 0, 1; \; l = 1, 2.$$

General equilibrium with across period budget constraints. A general equilibrium for this economy with combined budget constraints over periods is characterized by a price system and consumption of goods by countries $[(\pi_l^t : t = 0, 1; l = 1, 2), (X_{il}^t : t = 0, 1; i = 1, 2; l = 1, 2)]$ such that (1) given $(\pi_l^t; t = 0, 1, l = 1, 2)$, for $i = 1, 2, (X_{il}^t; t = 0, 1, l = 1, 2)$ solves the utility maximization problem subject to the combined across period budget constraint (6), and (2) markets clear:

$$\sum_{i=1}^{2} X_{il}^{t} = \sum_{i=1}^{2} E_{il}^{t}, \quad t = 0, 1; \; l = 1, 2.$$

The combined across periods budget constraint (6) for each individual in each country can also be written as

$$\sum_{l=1}^{2} (1 + T_{il}^{0}) \pi_l^0 X_{il}^0 + F_i = \sum_{l=1}^{2} (1 + T_{il}^{0}) \pi_l^0 E_{il}^0 + R_i^0, \tag{7}$$

$$\sum_{l=1}^{2} (1 + T_{il}^{1}) \pi_l^1 X_{il}^1 = \sum_{l=1}^{2} (1 + T_{il}^{1}) \pi_l^1 E_{il}^1 + R_i^1 + F_i, \tag{8}$$

where F_i represents the amount that country i (or the representative consumer in that country) lends (rather than borrow) to the other country in period 0.

The across period budget constraint equilibrium is the same as an equilibrium characterized by a price system and consumption of goods by countries $[(\pi_l^t : t = 0, 1; l = 1, 2), (X_{il}^t : t = 0, 1; i = 1, 2; l = 1, 2)]$ such that (1) given $(\pi_l^t; t = 0, 1, l = 1, 2)$, for $i = 1, 2, (X_{il}^t; t = 0, 1, l = 1, 2)$ solves the utility maximization problem subject to the budget constraints (7)–(8), and (2) markets clear

$$\sum_{i=1}^{2} X_{il}^{t} = \sum_{i=1}^{2} E_{il}^{t} \quad \text{for } t = 0, 1 \quad \text{and} \quad l = 1, 2 \quad \text{and} \quad \sum_{i=1}^{2} F_i = 0.$$

Denoting an interest rate (for both lenders and borrowers) in the two countries as r, the combined budget constraints become

$$\sum_{l=1}^{2}(1+T_{il}^{0})\pi_l^0 X_{il}^0 + F_i = \sum_{l=1}^{2}(1+T_{il}^{0})\pi_l^0 E_{il}^0 + R_i^0, \tag{9}$$

$$\sum_{l=1}^{2}(1+T_{il}^{1})\pi_l^1 X_{il}^1 = \sum_{l=1}^{2}(1+T_{il}^{1})\pi_l^1 E_{il}^1 + R_i^1 + [1+r]F_i. \tag{10}$$

Thus, the across period equilibrium is equivalent to an equilibrium characterized by the same lending and borrowing interest rate r, and a price system and consumption of goods by countries $[(\pi_l^t : t = 0,1; l = 1,2), (X_{il}^t : t = 0,1; i = 1,2; l = 1,2)]$ such that (1) given $(\pi_l^t; t = 0,1, l = 1,2)$, for $i = 1,2, (X_{il}^t; t = 0,1, l = 1,2)$ solves the utility maximization problem subject to the budget constraints (9)–(10), and (2) markets clear

$$\sum_{i=1}^{2} X_{il}^t = \sum_{i=1}^{2} E_{il}^t \quad \text{for } t = 0,1 \quad \text{and} \quad l = 1,2 \quad \text{and} \quad \sum_{i=1}^{2} F_i = 0.$$

If tariff rates are zero on both products in both countries at both dates ($T_{il}^t = 0$ for $t = 0,1$ and $i = 1,2$ and $l = 1,2$), then these equilibria are also free trade competitive equilibria.

Comparing across these equilibria in this simplified world enables us to consider the effects of financial services liberalization (in the sense assumed here) in the presence of restrictions on goods trade.

3. Numerical Analysis with the Two-Country Model

We use the equilibrium structures set out in the previous section in numerical equilibrium analyses which compare across equilibria for particular parametrizations and assess the welfare effects of alternative trade liberalizations. To compute equilibria for these we need to assume that the direction of trade is predetermined. This may be that country 1 imports good 1 ($X_{11}^t \geq E_{11}^t$ and $T_{11}^t \geq 0$) and exports good 2 ($X_{12}^t \leq E_{12}^t$ and $T_{12}^t = 0$), while country 2 exports good 1 ($X_{21}^t \leq E_{21}^t$ and $T_{21}^t = 0$) and imports good 2 ($X_{22}^t \geq E_{22}^t$ and $T_{22}^t \geq 0$). In this case, the price of good 1 is $P_{11}^t = (1 + T_{11}^t)\pi_1^t$ for buyers in country 1 and $P_{21}^t = \pi_1^t$ for sellers from country 2, and the price of good 2 is $P_{12}^t = \pi_2^t$ for sellers from country 1 and $P_{22}^t = (1 + T_{22}^t)\pi_2^t$ for buyers in country 2.

Table 1. A Parametrization of a Cobb–Douglas Spatial and Intertemporal Economy Used to Analyze Joint Goods and Services Liberalization.

Intertemporal discount factor by country $\rho_1 = 0.10$ and $\rho_2 = 0.10$

	Period 0		Period 1	
	Good 1	Good 2	Good 1	Good 2
Share parameters, α_{il}^t				
Country 1	0.70	0.30	0.60	0.40
Country 2	0.40	0.60	0.30	0.70
Initial endowments, E_{il}^t				
Country 1	40	80	40	80
Country 2	80	40	80	40
Initial tariff rates, T_{il}^t				
Country 1	0.10	0.00	0.05	0.00
Country 2	0.00	0.05	0.00	0.10

In this case, tariff revenues at date t are given by

$$R_1^t = T_{11}^t \pi_1^t (X_{11}^t - E_{11}^t) \quad \text{and} \quad R_2^t = T_{22}^t \pi_2^t (X_{22}^t - E_{22}^t). \tag{11}$$

Table 1 sets out a parametrization for a Cobb–Douglas intertemporal-spatial two-country economy with and without tariffs. The parameter values used here have been selected to generate cases for which services liberalization is welfare worsening. This is a symmetric specification across countries except for the share parameters, including the intertemporal discount factors used in the two countries. Tariff rates are specified as positive when the direction of trade implies an import by that country. We later perform parametric variation around this specification in an effort to explore the likelihood of such an outcome occurring.

In Table 2, we report Hicksian equivalent variation money metric welfare measures of the impacts of various liberalizations both for individual economies and for the world using the parametric specification in Table 1. In this table, Hicksian measures are expressed as a percentage of reference (pre-liberalization) equilibrium incomes. Here, results show that goods liberalization yields a welfare gain, while services liberalization in the presence of tariffs yields a welfare loss. Larger gains occur if tariffs and services are jointly removed, implying these two liberalizations have nonadditive effects. Services liberalization, if tariffs are already zero, yields gains instead of losses. Goods liberalization when services are already liberalized yields considerably larger gains.

Table 2. Impact of Alternative Liberalization Using the Cobb–Douglas Economy Parametrization from Table 1.

	Hicksian equivalent variation as % of original equilibrium income from		
	Country 1	Country 2	Both countries (the World)
Moving from base case to goods liberalization	0.037338	0.076633	0.056985
Moving to services liberalization when goods are already liberalized	0.006973	0.006891	0.006932
Moving from base case to services liberalization	−0.152988	−0.153513	−0.153250
Moving to goods liberalization when services are already liberalized	0.197604	0.237406	0.217514
Moving from base case to joint goods and services liberalization	0.044313	0.083529	0.063921

The intuition for our main result is as follows.[e] Liberalization of financial services leads to an increase in trade between countries; in turn, the resulting trade expansion increases the costs of the misallocation of resources brought about by the existence of tariffs. This result is perhaps not surprising in second best theory, which shows that a policy that would be optimal in the absence of any distortion may not be second-best optimal if other policies are constrained. What is more interesting, however, is that, in the framework described in this chapter, the desirability of service liberalization depends on the extent of goods liberalization that has already occurred, while the opposite is not true, i.e., goods liberalization is always welfare improving, independently of the degree to which services have already been liberalized.

Numerical results however are not robust. Country 1 has a stronger preference for good 1 relative to country 2 and this preference is even stronger in the first period; on the other hand, its endowment of good 1 is relatively low. These claimfurstics imply that country 1 imports good 1 and when financial markets are liberalized becomes a borrower so that it can consume relatively more of good 1 in period 1. If tariffs in period 1 are higher than in period 2 (in country 1) and financial liberalization boosts imports in period 1 when tariffs are higher. Here we have a welfare

[e]We are grateful to our two referees for offering the intuition on the interpretation in this and the following paragraphs.

enhancing effect (the direct effect of liberalization) and a welfare reducing effect because more trade takes place in the period when tariffs are higher. Thus, for this particular specification the second effect dominates the first.

The size of welfare effects when moving from the base case equilibrium to services liberalization using different parameter setting for the base case also varies. If we increase all initial tariff rates by good and by country, welfare losses from service liberalization increases, lowering initial tariff rates causes them to fall. Increasing the discount rate only in country 2 to increase gains from intertemporal intermediation produces smaller losses, while lowering the discount rate in country 2 has a similar effect since it is asymmetry of the discount factors that determines gains from intertemporal intermediation. Finally, more extreme endowments or share parameters yield larger losses since the trade impacts of incremental financial intermediation are larger.

These point in the direction that, while it is the interaction between intertemporal intermediation and trade that determines whether a loss from financial services liberalization occurs, this outcome is made more or less likely by various model features. One is the size of the trade restrictions with higher restriction raising the likelihood of loss. Another is features of the parametrization which increase the size of commodity trade, such as endowment or share specifications. In contrast, differences in factors across countries which increase the size of intermediation gains will reduce the likelihood of loss, since the direct intermediation gain is more likely to dominate the interaction effect with commodity trade.

We have used parametric variation around this base case specification to explore how welfare impacts vary continuously with parametric changes, and we find changes in the sign of the effect. Table 3 reports the sensitivity of welfare measures of alternative liberalizations to tariff rates. Table 3 reports Hicksian equivalent variation as % of original equilibrium income from the six settings from $T_{11}^0 = 0.10, T_{22}^0 = 0.05$, and T_{11}^1 and T_{22}^1 decreasing to free trade.

The goods liberalization here involves tariff rates which only change from $T_{11}^0 = 0.10, T_{22}^0 = 0.05$, and (1)–(6) to free trade ($T_{11}^0 = T_{22}^0 = T_{11}^1 = T_{22}^1 = 0.00$) for case of numerical solution of the model. The six settings are (1) $T_{11}^1 = 0.05$ and $T_{22}^1 = 0.10$, (2) $T_{11}^1 = 0.04$ and $T_{22}^1 = 0.09$, (3) $T_{11}^1 = 0.03$ and $T_{22}^1 = 0.08$, (4) $T_{11}^1 = 0.02$ and $T_{22}^1 = 0.07$, (5) $T_{11}^1 = 0.01$ and $T_{22}^1 = 0.06$, and (6) $T_{11}^1 = 0.00$ and $T_{22}^1 = 0.05$.

For case (1) moving from base case to goods liberalization, the country 1 EV gains and increases, the country 2 EV decreases from positive

Table 3. Sensitivity of Welfare Measures of Alternative Liberalizations Using the Cobb–Douglas Economy Parametrization from Table 1 to Tariff Rates.

	Hicksian equivalent variation as % of original equilibrium income from		
	Country 1	Country 2	Both countries (the world)
Moving from base case to goods liberalization	(1) 0.037338	(1) 0.076633	(1) 0.056985
	(2) 0.044684	(2) 0.055664	(2) 0.050174
	(3) 0.053243	(3) 0.035288	(3) 0.044266
	(4) 0.063043	(4) 0.015522	(4) 0.039286
	(5) 0.074119	(5) −0.003618	(5) 0.035257
	(6) 0.086503	(6) −0.022113	(6) 0.032206
Moving to services liberalization when goods are already liberalized	(1) 0.006973	(1) 0.006891	(1) 0.006932
	(2) 0.006973	(2) 0.006891	(2) 0.006932
	(3) 0.006973	(3) 0.006891	(3) 0.006932
	(4) 0.006973	(4) 0.006891	(4) 0.006932
	(5) 0.006973	(5) 0.006891	(5) 0.006932
	(6) 0.006973	(6) 0.006891	(6) 0.006932
Moving from base case to services liberalization	(1) −0.152988	(1) −0.153513	(1) −0.153250
	(2) −0.208111	(2) −0.085226	(2) −0.146671
	(3) −0.260803	(3) −0.019745	(3) −0.140285
	(4) −0.311197	(4) 0.042978	(4) −0.134133
	(5) −0.358948	(5) 0.102867	(5) −0.128080
	(6) −0.404424	(6) 0.160031	(6) −0.122256
Moving to goods liberalization when services are already liberalized	(1) 0.197604	(1) 0.237506	(1) 0.217514
	(2) 0.260313	(2) 0.147910	(2) 0.204059
	(3) 0.321862	(3) 0.061939	(3) 0.191716
	(4) 0.382408	(4) −0.020555	(4) 0.180550
	(5) 0.441631	(5) −0.099492	(5) 0.170449
	(6) 0.499928	(6) −0.174975	(6) 0.161565
Moving from base case to joint goods and services liberalization	(1) 0.044313	(1) 0.083529	(1) 0.063921
	(2) 0.051661	(2) 0.062559	(2) 0.057109
	(3) 0.060219	(3) 0.042182	(3) 0.051201
	(4) 0.070021	(4) 0.022414	(4) 0.046221
	(5) 0.081097	(5) 0.003273	(5) 0.042192
	(6) 0.093482	(6) −0.015224	(6) 0.039141

to negative, the world (two countries) EV gains and decreases; for case (2) moving to services liberalization when goods are already liberalized, the country 1, country 2, and the world EV gains and unchanged; for case (3) moving from base case to services liberalization, the country 1 EV losses and decreases, the country 2 EV increases from negative to positive, the world (two-countries) EV losses and increases; (4) moving to goods liberalization when services are already liberalized, the country 1 EV gains and increases, the country 2 EV decreases from positive to negative, the world (two-countries) EV gains and decreases; and for case (5) moving from base case to joint goods and services liberalization, the country 1 EV gains and increases, the country 2 EV decreases from positive to negative, the world (two-countries) EV gains and decreases.

4. A Model with Costly Intermediation Services

The model used in the previous section is highly simplified in that it considers a case with no intermediation in autarky and costless foreign supplied intermediation services under financial service trade liberalization. Where intermediation occurs under liberalization, the same interest rate for lenders and borrowers applies in both countries: Equivalent to an across period budget constraint equilibrium for the two countries combined. A more realistic case involves costly intermediation with different costs faced by service providers in the two countries. Under liberalization of service trade more efficient foreign service providers then displace domestic service providers in one of the country markets. Developing such a structure, in which interest rates differ between borrowers and lenders, is more complex since the use of intermediation services will now use real resources which in turn will impact the incomes of consumers which, in turn, will affect both commodity demands and intertemporal trade. To deal with the simultaneities involved, unlike in the costless intermediation case, either the amount of borrowing (lending) must be exogenously specified with the borrowing and lending rates endogenously determined, or borrowing and lending rates are exogenous and the amounts involved are endogenous.

If intermediation across countries within the period is allowed up to some level F_i, but when a separate and different interest rate applies in each country to be paid by borrowers, the budget constraint for each country i then becomes

$$\sum_{l=1}^{2}(1+T_{il}^{0})\pi_l^0 X_{il}^0 + F_i = I_i^0 = \sum_{l=1}^{2}(1+T_{il}^{0})\pi_l^0 E_{il}^0 + R_i^0, \tag{12}$$

$$\sum_{l=1}^{2}(1+T_{il}^{1})\pi_l^1 X_{il}^1 = I_i^1 + [1+r_i]F_i$$

$$= \sum_{l=1}^{2}(1+T_{il}^{1})\pi_l^1 E_{il}^1 + R_i^1 + [1+r_i]F_i, \tag{13}$$

where F_i is the amount borrowed by a consumer in one country from the other country's consumer via banks supplying intermediation services. With costless intermediation, r_i is the lending and borrowing interest rate in country i. In this structure, F_i can be set by policy (allowable credit, or money issuance) with the r_i endogenously determined, or r_i can be set with F_i endogenously determined. The difference from the previous section is the use of different interest rates in each country.

In this costless intermediation case, a general equilibrium for this economy (with the interest rate for lending and borrowing r_i for $i = 1, 2$) is characterized by a price system and consumption of goods by countries $[(\pi_l^t : t = 0, 1; l = 1, 2), (X_{il}^t : t = 0, 1; i = 1, 2; l = 1, 2)]$ such that (1) given $(\pi_l^t; t = 0, 1, l = 1, 2)$, for $i = 1, 2$, $(X_{il}^t; t = 0, 1, l = 1, 2)$ solve the utility maximization problem subject to the budget constraints (12)–(13), and (2) markets clear $\sum_{i=1}^2 X_{il}^0 = \sum_{i=1}^2 E_{il}^0$ and $\sum_{i=1}^2 X_{il}^1 \leq \sum_{i=1}^2 E_{il}^1$ for $l = 1, 2$, and $\sum_{i=1}^2 F_i = 0$.

We can then move on to consider the case of costly intermediation services with (in the no services trade case) different interest rates for lending and borrowing for each country and the budget constraints for each country i are

$$\sum_{l=1}^{2}(1+T_{il}^0)\pi_l^0 X_{il}^0 + F_i = I_i^0 = \sum_{l=1}^{2}(1+T_{il}^0)\pi_l^0 E_{il}^0 + R_i^0, \tag{14}$$

$$\begin{aligned}\sum_{l=1}^{2}(1+T_{il}^1)\pi_l^1 X_{il}^1 &= I_i^1 + [1+r_i(F_i)]F_i \\ &= \sum_{l=1}^{2}(1+T_{il}^1)\pi_l^1 E_{il}^1 + R_i^1 + [1+r_i(F_i)]F_i,\end{aligned} \tag{15}$$

If we represent deposit and borrowing rates as

$$r_i(F_i) = \begin{cases} r_i^D, & \text{if } F_i \geq 0, \\ r_i^B, & \text{if } F_i \leq 0, \end{cases} \tag{16}$$

where r_i^D and r_i^B are the interest rates for lending (deposits or saving) and borrowing in country i, and $[1+r_i(F_i)]F_i = [1+r_i^D]F_i^+ - [1+r_i^B]F_i^-$. The budget constraints (14) and (15) can then be written as

$$\sum_{l=1}^{2}(1+T_{il}^0)\pi_l^0 X_{il}^0 + F_i = \sum_{l=1}^{2}(1+T_{il}^0)\pi_l^0 E_{il}^0 + R_i^0 \tag{17}$$

$$\sum_{l=1}^{2}(1+T_{il}^1)\pi_l^1 X_{il}^1 = \sum_{l=1}^{2}(1+T_{il}^1)\pi_l^1 E_{il}^1 + R_i^1 + [1+r_i^D]F_i^+ - [1+r_i^B]F_i^-. \quad (18)$$

Since in the presence of costly intermediation, $r_i^B \geq r_i^D$ for $i = 1, 2$, we can represent intermediation costs in country i by the a parameter λ_i such that $r_i^B = (1+\lambda_i)r_i^D$. If intermediation services are provided by banks in country i, $\lambda_1 > \lambda_2$ implies that banks in country 2 are more efficient than in country 1; while $\lambda_2 > \lambda_1$ implies that banks in country 1 are more efficient than in country 2.

This then allows us to again characterize two equilibria, but now in the presence of costly banking services — one with no trade in banking services (autarky in banking) and one with free trade in banking services. Now F_i will be parameters rather than endogeneous variables.

Table 4 sets out a parametrization for a Cobb–Douglas economy with tariffs for this model, which is the same as Table 1 except that the F_i are exogenous and set (arbitrarily) at 32 and intermediation cost factors are specified in each country. The intermediation cost factors are assumed to be $\lambda_1 = 0.25$ and $\lambda_2 = 0.50$. The value of interest rates are $r^D = r_1^D = r_2^D = 0.03995$, $r_1^B = 0.04994$ and $r_2^B = 0.05993$ in the equilibrium with autarky in

Table 4. A Parametrization of a Cobb–Douglas Spatial and Intertemporal Economy with Costly Intermediation used to Analyze Joint Goods and Services Trade Liberalization.

Intertemporal discount factor by country $\rho_1 = 0.10$ and $\rho_2 = 0.10$

	Period 0		Period 1	
	Good 1	Good 2	Good 1	Good 2
Share parameters, α_{il}^t				
Country 1	0.70	0.30	0.60	0.40
Country 2	0.40	0.60	0.30	0.70
Initial endowments, E_{il}^t				
Country 1	40	80	40	80
Country 2	80	40	80	40
Initial tariff rates, T_{il}^t				
Country 1	0.10	0.00	0.05	0.00
Country 2	0.00	0.05	0.00	0.10

Amount borrowed/lent $F_1 = 32$ and $F_2 = -32$
Intermediation cost factor $\lambda_1 = 0.25$ and $\lambda_2 = 0.50$

Table 5. Welfare Consequences of Alternative Liberalizations Using the Cobb–Douglas Economy Parametrization from Table 1, but with Costly Intermediation.

	Hicksian equivalent variation as % of original equilibrium income from		
	Country 1	Country 2	Both countries (the World)
Moving from base case to goods liberalization	0.093343	0.079184	0.086260
Moving to services liberalization when goods are already liberalized	−0.000276	−0.000276	−0.000276
Moving from base case to services liberalization	−0.001471	−0.001402	−0.001437
Moving to goods liberalization when services are already liberalized	0.094540	0.080310	0.087422
Moving from base case to joint goods and services liberalization	0.093067	0.078907	0.085984

intermediation services, and $r^D = r_1^D = r_2^D = 0.08032$, $r_1^B = 0.10040$ and $r_2^B = 0.12049$ in the equilibrium with free trade in intermediation services.

In Table 5, we report Hicksian Equivalent Variation money metric welfare measures of the impacts of goods and services liberalization both for individual countries and the world for this model. Hicksian measures are expressed as a percentage of reference equilibrium (pre-liberalization) incomes. This is a more complex structure to work with computationally and so we only consider incomplete goods liberalization and changes tariff rates from $T_{11}^0 = T_{22}^1 = 0.10$ and $T_{22}^0 = T_{11}^1 = 0.05$ to $T_{11}^0 = T_{22}^1 = 0.05$ and $T_{22}^0 = T_{11}^1 = 0.00$. In this case, results are different from those in Table 2 and show that moving to services liberalization even when goods trade is liberalized implies a welfare loss. A result is similar to that in Chia and Whalley (1997) for the one good case. This result occurs due to the real resources involved in providing intermediation services, which, from Foley (1970), imply the two fundamental theorems need not hold and hence, even without trade restrictions, financial service liberalization can be welfare worsening. We can also conduct parametric variation around this base case specification and reevaluate the gains from alternative liberalizations.

The goods liberalization here involves tariff rates which only change from $T_{11}^0 = T_{22}^1 = 0.10$ and $T_{22}^0 = T_{11}^1 = 0.05$ to $T_{11}^0 = T_{22}^1 = 0.05$ and $T_{22}^0 = T_{11}^1 = 0.00$, for case of numerical solution of the model.

5. Concluding Remarks

Our discussion of financial services liberalization focuses on the issue of whether broader services trade liberalization in the WTO under the GATS need necessarily be globally welfare improving if free trade in goods does not already apply. Here we use a numerical simulation approach which we apply to two models that differ in their complexity. They each involve joint liberalization of spatial and intertemporal trade in a multi-good multi-period numerical model. In our first model, there is costless banking and we consider services liberalization to imply foreign banking entry where, in autarky, no domestic banks exist. Their entry relaxes period by period budget constraints. A more complex model considers domestic and foreign service providers with different (but constant) costs. Liberalization in banking service trade allows domestic residents full access to foreign banks. We consider the cases with both Cobb–Douglas preferences over goods within the period, and draw on a formalization on asset and spot market equilibrium literature originating with Arrow. We are relatively easily able to produce examples where in the presence of tariffs banking liberalization can be welfare worsening. The intuition is that banking liberalization increases intertemporal trade, which, in turn increases international trade in goods, which can increase the welfare cost of a pre-existing tariff.

It may also be interesting to mention the implications of our analysis for service liberalization within preferential trade agreements. In particular, EU members created the so-called Single Market for Financial Services well in advance of the GATS negotiations. The model presented here suggests that service liberalization may be particularly desirable within existing free trade areas or customs unions, since these should be characterized by zero tariffs among member countries (this is particularly true for preferential trade agreements that involve little or no trade diversion). The welfare gains experienced during the process of regional financial integration may explain why EU member countries were extremely supportive of multilateral service liberalization during the GATS negotiations.

Under this view of the world, then, depending on cost differentials across domestic and foreign services providers there could be net benefits from significant global liberalization in financial services independently of further tariff liberalization. But whether this is so needs to be more firmly established rather than simply asserted as at present.

References

Arrow, KJ (1964). The role of securities in the optimal allocation of risk-bearing. *Review of Economics Studies*, **31**, 91–96.

Chen, Z and L Schembri (2002). Measuring the barriers to trade in services: Literature and methodologies. In *Trade Policy Research*, JM Curtis and DC Ciuriak (eds.). Canada: Development of Foreign Affairs and International Trade.

Chia, NC and J Whalley (1997). A numerical example showing globally welfare worsening liberalization of international trade in banking services. *Journal of Policy Modeling*, **19**, 119–127.

Debreu, G (1959). *Theory of Value — An Axiomatic Analysis of Economic Equilibrium*. London: Yale University Press.

Duffie, D (1987). Stochastic equilibria with incomplete financial markets. *Journal of Economic Theory*, **41**, 405–416.

Duffie, D and W Shafer (1985). Equilibrium in incomplete markets: I — A basic model of generic existence. *Journal of Mathematical Economics*, **14**, 285–300.

Foley, DK (1970). Equilibrium with costly marketing. *Journal of Economic Theory*, **2**, 276–291.

Francois, J and L Schuknecht (2000). International trade in financial services, competition and growth performance. Centre for International Economic Studies, No. 6 (2000).

Geanakoplos, JD (1990). An introduction to general equilibrium with incomplete asset markets. *Journal of Mathematical Economics*, **19**, 1–38.

Geanakoplos, JD and DP Tsomocos (2002). International finance in general equilibrium. *Resource Economics*, **56**, 85–142.

Hart, OD (1975). On the optimality of equilibrium when the market structure is incomplete. *Journal of Economic Theory*, **11**, 418–443.

Huang, H, J Whalley and S Zhang (2004). Trade liberalization in a joint spatial intertemporal trade model. Research Paper, The University of Western Ontario.

Kalirajan, K, G McHuire, D Nguyen-Hong and M Schuele (2001). The price impact of restrictions on banking services. In *Impediments to Trade in Services: Measurement and Policy Implications*, C Findlay and T Warren (eds.). New York: Routledge.

Kamiya, K and T Shimizu (2007). Existence of equilibria in matching models of money: A new technique. *Economic Theory*, **32**, 447–460.

Magill, M and M Quinzii (1996). *Theory of Incomplete Markets*. Cambridge: MIT Press.

Magill, M and W Shafer (1991). Incomplete markets. In *Handbook of Mathematical Economics*, W Hildenbrand and H Sonnenschein (eds.), Vol. 4, pp. 1523–1614. New York: Elsevier Science.

Mattoo, A (1999). Financial services and the WTO: Liberalization commitments of the developing and transition economies. Policy Research Working Paper No. 2184, Developing Research Group, World Bank, Washington, DC.

Radner, R (1972). Existence of equilibrium of plans, prices and price expectations in a sequence of markets. *Econometrica*, **40**, 289–303.

Vayanos, D and J Vila (1999). Equilibrium interest rate and liquidity premium with transaction costs. *Economic Theory*, **13**, 509–539.
Werner, J (1985). Equilibrium in economies with incomplete financial markets. *Journal of Economic Theory*, **36**, 110–119.
World Trade Organization (WTO) (2007). Annual Report. Geneva.

Part V

The Trade and Wages Debate

Chapter 19

Goods Market Responses to Trade Shocks and Trade and Wages Decompositions*,†

Lisandro Abrego
International Monetary Fund

John Whalley
University of Western Ontario, Canada
National Bureau of Economic Research, U.S.A.

Trade and wages literature asks whether trade or technology has been the major factor behind increases in wage inequality in OECD countries since the 1980s. In this literature, little attention has been paid to how goods market responses to trade shocks affect conclusions. Using an Armington heterogeneous goods trade model we capture demand side effects, and show how trade shocks affecting the price of unskilled-intensive importable goods can be absorbed on the demand side of goods markets, with little or no impact on relative wage rates. No wage impact occurs if the elasticity of substitution in preferences between imports and import substitutes is one. As this elasticity increases, trade plays an ever larger role in explaining wage inequality changes, and as the elasticity goes below one the sign of the effect changes. We present some results of general equilibrium decompositions of total wage change into trade and technology components using U.K. data. We suggest that since many import demand elasticity estimates are in the neighborhood of one, there is a prima facie case that goods market considerations further lower the significance of trade as an explanation of recent trends in OECD wage inequality beyond that claimed in the literature.

*This chapter draws on work executed under a project on Globalization and Social Exclusion supported by the Targeted Socio Economic Research program of the European Union. The second author acknowledges support from SSHRC for finalization of the chapter. The work was undertaken while the first author was at the University of Warwick. We are grateful to Paul Brenton, Huw Edwards, Matthias Luecke, Carlo Perroni, Ted To, and two helpful referees for discussions and comments.
†This chapter was first published in (2003). *Canadian Journal of Economics*, **36**(3), 747–757.

1. Introduction and Background

Most trade and wages literature explores, the factors behind the sharp increase in wage inequality between the 1980s and the early 1990s in OECD countries.[a] Two major factors have been identified as primarily responsible: Increased trade volumes (imports) in low-skill-intensive products (particularly from low-wage developing countries) and technological change biased against unskilled labor. The issue has been the relative importance of these two. Most literature concludes that technological change is more important. The outcome of the debate is important because of pressures for protection if trade is the main source of added wage inequality.

Early papers in this area analyzed how increased trade changes labor demand via the factor content of trade (e.g., Borjas *et al.*, 1991; Katz and Murphy, 1992; Murphy and Welch, 1991). Their conclusion, was that trade was a secondary factor, although this was later criticized by Wood (1994). Subsequent papers related relative product price changes to relative wage changes used estimating equations derived from general equilibrium models of a Heckscher–Ohlin type (Baldwin and Cain, 1997; Harrigan and Balaban, 1999; Haskel and Slaughter, 1999; Lawrence and Slaughter, 1993; Leamer, 1998) and echoed the earlier conclusion that trade is a smaller source of inequality change than technology. Other work relates relative factor shares to outsourcing and other factors (Anderton and Brenton, 1998; Autor *et al.*, 1998; Feenstra and Hanson, 1996; Gaston and Trefler, 1994).[b] How goods market responses propagate world price shocks onto labor markets and how this affects conclusions is not discussed in this literature.

Here, we argue that, either implicitly or explicitly, the framework used in much of the literature discussing this issue is that of a homogeneous goods trade model in which changes in world prices are fully transmitted to

[a]Increases in wage inequality have been documented for a number of OECD countries, most notably the U.S. and the U.K. (e.g., Davis, 1992; Gottschalk and Smeeding, 1997; Kosters, 1994; OECD, 1997). This pattern has been observed across different types of workers (low versus high skill), education levels (college versus noncollege graduates), and experience. Even among "observably similar workers" wage inequality has increased (e.g., Davis, 1992). There has also been documentation of a rise in unemployment in some European countries without major increases in wage inequality (Dewatripont *et al.*, 1998; Kosters, 1994; OECD, 1997) — as well as of a decline in wage inequality in some key developing countries (Korea, Venezuela, Colombia and Brazil) (Davis, 1992; UNCTAD, 1997; Wood, 1997).

[b]Gaston and Trefler, for instance, argue that the empirical evidence is that tariffs in the U.S. have a significant negative effect on wages for low paid workers.

domestic prices, and from there (via zero profit conditions) to factor prices. Our contribution is to present a model with heterogeneous goods across countries, for which the homogeneous goods model is a special case, noting that in this model there may be no or little transmission of international price shocks onto relative wages depending upon substitution elasticities in preferences. We then cite empirical estimates of trade elasticities to argue that the effects of trade shocks on relative wage inequality may be even smaller than currently believed.

2. Trade and Wages in a Differentiated Goods Model[c]

We analyze the relative importance of trade and technology in explaining relative wage changes in OECD countries in a trade model with differentiated goods, similar to that set out in de Melo and Robinson (1989) and Thierfelder and Robinson (2002), and also discussed by Bhattarai *et al.* (1999). In this model, imports and domestically produced goods are imperfect rather than perfect substitutes. The model has two traded and two produced goods, but embodies three goods in aggregate when the consumption side is included, since imports are not produced domestically and the domestically produced good which substitutes for imports in consumption is not traded. On the production side, the model has a domestically produced good — the imperfect substitute for imports — and an exportable. Each of the produced goods uses two factor inputs: low skill and high skill labor. Imports, the (nonexportable) domestic good and the exportable enter consumption. Imports and exports are traded at fixed world prices.

As imports and the domestically produced import substitute become perfect substitutes in preferences in this structure, the model approaches the conventional homogeneous goods form, with only two traded and produced goods.[d] The model, therefore, is a generalization of the conventional homogeneous goods trade model, which stands as a special case when the elasticity of substitution in preferences between imports and the domestically produced import substitute is infinite. For finite

[c]This section draws on a related model discussion in Abrego and Whalley (2000).
[d]This is the case when the number of goods is the same as the number of factors. When there are more factors than goods, the domestic price system is not fully tied to world prices (see Bilal *et al.*, 1998).

elasticities, demand side effects from world commodity price changes will be reflected in substitution in consumption between these two goods.

More formally, denoting consumption of imports by M, the exportable by E, and other domestically produced goods by D, preferences are defined as

$$U(M^C, E), \tag{1}$$

where M^C is a composite function of M and D; i.e.,

$$M^C = C(M, D). \tag{2}$$

We use Cobb–Douglas and CES functions respectively for U and C in later empirical implementation of the model using U.K. data.[e]

With D and E being the two produced goods, and H and L (high and low skilled labor) the two factor inputs, technology is represented by

$$D^S = D^S(L_D, H_D), \tag{3}$$

$$E^S = E^S(L_E, H_E), \tag{4}$$

where D^S and E^S represent production of the (imperfect) import substitute domestic good and the exportable respectively and L_D, L_E, H_D, and H_E denote the use of high and low skilled labor in domestic good and export production. In later empirical implementation of the model, technologies are modeled through CES production functions.

For simplicity, we assume that the economy is a taker of prices $\overline{P}_E, \overline{P}_M$, for exports and imports while the price of the domestic good, P_D is endogenously determined. Thus, in contrast to a simple homogeneous goods trade model, a product price adjusts to clear the domestic market even in the small-country case. We model trade shocks as changes in world prices, i.e., of imports relative to exports.

Given the above, the per unit cost functions for the production of E and D, consistent with zero profits, are given by

$$P_D = g_D(W^H, W^L), \tag{5}$$

$$\overline{P}_E = g_E(W^H, W^L), \tag{6}$$

[e]Cobb–Douglas and CES are the most widely used functional forms in the numerical simulation literature, and we follow that tradition here. Flexible functional forms, such as translog or generalized Leontief, do not satisfy global concavity conditions and can lead to numerical problems in computation of equilibria, and so are not used here.

where W^H and W^L are the wage rates of high and low skilled labor, and g_D and g_E are per unit costs functions for D and E.

Full employment conditions for factors yield

$$f_D^H \cdot D^S + f_E^H \cdot E^S = \overline{H}, \tag{7}$$

$$f_D^L \cdot D^S + f_E^L \cdot E^S = \overline{L}, \tag{8}$$

where $f_D^H, f_E^H, f_D^L, f_E^L$ are per unit cost minimizing factor demands for H and L in the production of the domestic import substitute and the exportable.

To generate commodity demands, the representative household in this economy maximizes the utility function (1) subject to the budget constraint

$$P_D D + \overline{P}_M M + \overline{P}_E E^D = W^L \overline{L} + W^H \overline{H}, \tag{9}$$

where D, E, and M denote domestic consumption of the domestic substitute, imports, and the exportable.

In equilibrium, the price of the domestically produced good P_D^*, is determined such that market clearing occurs in D, i.e.,

$$D = D^S. \tag{10}$$

No market clearing in either E or M is required in this model since these are internationally traded at fixed prices. Walras' Law, which automatically holds for economies with demand functions generated from utility maximization subject to a budget constraint, also implies that trade balance will hold in equilibrium, i.e.,

$$\overline{P}_M M = \overline{P}_E E, \tag{11}$$

where M and E represent imports and exports.

The feature of this structure that is relevant to the trade and wages debate is that changes in world prices of imports can be partially or even fully accommodated by changes in import volumes without necessarily impacting the rest of the economy. Hence, if changes in $\overline{P}_M$ occur but yield offsetting changes in M which are consistent with the other equilibrium conditions of the model, trade balance will still hold but these price changes will have no impact on domestic production. The domestic output of each product will remain the same, as will the use of factors by sector and relative factor prices, and no impacts on the wages of skilled and unskilled labor will occur from a trade shock. More generally, imperfect pass through of world price changes onto domestic product prices in a heterogeneous goods trade model will tend to lessen the impact of trade on wage inequality.

An outcome in which world price changes have no impact on wage inequality will occur when the elasticity of substitution between M and D in preferences [Eq. (2)] is unity, since demand-side substitution effects will fully accommodate to the world price change. If this substitution elasticity is close to one, world price changes affecting low skill intensive goods will still largely be accommodated by the demand side of the model, weakening the role of trade in explaining increased wage inequality compared to the conventional homogeneous goods model.

Empirical studies yielding import demand elasticities (see, for example, Marquez, 1994; Reinert and Roland-Holst, 1992; Shiells and Reinert, 1993) consistently produce estimates in the neighborhood of one.[f] The role of trade in explaining recent increases in OECD wage inequality thus seems to be weakened once goods market behavior considerations are added to conventional trade models. And demand functions generated by maximizing a CES utility function subject to a budget constraint imply that the own price elasticity of demand approaches the negative of the substitution elasticity as the relevant share parameter approaches zero, and so import demand elasticities and substitution elasticities in preferences are interrelated in this way.

3. Some Calculations on the Role of Trade in U.K. Wage Inequality Using a Heterogeneous Goods Trade Model

We have used the heterogeneous goods general equilibrium trade model set out above U.K. data to quantitatively investigate the impact of goods market considerations on trade and wage decompositions.[g] In these, we use data on production, consumption, and trade for 1990 to represent an equilibrium after the increase in wage inequality in the 1980's, and data for 1976 to represent pre-trade and technology change equilibrium. We then calibrate the model to these two data sets, and compute counterfactuals for cases where only one of the two shocks we consider (trade and technology) occurs.

[f]Using a GNP function approach, Kohli (1999) also finds the import demand elasticity for Switzerland to be close to unity.
[g]The data we use here draws on Abrego and Whalley (2000), where the application of Heckscher–Ohlin-type models in other related decomposition calculations is discussed.

The U.K. data we use show a fall in the relative price of internationally traded unskilled-intensive to skilled-intensive goods of 7.9% over the period 1976–1990 (based on information from Neven and Wyplozs, 1999), and a fall in the wage rates of low skilled relative to high skilled workers of 15% over the same period (from U.K. Office for National Statistics' *Employment Gazette*). Technological change over the period is calculated residually in the decomposition experiments; i.e., determined via calibration such that in combination with the given product price change of −7.9% it produces a decline of 15% in W^L/W^H.

Unlike in the conventional homogeneous goods model (see, e.g., Krugman, 2000; Leamer, 1998), factor-biased technological change can be accommodated by the heterogeneous goods structure used here since the price of the domestic import substitute is endogenously determined, and in making our residual calculation we assume that technological change is biased against unskilled labor. We consider alternative values for the elasticity of substitution in preferences between the domestic good and imports which lie in the interval 0.2 to 20. We initially set the value for the elasticity of substitution between skilled and unskilled labor in production of both goods equal to 1.25.

We conduct decomposition experiments with the model and data, first by calibrating the model in the presence of the joint trade and technology shock and then computing counterfactual equilibria with only the trade shock present. The experiments are repeated with different values of the substitution elasticity in preferences, so that in repeated calibrations of the model to the same data, share parameters change as elasticities vary. In other decomposition experiments, we vary production-side elasticities between 0.5 and 5, and hold the consumption-side elasticity at 1.25. In all these experiments, technological change is obtained residually through calibration, and as parameter values change its size changes. For each model specification we conduct the same experiment of removing the world price change that occurred between 1976 and 1990 from the model and computing the implied equilibrium wage change. We then compare this to the actual change. Results of these computations are presented in Table 1.

For cases where the elasticity of substitution in preferences (σ) is close to unity (consistent with available empirical estimates), the contribution of trade to wage inequality is small. For values of σ equal to one, trade shocks have no impact on wage inequality. For values which are large (20), the impact of trade dominates that of technology.

Table 1. U.K. Technology-Trade Decompositions for Alternative Values of the Elasticity of Substitution in Preferences (σ).*

	σ							
	0.2	0.5	1.0	2.0	5.0	10	15	20
Percentage of change in U.K. W^L/W^H between 1990 and 1976 due to technology	102.5	101.5	100.0	97.4	87	70.3	53.9	38.9
Percentage of change in U.K. W^L/W^H between 1990 and 1976 due to trade	−2.5	−1.5	0.0	2.6	12.9	29.7	46.1	61.1

*Production-side elasticities are held constant across these cases, and set equal to 1.25.

These effects occur in this model because imports and their domestic counterparts are imperfect substitutes, and changes in relative commodity prices can (depending on σ) be accommodated wholly or partially through changes in consumption rather than production. Indeed, for the contribution of trade to increased wage inequality to exceed that of technology, high values (of around 17) are needed for the elasticity of substitution in preferences. These are considerably in excess of empirical estimates for import demand elasticities reported in the literature. These results thus suggest that the role of trade in driving increased OECD wage inequality may be even smaller than currently thought.[h]

Results in Table 1 also emphasize that the contribution of trade to wage inequality changes sign as the elasticity of substitution in preferences moves below one. With an elasticity of substitution in preferences of less than one, when the world price of imports falls, the resulting increase in the volume of imports is insufficient to offset the price fall. In this case, if trade is to remain balanced, exports — and the production of E — must fall. This implies that the production of the import-competing good, D, will increase, and since D is intensive in L, W^L/W^H increases. In contrast, with a consumption elasticity above one, the trade shock causes the production of D to decrease, and W^L/W^H falls.

[h]Recent studies implicitly using models based on a homogeneous goods structure and reporting a relatively small trade contribution to increased wage inequality include Feenstra and Hanson (1999), and Baldwin and Cain (1997) (both for the U.S.). The former provides an estimate of 15% (base specification), while the latter reports a 19% figure for the contribution of trade. These stand in contrast to estimates in Table 1 of around 2% for preference substitution elasticities between one and two.

Table 2. U.K. Technology-Trade Decompositions for Alternative Values of the Elasticity of Substitution in Production (η) for a Given Value of σ.*

	η			
	0.5	1.25	2.5	5.0
Percentage of change in U.K. W^L/W^H between 1990 and 1976 due to technology	98.1	99.2	99.6	99.8
Percentage of change in U.K. W^L/W^H between 1990 and 1976 due to trade	1.9	0.8	0.4	0.2

*The consumption-side elasticity is held constant, and set equal to 1.25.

Less sensitivity occurs in these decompositions as other model parameters change. Table 2 reports results for a second set of decomposition experiments in which we vary production-side elasticities, keeping the demand-side elasticity unchanged at 1.25. These results suggest that, given consumption-side elasticities between imports and import substitutes, the role of trade in accounting for wage inequality grows as the elasticity of substitution between high and low skill labor inputs decreases. These effects are, however, small, but, not surprisingly, confirm that the impact of introducing goods market responses into trade and wage decompositions will also vary with non-demand side parameter values.

4. Conclusions

This chapter discusses recent literature on the role of trade in explaining recent increases in OECD wage inequality. It highlights the absence of discussion of how goods market responses affect conclusions in this literature. Specifically, we argue that in a single country heterogeneous goods trade model, demand-side substitution effects can wholly or partially absorb trade shocks and insulate the production-side of economies, and hence wage rates of high and low skilled labor can remain little changed as world prices change.

We present a simple heterogeneous goods model in which we are able to vary the elasticity of substitution between imports and domestically produced import substitutes. As this elasticity approaches infinity a homogeneous goods trade model is approached. Using this model and U.K. data for 1976 and 1990, we conduct trade-technology decomposition experiments which isolate this separate influences on wage inequality. Our results show little role for trade when elasticities are in the neighborhood of one, and a much more prominent role under larger elasticities. Given literature estimates of trade elasticities in the neighborhood of one, we conclude that demand side considerations will tend to further dampen the perceived role of trade in explaining recent increases in OECD wage inequality relative to current literature.

References

Abrego, L and J Whalley (2000). The choice of structural model in trade-wages decompositions. *Review of International Economics*, **8**, 462–477.

Anderton, B and P Brenton (1998). The dollar, trade, technology and wage inequality in the U.S.A. Center for European Policy Studies, Brussels, mimeo.

Autor, D, L Katz and A Krueger (1998). Computing inequality: Have computers changed the labor market. *Quarterly Journal of Economics*, **113**, 1169–1213.

Baldwin, RE and GG Cain (1997). Shifts in US relative wages: The role of trade, technology and factor endowments. *NBER Working Paper No.* 5934.

Bhattarai, K, M Ghosh and J Whalley (1999). On some properties of a trade closure widely used in numerical modelling. *Economics Letters*, **62**, 13–21.

Bilal, S, J-M Grether and J de Melo (1998). Determinants of attitude towards immigration: A trade-theoretic approach. CPER Discussion Paper 1877.

Borjas, G, R Freeman and L Katz (1991). On the labour market effects of immigration and trade. In *Immigration and the Work Force*, G Borjas and R Freeman (eds.). Chicago: The University of Chicago Press.

Davis, S (1992). Cross-country patterns of changes in relative wages. *NBER Macroeconomics Annual*, **7**, 239–291.

Dewatripont, M, A Sapir and K Sekkat (1998). Labour market effects of trade with LDCs in Europe. In *Trade and Jobs in Europe: Much Ado about Nothing*, M Dewatripont, A Sapir and K Sekkat (eds.), Oxford: Clarendon Press.

Feenstra, R and G Hanson (1996). Globalization, outsourcing and wage inequality. *American Economic Review*, **86**, 240–245.

Feenstra, R and G Hanson (1999). The impact of outsourcing and high-technology capital on wages: Estimates for the United States, 1979–1990. *Quarterly Journal of Economics*, **113**, 907–940.

Gaston, N and D Trefler (1994). Protection, trade, and wages: Evidence from U.S. manufacturing. *Industrial and Labor Relations Review*, **47**(4), 574–593.

Gottschalk, P and T Smeeding (1997). Cross national comparisons of earnings and income inequality. *Journal of Economic Literature*, **35**, 633–687.

Harrigan, J and R Balaban (1999). U.S. wages in general equilibrium: The effects of prices, technology, and factor supplies, 1963–1991. *NBER Working Paper No.* 6981.

Haskel, J and M Slaughter (1999). Trade, technology and U.K. wage inequality. *NBER Working Paper No.* 6978.

Katz, L and K Murphy (1992). Changes in relative wages, 1963–1987: Supply and demand factors. *Quarterly Journal of Economics*, **107**, 35–78.

Kohli, U (1999). Trade and migration: A production theory approach. In *The Controversies and the Evidence*, R Faini, J de Melo and K Zimmermann (eds.), Cambridge: Cambridge University Press.

Kosters, M (1994). An overview of changing wage patterns in the labour market. In *Trade and Wages: Levelling Wages Down?*, J Bhagwati and M Kosters (eds.). Washington: AEI Press.

Lawrence, R and M Slaughter (1993). International trade and American wages: Giant sucking sound or small hiccup. *Brookings Papers of Economic Activity*, **1993**(2), 161–226.

Leamer, E (1998). In search of Stolper–Samuelson linkages between international trade and lower wages. In *Imports, Exports and the American Worker*, SM Collins (ed.), Washington, D.C.: Brookings Institution.

Krugman, P (2000). Technology, trade and factor prices. *Journal of International Economics*, **50**, 51–71.

Marquez, J (1994). The econometrics of elasticities or the elasticity of econometrics: An empirical analysis of the behavior of U.S. imports. *Review of Economics and Statistics*, **76**(3), 471–481.

de Melo, J and S Robinson (1989). Product differentiation and the treatment of foreign trade in computable general equilibrium models of small economies. *Journal of International Economics*, **27**, 47–67.

Murphy, K and F Welch (1991). The role of international trade in wage differentials. In *Workers and Their Wages: Changing Patterns in the United States*, M Koster (ed.). Washington: AEI Press.

Neven, D and C Wyplosz (1999). Relative prices, trade and restructuring in European industry. In *Trade and Jobs in Europe: Much Ado about Nothing?*, M Dewatripont, A Sapir and K Sekkat (eds.), Chapter 3, pp. 60–78. Oxford: Oxford University Press.

OECD (1997). Trade, earning and employment: Assessing the impact of trade with emerging economies on OECD labour markets. *Employment Outlook*, OECD.

Office for National Statistics (various years). *Employment Gazette*. London: Office for National Statistics.

Reinert, K and D Roland-Holst (1992). Armington elasticities for United States manufacturing sectors. *Journal of Policy Modelling*, **14**, 631–639.

Shiells, C and K Reinert (1993). Armington models and terms of trade effects: Some econometric evidence for North America. *Canadian Journal of Economics*, **26**, 299–316.

Thierfelder, K and S Robinson (2002). Trade and tradability: Exports, imports and factor markets in the Salter–Swan model. Working Paper No. 93, Trade and Macroeconomic Division, International Food Policy Research Institute, Washington, D.C.

UNCTAD (1997). *Trade and Development Report*. Geneva: UNCTAD.

Wood, A (ed.) (1994). *North–South Trade, Employment and Inequality*. Oxford: Clarendon Press.

Wood, A (1997). Openness and wage inequality in developing countries: The Latin American challenge to East Asian conventional wisdom. *World Bank Economic Review*, **11**, 33–57.

Chapter 20

The Choice of Structural Model in Trade-Wages Decompositions*,†

Lisandro Abrego
University of Warwick, Coventry, U.K.

John Whalley
University of Western Ontario, Canada
National Bureau of Economic Research, U.S.A.

This chapter explores the use of structural models as an alternative to reduced form methods when decomposing observed joint trade and technology driven wage changes into components attributable to each source. Conventional mobile factors Heckscher–Ohlin models typically reveal problems of specialization unless price changes accompanying trade shocks are small, and can also produce wide ranges for the decomposition for parametrizations consistent with the joint change. A differentiated goods model which generalizes Heckscher–Ohlin removes problems of specialization and concentrates the range of decompositions more narrowly, but introduces larger demand side responses to trade shocks which greatly reduce the effect of trade. The conclusion offered is that the choice of structural model matters for decomposing observed wage changes into trade and technology components, and that reduced-form methods which do not discriminate between alternative structural models may not be that informative for such decompositions.

1. Introduction

This chapter addresses the ongoing debate on the principal sources of increased wage dispersion in the form of an elevated premium paid to

*This chapter forms part of a project on Globalization and Social Exclusion supported by the Targeted Socio-Economic Research Program of the European Union. An earlier version was presented at a conference at Nottingham, March 27/28, 1999. We are grateful to Bob Anderton, Paul Brenton, Johnathan Haskel, Matthias Luecke, and Ken Wallis for helpful comments on an earlier draft.
†This chapter was first published by National Bureau of Economic Research, Inc. in its series NBER Working Paper 7312.

skilled labor in OECD countries in recent years. Many papers have been written on the subject, and most focus on increased trade and skill-biased technological change as the two principal causes.[a] Baldwin and Cain (1997), Krugman and Lawrence (1993), Lawrence and Slaughter (1993), Leamer (1996), and others conclude that the role of trade is small; Wood (1994) points to a dominant role for trade. Conclusions in this literature rest largely on reduced form regressions. Some, such as Borjas *et al.* (1991), and Murphy and Welch (1991) estimate the factor content of trade and use these estimates via exogenous (literature-based) labor demand elasticities to infer the wage change attributable to trade. They then compare this to observed wage changes. Others, such as Baldwin and Cain (1997) and Leamer (1996) use estimating equations derived from explicit general equilibrium models.

Our purpose here is to explore the use of structural models as an alternative to reduced form methods when decomposing observed joint trade and technology driven wage changes into the components attributable to each source. We first use a Heckscher–Ohlin type trade model with two factor inputs (skilled and nonskilled labor) and two outputs (skilled labor intensive, and nonskilled labor intensive outputs), where the economy in question is a taker of goods prices on world markets.[b] Skilled and unskilled labor are mobile between sectors, but are internationally immobile. In this model, trade shocks are modeled as world price changes, and technology shocks as factor specific shocks. We model these as changes in production function parameters in our two sectors. We calibrate the model both to U.K. data for 1990, and to the relative wage changes observed for the joint technology/trade shocks over the period 1980–1995. We then explore the use of the model for decomposition experiments by first removing technology only, and then subsequently removing trade, and computing equilibria for each case. These allow for an assessment of the separate role of trade and technology in contributing to observed changes in wage inequality over the period.

Results using simple Heckscher–Ohlin as the structural model for decomposition suggest that with conventional functional forms this model

[a]Immigration enters as a third factor in some literature.

[b]The structure differs from the two-country, two-good, two-factor Heckscher–Ohlin model in which relative factor abundance across countries determines the pattern of trade. Our model contains two goods, two factors and homogeneous products, but there is only one (small price-taking) country and our base case pattern of trade is determined by the own country comparative advantage, not relative factor abundance.

is unlikely to be suitable for analysis of actual country experiences. First, the model can only be solved for relatively small shocks with the CES functional forms used in the model (or indeed any convenient functional form), since the production frontier is close to linear and so specialization accompanies even small changes.[c] Second, there are significant degrees of ambiguity associated with the decompositions for the small changes that the model is able to be solved for. These indicate that there is a range of parametrizations for the model which are consistent with the same reduced form data, but these parametrizations yield divergent decompositions of the same joint change. Estimated reduced forms do not allow for discrimination between these alternative parametrizations for use in decomposition.

We then consider an alternative differentiated goods model of which the Heckscher–Ohlin model is a special case. In this, imported goods and nonexportable domestic products are imperfect substitutes in demand, and as the substitution elasticity between domestic products and imports approaches infinity the model reverts to the more classical Heckscher–Ohlin form. For finite substitution elasticities, this model weakens, and typically removes the specialization properties of simple Heckscher–Ohlin models, allowing actual joint technology and wage changes to be decomposed into constituent parts. It also incorporates endogenous domestic price determination in response to world price changes within imperfect pass through of world price changes onto prices of domestically produced goods (in simple Heckscher–Ohlin models all external shocks fully impact domestic goods prices). It also allows for direct model calibration to import demand elasticity estimates, something that in simple Heckscher–Ohlin is considerably more difficult.

Analyzing decompositions of the same U.K. data with this model reveals strikingly different results relative to simple Heckscher–Ohlin specialization problems recede, and the range of decomposition results for given joint changes is substantially narrowed, in part because trade shocks can now be absorbed on the import demand-side of the model without full transmission to domestic producer prices. The increase in inequality attributed to trade changes can change sign depending upon whether the demand side substitution elasticity between domestic and foreign goods is

[c]Fixed-factor variants of the same model can be used to remove specialization, but these have the property that price shocks are largely borne by the fixed factors, rather than by the mobile skilled and unskilled labor types.

greater or less than one. These demand side effects thus play a key role in trade-wages decompositions.

We interpret our results as showing how alternative structural models with different properties can be built for decompositional analysis, each consistent with the same joint shock, but with sharply different results. Using a simple Heckscher–Ohlin type model, close to what is found in some of the trade and wages literature, only small changes can be analyzed and these, in turn, offer a wide range of decompositions from alternative data consistent parametrizations. With a product differentiation model, large changes can be analyzed and across alternative parametrizations decomposition results are relatively robust, but with demand side effects entering the model the contribution of trade to inequality is much reduced. We suggest that exploration of alternative structural models rather than reduced forms may be the way forward to more satisfactorily sort out trade and technology effects on wage dispersion.

2. The Trade and Wage Inequality Debate

Recent literature on trade and wages focuses on understanding the quantitative significance of trade in explaining the sharp increase in OECD wage inequality which has occurred during the 1980s. This issue is important because of the associated pressures for protection which arise if trade is deemed to be the main source of increased inequality. This increase in inequality has been documented for a number of OECD countries, most notably the U.S. and the U.K. (e.g., Davis, 1992; Kosters, 1994). The pattern has been observed across different types of workers according to their skills (low versus high skill), education level (college versus noncollege graduates), and experience. Even among "observably similar workers" wage inequality has increased (e.g., Davis, 1992). There has also been some documentation of a rise in unemployment in European countries without major increases in wage inequality (Kosters, 1994) — as well as of a decline in wage inequality in some key developing countries (Korea, Venezuela, Colombia, and Brazil) (Davis, 1992). A large literature has evolved on the explanation of increased wage inequality, especially for the U.S. case.[d]

[d]See, for instance, the surveys by Brenton (1998). Also see Deardorff and Hakura (1994).

Two major factors have been identified as responsible for this phenomenon: Increased trade with developing countries and technological change biased against unskilled labor. The great majority of research has concluded that unskilled-biased technological change, rather than increased trade, is the main source of the surge in wage inequality in the 1980s.[e]

This literature uses a variety of econometric models.[f] Early papers focused on how trade changes labor demand via the factor content of trade (e.g., Borjas *et al.*, 1991; Katz and Murphy, 1992; Murphy and Welch, 1991). They typically ran regressions which linked labor demand (by type of labor) and trade flows, and then used actual trade flows to infer the changes in labor demand they imply. They then combined these labor demand changes with wage elasticity of labor demand estimates culled from the literature to infer what portion of actual wage changes are due to trade changes. This work generally came to the conclusion that the portion of actual wage change attributable to trade is small.

These estimates, based on factor content of trade calculations, were later criticized by Wood (1994) who argued that trade is a considerably more important factor than these analyses show. He argued that, for many products and especially those from developing countries, there is no comparable domestic product, and so factor substitution effects attributed to trade using conventional elasticities are understated. He also argued that technological response to trade will occur in expectation of future trade surges, and so some of what is attributed to technology in factor content analyses should in reality be attributed to trade.

Later papers in the area (Baldwin and Cain, 1997; Lawrence and Slaughter, 1993; Leamer, 1996) take a different approach and work with estimating equations derived from explicit general equilibrium models of a Heckscher–Ohlin type. Lawrence and Slaughter, for instance, relate changes in relative skilled and unskilled wage rates to changes in prices of skilled and unskilled labor intensive products. Highlighting key measurement issues, they suggest that for the U.S. the changes in product prices appear to be opposite from those needed to generate increased wage inequality (i.e., unskilled intensive product prices rise rather than fall). Their conclusion is

---

[e]Exceptions to this conclusion include Borjas *et al.* (1991), Wood (1994), and Feenstra and Hanson (1996). The latter identify outsourcing as a significant cause.

[f]Francois and Nelson (1998) are seemingly the other authors who use an applied general equilibrium model to look at the effects of trade and technology on wage inequality. They set out a modeling approach, rather than analyze decompositions in detail.

that unskilled-biased technical change is the main source of increased wage inequality and that trade is relatively unimportant.

Finally, more recent work regresses measures of factor shares on measures of outsourcing (Anderton and Brenton, 1998; Feenstra and Hanson, 1996) concluding that trade may be more important than in earlier analyses. Anderton and Brenton (1998), in particular, find that trade is more important when only trade with developing countries rather than with all countries is used as an explanatory variable.

Virtually all of these analyses use reduced-form data in their estimations, with little or no work explicitly employing structural models[g] even though structural models are needed to make a meaningful decomposition of an observed relative wage change into a portion due to trade and a portion due to (skill-biased) technological change. Because the model parameters which are consistent with given reduced-form data are not unique, different parametrizations can generate a different decomposition between trade and technological change as sources of an observed combined change in inequality. Some attention to structural models may be required.

3. A Heckscher–Ohlin Inequality Decomposition for the U.K.

We first explore decompositions of combined wage and technology shocks using some numerical simulations from a simple and theory-consistent Heckscher–Ohlin general equilibrium model calibrated to U.K. data. We describe this data in more detail in an Appendix. We use 1990 data on production, consumption, factor use, and trade, aggregated into a two commodity unskilled labor intensive and skilled labor intensive product and industry classification to calibrate the model. Data on trade shocks and wage changes cover the period 1976–1990 and 1980–1995, respectively. Technology shocks are implied for the model by the wage outcome over the period and the data on trade shocks.

We use a two-good (importable/exportable), two-factor (skilled/unskilled labor) Heckscher–Ohlin CES model to incorporate both trade shocks and changes in skilled-biased technological change. We perform decompositional analysis by first generating a parametrization for the model which is consistent with the combined trade and technology shock (as

[g]An exception is Leamer (1996), where a structural form is estimated.

reflected in data on wage change). We then remove individual components of the joint change from the model to assess the contribution of each to the observed total change generated by the joint shock.

There are, however, alternative parameter values which can be chosen for the functional forms used in the model which imply that this structural model form can be parametrized in different ways, even though each of which gives the same wage inequality change for a combined trade and technology shock. There are in fact many such parametrizations, while each potentially gives different decompositional results and we are able to show substantial ambiguity in the resulting decompositions using this model for different parametrizations. In the simple Heckscher–Ohlin case, specialization also occurs even for only small goods price changes since the production frontier in such models is close to linear for convenient functional forms (see Johnson, 1966).

The ambiguity for the small size decompositions that we can perform with the model can be reduced either by restricting key elasticity parameters — such as production substitution elasticities between skilled and unskilled labor — to a narrow range of values, appealing to literature estimates (Hamermesh, 1993) or by moving to increasingly constrained calibration in which we require more than calibration to only the combined wage change over the period. Experience with the model nonetheless suggests that the simple Heckscher–Ohlin model is a poor performer in decompositional analysis.

3.1. *Production*

For our simple Heckscher–Ohlin case, we consider a small open price-taking economy that produces two goods, M and E (importable and intensive in unskilled labor, and exportable and intensive in skilled labor, respectively), both of which are traded at fixed world prices. The production of each good requires the use of two factors: Skilled labor, S, and unskilled labor, U. Each good is produced using a constant returns to scale CES technology, with constant elasticity of substitution between S and U.

$$Y_i = \gamma_i[\beta_i U_i^{-\rho_i} + (1-\beta_i)S_i^{-\rho_i}]^{-\frac{1}{\rho_i}}, \quad i = M, E \tag{1}$$

where Y_i represents output, γ_i denotes units of measuremen, β_i is a share parameter, and ρ_i determines the elasticity of substitution, η_i, between U_i and S_i, with $\eta_i = \frac{1}{1+\rho_i}$.

3.2. *Labor market*

We take the endowment of unskilled and skilled labor to be fixed (there is no labor-leisure choice), and equal to $\overline{U}$ and $\overline{S}$, respectively. Full employment of each type of labor is assumed. We also assume competitive labor markets so that each type of labor is paid its marginal value product, i.e.,

$$W_U = \gamma_i \beta_i U_i P_i Y_i^{1-\rho_i} \quad (i = M, E) \tag{2}$$

$$W_S = \gamma_i (1-\beta_i) S_i P_i Y_i^{1-\rho_i} \quad (i = M, E) \tag{3}$$

where W_U and W_S denote unskilled and skilled wage rates respectively, and P_i is the (fixed) world price of good i.

3.3. *Trade*

Imports and domestically produced goods are homogeneous, as is also the case with exports (i.e., trade is of Heckscher–Ohlin form). This homogeneity assumption implies that trade flows involving any good are only one-way, i.e., one of the goods is exported and the other imported.

In equilibrium trade balance will hold, i.e.,

$$\sum_{i=M,E} P_i T_i = 0 \tag{4}$$

where the T_i denote the net trade of the country in the two goods, M and E. If good i is exported, domestic production less consumption is positive; if good i is imported, this difference is negative.

3.4. *Equilibrium and market clearing conditions*

Given the small open economy assumption, equilibrium in this model is given by unskilled and skilled wage rates, such that the two domestic labor markets clear, i.e.,

$$\sum_i U_i = \bar{U}, \quad i = M, E \tag{5}$$

$$\sum_i S_i = \bar{S}, \quad i = M, E \tag{6}$$

Consumption of each good i is given by the difference between production and trade, i.e.,

$$C_i = Y_i - T_i, \quad i = M, E \tag{7}$$

where C_i denotes consumption of good i.

Production of each good, in turn, is given by using Eqs. (2), (3), (5), and (6) and solving for, Y_i along with, W_U and W_S as part of the equilibrium.

3.5. *Decomposing the effects of trade and technology on wage inequality*

We can use the Heckscher–Ohlin model presented above to investigate the decomposition of a total wage rate effect from a joint trade-technology shock into a separate trade related and technology components. To do this, we consider trade shocks to be represented by world price shocks which generate more trade. We take such shocks to be given by falls in the relative price of unskilled intensive to skilled intensive products. Our data for the U.K. indicate a relative price fall of 7.9% for unskilled-intensive products over the period 1976–1990.[h] Given the data on wage change over the sample period, we determine the technology shock by residual as that needed to yield the observed wage change as a model solution in the presence of the combined trade and technology shock. We then treat technology shocks as changes in the share parameters applying to skilled and unskilled labor in sector production functions. We focus on technological change which is factor specific, assuming in our analysis that such changes occur only for unskilled labor. As share parameters in each production function sum to one, an adverse shock-biased against unskilled labor, lowers the share parameter on unskilled labor relative to that for skilled labor for the same sector.

3.6. *Specialization and simple Heckscher–Ohlin*

This simple Heckscher–Ohlin-type model immediately proves unsatisfactory for the task of decomposing U.K. data on wage inequality into separate trade and technology components because of the near linearity of the production frontier alluded to above, and the associated problems of specialization. This is a well known numerical property of production frontiers generated from conventional functional forms and fixed economy wide endowments (see Johnson, 1966). If alternatively a production frontier with sufficient curvature to present specialization were directly specified, the problem would remain that there is no known way to recover sector

[h]This estimate is based on information from Neven and Wyplosz (1996), as set out in the Appendix.

production functions consistent with such a frontier, and they anyway would be inconsistent with the observed base case (1990) equilibrium data.

We can, however, solve the model for smaller trade and technology changes than those observed, and such solutions raise further problems since they also indicate ambiguity in decomposition for such changes. To illustrate this, we have simulated the effects of a joint 1% fall in the world price of the unskilled-intensive good relative to the skilled intensive good, and a 1% technological change adverse to unskilled labor to provide some sense of model behavior under such changes. We represent this latter change by a 1% reduction in the share parameter on unskilled labor in the production of both goods, so as to represent pervasive unskilled-biased technological change, which, as we indicated earlier, the bulk of the literature finds to be responsible for the surge in wage inequality during the 1980s (e.g., Baldwin and Cain, 1997; Berman *et al.*, 1994).

3.7. *Results*

In Table 1, we report two alternative model parametrizations chosen such that, given the combined trade and technology shocks, both generate the same change in relative wages (−6.67% in Table 2), but with different decomposition results for the portion due to trade and to technological change. As we note above, there are, in fact, many such parametrizations that can be determined, and Table 1 presents merely two that we have been able to find using a GAMS (Generalized Algebraic Modeling System) Code which endogenously determines model parametrizations consistent with the combined change we specify.

Table 1. Two Parametrizations of a U.K. Trade Model Each Giving the Same Joint (Trade and Technology) Wage Changes.

	A		B	
Share parameters	Good M	Good E	Good M	Good E
Production				
Unskilled labor	0.86	0.29	0.81	0.45
Skilled labor	0.14	0.71	0.19	0.56
Consumption	0.52	0.48	0.52	0.48
Elasticities of substitution				
Production	0.4	0.6	0.5	2.5
Consumption	1.25		1.25	

Table 2. Decomposition Results on the Relative Importance of Trade and Technology for a Total Wage Change of −6.67% (Implied by a 1% Trade and a 1% Technology Shock).

	A	B
% Change in W_U/W_S for joint trade and technology change	−6.67	−6.67
Fraction of change in W_U/W_S due to technology	0.58	0.43
Fraction of change in W_U/W_S due to trade	0.42	0.57

Table 1 presents these two model parametrizations. They differ substantially in share parameters and production-side elasticities. In both parametrizations, the importable good utilizes unskilled labor intensively — which we, for now, take as a stylized fact for the U.K. and other OECD economies. We have only varied production parameters elasticities of substitution and labor shares, leaving demand parameters unaltered since this is a small open economy model.

Table 2 presents decomposition results for each of the two model parametrizations. These are obtained by first only allowing technology to change, and then only the world price change to occur, and computing a new equilibrium in each case. The resulting wage change is compared to that observed under the joint shock (shown in Table 2). Although the overall change in wage inequality is the same for both parametrizations, the relative importance of trade and technology in each case is different. For parametrization A, the technology shock is dominant, whereas for parametrization B the opposite occurs. Were we to regress, say, factor price changes from the joint shock on goods price changes (the trade shock) and some measure of the technology change, such a regression does not allow differentiation to be made between competing parametrizations of the structural model, all of which are consistent with reduced form data, but each of which gives a different decomposition.

In passing, we also comment on a further feature of Heckscher–Ohlin that large wage changes occur from only relatively small product price changes. This reflects the same feature alluded to earlier, that with a production frontier close to linear, a small change in output prices from a trade shock (1% here) moves the economy a substantial distance along the frontier with a large change in output composition and hence a large relative wage change. In our U.K. simulations, the result of this is that changes in goods prices that constitute only a small fraction of the actual change over the period we consider here, nonetheless generate wage effects stronger than those observed. Thus, using Heckscher–Ohlin models to analyze decomposition for economies in which significant output price and relative wage changes have simultaneously occurred is a further problem for such models.

4. Trade and Technology Decompositions in a Differentiated Goods Model

As we note above, the most commonly used structure in which to conduct analyses of the contribution of trade and technology to wage inequality is a two-factor (high/low skilled labor), two-good (high skilled intensive, low skilled intensive) Heckscher–Ohlin trade model. In this structure, the key parameters affecting the decomposition of the total wage effect into component parts are production side parameters — shares and elasticities. But the results in the preceding section suggest that this model may be inappropriate for the conduct of such analyses. This is because such models typically have close to linear production frontiers, and so for a small shock complete specialization can occur, and also wide variations in decompositions occur across parametrizations.

In this section, we examine an alternative structural model with differentiated goods, similar to the one set out in de Melo and Robinson (1989), and recently discussed in Bhattarai *et al.* (1999). In this model, imports and domestically produced goods are imperfect rather than perfect substitutes. Imports are not produced domestically, and one of the domestically produced goods is not traded. The model remains a two-produced goods, two-factor model with two traded goods, but embodies three goods in aggregate when the consumption side is included.[i] Imports and exports are traded at fixed world prices. The domestic good — which is an imperfect substitute for imports — and the exportable are the two produced goods. Each uses skilled and unskilled labor. Imports and the (nonexportable) domestic good enter consumption. This structure removes the problems with specialization associated with the simple Heckscher–Ohlin model when performing trade-technology decompositions since imports are not produced domestically. This differentiated goods

[i] In de Melo and Robinson's model, three goods are also considered — two of which are domestically produced — but only two of them (the imported and the domestic good) enter preferences.

model generalizes the Heckscher–Ohlin model, since as the elasticity of substitution in demands between domestically produced goods and imports approaches infinity, it asymptotically approaches Heckscher–Ohlin.

Model results using the same U.K. data as above show both that large change decompositions can now be made and that demand-side parameters are critical for the results of such decompositions. When the substitution elasticity in preferences between domestic products and imports is one, terms of trade shocks can be fully accommodated on the demand-side by an offsetting quantity adjustment in the imported goods not domestically produced. No impacts on wage rates of skilled and unskilled workers occur since all the adjustment is now in consumption of the nonproduced traded good. The sign of the wage rate impact also changes as this elasticity goes above or below one. These are radically different properties to those found for simple Heckscher–Ohlin models, indicating how critical the choice of structural model is for wage-technology decompositions.

4.1. *Model*

Denoting imports by M, exports by E, and domestic goods by D, preferences are defined over M, D, and E, with D and E being the produced goods. Using the same two-factor inputs U and S, high and low skilled labor, production occurs for only two of the three goods, D and E. Effectively the same two-by-two structure is preserved, but differentiated goods are imported and domestically produced. Unlike in the Heckscher–Ohlin model above, preferences now enter the picture and a product price is endogenously determined, even in the small country case.

Thus, preferences are denoted by

$$U(M^D, E^D), \tag{8}$$

where E^D denotes demands for the exportable good, M^D is the composite of imports, M, and the domestic import substitute, D^D, i.e.,

$$M^D = h(M, D^D)$$

and technology by

$$D^S = D(U^D, S^D) \tag{9}$$

$$E = E(U^E, S^E) \tag{10}$$

where U^D, S^D, U^E, and S^E denote inputs of high and low skilled labor used in domestic good and export production; D^S is production of the imperfect substitute domestic good.

The economy is a taker of prices for exports and imports, $\bar{P}_E, \bar{P}_M$, but now the price for the domestic good P_D is endogenously determined. The per unit cost functions for the production of E and D, consistent with zero profits, are

$$P_D = g_D(W^U, W^S) \tag{11}$$

$$\bar{P}_E = g_E(W^U, W^S) \tag{12}$$

where W^U and W^S are the wage rates of high and low skilled labor, and g_D and g_E are per unit costs functions.

Full employment conditions for factors yield

$$f_D^U \cdot D^D + f_E^U \cdot E = \bar{U} \tag{13}$$

$$f_D^S \cdot D^D + f_E^S \cdot E = \bar{S} \tag{14}$$

where $f_D^U, f_E^U, f_D^S, f_E^S$ are per unit cost minimizing factor demands for U and S in the production of D and E.

The representative household in this economy maximize the utility function (8) subject to the budget constraint

$$P_D D^D + \bar{P}_M M + \bar{P}_E E^D = W^U \bar{U} + W^S \bar{S}. \tag{15}$$

In equilibrium, the price of the domestically produced good P_D^*, will be determined such that market clearing occurs in D, i.e.,

$$D^D = D^S. \tag{16}$$

No market clearing is required in either E or M. Walras' Law, which holds for demand functions generated from utility maximization subject to a budget constraint, also implies that trade balance will hold, i.e., in equilibrium

$$\bar{P}_M M = \bar{P}_E E. \tag{17}$$

In this model, relative to the simple Heckscher–Ohlin model discussed earlier, one additional endogenous variable, P_D, enters the model. Additional parameters enter the model in terms of preferences over D^D and M. Thus, in the case where the elasticity of substitution in preferences between D^D and M is unity, changes in world prices of imports can be fully accommodated by changes in import volumes. In this case, trade shocks have no impact on domestic production patterns, and hence no impact on the relative wages of skilled and unskilled labor. In such a case in trade and technology decompositions, the role of trade in affecting the relative wages of the skilled and unskilled will be zero. In addition, we note that empirical studies of import demand elasticities (Reinert, 1992; Shiells and Reinert, 1993; Stern *et al.*, 1976) consistently produce estimates in the neighborhood of one; and in a CES function the own price demand elasticity approaches the negative of the substitution elasticity as the relevant share parameter approaches zero.

4.2. *Results*

With specialization problems removed in the model, we are able to consider the full change in relative wages and goods prices for in a decomposition exercise for the U.K. economy. The number we use for the change in the relative price of the unskilled-intensive good is −7.9% [based on Neven and Wyplosz (1996)], and for the fall in wages of the unskilled relative to the skilled is −15% (Haskel, 1996).[j] In the absence of estimates of technological change fully consistent with the units of measurement used in the production functions in our model, we determine the size of technological change residually, given the observed relative wage and product price changes. As in the previous section, we assume that technological change is biased against unskilled labor.

Table 3 reports results for a decomposition experiment of this data conducted for this model with a substitution elasticity in preferences of unity. In this case, independently of the parametrization used for the model, the fraction of the change in W_U/W_S due to trade is zero because trade shocks are fully accommodated on the demand-side of the model. In Table 4, we report of decomposition results for parametrizations where the elasticity of substitution in preferences ranges departs from unity. We consider elasticity values above and below unity, and roughly consistent with literature estimates of import demand elasticities. In all cases, the contribution of trade to wage inequality is small, but changes sign as the elasticity of substitution in consumption moves below one.

[j]Both estimates are for the U.K., and are discussed in more detail in the Appendix.

Table 3. Trade-Technology Decomposition in Differentiated Goods Model Where the Substitution Elasticity in Preferences Equals One.

(1) *Parametrizations*	Parametrization A		Parametrization B	
Share Parameters	Good D	Good E	Good D	Good E
Production				
Unskilled labor	0.41	0.21	0.55	0.30
Skilled labor	0.59	0.79	0.45	0.70
Consumption	0.56	0.28	0.56	0.28
Elasticities				
Production	1.25	1.25	2.0	2.0
Consumption	1.0		1.0	

(2) *Decomposition results on the relative importance of trade and technology for a total wage change*

	A	B
% change in W_U/W_S in U.K. data for joint technology and trade change	15.0	15.0
Fraction of change in W_U/W_S due to technology	1.0	1.0
Fraction of change in W_U/W_S due to trade	0.0	0.0

Table 4. Range of Technology-Trade Decompositions over Alternative Values for the Elasticity of Substitution in Preferences (σ).

	$\sigma = 0.5-1.0$	$\sigma = 1.0-2.0$
Range for fraction of change in W_U/W_S due to technology	1.03–1.00	1.00–0.94
Range for fraction of change in W_U/W_S due to trade	−0.03–0.0	0.0–0.06

From this, we conclude that the choice of structural model makes a significant difference to the conclusions of any trade-technology decomposition experiment analyzing the sources of recent changes in wage inequality for OECD countries. For the simple Heckscher–Ohlin case widely discussed in the literature, only small shocks can be analyzed because of specialization problems, and along with these restrictions wide ranges for decompositions are obtained for model parametrizations consistent with the observed combined wage change. Using a differentiated goods model, large changes can be analyzed since specialization is not a problem but much (or most) of the trade shock is absorbed on the demand-side, sharply raising the contribution of technology.

5. Summary and Conclusions

This chapter uses general equilibrium numerical simulation techniques to explore the significance of the choice of structural model when assessing the contribution of trade and technological change to the increased wage inequality documented for a number of OECD countries for the 1980's, (most notably the U.S. and the U.K.). Using a simple Heckscher–Ohlin model, we first show both how problems of specialization can occur for large trade shocks and different model parametrizations are consistent with a given change in wage inequality from trade and technology shocks which yield different decompositions of the combined change into trade and technology components. We also use a differentiated goods model with imports and domestically produced goods as imperfect rather than perfect substitutes, since this removes the problem of specialization. This model, however, also introduces demand side considerations through substitution in preferences between domestic goods and imports.

Our results with the second model indicate an ability to examine large rather than only small trade shocks in decomposition experiments, but also much reduced variation in results across parametrizations. This is because now, depending upon the value of the elasticity of substitution in consumption, the demand-side of the model can absorb a large portion of any trade shock (indeed all of the trade shock when this elasticity is one).

From these results we suggest that it is important to explicitly explore the properties of particular structural models in decompositions, rather than only appealing to them as theoretically consistent models for reduced form analyses. The choice of structural model, perhaps not surprisingly, seems to matter for such decompositions.

References

Anderton, B and P Brenton (1998). The dollar, trade, technology and wage inequality in the U.S.A. CEPS, Brussels, Mimeo.

Baldwin, RE and GG Cain (1997). Shifts in US relative wages: The role of trade, technology and factor endowments. *NBER Working Paper No.* 5934.

Bhattarai, K, M Gosh and J Whalley (1999). On some properties of a trade closure widely used in numerical modeling. *Economics Letters*, **62**, 13–21.

Brenton, P (1999). Rising trade and falling wages: A review of the theory and the empirics. In *Global and European Workers*, P Brenton and J Pelkmans (eds.). Houndmills, Basingstoke, Hampshire: Macmillan Press; New York: St. Martin's Press (in association with European Institute of Asian Studies).

Berman, E, J Bound and Z Griliches (1994). Changes in the demand for skilled labor within US manufacturing: Evidence from annual survey of manufactures. *Quarterly Journal of Economics*, **109**, 367–398.

Borjas, G, R Freeman and L Katz (1991). On the labor market effects of immigration and trade. In *Immigration and the Work Force*, G Borjas and R Freeman (eds.). Chicago: The University of Chicago Press.

Davis, S (1992). Cross-country patterns of changes in relative wages. *NBER Macroeconomics Annual*, **7**, 239–291.

Deardorff, A and DS Hakura (1994). Trade and wages: What are the questions. In *Trade and Wages: Levelling Wages Down?*, J Bhagwati and M Kosters (eds.). Washington: AEI Press.

De Melo, J and S Robinson (1989). Product differentiation and the treatment of foreign trade in computable general equilibrium models of small economies. *Journal of International Economics*, **27**, 47–67.

Feenstra, R and C Hanson (1996). Globalization, outsourcing and wage inequality. *American Economic Review*, **86**, 240–245.

Francois, F and D Nelson (1998). Trade, technology and wages: General equilibrium mechanics. *Economic Journal*, **108**, 1483–1499.

Hamermesh, DS (1993). *Labor Demand.* Princeton: Princeton University Press.

Haskel, J (1996). Declining wages for unskilled workers. *CEPR Discussion Paper No.* 1490.

Johnson, HG (1966). Factor market distortions and the shape of the transformation frontier. *Econometrica*, **34**, 686–698.

Katz, L and K Murphy (1992). Changes in relative wages, 1963–1987: Supply and demand factors. *Quarterly Journal of Economics*, **107**, 35–78.

Kosters, M (1994). An overview of changing wage patterns in the labor market. In *Trade and Wages: Levelling Wages Down?*, J Bhagwati and M Kosters (eds.), pp. 28–31. Washington, DC: AEI.

Krugman, P and R Lawrence (1993). Trade, jobs and wages. *NBER Working Paper No.* 4478, National Bureau of Economic Research, Inc.

Lawrence, R and M Slaughter (1993). International trade and American wages: Giant sucking sound or small hiccup. *Brookings Papers of Economic Activity*, **1993**(2), 161–226.

Leamer, E (1996). In search of Stolper–Samuelson effects on US wages. *NBER Working Paper* 5427, National Bureau of Economic Research, Inc.

Murphy, K and F Welch (1991). The Role of international trade in wage differentials. In *Workers and Their Wages: Changing Patterns in the United States*, M Koster (ed.). Washington: AEI Press.

Neven, D and C Wyplosz (1996). Relative prices, trade and restructuring in European industry. *CEPR Discussion Paper No.* 1451.

Reinert, K (1992). Armington elasticities for United States manufacturing sectors. *Journal of Policy Modeling*, **14**, 631–639.

Shiells, C and K Reinert (1993). Armington models and terms of trade effects: Some econometric evidence for North America. *Canadian Journal of Economics*, **26**, 299–316.

Stern, RM, J Francis and B Schumacher (1976). *Price Elasticities in International Trade: An Annotated Bibliography.* London: Macmillan.

Wood, A (1994). *North–South Trade, Employment and Inequality.* Oxford: Clarendon Press.

APPENDIX

U.K. Data Used in Model-Based Trade and Technology Decompositions

This Appendix describes the U.K. data used for the parametrization of both the Heckscher–Ohlin and differentiated goods model. We have calibrated both model to a 1990 data set on U.K. production, trade, and factor use as well as data on relative wage and product price changes over the 1980s in the case of the differentiated goods model. Production and trade data come from the U.K. input–output matrix for 1990. The data on trade are adjusted for model consistency. Wage and employment data by sector and skill category have been obtained from *Labor Market Trends* and the *New Earnings Survey* for 1990. All these data are aggregated into the two-good, skilled and unskilled intensive classification.

The data on relative price changes for goods are taken from Neven and Wyplosz (1996). They disaggregate import price changes for manufacturing both by sector (which they also disaggregate according to different factor skill intensities) and origin of imports (between developed and developing countries), and cover the period 1976–1990. This source, together with information on the composition of U.K. imports by origin for 1990, gives a decline in the relative import price of the unskilled-labor-intensive good of 7.9%. The data on the decline of relative earnings by U.K. unskilled workers (15% over the period 1980–1995) that we use for the decomposition exercise in our differentiated goods model comes from Haskel (1996).

The definition of "unskilled" and "skilled" workers we utilize corresponds to manual and nonmanual workers as defined in U.K. official statistics. The production sectors included in our unskilled-intensive sector are those which at level of disaggregation in the 1990 U.K. input–output table were net importers of goods or services, plus nontraded sectors (public administration, utilities and construction). Our skilled-intensive sector is then made up of the remaining sectors. This aggregation produces a ratio of the value of unskilled to skilled labor inputs of 0.64 for the unskilled-intensive sector, and 0.18 for the skilled-intensive sector in our 1990 base year. The domestic and export good sectors in our differentiated goods model correspond to the unskilled-intensive and skilled-intensive sectors, as defined above.